Miki Kiyoshi's
The Logic of Imagination

Bloomsbury Introductions to World Philosophies

Series Editor
Monika Kirloskar-Steinbach

Assistant Series Editor
Leah Kalmanson

Regional Editors
Nader El-Bizri, James Madaio, Ann A. Pang-White, Takeshi Morisato, Pascah Mungwini, Mickaella Perina, Omar Rivera and Georgina Stewart

Bloomsbury Introductions to World Philosophies delivers primers reflecting exciting new developments in the trajectory of world philosophies. Instead of privileging a single philosophical approach as the basis of comparison, the series provides a platform for diverse philosophical perspectives to accommodate the different dimensions of cross-cultural philosophizing. While introducing thinkers, texts and themes emanating from different world philosophies, each book, in an imaginative and path-breaking way, makes clear how it departs from a conventional treatment of the subject matter.

Titles in the Series

A Practical Guide to World Philosophies, by Monika Kirloskar-Steinbach and Leah Kalmanson
Daya Krishna and Twentieth-Century Indian Philosophy, by Daniel Raveh
Māori Philosophy, by Georgina Tuari Stewart
Philosophy of Science and The Kyoto School, by Dean Anthony Brink
Tanabe Hajime and the Kyoto School, by Takeshi Morisato
African Philosophy, by Pascah Mungwini
The Zen Buddhist Philosophy of D. T. Suzuki, by Rossa Ó Muireartaigh
Sikh Philosophy, by Arvind-Pal Singh Mandair
The Philosophy of the Brahma-sūtra, by Aleksandar Uskokov
The Philosophy of the Yogasūtra, by Karen O'Brien-Kop
The Life and Thought of H. Odera Oruka, by Gail M. Presbey
Mexican Philosophy for the 21st Century, by Carlos Alberto Sánchez
Buddhist Ethics and the Bodhisattva Path, by Stephen Harris
Contextualizing Angela Davis, by Joy James
The Philosophy of No-Mind, by Nishihira Tadashi and translated by Catherine Sevilla-Liu and Anton Sevilla-Liu
Miki Kiyoshi's The Logic of Imagination, introduced and translated by John W. M. Krummel

Miki Kiyoshi's
The Logic of Imagination

A Critical Introduction and Translation

Introduced and Translated by John W. M. Krummel

BLOOMSBURY ACADEMIC
LONDON • NEW YORK • OXFORD • NEW DELHI • SYDNEY

BLOOMSBURY ACADEMIC
Bloomsbury Publishing Plc
50 Bedford Square, London, WC1B 3DP, UK
1385 Broadway, New York, NY 10018, USA
29 Earlsfort Terrace, Dublin 2, Ireland

BLOOMSBURY, BLOOMSBURY ACADEMIC and the Diana logo are trademarks
of Bloomsbury Publishing Plc

First published in Great Britain 2024

Copyright © John W. M. Krummel, 2024

John W. M. Krummel has asserted his right under the Copyright, Designs and Patents Act, 1988,
to be identified as Translator of this work.

Series design by Louise Dugdale
Cover image © bgblue / Getty Images

All rights reserved. No part of this publication may be reproduced or transmitted in any form or by any
means, electronic or mechanical, including photocopying, recording, or any information storage or
retrieval system, without prior permission in writing from the publishers.

Bloomsbury Publishing Plc does not have any control over, or responsibility for, any third-party websites
referred to or in this book. All internet addresses given in this book were correct at the time of going to
press. The author and publisher regret any inconvenience caused if addresses have changed or sites
have ceased to exist, but can accept no responsibility for any such changes.

A catalogue record for this book is available from the British Library.

Library of Congress Cataloging-in-Publication Data

Names: Miki, Kiyoshi, 1897–1945, author. | Krummel, John W. M. (John Wesley Megumu), 1965–
translator, writer of introduction.
Title: Miki Kiyoshi's The logic of imagination : a critical introduction and translation /
introduced and translated by John W. M. Krummel.
Other titles: Kōsōryoku no ronri. English | Logic of imagination
Description: London ; New York : Bloomsbury Academic, 2024. |
Series: Bloomsbury introductions to world philosophies | Translation of: Kōsōryoku no ronri. |
Includes bibliographical references and index. |
Summary: "One of the central figures in the Kyoto School, Miki Kiyoshi wrote Logic of Imagination as a
series of articles between 1937 and 1943. Translating this seminal work into English for the first time,
with contextual notes throughout, this book features an introduction and biographical information about
the author. Miki's thinking about the imagination illuminates our contemporary understanding of
technology and how we behave in the world"– Provided by publisher.
Identifiers: LCCN 2023055804 (print) | LCCN 2023055805 (ebook) |
ISBN 9781350449916 (HB) | ISBN 9781350449909 (PB) | ISBN 9781350449923 (ePDF) |
ISBN 9781350449930 (eBook)
Subjects: LCSH: Kyoto school. | Miki, Kiyoshi, 1897-1945. | Logic. | Imagination (Philosophy). |
Philosophy, Japanese–20th century.
Classification: LCC B5243.K96 K56413 2024 (print) | LCC B5243.K96 (ebook) |
DDC 181/.12—dc23/eng/20240308
LC record available at https://lccn.loc.gov/2023055804
LC ebook record available at https://lccn.loc.gov/2023055805

ISBN: HB: 978-1-3504-4991-6
       PB: 978-1-3504-4990-9
       ePDF: 978-1-3504-4992-3
       eBook: 978-1-3504-4993-0

Series: Bloomsbury Introductions to World Philosophies

Typeset by RefineCatch Limited, Bungay, Suffolk
Printed and bound in Great Britain

To find out more about our authors and books visit www.bloomsbury.com
and sign up for our newsletters.

Contents

Series Editor Preface	vi
Translator's Introduction	1
Introduction	15
1 Myth	21
2 Institution	57
3 Technology	93
4 Experience	123
Notes	225
Index	255

Series Editor's Preface

The introductions we include in the World Philosophies series take a single thinker, theme or text and provide a close reading of them. What defines the series is that these are likely to be people or traditions that you have not yet encountered in your study of philosophy. By choosing to include them you broaden your understanding of ideas about the self, knowledge and the world around us. Each book presents unexplored pathways into the study of world philosophies. Instead of privileging a single philosophical approach as the basis of comparison, each book accommodates the many different dimensions of cross-cultural philosophizing. While the choice of terms used by the individual volumes may indeed carry a local inflection, they encourage critical thinking about philosophical plurality. Each book strikes a balance between locality and globality.

John W.M. Krummel's translation *Miki Kiyoshi's* The Logic of Imagination: *A Critical Introduction and Translation* illustrates the complex thinking of the later Miki Kiyoshi (1897–1945) on the logic of cultural form. This logic unfolds for Miki when human beings who are grounded upon nothingness, relate to their environment through technology. Through their conceptual and mental as well as material and industrial activity, they creatively produce a real picture of being in the world. Cut short by his premature death in a Japanese prison in 1945 after the war had ended, Miki's thinking on the logic of forms remained incomplete in his lifetime. Krummel's book promises to make this key figure of the Kyoto School's intriguing thoughts about creative nothingness more accessible to a wider philosophical audience.

Monika Kirloskar-Steinbach

Translator's Introduction

You are holding the first English translation of an originally two-volume work by the Japanese philosopher, Miki Kiyoshi (三木清) (1897–1945),[1] *The Logic of Imagination* (*Kōsōryoku no ronri* 『構想力の論理』), put into a single volume. In the following I briefly outline his life and oeuvre, making use mostly of Akamatsu Tsunehiro's commentary, to provide an idea of who the philosopher Miki was and then discuss the content of this work and its relevance for us today. I close with a word on the translation and acknowledgments.

Miki's Biography and Oeuvre

Who was Miki? He was born in Hyōgo prefecture of Japan in 1897 and died in prison shortly after the end of World War II in 1945 at the age of 48. His philosophical career began while he was a student at Kyoto Imperial University (京都帝国大学). Borrowing from Akamatsu Tsunehiro's schema, we may divide the development of Miki's work into six thematic periods: 1) Neo-Kantianism during his student years; 2) hermeneutic ontology while researching in Europe; 3) Marx studies, moving towards a practical ontology; 4) development of his own historical social ontology; 5) the unfolding of his philosophy of technological-productive action; and 6) pursuit of a philosophy of the imagination and forms.[2]

Miki began his undergraduate studies in 1917 at the Dept. of Philosophy in the Faculty of Literature of Kyoto Imperial University. Nishida Kitarō (西田幾多郎) (1870–1945), who was at the beginning of his long career of philosophical writing—his *Inquiry into the Good* (『善の研究』) was published in 1911 and *Intuition and Reflection in Self-Awareness* (『自覚における直感と反省』) was published in 1917—was the head of the department and exerted a predominant influence on Miki's thinking at the time. Nishida will subsequently be regarded as the founder of the so-called Kyoto School (京都学派) of philosophy, of which Miki will be considered to be a prominent member. But Miki also studied under Tanabe Hajime (田辺元) (1885–1962), who will also subsequently become known as a co-founder of the Kyoto School, and under Hatano Seiichi (波多野精一) (1877–1950), a philosopher of religion, both teaching at Kyoto Imperial University. After graduating in 1920, Miki entered the Army as a student conscript but in the same year also began his (post-)graduate studies at Kyoto Imperial University, where he focused his research on the philosophy of history.

During this period, he also became a lecturer in philosophy at Ryūkoku University (龍谷大学) and Ōtani University (大谷大学), both in the city of Kyoto.

Miki's primary philosophical orientation at Kyoto during his student years, undergraduate and graduate, was Neo-Kantianism. He was interested in what it means for a human being to be an individual and the issue of historical progression in human history. The two problems fused into the question of "the role of the individual in history," and how the accumulation of the actions of free individuals constitutes ethnic, civic, and universal human cultures. Miki found the conceptual apparatus of Neo-Kantianism useful for tackling these topics, but he also appropriated Plato's theory of the *ideas*, Leibniz's monadology, and the philosophy of his mentor at Kyoto, Nishida Kitarō, and therefore did not restrict himself to Kantian rationalism when he emphasized an irrationality at the root of humanity.

After graduating Miki received a scholarship that was funded by the publisher Iwanami, and spent the years from 1922 to 1925 studying and doing research in Europe. He started in Germany, where at the age of 25 he studied under Heinrich Rickert in Heidelberg and then under Martin Heidegger in Marburg. In Rickert's seminars, he worked on the philosophy of history. In the seminars conducted at Rickert's house, Miki also came to associate with future philosophical notables like Karl Mannheim, Eugen Herrigel (who would go to Japan to teach in 1924), and Hermann Glockner. During his stay in Heidelberg, he kept in touch with other Japanese colleagues, studying in Germany, like Abe Jirō (阿部次郎), Kuki Shūzō (九鬼周造), and others. Unsatisfied with Rickhert, Miki transferred in the summer of 1923 to Marburg to study with Heidegger. Heidegger told him to study Aristotle and introduced him to Hans-Georg Gadamer, with whom Miki studied Aristotle's *Metaphysics* and *Nichomachean Ethics*. Miki also came to associate with Heidegger's assistant (and student) Karl Löwith, who directed their readings of Schlegel, Humboldt, Dilthey, Nietzsche, and Kierkegaard, among others. This association with Löwith led Miki to alter his earlier philosophical positions and methods. (Löwith, like Herrigel, also ended up teaching in Japan some years later in 1936.) This was also a period when Neo-Kantianism was waning in post-World War I Europe and was no longer fashionable in Japan. Under the influence of Heidegger and his associates like Gadamer and Löwith, Miki freed himself from the Neo-Kantian conceptual apparatus of his student years to embrace the Diltheyan-Heideggerian approach of hermeneutic ontology. From Heidegger, who was in his pre-*Sein und Zeit* period, Miki learned the methodology of an "ontological hermeneutic of life" and studied the *Lebensphilosophie* ("philosophy of life") of people such as Friedrich Nietzsche and Georg Simmel, the hermeneutics of Wilhelm Dilthey among others, and the philosophical anthropology of Max Scheler, among other trends. Miki absorbed these various newer approaches from the post-war period that constituted a certain intellectual current in Germany at the time, but he would go on to create his own version of hermeneutic ontology, which was more affirmative of the public and the social in comparison to Heidegger's hermeneutic at the time.[3] The broad movement of the philosophy of life and hermeneutics to which Dilthey, Heidegger, and Scheler all belonged, and which provided a critique of the intellectual logicism of the Southwest School of Neo-Kantianism, was important to Miki's intellectual development at the time. He found himself more in sympathy with Heidegger's "ontology of life" that transcended the restrictions of reflective philosophy focusing on the interiority of "consciousness." He came to think of his own philosophical project to be the employment of this hermeneutical method to elucidate human existence from the perspective of an "ontology of life."[4]

Miki moved to Paris in August of 1924, where he learned French, and studied the works of Henri Poincaré, Ernest Renan, Hippolyte Taine, and Blaise Pascal. But among them, he especially developed an interest in Pascal and started working on him. Miki's endeavor to apply the hermeneutical method to human existence thus bore fruit in his work on Pascal, which he read from the standpoint of an "ontology of life" instead of taking Pascal as expressing the interiority of human consciousness or the psyche. It was here in Paris that Miki wrote his first book, *The Study of Man in Pascal* (『パスカルにおける人間の研究』), which was initially made up of three articles that he submitted to the journal *Thought* (『思想』), published by his scholarship sponsor in 1925. When his Iwanami-sponsored scholarship ended in October of 1925, he returned to Japan. The book version of his Pascal work was then published in June 1926. According to Akamatsu, Miki's philosophy at the time expressed a "cosmopolitan humanism," and resonated with the mood of Taishō (大正) liberalism and democracy and its culture of 1920s Japan.[5]

Between his return to Japan and before the book publication, Miki was appointed lecturer at the Third Higher School in April 1926. He also resumed lecturing at Ryūkoku University. Around this time Nishida recommended Miki to be an assistant to Kawakami Hajime (河上肇) (1879–1946) in the latter's research on Hegel's dialectic. Miki also started leading a seminar on Hegel's *Encyclopedia* at the Law School of Kyoto Imperial University. Kawakami was inclined toward Marxism, and the association sparked Miki's own interest in dialectical materialism and Karl Marx, thus beginning his Marxist period in 1926 or 1927. Nishida had also recommended Miki to a teaching position in Tokyo at this time, where he would eventually become tenured in 1927 as a professor of philosophy at Hōsei University (法政大学) while also lecturing at Nihon University (日本大学) and Taishō University (大正大学). He also traveled in December 1927 to Korea, Manchuria, and northern China with the president of Iwanami Publishing House (岩波出版社), Iwanami Shigeo (岩波茂雄) (1881–1946), working for the publisher.[6]

After publishing his first article on Marx in June 1927, "The Marxist Form of the Humanistic Sciences" in the journal *Thought* (*Shisō*), Miki began to focus on Marx to write several more essays on the topic. In 1928, he put together his published articles on Marx into a book, *Historical Materialism and Contemporary Consciousness* (『唯物史観と現代の意識』). But although he shifted his interest away from the religious humanism of Pascal and other French authors to become more involved in Marxism, Miki still viewed Marxism as another form of humanism. And his reading of Marx was still conducted under the lens of an ontological hermeneutic of life that prioritized fundamental experience (基礎経験) as foundational and giving birth to *logos*, but also contradicting *logos* when the latter becomes congealed and fixed, leading to its collapse and the rise of a new *logos*. With this, he developed a three-part scheme of 1) fundamental experience, 2) anthropology, and 3) ideology. Accordingly, fundamental experience is first followed by concepts (*logos*) that clarify the experience and which constitute what he called "anthropology," whereby we understand our human existence. But that anthropology, in turn, can become stagnant and fossilized as an "ideology."[7] "Experience" (経験) here has an ontological significance similar to how Nishida conceived experience in *Inquiry into the Good*. But Dilthey has also been pointed to as an important influence on Miki's notion of "experience."[8] But in Miki's Marx book, "experience" also has the sense of "dynamic correlation" in the relationships of negotiation (交渉的関係) among human beings or between them and other entities. *Logos* is born from out of this relationship—first "anthropology" as the *logos* of human self-comprehension, and then "ideology" as the *logos* of certain disciplinary fields of scholarship, science, social thought, and so on, belonging to a specific time and place. But *logos* is unstable and once established—anthropology and ideology—it can become rigid and inflexible or static, unable to respond to the ongoing flux of experience. When that happens *logos* collapses under the pressure of a new fundamental experience that contradicts it, which in turn gives birth to a new *logos*. Miki called this instability in their *kinesis*, "the dark" (闇). While on the one hand, Miki's understanding here appears to be based on Marx's schema of base and superstructure, Akamatsu thinks it may come from Simmel's philosophy of life that problematized the relationship between the established fixed forms of culture and life that overthrows it.[9] By taking fundamental experience as the foundation for human existence, Miki also came to assert the priority of "practice" over "theory." This also spurred the shift of his ontology from a hermeneutic ontology to an ontology founded on practice, a shift attributable to the influence of Marx. And yet, regardless of this shift in method, his focus, whether looking at Pascal or Marx, remained the human being—before it was Pascal's view of man, and now Marx's view of man.[10] Moreover, despite his interest in Marx's philosophy, Miki never embraced the Marxist standpoint of materialism and, rather, conducted his Marx studies from the perspective of a philosophy of life, and in that respect never became a full-fledged Marxist.[11] The unorthodoxy in his reading of Marx therefore will lead to him being ostracized and criticized by the orthodox Marxists of the Communist Party. Yet, although Miki thus never became a full-fledged Marxist, his interest in Marx did lead him beyond mere scholarly pursuits to become actively involved in the revolutionary movement, cooperating with Communist Party members. Such involvements will eventually result in his arrest under the Public Security Preservation Law for suspicion of donating money to the illegal (since 1925) Communist Party in May 1930 and subsequent imprisonment in November of that year together with his expulsion from all public academic employment, forcing him to resign his post as a professor.

His imprisonment did not prevent him from scholarly activity, however. After serving his sentence, Miki was appointed to represent the Japan section of the International Hegel League in February of 1931 and then began a series of roundtable dialogues with Nishida in 1932, two of which were published in the *Yomiuri Newspaper* (『読売新聞』).[12] 1932 is when we can date Miki's turn to historical-social ontology as represented by his work, *Philosophy of History* (『歴史哲学』) published in that year. Based on his study of Marx, he developed an ontology founded upon practice but through the addition of his own distinct understanding of historical-social ontology. With this turn to an historical-social ontology on the basis of practice, even while still retaining the aspect of a *Lebensphilosophie*, Miki's philosophizing comes into its own although previously Miki was engaging in the interpretations of Pascal or Marx as well as other philosophers like Plato, Aristotle, and Hegel, and had allowed himself to be influenced by the methodologies and thought of Neo-Kantianism, Heidegger, and Marx.[13] After his arrest he had distanced himself from the Marxist movement, but he retained the ontology, whereby history-making acts even while premised upon previous historical social realities remake the social realities into new ones. Borrowing the terminology of Nishida's dialectics, he called the relationship between the made and the making, a relationship of continuity and discontinuity, and described this dialectic in terms of mutual negation amidst mutual affirmation. He took this history-making act to be sensory and somatic and argued that this *soma* (body) is "social," so that social somaticity or social embodiment is at the basis of historical formation.[14] And this bodily nature is also entangled with history as the somatic acts shape history and are shaped by it in turn. Thereby human beings are subjects who make history. But this means that, in turn, history is also the subject forming itself via human beings as its constitutive elements.[15] We can hear in these ideas a resonance with Nishida's philosophy from the 1930s and it's hard to say who influenced who, or who is echoing who. In fact, it may be possible that these ideas developed in both thinkers together through their roundtable sessions. In any case, this emphasis on embodied action helped to concretize Miki's philosophy of practice and action and helped to clarify how human beings as embodied beings "construct the world through acts of technological production."[16] This historico-social ontology, therefore, will morph in a few years into a philosophy of technological-productive action before transmuting, after 1937, into a philosophy of the imagination and of the historical form.

Despite his alienation from Marxism, Miki still found himself interested and involved in political praxis coinciding with his scholarly interests. In January 1933, Miki wrote "The Literature of Contemporary Class Struggle," but the government forbade its sale and demanded that it be destroyed. When the "Takigawa Incident" (滝川事件) or "Kyoto University Incident" happened on July, 1933, in which Education Minister Hatoyama Ichirō declared Takigawa Yukitoki's theory of criminal law that pointed to the social roots of deviance as founded on Marxist doctrines and therefore suspended him from teaching, Miki formed the League for Academic Freedom with his colleagues in protest.[17] Nevertheless, having somewhat distanced himself from Marxism by the mid-30s made it easier for him to be more active within the academic world again. Miki had been pursuing the logic of cultural form as historical formation, but from 1934 on he begins to grasp this in terms of technological-productive action via human beings as embodied beings and discuss issues of technology and technological production in general. He comes to argue that human acts in general are acts of production mediated by technology, which include not only manufacture and tools but things like rhetoric as a technology of linguistic expression and techniques of artistic expression. That is, technology as social can be conceptual and mental as well as material and industrial. Moreover, he viewed technology as such to be regulated in the relationship or dialectic between subject and environment—not only the natural environment but also the social and cultural environments. Human beings, facing their environment, alter it to make it anew as a distinct environment. Technology mediates this relationship. Miki grasped this act of technological production to be, in some sense, a "creation out of nothingness." In transcending their environment, human beings are grounded upon this "nothingness" (無), whereupon they are seized by a demonic and primal urge to undertake creation. The nothingness here symbolizes the indeterminacy of this creativity. In this Miki is borrowing Nishida's concept of "nothingness" (無) to assert the groundlessness (無根拠性) of human existence, resulting in an ontology of life un/grounded upon the nothing.[18] From 1933 to 1937 Miki reworked his manuscript for *Philosophical Anthropology* (『哲学的人間学』) several times but it remained unpublished. Miki began writing the *Logic of Imagination* in 1937 in the form of twelve serially published essays. In these essays, he eventually comes to understand this formation of culture via technological-productive action that is a "creation from nothingness," further in terms of the formation of "forms" (形) by the imagination, uniting *pathos* and *logos*. Both of his philosophies of technological production and of the imagination involve the idea of this unifying of opposites within the framework of a self-forming force moving history and, perhaps, to that extent, as Akamatsu argues, also remain within the framework of a philosophy of life or *Lebensphilosophie*, even if now grounded more explicitly upon the nothing.[19]

In the meantime, from 1935 to 1937, Miki worked as a lecturer at the Bunka Gakuin (文化学院) institute. He also became editor of the *Catholic Encyclopedia* of Sophia University (上智大学) in 1935. The same year, he held another three-session dialogue for publication with Nishida. In 1936 he participated in two roundtable discussions, "On Nishida Philosophy" and "Life and the Philosophy of Life." He took part in a number of academic conferences during this time as well as continuing his close association with Tosaka Jun (戸坂潤) (1900–1945), who maintained a lifelong allegiance to Marxism, while participating in the same conferences. Miki finished a revised edition of a philosophy dictionary for Iwanami Publishers in 1937. And in 1938 he joined the Shōwa Research Association (昭和研究会) and its institute, the Shōwa-juku (昭和塾), serving as the president of its Culture section. The association was an informal think-tank, organized to inform Konoe Fumimaro (近衞文麿) (1891–1945), who served as prime minister from 1937 to 1941. Miki became a leading figure in the institute and its seminars. And in 1939, together with other philosophers associated with Kyoto University, including Nishida, Watsuji Tetsurō (和辻哲郎) (1889–1960), and Tanabe, among others, he became a member of the Civilian Academic Society (国民学術協会). In the late 1930s, Miki was also employed by the Japanese government to conduct lecture tours through China and Manchuria, and in 1940 he returned to China to attend conferences and hold dialogues with distinguished personalities and to Manchuria for two months where he lectured. But in October 1940, the Shōwa Research Association was dissolved following the Sorge Spy Incident, in which a Soviet Russian spy under the cover of a German journalist was caught reporting on Germany and Japan and was hanged by his Japanese captors. In 1942, Miki was drafted by the Army and sent to Manila as a member of the Army's propaganda section.

During this period, from the late 1930s to the 1940s, Miki published *Socrates* in June 1939, followed by the essays that will become *The Logic of Imagination Part 1* (『構想力の論理第一』). He also published *Introduction to Philosophy* (『哲学入門』) in March 1940, and in 1941 published *Notes on a Theory of Human Life* (『人生論ノート』) in

August, and the first volume of *Notes on Philosophy* (『哲学ノート』) in November. In 1942 he published *Philosophy of Knowledge* (『知識哲学』), *Learning and Human Life* (『学問と人生』) both in March, the second volume of *Notes on Philosophy* in April, *Reading and Human Life* (『読書と人生』) in June, and the *Philosophy of Technology* (『技術哲学』) in September.[20]

Despite his employment with the state, he was again arrested in March of 1945 by the Metropolitan Police Dept. and found guilty in June on the charge of sheltering and helping Takakura Teru, who was suspected of violating the Peace Preservation Law, allowing him to flee, thus himself breaking the Peace Preservation Law. He was imprisoned just as the war was ending, first sentenced to Sugamo Prison and then moved to Toyotama Prison in Nakano. There in September of 1945, a mere forty days after Japan's surrender to the US, Miki died in prison from sudden nephritis (acute kidney inflammation), his whole body covered with scabies, reportedly due to mistreatment under unhygienic conditions. Despite the war ending, he had not been released due to the turmoil and confusion of the transitional period immediately following the war. In fact, his death in prison had so astonished the General Head Quarters of the U.S. Occupation that it motivated it to issue, in October of that year, the directive ordering to release all political prisoners.[21] After his death a posthumous manuscript, which remained a fragmentary draft, entitled *Shinran* (『親鸞』) was discovered, in which Miki attempts to clarify his view of Shinran's religion from a variety of angles.[22]

The Logic of Imagination

As mentioned above, the *Logic of Imagination* was never completed by Miki. If Miki had lived longer, he may have revised and edited portions of it to polish the manuscript before publishing the final version, although it had already been serially published while he was alive. He was planning on writing the next section on language. And he certainly would have worked on further insights, whether in this or other works, in light of the post-war conditions and contemporary technological and social developments. In any case, this work remains representative of his philosophy during the last years of his life.

The work was first serialized, as mentioned above, in the journal *Thought* from 1937 to 1938, under the themes of "Myth," "Institution," and "Technology," which make up the first three chapters of the present book. After its serialization in the journal, the three chapters were brought together and published as the monograph, *Logic of Imagination Part One* in 1939 by Iwanami Pub. The next part, "Experience," was then also serialized in the same journal and Miki continued to work on it, writing it until 1943 when he announced his intention to address "Language" in the following chapter. He was unable to realize his plan due to his arrest and death in prison. The completed portion of "Experience" was then published by Iwanami as *Logic of Imagination Part Two* posthumously, after the war, in 1946.

By his own account in the Introduction, in terms of a methodology, Miki adopts the approach of a phenomenology with the intention of advancing this into a logic—

perhaps with Hegel in mind whose *Phenomenology of Spirit* chronologically preceded his *Logic*. The point was to observe the unfolding of the imagination in its formation of forms in the phenomena of myth, institution, technology, and experience, and to develop a logic (*Logik*) on that basis as the structure of that formation. He ends his Introduction by stating that his research for the moment remains phenomenological as a collection of notes and that the *logic* of imagination, however, has not yet been fully worked out and remains incomplete.

As evident from the title, the book deals with the imagination, by which he means the productive imagination responsible for creating our picture of the world and hence for shaping, in Heideggerian terms, our being-in-the-world. Imagination (*kōsōryoku*, 構想力) in the former sense is in reference to Kant's *productive* imagination, which adds the constructive or constitutive aspect to the, otherwise, merely fanciful imagination or phantasy (*sōzōryoku*, 想像力). Miki's claim is that the real (現実的なもの) as such, in contrast to Hegel's claim that the real is the rational, is "imaginary" (想像的) and follows the logic of imagination (構想力（想像力）の論理) (MKZ[23] 1: 209). It is imaginary, yet nonetheless real. Miki postulates that its formative act involves the union of *pathos* and *logos*—encompassing the oppositions and ambiguity between subjectivity and objectivity, ideality and reality, interiority and exteriority, the intellectual and the emotive, sensibility and understanding, being and becoming, time and space, and so on. Miki has in large part been inspired here by his reading of Kant's theories of the imagination (*Einbildungskraft*) in the first and third *Critiques*. For Miki, the forms (*Bilder*, 形) or form-images (形像), which the imagination (*Einbildung*)—as the faculty of formation (*Bildung*)—forms (*bilden*), are not merely ideal images but, as collectively meaningful, are ontologically constitutive of our world and can be materialized or embodied in physical reality to shape our environment. Hence the logic here is a logic of form (形の論理), which, moreover, involves the transformation of forms in history (MKZ 8: 6). The forms the imagination gives birth to, therefore, are not merely fanciful fictions but the very reality of our world (MKZ 8: 41), which is dynamic and never static. This synthetic act of *pathos* and *logos* gets played out in different ways through the media of myth, institution, and technology to which Miki devotes the first three chapters as well as experience in general which makes up the second part of the book. In ancient Greek terms, *mythos*, *nomos*, and *technē*, along with experience, thus all involve the *poiēsis* (production) of the imagination.

The first medium of the imagination that Miki analyzes is myth (神話), which contrary to common opinion does not belong solely to the ancient period or to primitive societies. Instead, it is a force that continues to move and make history today. Miki most certainly noticed the mythical aspects of the imperial-nationalist ideology propagandized by the Japanese state at the time. But he also referred to Georges Sorel's notion of myth as utilized by revolutionary movements as a counter to statist oppression. Through myth the imagination gathers and shapes the material of the environing world, thereby uniting *logos* and *pathos*, giving form to matter, to shape a meaningful picture of the world (MKZ 8: 75). Myth thereby expresses the hopes and fears, loves and hates, desires, passions, impulses, and so on of a people but in the form of intellectual representations and figures, which in turn motivate and guide action. Myth as such is the "symbolization of internal states by means of external form-images and the animation of an external actuality by means of internal states" (MKZ 8: 34). Today we ordinarily think of myths as unreal, but Miki argues that they are present, with a sense of reality, wherever and whenever their primeval power is felt to function in this world (MKZ 8: 27–28), moving people to action, and thereby "drawing out" a new reality out of the natural world, giving form to a new world.

The second medium Miki discusses is institution (制度). As forms produced by the imagination, institutions are systems of customary activity that help to adapt us to the environment. As "institution," Miki includes "language, convention, morality, law, art, and so on," signifying "culture" as a whole (MKZ 8: 102). He also includes the topic of the previous chapter, "myth," as such an institution (MKZ 8: 97). As products of custom or habit, they are "fictions," and yet despite being "fictions," they possess "reality." Miki gives three main characteristics of an institution: 1) it possesses a fictional character as an invention rather than being based on instinct; 2) as a social convention it is endowed with the character of being a custom or tradition, whereby its fictionality is forgotten and it becomes seen as natural and necessary, as "second nature"; and 3) it has the character of normativity in that it is coercive or constraining and authoritative for the individual (MKZ 8: 102–103). What at first was invented by one or a few individuals becomes imitated and then repeated by others to become a custom, which in turn becomes a tradition inherited by later generations to possess an imperative or normative character. This occurs from out of the interactivity of human beings with their environment (MKZ 8: 158, 159). But institutions, in turn, also constitute the environment itself (MKZ 8: 160). And as such working adaptations, they are not fixed but are variable. In relation to the environment of formed institutions, throughout history we go on forming new institutions to create new socio-cultural environments (e.g. MKZ 8: 180; MKZ 18: 248).

The following chapter deals with technology (技術) through which human beings transcend their environment to alter it and reshape it into a new one. It is "the skill used to mediate the subject with its environment when there is an opposition or alienation between them."[24] This occurs in the embodied behavior of human beings, such as in the production of things through the use of tools. Technological activity as such are productive acts that give birth to new forms by means of the imagination. There is some overlap here with another work of his, *The Philosophy of Technology* (『技術哲学』) of 1941, in which Miki states that technology is invention (発明), which in turn is forming (形成) or creation (創造) (MKZ 7: 224). By structurally assimilating existent elements, technological-productive action creatively adapts the subject to its environment, mediating the subject's relation to the environment and producing a new one with new forms. Such production involves the synthesis of two moments: the cognition of laws of nature as the objective element and the postulation of goals as the subjective element. The synthesis results in the production of definite forms. This technology realizes the synthesis of *pathos* and *logos* (MKZ 8: 241–43).

Miki, however, goes on to expand the meaning of technology to encompass biological nature in general for life evolves in relation to its environment by adapting to it: "In making forms, life is technological. To the extent that not only human beings but nature also makes forms, we can see it as technological. The human being simply continues what nature accomplishes" (MKZ 8: 234). This however also leads Miki to extend the meaning of the imagination beyond the human domain to nature as well: "We can admit that the imagination's creative logic is already operative even in nature ..." (MKZ 8: 236). While Miki began his analysis of the productive activity of the imagination at the root of the human being, we thus eventually see him extending this productivity to nature itself as technological and that human creativity imitates, participates in, and is an extension of nature's own *techné*. What defines the essence of technology, common to both humanity and nature, as such is "transformation" (転形): "Transformation is the fundamental act of technology" (MKZ 7: 253–54). That is, just as human history is the history of transformation, "the history of nature is the history of the transformation of forms" (MKZ 8: 237). They are both histories of alteration of forms (形の変化) (MKZ 8: 237). Human technology simply "takes up the construction of the universe at the point it had been abandoned by nature" (MKZ 8: 237). Borrowing a concept from Nishida, Miki states that they belong together in the unfolding of the "historical world" (歴史的世界) as inclusive of both humanity and nature. As if to quote Nishida, he says: "The historical world is creative and human beings are creative elements of the creative world" (MKZ 7: 223).[25] And "as formative elements of the formative world, we participate in the self-formation of the historical world" (MKZ 7: 236).

The dynamic logic of the imagination's formative act is played out in human somatic interactivity with the environment as a *praxis* that is technological. Technological productive action—not only industrial and mechanical technologies, but also social, conceptual, and psychological technics—mediates the subject to its environment by forming the environment anew as not simply natural but a cultural and social world, giving birth to the reality of our world. Certainly, technology has become much more extensive in contemporary times perhaps beyond Miki's imagination, stretching as far as information technology and the technology for manipulating biological life—whether this involves genetics, nanotechnology, or other means. But Miki's comprehensive concept of "form" may still be useful in such contemporary contexts. As we work upon the material surrounding us, they are trans*form*ed and given new form (MKZ 8: 7), a dynamism he describes as moving from chaos to form, darkness to light, nothingness to being. The root of this creativity is an indetermination (無限定) at the root of man, demanding determination (限定) with the *demonisch* urge to form or, in Schelling's terms, "der Hunger nach Wesen" ("hunger for being") (MKZ 8: 72). If *pathos*, as its verb form *paschein* (πάσχειν) indicates, is something to be *suffered*, *received*, as singular, multiple, and contingent, preceding any conceptual or determinative grasp, *logos* as indicated by its verb form of *legein* (λέγειν) is the "gathering" of that formlessness, the "raking together" (掻き集める) of the manifold chaos, that Miki had previously called "the dark" (闇) or "the nothing" (無), to give it form, bringing it into the light as "being." This ongoing creation and transformation of forms is the process of history, which Miki thus describes as a "logic of history" (歴史の論理), a "logic of historical forms" (歴史的形の論理), and "logic of historical creation" (歴史的創造の論理) (MKZ 8: 18).

Beginning with Miki's hermeneutical approach in looking at human existence, his philosophy, it is often said, was a philosophy of cosmopolitan humanism, perhaps under the influence of the mood of democracy and Taishō liberal arts or liberalism as its backdrop.[26] He himself claims in his Introduction that his philosophy had developed from an anthropology to a humanism that acknowledges things of both *pathos* and *logos*. Akamatsu thus makes the claim that Miki's philosophy consistently has been a philosophy of humanism.[27] Be that as it may, we need also to recognize how his thought dug deep into the roots of that humanity and, further, behind it, to the abyssal prehuman root beneath the human essence, to what he called "the dark," "nothingness"— the *pathos* that we suffer beyond our supposedly autonomous rationality, and which we are not in control of. Miki pursued this to the extent of attributing the creativity of history[28]—beyond the confines of the human—to be operative in the middle voice in nature itself, as the sinograph for "nature" (自然) implies. This act or event, formation, can no longer be said to be simply of the subject or of the object.

The final chapter that originally made up the entirety of Part Two of the book bears its title from the word *experience* (経験). Here Miki problematizes experience in David Hume and Immanuel Kant as well as other thinkers but discusses especially Kant's reexamination of the imagination in this context, not only in the first *Critique* (*Kritik der reinen Vernunft*) with its three-fold synthesis and the schematism but also in relation to the faculty of judgment and common sense in the third *Critique* (*Kritik der Urteilskraft*). He thus takes the imagination here as responsible for experience in general. This final chapter or Part Two may in fact be the most foundational and important in terms of what Miki has to offer of a philosophy of the imagination. Miki inherited Heidegger's reading of Kantian imagination as the root of the faculties. But he takes this further in ontological terms, concretizing it, by relating it explicitly to technology, embodiment, society, and history, in the constitution of our being-in-theworld. The connection Miki makes here between the imagination in Kant's first and third *Critiques* at the time was unusual and makes explicit what he may have discerned as implicit in Heidegger's interpretation of Kant.

Miki's Contribution and Relevance

How relevant is Miki's philosophy of the imagination for us today in our contemporary context? Does it serve to make any contribution to philosophy or to our lives in general? Or is it only of historical interest, especially since the work remained unfinished? Miki's philosophy of the imagination anticipated later theories of the productive imagination as embodied and social or collective and historical that would take Kant's productive imagination in a more radical direction beyond mere transcendental subjectivity, tying the imagination explicitly to the *sensus communis* and history. These later theories we find, first, in Hannah Arendt, and then in Paul Ricoeur and Cornelius Castoriadis, in Benedict Anderson, as well as most recently in Charles Taylor. The connection Miki makes of the imagination with technology anticipates ideas of the technological imagination in Don Ihde and Bernard Stiegler, for example, and the digital imagination in more recent authors. Miki, however, distinctly provides a sober ontological grounding for this formative function of the imagination in an abyss that accounts for its unpredictable nature, relating Nishida's nothingness to the imagination's creativity and the emergence of novelty in history.

The above question of relevance leads to the issue of viability. The question may especially pertain to the issue of technology. Whether his account of technology possesses any viability today depends on whether, or not, it can resolve the fundamental issues of ecology, the Anthropocene, and the so-called destruction of nature that scientific technology faces today. For example, we would need to consider whether Miki's account inherits the Greek dualism of form and matter and to what extent Miki's theory can respond to the violent imposition of form, on the part of human beings, upon nature. How can we overcome the violation of nature that treats it, in Heideggerian terms, as mere standing-reserve? On the other hand, if the imagination in Miki is ultimately rooted in the historical world's self-formation that moves in the middle voice, escaping reduction to human subjectivity or autonomy but without thereby leading to materialist determinism, perhaps then the issue of dualism becomes a non-issue. Akamatsu argues that it may be necessary to reconstruct Miki's account of technology in a way so as to incorporate this topic of form/matter. But he adds that to bring it to life, we would need to grasp his philosophy anew in light of the more recent discoveries of the life sciences and information sciences.[29] We may also add to this the wartime and post-war development of nuclear technology as well as of computer and digital technology, the Internet, cyberspace, virtual reality, AI technology, social media, and so on. With these developments in technology that did not exist in Miki's time, but which certainly condition our imagination and imaginaries today, the very concepts of subject and environment, form, production, even *pathos* and *logos*, and of course, technology and the imagination themselves, have inevitably altered. The imagination in Miki's philosophy would nevertheless be well worth investigating in light of these transformations in our way of living. Although he was unable to realize the completion of this book, his thinking about the imagination, inherited critically, would provide clues for further development that can illumine our contemporary understanding of the imagination and technology and our comportment to the world.[30] His association of technology with imagination in relation to nature and its history, for example, provides a source for cross-disciplinary discourse on the ecological crisis today. In that respect Miki has much to contribute to our contemporary understanding of our situatedness in the world.

Note on the Translation

The current translation was made from the Japanese original as it appears in *The Collected Works of Miki Kiyoshi* vol. 8 (『三木清全集第八巻』) published in 1967 by Iwanami Publishers. Under Japanese copyright laws, this work falls under the public domain as the 70-year term, after the author's death, for copyright has passed. I have provided the pagination from this version in square brackets only at the beginning of each section for scholars and students who want to check the Japanese. This is the first English translation of the entire volume although an earlier version of the translation of chapter one ("Myth"), by the same translator, was published in *Social Imaginaries* vol. 2, no. 1 (2016).

Acknowledgements

This publication would not have been possible without the many people who have helped and supported me in one way or another. It would be impossible to name all of them, but among them, I am grateful, first and foremost, to Stephen Lofts, who read and edited the manuscript and provided suggestions for improving the English translation. I am also indebted to the support given to me by the Social Imaginaries Editorial Collective, editors of the journals *Social Imaginaries* (Zeta Books, 2014–21) and *The International Journal of Social Imaginaries* (Brill, 2022–), which in its different incarnations have included Suzi Adams, Jeremy Smith, Natalie Doyle, Paul Blokker, and Saulius Geniusas. As mentioned above a very early version of my translation of chapter 1 ("Myth") was published in *Social Imaginaries* vol. 2, no. 1 (2016). I was also spurred on to finish this translation by the interest shown by a number of people, including Saulius Geniusas, Dennis Stromback, Stephen Lofts, and Kevin Lam, who had asked me over the years when the translation will be finished and published. I also would like to thank the interest in my work on Miki in general shown by Fernando Wirtz and Stephen Lofts who organized the International Workshop on the Contemporary Significance of the Philosophy of Miki Kiyoshi held December 17, 2022 at Kyoto University in Kyoto, Japan; and also Enrico Fongaro and Stephen Lofts who organized the Workshop on Miki Kiyoshi's *Logic of Imagination* held December 19, 2022 at Nanzan University in Nagoya, Japan, in both cases inviting me to participate. I am grateful to the participants in both conferences for their thought-provoking questions and stimulating conversations, including Takushi Odagiri, Joseph O'Leary, Sova Cerda, Yoko Arisaka, and James Heisig. I also want to thank the anonymous reviewers of this manuscript for providing useful suggestions to improve the translation and the introduction. I am lastly grateful to the book series editors, Monika Steinbach and Takeshi Morisato, at Bloomsbury Publishing for their interest and suggestions in regard to the manuscript's publication. I also want to thank the entire production team at Bloomsbury for their excellent job. And finally, I would like to express my gratitude to Shigenori Nagatomo, who first introduced me to Miki Kiyoshi some twenty years ago and who also coached me back then when I was having my start in translating Japanese philosophy. I take full responsibility for any errors in the translation.

Introduction[1]

[3][2] This treatise on the logic of imagination [*kōsōryoku no ronri*, 構想力の論理], whose first volume is being brought into the world here, was originally published as a serial in the journal, *Thought* [*Shisō*,『思想』]. As I returned to writing after an unavoidable interruption due to various circumstances I felt the necessity, for the sake of the readers, but above all for my own sake, to arrange the first three chapters that had already been published into a single volume. These were originally written in the form of research notes, but I decided to publish them in their original form, limiting myself to minimum revisions. A complete systematic narrative must necessarily begin from where this investigation left off. The narrative here first adopts a phenomenological form; however, it will then advance to a purely logical form.

In order to show the way within to the somewhat intricate discussions of this treatise which began initially as research notes, I would like to briefly explain in this Introduction my intention. Needless to say, as I go on writing this treatise, the path I take will likely change and be developed. This is a matter of course for those who, like myself, have the habit of thinking while writing instead of writing after thinking.

What ceaselessly passed through my thoughts after the publication of my previous work, *Philosophy of History* [*Rekishi tetsugaku*,『歴史哲学』] (1932), was the question as to whether it was possible to combine the objective and the subjective, the rational and the irrational, the intellectual and the emotional. At the time I formulated this problem as a matter of the unity of *logos* and *pathos* and it was my main task to analyze the element of *logos* [*rogosuteki yōso*, ロゴス的要素] and the element of *pathos* [*patosuteki yōso*, パトス的要素] within everything historical, and thereby discuss their dialectical unity. The issue at this time is especially seen in my collection of essays, *The Standpoint of Man in Crisis* [*Kiki ni okeru ningen no tachiba*,『危機に於ける人間の立場』] (1933). Although I am drawn to the rational, to things of *logos*, I have always found the problems of subjectivity, interiority, and things of *pathos* too difficult to deal with. This is why I found myself seized by Pascal (*The Investigation of Man in Pascal* [*Pasukaru ni okeru ningen no kenkyu*,『パスカルに於ける人間の研究』], 1926) and also why Heidegger exerted an influence on me. Even during the period when I became absorbed in the investigation of historical materialism from my original interest in the philosophy of history (*Historical Materialism and the Consciousness of the Contemporary Period* [*Yuibutsushikan to gendai no ishiki*,『唯物史観と現代の意識』], 1928), I searched for a human basis for historical materialism, indeed, from out of the same spirit. My demand to not lose sight of the things of *pathos* for the sake of the things of *logos*, but also to not forget the things of *logos* for the sake of the things of *pathos*, eventually took shape in the affirmation of humanism. I advanced, so to speak, from anthropology to humanism and this is exemplified in my collection of critical essays, *On Anthropological Literature* [*Ningengakuteki bungaku ron*,『人間学的文学論』] (1934) of that period.

As I stated before, even if it is not a mistake to conceive of the unity of *logos* and *pathos* as a dialectical unity qua unity of opposites, I myself had always felt that this way of thinking was too formal. I am a person who cannot but feel an aversion towards the reduction of dialectics in the hands of many into a kind of formalism, into a new formal logic, or even into an expediency, as it were. Even if the things of *logos* and the things of *pathos* are dialectically united, where can we concretely discover that unity? Where is that synthesis that does not stop at mere logical constitution given in actuality? In pursuing this issue and recollecting that Kant recognized a faculty that conjoins understanding and sensibility in the imagination, I came to think of the logic of imagination. And so guided by the premonition that perhaps I might approach the solution to my long-standing question of many years, I began writing these research notes (*Thought* [*Shisō*,『思想』] May 1937). However, it can be said that during the period when I was writing the first chapter, "Myth," I was apprehensive that the imagination was only being thought of as a faculty of synthesis of *logos* and *pathos* and could very well fall into a kind of irrationalism or subjectivism. I can say that what supported me vis-à-vis this uncertainty was nothing more than the view that something objective and rational that can be called technology [or: technics; *gijutsu*, 技術], in its universal essence, forms the unity of the subjective and the objective. However, as I eventually began my investigations into "institutions [*seido*, 制度]," it became clear, little by little, that what I had been thinking of as a logic of imagination was in fact a "logic of form [*katachi no ronri*, 形の論理]." In taking up Greek philosophy, recently in particular Aristotle (*Aristotle's Metaphysics* [*Aristoteresu keijijōgaku*,『アリストテレス形而上学』], 1935; *Aristotle* [*Arisutoteresu*,『アリストテレス』], 1936), my thinking advanced with respect to this point. My idea has now stabilized with the discovery of the logic of imagination as subjective expression, and objective expression in the logic of form. In this way, I see that from my own problem of the human, I have come into contact with Nishidian philosophy [*Nishida tetsugaku*, 西田哲学]. Nishidian philosophy has, consciously or unconsciously, continuously guided me in my research. Nevertheless, there is another problem concerning the relationship between my logic of imagination and the logic of Nishidian philosophy that should probably be thought through at some point.

For the time being, in order to remove misunderstanding, and to provide some perspective, concerning the intent of this treatise, I will discuss the following two or three points.

What I am attempting to conceive by means of a logic of imagination is a philosophy of action [*kōi*, 行為]. Up to now, when speaking of the imagination, one almost always considered only artistic activity. And where it comes to form [*katachi*, 形], it is as well considered only from the standpoint of thought. Here, I free the imagination from this restriction and relate it to action in general. In this case what is important is to understand action, not abstractly as something to do with the will, as in conventional subjectivist idealism, but to understand action as making things. All action, in a broad sense, has the meaning of making things, namely, the sense of production. The logic of imagination is such a logic of production. Everything made has form. To act means to make a new form by working upon something and altering (*transforming*) its form. As a thing made, form is historical and continues to change historically. The form is not only objective but the unity of the objective and the subjective, the unity of *ideas* and reality, being and becoming, time and space. The logic of imagination is a logic of historical form. Moreover, even if I say that action is to make things, history is inconceivable unless to make (ποίησις) at the same time has the sense of to become (γένεσις). History becomes thinkable where production (*poíēsis*) at the same time has the meaning of becoming (*génesis*). The logic of imagination is the logic of the transformation of form. But what I call the philosophy of form is not the same as what had previously been called morphology. Morphology is a philosophy of interpretation and not a philosophy of action. And in contrast to the fact that much of morphology had been irrationalist, what I call the philosophy of form is rather a unity of eidology (*Eidologie*) and morphology (*Morphologie*) and, furthermore, aims for this within the standpoint of action.

We can probably say that up until now all logic, with the exception perhaps of the logic that sought to ground modern science, has been the logic of form. Aristotle's logic, which is claimed to have perfected formal logic, was originally a logic of form tied to Greek ontology that viewed form or idea (*idea, eidos*) as reality. In this case, however, form was thought to be unchanging and not historical. Hegel's logic, which is said to have completed dialectics, is ultimately also a logic of form. Although Hegel introduced a historical perspective to it, he remains within the standpoint of thinking of Greek ontology and does not take up the position of action. His dialectic is a logic of reflection or logic of thinking-over [*tsuikō*, 追考; *Nachdenken*], and not a logic of action or logic of creation. The logic of imagination, as a logic of form, is tied to the logic of Aristotle and that of Hegel, but it grasps form from the standpoint of historical action. The logic of imagination, however, does not simply reject formal logic and Hegelian dialectics: rather, it encompasses them. As an originary logic (*Urlogik*), the logic of imagination spins them out of itself as a form of its self-reflection.

By taking the standpoint of enactive intuition [*kōiteki chokkan*, 行為的直観],[3] the logic of imagination will presumably recognize an originary meaning in intuition that had hitherto been unjustly neglected. And yet, this cannot be a simple intuitionism. Real intuition is something mediated in many layers by reflection. It is a single point of the present that gathers together the infinite past and leaps into the future. The logic of imagination is, however, not simply the logic of mediation. In the end, the logic of mediation remains a logic of reflection and therefore cannot be a logic of action, in that it takes every mediation as ultimately something abstract and misses the point where it can make the utmost lived leap. This is presumably clear in creative action in art and in general in invention in technology [*gijutsu*, 技術]. And it must be said that all human action, when viewed as operative adaptations, is all technological [or: technical; *gijutsuteki*, 技術的]. The basic idea of technology [technics] is form. If we think about the logic of imagination with technology in this way, we can understand the relationship between the logic of form and science. As technology is based on science, the remarkable progress of modern technology was made possible by the development of modern science. Considered from here, the logic of imagination can be developed into an actual logic by being mediated by the logic of science.

In this sense, the idea of science was born in modern times, but technology had existed prior to that. It existed even in the East, where science had allegedly not developed. Technology, together with human culture, is ancient and universal. Modern science too was born from technological demands and was always being adapted for technological ends. The idea of culture was, therefore, oriented towards the idea of form, whereas the idea of technology, which was more general than the idea of culture, was oriented towards the idea of science. And science as well was also comprehended within it as an element. It can be seen that the idea of culture as *Gemeinschaft* preceding the modern *Gesellschaft* was an idea of form. Today, when the abstract nature of the modern culture of *Gesellschaft*, oriented towards the idea of science, is shown and we require a new culture in terms of a *Gemeinschaft*, the logic of imagination can provide a philosophical foundation for the creation of a new culture. But just as this new *Gemeinschaft* is not abstract, in opposition to *Gesellschaft*, but must be that which sublates *Gesellschaft*, the logic of form must be that which is mediated by science rather than abstractly opposed to it.

The logic of form is not only a universal logic of culture. It is a logic that ties nature and culture, the history of nature and the history of the human being together. Nature is both technological and makes form. Human technology continues the work of nature. In contrast to the view that would abstractly separate nature, culture, and history, the logic of imagination makes it possible to grasp both in terms of the *transformation* of form. Instead of thinking of history from nature, we are thinking of nature from history. From this, the logic of imagination will presumably be able to provide an appropriate position for the descriptive sciences of nature along with the sciences of culture that have not been adequately addressed in contrast to mathematical natural science.

Just as the idea of culture as *Gemeinschaft* is generally a form, we can say that the idea of Eastern culture was also a form. However, whereas in Greece form was viewed objectively and came to mean "concepts" and so that form was ultimately connected to modern science, in the East form was grasped subjectively and thus seen as symbolic. This subjective viewpoint has been thoroughly pursued through the idea of the "formless form" [*katachinaki katachi*, 形なき形],[4] the idea that what has form is an image [*kage*, 影][5] of the formless. This idea is significant for us. Form is form vis-à-vis form, and every form is independent. What lies at the root of such forms and ties them together is not something like the laws of modern science, it cannot be something objectively graspable; rather, it must be a form beyond form, a "formless form." Even though I say that form is the unity of the subjective and the objective, the logic of imagination does not take the standpoint of the so-called union of subject/object but rather is thinkable only where the subjective/objective has been transcended. Only then can we say that the logic of imagination is a logic of action, a logic of creation. And yet, even if one says that Eastern logic takes up the standpoint of enactive intuition, we must be wary of its tendency to remain within a mental framework; the technology it has in mind, without stepping forward into the practice that actually works upon things to alter their form and make new forms, ultimately ends in contemplation. Here it needs to be mediated by the concept of the technology of science and of things.

The above ideas must, of course, be fully developed. For the moment, my research is phenomenological, and has only just gotten underway. Although I had first taken up the three factors of myth, institution, and technology, because my aim was to treat them mainly from the perspective of the logic of imagination, as independent theories of myth, institution, and technology, it is unavoidable that they would be incomplete. For my purpose, there are probably a variety of issues that I need to consider, but I will make up for any inadequacies as I proceed.

Miki Kiyoshi
July 1939
Tokyo

1

Myth

1.

[13] The term "logic of imagination" (*Logik der Einbildungskraft*) is derived from Baumgarten.[1] It has also been called the "logic of phantasy" [*sōzō no ronri*, 想像の論理] (*Logik der Phantasie*). According to [Ernst] Cassirer,[2] the concept of the logic of imagination [*sōzō*; phantasy] took root in German psychology through Meier (Georg Fr. Meier) and Tetens, disciples of Baumgarten, and even the "critique of judgment" (*Kritik der Urteilskraft*) in Kant is related to this. Pascal had already discovered a "logic of the heart" (*logique du couer*) unknown to reason. In the present age [*gen'dai*, 現代] as well, as in the theories of Ribot's "logic of emotions" (*logique des sentiments*) and Heinrich Maier's "psychology of emotional thought" (*Psychologie des emotionalen Denkens*), both speak of a logic distinguished from the logic of abstract thought. Does this kind of logic really differ from the logic of reason? And if a difference does exist, what is it like? These are the questions that I wish to investigate here by reviving the term "logic of imagination." How does the logic of imagination, as we mean it, relate to Ribot's logic of emotions or Maier's psychology of emotional thought? Retrospectively, how does it relate to formal logic? An even more significant question to be clarified is the relationship between what is normally referred to as dialectics and what we call the logic of imagination. Indeed, dialectics are generally acknowledged to be a logic distinct from formal logic.

There are probably several reasons why we must consider a logic that differs from formal logic. The details will have to be discussed later, but let me give a few reasons in order to show the problem we are facing at the starting point of our research.

To begin with, once the abstractness of formal logic is shown, we demand in contrast some sort of concrete logic. Where does this so-called abstractness of formal logic lie? Formal logic, at its source, is intimately tied to Greek ontology that viewed form [*keisō*, 形相] (*forma*) as reality. The formal [*keishiki*, 形式] in formal logic [*keishiki ronri*, 形式論理] was originally related to the ontology of form. Hence if concrete things are constituted from form and matter, one might then say that formal logic is not a logic of things, or that as a logic of things it is abstract. In Aristotle, *logos* or *nous* was conceived as the capacity to receive form from things by stripping them of matter. To put it simply, formal logic is a logic in terms of *logos*. Nevertheless, it is through our bodies that we collide with things themselves in their materiality. As things, we collide with things. If we here give the designation of *pathos* to the body in its subjectivity, the logic of things is not simply a logic of *logos* but at the same time would have to be related to things of *pathos*. In previous logic, perception was placed at the foundation of thought or its preceding stage, and sensation [*kankaku*, 感覚] whereby we come in touch with things themselves was hardly reflected upon. Even when sensation was made an issue, like perception and thought, it was only grasped in an intellectual sense. The issue of whether sensation at the same time possesses the meaning of *pathos* was not raised. In cases where one "thinks with the body," where one thinks through action as a human being possessing a body, we can say that formal logic is abstract. I believe that here there must be something like a logic of emotions [*kanjō*, 感情] in contrast to the Greek logic of intellectualism.

Even if formal logic is a logic of the intellect, it presumably cannot be a logic of action. When we act, we collide through our bodies with things themselves. Action requires a body, and the objects of action are not abstract universals but rather individual concrete things. The logic of action must therefore be a logic that somehow differs from formal logic. But can this be something like the logic of imagination? When we speak of the logic of emotions or the logic of imagination, we ordinarily think of the realm of beauty or art. Baumgarten grounded aesthetics in the logic of phantasy [想像]. What Kant sought in the transcendental structure of the faculty of judgment was the ground for the principles of beauty. In this way, even if we acknowledge something like a logic of imagination, we regard it as a logic of beauty or logic of art and find it difficult to think of it as a logic of action. Nevertheless, if, as I will argue shortly, all acts possess the sense of *poiēsis* (production) or put differently, expressive action, then perhaps we can say that the logic of action is the logic of imagination, hitherto conceived merely in regard to artistic expression. Needless to say, we are not setting out to consent to the standpoint of so-called aestheticism. On the contrary, the issue for us is to comprehend not only art but all action, including the act of cognition, at its root by clarifying the fundamental meaning of expression, thereby liberating the logic of imagination as a logic of the expressive world in general from its restriction to the realm of beauty, and to display it in its relationship to morality and theory, especially to theory and practice.

Action, incidentally, is essentially social. And it is particularly in regard to group psychology that a logic distinct from formal logic came to be required. One might say that formal logic is not simply of the individual but rather possesses a supra-individual universality. By means of this, however, it assumes precisely that the human being is divorced from historical determination, that the human is an eternal, abstract essence. The concrete operations of the historical psychology of society, and of the psychology of human beings constrained by that historical psychology, transcend formal logic. Everything that can be understood to be a product of group psychology, such as language, myth, manners, convention, institutions, etc., cannot be grasped by formal logic. Formal logic cannot be the logic of history if we take the subject of history primarily to be the so-called objective spirit [精神]. Even though dialectics has been seen as the logic of history, the reason why we are proposing a logic of imagination at this point is not from the desire to reduce history to something private. On the contrary, it is quite the opposite. The subject of history is not an abstract universal nor mere spirit; it is something equipped with the so-called social body and individualized through corporality. And everything historical exists in an environment, and when acting upon the environment is acted upon by it. It is determined by the environment as it determines the environment and, at the same time, it determines itself by means of itself as a subject. In this way, historical form [形] is made. We can think of the logic of imagination as the logic of historical form of this sort.

Formal logic is a logic of the object [対象], not a logic of the subject. To put it another way, it is a logic about something already there. We can say that even Hegel's dialectics was still objective or concerned with objects [対象的あるいは客体的]. Logic that takes the standpoint of the subject or the standpoint of action must be one that surpasses not only formal logic but even Hegelian dialectics. In a broad sense, to act is to make something and if this means to make something new, then presumably the logic of action as a logic of creation [sōzō, 創造] must be something like the logic of imagination. It would have to take the standpoint of the imagination that differs not only from the standpoint of the understanding but also from the standpoint of what Hegel calls reason. When I say that the logic of imagination is the logic of history, I am thinking of this not simply from the standpoint of understanding history, but from the standpoint of making history. Indeed, Baumgarten's logic of phantasy [想像] and Kant's critique of judgment were not only conceived primarily in relation to the realm of beauty, but from the standpoint of the enjoyment or comprehension of beauty without taking the standpoint of the productive activity of art itself. But the fact that we see the imagination as a faculty peculiar to artists is probably related to the fact that we view artistic activity in particular as creative work [sōsaku, 創作]. Our job is to elucidate the logic of imagination as a logic of historical creation, while releasing it from its confinement to the realm of beauty and introducing it broadly into the world of action.

As I have already mentioned, formal logic was originally not only simply formal [keishikiteki, 形式的] but was tied to the Greek ontology of form [keisō, 形相]; in other words, it was a logic of form. But this ontology lacked the historicist way of thinking. Hegel's dialectic in a certain sense is also a logic of form but one that possesses the special feature of including a historical approach. However, Hegel's philosophy, like Greek ontology, also takes the standpoint of contemplation [観想] and does not really take the standpoint of action. The logic of imagination is a logic of historical form, and so it is a logic from the standpoint of making form. Although I speak of this as a logic of things, what I mean by things are historical things, and as expressive things, they possess form. And when I speak of creation, it means that things with form are made externally. Historical form is not simply of *logos*, but rather a unity of things of *logos* and *pathos*. In this way, the logic of imagination arises out of the unity of *logos* and *pathos*.

What, then, is the imagination? And what sort of thing is the logic of imagination itself? I will leave a generalizing answer for later, and proceed here with a phenomenological investigation. Following the path Hegel took from phenomenology to logic, we shall pursue the logic amidst an analysis of phenomena.

2.

[19] Myth is seen as the most primitive thought-form [観念形態]. Enlightenment philosophy of the eighteenth century and positivist philosophy of the nineteenth

century conceived myth as a mere stage preceding science and as nothing but an unscientific substitute for science without recognizing its uniqueness. Comte's theory of three stages is a classic example of this. The error in this view has gradually been corrected. According to Malinowski, myth is neither useless rhapsody nor the purposeless effusion of empty phantasy, but an immensely significant cultural force of hard work. All its concerns are directed toward practical aims. Myth is neither an intellectual explanation nor a figure of art, but the practical charter of belief and ethical wisdom of the primitive human being.[3] And Lévy-Bruhl claims, on the basis of the empirical investigations of the psychology of primitive peoples, that just as the relationship between their psychology and the psychology of civilized people is not like the relationship between a child's psychology and an adult's, we ought not to view their myths as preceding the stage to science.[4] Although the myths of primitive humans are not particularly our concern, let us first examine this theory in order to obtain from it some suggestions.

The psychology of the primitive human, according to Durkheimian sociologists, is nothing more than a question of collective representation [*shūgō hyōshō*, 集合表象] (*représentations collectives*). A collective representation is a certain representation common to the members of a certain social group that is transmitted from generation to generation. It possesses a quality that we cannot explain by viewing individuals as mere individuals; instead, it presses upon the individual and at all times awakens the feelings of respect, fear, adoration, and so on within the individual. We cannot conceive of collective representations in the same way we conceive of what we ordinarily call representation. When we speak of representations, we ordinarily mean intellectual phenomena having to do with cognition. Hence, in the psychology of the primitive human, representations are mixed with emotive and kinetic (*émotionnel et moteur*) elements and are colored and penetrated by them. In relation to their represented objects, they thus take a bearing distinct from purely intellectual representations. Emotive and kinetic elements are constitutive parts of this representation. Lévy-Bruhl recognized this characteristic of the psychology of the primitive human where it is mystical (*mystique*) as well as pre-logical (*prélogique*).[5] The mystical signifies a belief in a power, influence, or function that is real although the senses fail to comprehend it. In the collective representation of the primitive human, whatever the being, thing, or phenomenon, it is not identical to what appears to us. Rather, the reality itself is mystical. The primitive human is for the most part uninterested in the objective relationships of things and instead directs its attention, more than anything else, to mystical links. The natural relations of causality between events either go unnoticed or only have an extremely small significance. The mode of thinking of the primitive human is pre-logical. Pre-logical does not mean that it constitutes a stage prior in time to the emergence of logical thought. The collective representations of the primitive are said to be pre-logical in the sense that they are not constrained [by the tendency] of our thinking to avoid contradiction. According to Lévy-Bruhl, collective representations and their combinations are governed primarily by "the law of participation" (*loi de participation*) and are unconcerned with the law of contradiction based on logic. That is, things, beings, and phenomena are themselves, and at the same time something other than themselves. Without ceasing to be themselves, they emanate and receive the forces, faculties, qualities, and mystical activities that can be felt outside of oneself. For example, the Bololo clan boasts that they are red parrots, but they do not mean that they become red parrots after they die or that they are people into whom red parrots had transformed. Rather, the Bololo people truly think that they are red parrots in the sense of an essential identity. At the same time that they are human beings, they are birds of scarlet plumage. In every totem society, between the individual belonging to a totem tribe and that totem, there is a collective representation signifying an identity analogous to this in accordance with the law of participation.[6] Not only from a static view, but from a dynamic view as well, the becoming of a certain being or phenomenon or appearance of a certain event is the result of a mystical function transmitted from one thing to another on the basis of mystical conditions. They depend on participation that is represented in various forms, such as contact, transfer, empathy, action at a distance, and so on. In a great number of primitive societies, the abundance of game for hunting or fishing, or the regularity of the seasons or rain, are tied to the performance of certain ceremonies by certain human beings, or to the existence or health of a holy man who possesses special mystical powers. The mind of the primitive human does more than merely represent objects, it possesses objects and is possessed by objects. It communicates with objects. It participates in objects, not only in the sense of representation but rather, at the same time, in a somatic and, moreover, mystical sense. It not only thinks objects but lives objects. Rites and rituals possess the effect of realizing a true symbiosis (*symbiose*) between a totem tribe and their totem. In such cases, collective representations are extremely intense emotive mental states and, without differentiations therein from movement or action, the representations bring about the desired communion (*communion*) vis-à-vis the social group.

In this way, in the psychology of the primitive human in its most pure form, a participation is felt and lived between the individual person and the social group, and furthermore, at the same time, between the social group and the grouping of surrounding things. This two-folded participation is joined and change on one side is echoed in the other. As the individual consciousness of each person, who is a member of the tribe, increases, the feelings of mystical symbiosis between the social group and the group of surrounding beings or things become less internalized, less immediate, and less constant. Whether one side or the other, external connections more or less begin to replace immediate emotions of communion. In other words, when this happens, participation tends to be represented. The communion that is no longer actually lived and, furthermore, constantly demanded is now sought in an indirect manner. Because participation is no longer immediately felt by each member of the social group, it is achieved by incessantly expanding the religious and magical activities, sacred beings and things, ceremonies performed by priests or members of secret societies, and so on. Lévy-Bruhl recognizes the beginning of myth in precisely this location.[7] In cases where the individual's participation in the social group is felt more immediately and in cases where the participation of the social group in the grouping of surrounding beings is lived with greater actuality, in other words, to the extent that the period of symbiosis is holding out, myths are uncommon and meager. By contrast, in societies of a more advanced form, myths become abundant by degrees. Myths are products of the psychology of primitive peoples in cases where the power of a mediator is borrowed to actualize a participation no longer felt as something immediate and to secure the no-longer-lived communion by means of that actualized participation. Myths are expressions of solidarity with the past of the social group and at the same time with the group of surrounding things, it is a means for maintaining the feeling of this solidarity and for ceaselessly renewing it. In the psychology of the primitive human dominated by the law of participation, myth is accompanied by the extremely powerful emotion of communion with the mystical reality it expresses. Mystical elements occupy therein a much more significant position than objective elements. Even natural history is included within sacred history. The attributes we call objective and that for us define and classify for us beings are, for primitive peoples, enveloped within the emotive and, further, kinetic elements, and their attention is chiefly directed towards the latter.

Now, as society develops, logical thought develops, and [in turn] concepts develop. However, do pre-logical modes of thinking vanish as a consequence? Lévy-Bruhl states that this is impossible. Even in advanced societies, traces of pre-logical ways of thinking remain within the majority of concepts, rather than vanishing. Only a small number of concepts employed in scientific thought express purely objective qualities and relationships of beings and phenomena, and such concepts are in general still abstract and only express specific qualities of phenomena and their specific relations. Other concepts that are used most ordinarily hold traces of what belonged to collective representations suited to them in pre-logical modes of thinking. For example, if we were to analyze concepts such as soul, life, death, society, order, kin, beauty, and so on, we would discern in them that they contain certain relationships that depict the law of participation. Even if we grant that mystical pre-logical elements have been removed from a greater portion of concepts, this does not mean that as a consequence the mystical pre-logical mode of thinking has completely disappeared. For pure concepts and the logical thought realized by means of their rational system do not extend over the same sphere as that of the psychology expressed among previous representations. The latter do not possess a purely intellectual function; rather, the intellectual faculty, as an undifferentiated element therein, shapes a complex whole by fusing with kinetic, and especially emotive, elements. Therefore, even if the cognitive faculty becomes differentiated and separated from other elements contained within the collective representation in the course of society's development to thus acquire a kind of independence, it fails to supply anything equivalent to the excluded elements. A portion of these elements continues outside of it in an undetermined form adjacent to it. The advancement of logical thinking would not stand cases where a representation formed on the basis of the law of participation contains a contradiction. In contrast to how logical thinking is in this way intolerant, pre-logical mystical psychology is indifferent towards logical elements. While it does not seek contradiction, neither does it avoid it. The fact that it is adjacent to the system of concepts that had been strictly ordered in accordance with the laws of logic has almost no affect on it at all. Logical thinking can, by no means, be the universal heir to pre-logical psychology. A collective representation, expressing strongly felt and lived participation, is constantly maintained despite evidence of its logical contradiction. The internal and lively felt emotions of participation are equal to the force of logical demands and, moreover, surpass them. Many institutions—institutions of religion, morality, and politics—take such collective representation as their foundation and are its expression. Even in our society, representations and their combinations, controlled by the law of participation, continue in juxtaposition with representations and their combinations that obey logical laws without vanishing in any way. Indeed, "our mental behavior is rational and at the same time irrational." Lévy-Bruhl states that, furthermore, therein lies the key to explaining the doctrines of religion and the history of philosophical systems.

3.

[27] Now if, as Lévy-Bruhl states, collective representations continue even in more advanced societies up to our society, myths would presumably have to belong not only to the primitive stage of development of the human race but would have to always exist in every society. For if, as he states, myths are rare according to the extent that the participation of individuals in society is immediately felt and actually lived, and they are born in cases when that participation in demand has to be obtained by indirect means, in cases where individual consciousness has developed along with the development of society, then the expressions of collective representation would have to take the form of myth more than anything else. Not only did myths exist in antiquity, but each period also has its own myths. Freedom and equality were myths of the eighteenth century. In the present age, there are myths for the present age, e.g., the so-called "myth of the twentieth century."[8] Today, the importance of myths is conceived not only by irrationalists like Rosenberg, but even someone like Valéry, who has been called an intellectualist, writes that "in the beginning, was the myth!" (*Au commencement était la Fable!*).[9] Moreover, this is true not only in its temporal sense but also in its logical sense. We can say that the institutions in this society already contain some sort of mythical significance. The question for us is to determine the sort of myth that still exists and is created even today. Understanding myth in this way, what is its relationship to the imagination?

Myth is not the simple product of cognition; rather emotive and, moreover, kinetic elements occupy an important position within it. Something like the law of participation is presumably active in the formation of myths. But if myths are born in cases where participation, in Lévy-Bruhl's words, "possesses the tendency towards being represented," then instead of being immediate and, so to speak, instinctive, a certain logic must be inherent in myth. This logic is a logic of emotion and, further, we can call it, more properly, the logic of phantasy [*sōzō*] or the logic of imagination [*kōsōroku*].[10] According to Ribot, as soon as human beings transcend immediate knowledge of external and internal sensation, as soon as they attempt to venture beyond what can be given by immediate experience or its recollection, they possess only two procedures of explanation, namely conjecture or anticipation, that is, to infer (*raisonner*) or to imagine (*imaginer*). And although the two were originally intermingled, as can be seen in children and ethnicities without intellectual culture, following the development of the human mind, they became differentiated bringing about the separation between rational logic and the logic of emotions. In other words, even what Ribot refers to as the logic of emotions is nothing other than the logic of imagination [*sōzō*]. He writes that in many cases emotive inferences are the work of the imagination [*sōzō*], in particular of the creative imagination [*sōzōteki sōzō*, 創造的想像].[11] And according to Lévy-Bruhl, myths and dreams possess completely analogous characteristics for the primitive human. In their psychology, the visible world and the invisible world are one. There is a ceaseless traffic between sensible reality and mystical forces. This sort of thing is presumably the most immediately and the most completely realized while dreaming. For primitive peoples, what is seen in dreams is equal in value to the perception gained when one is awake. They are also not deceived by unrefined psychological hallucinations. They are able to distinguish between dreams and perceptions when awake and know that they do not dream unless they are asleep. But even if what is seen in dreams contains many contradictions, the principle of contradiction does not have much weight in the psychology of primitive peoples. It is not that they believe in dreams indiscriminately; rather, they take certain dreams as true dreams (*vision*) that one ought to believe and take others as mere dreams (*réve*). With that proviso, however, in the eyes of primitive peoples, what one sees in dreams is as real as, or even more real than, what one recognizes in the waking state. For they believe that what is revealed in dreams belongs to a higher order and exercises an irresistible influence upon the course of thing-events. Lévy-Bruhl thus writes that they hardly distinguish the world one enters through dreams and the world of the mythological age.[12] Nevertheless people have been speaking of the likeness between the imagination and dreams since ancient times. What the sociologists refer to as collective representation has been maintained and purified in the imagination, and we can consider myth as but one such example.

The kinship between acts of the imagination and dreams, illusions, or even madness, has been previously discussed particularly with regard to the imagination of poets. Characteristics common to them are the intensity of the imaginary representation, their sensory clarity, and their free formations transcending the bounds of the actual. Poets see various forms and various states that are products of their imagination clearly as in perception. They live with the characters of their creation as if they were actual human beings and feel their pain as if it were actual pain. Flaubert states that when he was depicting the scene where Madame Bovary drinks poison, he clearly felt the taste of arsenic on his tongue and vomited his food twice in a row. And Goethe told Schiller that just by planning to write a tragedy he became frightened and felt he might destroy himself through this project. In all of these cases, we can recognize a certain kind of deep participation. Now [Wilhelm] Dilthey attempted to analyze and describe the laws followed in cases where mental images [*shinzō*, 心像] (*Bild*), on the basis of the poet's imagination, develop freely by transcending what is actual.[13] Although, of course, the function of the imagination in art needs to be distinguished from its function in cognition as well as from its function in myth, his theory, viewed broadly, contains clues that can help advance our research.

In previous theories of psychology that had been dominant, representations were treated as fixed facts, and laws were posited whereby these representations reproduce one another and press upon and remove each other. But such laws are mere abstractions. In the actual life of the mind, the fate of a mental image, namely, a singular representation that had not been dissolved depends on the distribution of emotion and attention. A mental image can thus have an impulsive force. It is life and an event. It arises, unfolds, and again vanishes. Mental images change as their compositional elements drop out or are removed. When a physicist dreams about flying in the sky, the experience of gravity is lost to him, and when a painter begins to paint the Madonna on the basis of a model, he removes the resistant characteristics. And mental images change by expanding or shrinking as the intensity of sensations composing them increases or decreases. In a dream, the sound of a book falling from a shelf becomes a canon boom, the snore of the next person becomes roaring and raging waves, and, by touching the foot-warming bottle of hot water with the sole of one's foot, one thinks one is hovering above the summit of Mt. Etna. Furthermore, mental images and their combinations change as new compositional elements and combinations enter into their most inner core and supplement them. The association of ideas leads to a variety of such alterations. In this way, what we might refer to as "the originary phenomenon of the imagination" (*Urphänomen der Einbildungskraft*) consists in the unfolding of mental images that Goethe had observed in himself. Goethe states:

> I had this gift, if I closed my eyes and let my head droop and think of a flower in the middle of my eyes, the flower, without remaining even for a moment in its first form, unravels, and from its interior, a new colorful flower with green leaves again unfolds. Although it is not a flower of nature but a flower of fancy, it is orderly just like a rose-shaped figure made by a sculptor. It was impossible to fix the sprouting creation.[14]

And Otto Ludwig confesses:

> My procedure is the following: There precedes a feeling, a musical feeling. This becomes for me a color. And then I see one or several shapes in some position or gesture, alone or towards one another ... Strangely enough, these images or that cluster [*jene Gruppe*] ordinarily is not the image of a catastrophe but is sometimes only a characteristic figure in some pathetic position ... [F]rom the first witnessed scene ..., at times moving forward, at other times coming to the end ... new plastic farcical forms and clusters ceaselessly shoot out until I finally have an entire drama ... All of this happens in great haste, during which my consciousness is in a completely passive state ...[15]

According to Dilthey, a mental image is one event in the mind and at the same time a process of formation (*Bildungsprozess*) that is restricted and founded by the connections of the whole of mental life. The representations or their compositional elements are internally altered on the basis of the functioning of these connections. As a single whole, mental connections are always actively in control even if ordinarily they are not raised to consciousness. Nevertheless, in dreams or madness, this control is diminished or is lost, and the mental images unfold and combine in an unfettered manner. In the imagination of poets, by contrast, such connections are at work, but the unusual force of emotions, feelings, and the system of sense organs freely unfold mental images by transcending the limits of the actual. Genius is in no way a pathological phenomenon, but, on the contrary, an eye toward something essentially emanating from the completeness and force of such mental connections. We must avoid here falling into the misunderstandings of psychologism. And yet, what is admitted in psychology can presumably be admitted in logic as well. In classical psychology, representations were viewed as individual fixed facts. This stands upon the axiom of so-called atomism.[16] Likewise in classical logic, representations were also thought to possess fixed content. We can say that Bolzano's idea of a "representation in-itself" was a purification of this sort of view in terms of object logic. This view, with regard to representation, is tied in formal logic to the principle of identity or the principle of contradiction. The logic of Greece was a logic of representation in this sense as well. Nevertheless, in the logic of imagination, we can conceive the mental image itself as something dynamic and formative. Representations are not isolated as form-images [keizō, 形像],[17] but internally combine with emotions and are vitalized by a single whole. In contrast to the axioms of atomism, its foundation is the axiom of wholeness.

Next, according to Dilthey, the relationship between what is internal and external to us is given within our psychophysical being, and we transpose this relationship everywhere. We interpret our internal states or render them sensible by means of external figures [keishō, 形象],[18] and animate or spiritualize external figures by means of internal states. Dilthey maintains that herein lies the powerful source of myth, metaphysics, and above all poetry. The ideality constituting the core of artworks consists in this way of the symbolization of internal states by means of external form-images and the animation of an external actuality by means of internal states. We can say that the logic of imagination is the logic of symbols [shōchō, 象徴]. What Cassirer refers to as "the philosophy of symbolic forms"[19] needs to be rewritten in accordance with the logic of imagination. In previous logic, the laws of logic were defined abstractly as laws or forms of thought; hence, abstractly as laws or forms of the (epistemological) subject. Or, on the other hand, they were defined, likewise abstractly, as the laws or forms of objects or objectivity.[20] Put differently, logic is not grasped on the basis of the lived point of conjunction or point of agreement between subject and object. Yet the logic of imagination can be seen precisely at that point. Instead of belonging to the activity of mere consciousness, it takes root in our psychophysical being.

In connection with the symbolization of the imagination, Dilthey further relates that it follows that the imagination produces something like a form or type [kata, 型] (type), something ideal, from the regularity of the imagination active in poets.[21] Already in dreams and even in madness, we can discern that in sensations and internal states uniform figures that expound, explain, and express these states are tied together with remarkable regularity. It is a meager and withered kind of symbol. However, the symbols of myth, metaphysics, and poetry, among the human race, develop abundantly and, moreover, lawfully. A symbol is a typological figure. A type is not something like the genus in formal logic. A type is individual and, at the same time, universal. It indicates something that is thoroughly individual and yet always universal. The logic of imagination is a logic of type [kata, 型]. A type is not simply something objective. It is not merely a copy or abstraction or generalization of something outside. Instead, it is produced from within, from the passion of the self. As Hugo stated that a type is a creation of inspiration mixed with observation, it is a form [*katachi*, 形] as the unity of what belongs to *logos* and *pathos*.

The concepts of development, totality, symbol, type [*kata*, 型], and so on, are presumably what is fundamental to the logic of imagination. But it cannot accept the theory of immanence belonging to *Lebensphilosophie* [生の哲学, philosophy of life].[22] Even if the logic of imagination escapes the abstract nature of subjectivism along with objectivism, it does not take the standpoint of so-called subject-object unity but instead takes a standpoint transcending that. However, before we critique the Diltheyian theory of immanence, we now need to return once again to the issue of myth and examine its character and philosophical foundation.

4.

[36] We probably cannot view the myths of the primitive human and what is ordinarily known as myth, namely, Greek mythology, Egyptian mythology, Indian mythology, and so on, and even less what is considered to be contemporary mythology, as immediately identical. Therein we might consider the difference in what Brunschvicg called "the age of intelligence," and correspondingly the difference in the age of the imagination, or rather the difference in stages in the logic of imagination. But as Lévy-Bruhl also states, if we are to admit that these pre-logical modes of thinking have continued until today even in societies with culture and that they are the source of myths, there would have to be some common structure contained within all myths. And even if the function of the imagination of poets and that of the imagination in the creation of myths are not immediately identical, we can presumably see something like the laws of what Dilthey calls the poetic imagination acting in a certain way in the myths of primitive peoples as well. In the first place, Lévy-Bruhl stresses that among collective representations, the representation is not something isolated but instead is one with emotive and kinetic elements. The mental image there is something animated by the whole. Next, we can say that the logic of myth is a kind of logic of symbols; that in the collective representations of the primitive human being, following the law of participation, things are themselves and at the same time other than themselves, and that "all things have an invisible being just as they have a visible being," indeed would be in reference to symbols. As Brunschvicg also points out, the concept of what Lévy-Bruhl calls participation reminds us of the philosophy of Plato as well as of Malebranche.[23] Already before the end of the sixteenth century, one Spanish Jesuit monk, discussing the mythical thoughts of the Indians of Peru, declared that therein lies something reminiscent of Plato's theory of *ideas*. Symbolism in the interpretation of myths is said to have originated in the Neo-Platonism of the Alexandrian school. According to Creuzer,[24] myths are nothing more than symbols and while these symbols were originally established to encapsulate philosophical doctrines and moral ideas, the meanings of symbols were later lost, and myths came to be understood as real facts and developed on the basis of historical forms. We probably cannot, however, admit the same sort of origin and genesis for all myths that we find in Plato's myths. Moreover, as a criticism that penetrates the shortcomings of this sort of symbolism, Toutain[25] cites the following words of Renan:

To suppose that the human race in ancient times created symbols in order to conceal doctrines by distinguishing doctrine and symbol is an extremely grave error. All of this, as in the cases of thought and language, ideas and their expressions, were born at the same time, in an indivisible moment in one leap. Myth does not contain two elements, the enveloping and the enveloped; it is undivided. There is no merit in the question of whether primitive man understood or not the meaning of the myths he created, for in myths intention is not distinguished from the thing itself. People understood myths, without seeing anything beyond, as simply one and not as two things.[26]

Indeed, this remark of Renan does not deny the symbolism that myths possess but rather indicates the still deeper meaning of symbols. Symbols mean that inner and outer are one. There is not an interior that exists apart from the exterior, nor an exterior separate from the interior. The symbol is formed when the inner is outside and the outer is inside. What we ordinarily consider to be the symbolized meaning in symbols is nothing but what had been, so to speak, derivatively abstracted out subsequently. The meaning of a symbol is not something that can be simply grasped objectively. In Plato as well, myths were not simply illustrative (*illustrative*) and were not allegories for depicting in pictures the results already obtained through demonstration.[27] Even for Plato, myths were created, beyond the theory of *ideas*, by relating the *ideas* to the issue of generation along with that of the (embodied) subject. A symbol is that wherein inner and outer are one, and if we were to still refer to that as a symbol, the deepest meaning of a symbol would have to be symbolization without a thing symbolized. The theory of personification taken to characterize myths only applies to the lowest stages of the symbol. A true symbol is not a symbol of something; rather, the essence of a symbol is to symbolize without something symbolized. But what does this mean? Therein lies the transcendental problem of the imagination.

Renan's statement that in myth we cannot distinguish between intention and the thing itself in myths would presumably clarify the activity of the imagination in the creation of myths. The imagination (*Einbildungskraft*, *imagination*) is the faculty that produces an image (*Bild*, *image*), but this image is not something essentially illustrative (*illustrierend*). In an illustrative image, the objective meaning exists as an *idea* independent of it, and we can think of the sensible image as nothing more than constituting the activity of demonstration (*Veranschaulichung*) in relation to it. According to Husserl, in phantasy images (*Phantasiebild*) are such illustrations and do nothing more than exemplify in intuition the meaning thought without falling under any meaning-giving function; and images in *imaginatio* (imagination) do nothing more than simply give clues for *intellectio* (the intellect) and, even if they support the understanding, they themselves are not active as meanings or bearers of meaning.[28] We cannot grasp the essence of the imagination by means of this sort of Platonism or Cartesianism. The imagination is more originary than reason. What constitutes the first distinction between man and animal is not reason but imagination. Jowett states: "In the lower stages of civilization imagination more than reason distinguishes man from the animals; and to banish art would be to banish thought, to banish language, to banish the expressions of all truth."[29] Instead of viewing the images of the imagination as symbols of thought, we ought, in reverse, to view thought as symbols of those images. In the imagination, the subjective and the objective are one, and the logic of imagination is such that the subjective is objective and the objective is subjective. As Maine de Biran [François Pierre Gontier de Biran] stated that "a ceaseless harmony between the emotional faculty and the intellectual faculty is constructed by means of the imagination," our subjective faculty and objective faculty are immediately tied together in the imagination as one. Therein lies an inner unity between *pathos* and *logos*. And just as [Rudolf] Kassner has stated that "the body and the mind are connected by means of the imagination," the positive essence of the imagination cannot be understood through a dualism that separates body and mind. In the sense that the subjective is the objective, we can probably view the imagination as "the metaphysical faculty *par excellence*" (*faculté métaphysique par excellence*) or as an "ontological faculty."[30] Fichte's thought, which attempted to explain the reality of the external world as a resistance to the will, and Dilthey's transformation of it, had not yet escaped subjectivism and were further oriented toward natural beings, and generally failed to explain the reality of the historical and expressive world, starting with the reality of works of art. I think that the reality of this world must be founded by means of the logic of imagination. Even if we say, however, that the subjective and the objective are one in the imagination, this does not mean that problems such as the existence of the outer world can be considered from the standpoint of the union of subject-object. Instead, we must view the logic of imagination where it transcends the subjective/objective as a whole. Therefore the transcendental [*chōetsuronteki*, 超越論的] character of the imagination must become the issue here as well. The mixture in myth of the supernatural and the natural is this sort of primitive form-image of transcendence [*chōetsu*, 超越].[31]

For the imagination, the concept of participation in the sense of harmony between the subjective and the objective is more important than the concept of empathy or other concepts. As I have already mentioned, this meaning cannot be fully understood within the scope of Plato's theory of *ideas*, but Brunschvicg theorizes that participation in cases that can be extended to the sense of the psychology of primitive man has the meaning of something like the total mixing (*panmixie*) of Stoic philosophy. Participation clearly signifies a state of non-division. Yet just as the harmony of body and mind in the imagination cannot be conceived from the standpoint of so-called monism, participation cannot be understood on the basis of the total blending of Stoicism. According to Toutain, although the distinctive character of myth consists in a partial amount of supernatural and irrational events, it is not grounded in fetishism or animism, nor in pantheism or monotheism either. Rather, the necessary condition for the abundant and variegated existence of myth is polytheism. We cannot view the myths of primitive peoples as polytheistic in the same sense as Greek mythology, but neither can we say that it involves no elements of fetishism or animism. Nevertheless, many have noted that in their societies the various myths are pluralistic in the sense that they possess no general logical correspondence with one another. The desire for concrete expression and the fertility of a vocabulary that expresses particular things and activities are common characteristics of their societies. The abundance of the concrete particularity of their mental images itself causes a lack in the transition from particular mental images to universal ideas. In this way, if we admit the function of the imagination in the creation of myths, the imagination is always tied to the particular. And this is not limited to the case of primitive man. What the imagination produces are not concepts but forms, and the root of the imagination is the "manifoldness of form" (*Mannigfaltigkeit der Form*). A form is not one; rather, it is a form only vis-à-vis other forms, by being one of many. The logic of imagination is the logic of individuals. Of course, to the extent that we refer to this as a logic, particulars must be related to something universal, and individuals must be related to one another by means of a universal. Nevertheless, that universal is not something that we can grasp objectively, and individuals are not tied together by a universal that is objective. The one that ties together the many forms is formless rather than being a form. It is, so to speak, a "formless form."[32] "Everything that happens is a symbol, and it points to the others by expressing itself completely" (Goethe).[33] An individual, by completely expressing itself as an individual, is endlessly connected to other individuals that are likewise independent. The logic of imagination must be recognized where individuals are reciprocally related in a universal completely different from themselves, even while their independence is thoroughly acknowledged. We may understand the relationship between particular and universal, for the present, in the following manner. The imagination is the faculty that makes images but such images are always individual. As images, they are intellectual things, and we may think of the imagination as something intellectual. On the other hand, however, the imagination is not simply an intellectual faculty; rather to the contrary, it is an emotion, and we can view the character of emotions to be universality (wholeness). Accordingly, within the imagination, intellectual images pertaining to individual things always possess, at the same time, universal meanings. Opposites, such as the individual and the universal, therein are immediately joined together as one. The logic of imagination is such that the individual is universal and the universal is individual. In this case, we should not understand the imagination, from the outset, in a psychological sense. What is at issue here is rather its transcendental sense. Nor should we think of the logic of imagination as being manifested in the myths of primitive or ancient peoples in the same way it is in artistic production. The true universal is not the universal restricted to collective representations to constitute their foundation. We can probably recognize the limitation of myth, instead, where the universal negates the independence of the individual.

According to Usener, ensouling (*Beseelung*) and figuration [形像化] (*Verbildlichung* [picturing]) are two principal processes in every act of mythical representation.[34] It would be a mistake to think that myths are given simply through ensouling or personification. At the same time, form-images must arise from the depths of consciousness to be tied to ensouling. The two processes are conjoined and within this source filled with mystery is the foundation of every religious representation as well as language and poetry. Such psychological and kinetic forms, in contrast to intellectual thought and science, are called "mythical" (*mythisch*). As in the function of physiological stimulus, this process functions without volition or consciousness, stands apart from all laws of thinking, excepting cases of fallacious reasoning, and furthermore possesses immediate certainty and actuality vis-à-vis the mind. For the function of mythical representation, thing and image are completely one. In what Usener refers to as ensouling and picturing [rendering into form-images], the former can be viewed as emotional and the latter as intellectual, and we conceive the imagination to be their connection as one or what ties them together as one. Usener, moreover, found Schleiermacher's distinction between religion and science as intuition and reason respectively to be inadequate. The two are fundamentally distinct even in the intellectual process that emerges in our consciousness with no point of unification between them. Usener states that even with new ideas coming to a scientist, there is something analogous to the imagination of a poet, and both are engendered by means of a mental faculty identical to the function of mythical representation. And it is here that we find the logic of imagination to be operating.

5.

[46] The intellectual and the emotional are tied together in the imagination as one. According to Ribot, the imagination always contains an intellectual element and an emotional element and forms their inner unity.[35] The imagination is distinguished from mere emotion in that it internally and, moreover, generatively contains within itself intellectual elements. Accordingly, the philosophy of the imagination is neither simply rationalism nor simply irrationalism. The logic of imagination is a logic of form-images [keizō, 形像] and not the logic of emotions. Form-images are dynamic and developmental. The logic of imagination is not a static logic. Form-images are dynamic and developmental because they are primarily generated as syntheses of the emotional and the intellectual, the subjective and the objective. Now one person who attempted to remove all the intellectual elements from myth is Sorel, who merits our notice as a contemporary theorist of myth.[36] Sorel regarded the philosophy of intellectualism to be fundamentally powerless when it comes to explaining the great movements of history. In every revolutionary period, myths of various distinct forms prepared people for revolution, who therefore acted by relying on myth. In such cases, it would be meaningless to theoretically compare the myths accepted prior to action and the facts accomplished by means of action. Myth as a historical force ought to be grasped as a whole. We fail to grasp its actual meaning when we break it down it into various elements. Sorel thus rigidly distinguishes utopia and myth. Myth is not a description of thing-events but an expression of the will. By contrast, utopia is a product of intellectual labor. The theorist attempts, through observing, reflecting on, and discussing facts, to create a model to which existent society can be compared. Although the utopian model would be a fanciful institution, it offers an analogy with present institutions, enough to permit speculation on it. Myths are, nevertheless, expressions in words of the movement of conviction of a definite society, and rouse the whole of emotions corresponding to actions, all together, by a singular intuition preceding any reflective analysis. In the creative movement of history, each moment is refused any kind of foreknowledge. To predict is self-contradictory for the reason that it is to create prior to the creation of things. Sorel claims that his theory of myth is grounded in Bergson's philosophy, but it contains various important insights. First, of all, myth has been previously investigated in many cases from the viewpoint of aesthetics. Accordingly, for Sorel myth as a historical force is related to action and

evaluated from that standpoint. Second, whereas myth is ordinarily seen as something belonging to the past, and hence as something traditional and conservative, Sorel, by contrast, considers contemporary myths (socialist revolution, the syndicalists' general strike) and comprehends their sense as acting upon present actions and thus upon the future. The emphasis on the historical creativity of myth is a noticeable characteristic of his theory of myth. Furthermore, we ought to pay attention to his distinction between myth and utopia. Just as Bergson stated that people do not anticipate concerning the future other than what resembles the past or what can be reassembled with elements resembling elements of the past, utopia is not actually something that paints an image of the future; rather, it only projects the past into the future. Sorel, moreover, deemed the optimism of utopias as reactionary and believed that without pessimism, nothing can be accomplished, no matter how sublime.

Despite the importance of the distinction between myth and utopia, it would nevertheless be impossible to remove all intellectual content from myth. Just as a utopia without mythical elements does not exist, myth without utopian elements would presumably not exist. The intellectual element in myth does not refer to something like objective and universal knowledge. When Sorel himself speaks of myth as a mental image (*image*) or as representation (*representation*), this must mean the image of the imagination. The imagination is a faculty that produces not merely emotions but at the same time intellectual images. That the imagination is active in the formation of myth is evident in the sort of myths conceived by Sorel. Sorel states that myth is an expression of the will, and appropriates while affirming, the following words of Newman:

> Strictly speaking, it is not the imagination [phantasy] that causes action; but hope and fear, likes and dislikes, appetite, passion, the stirrings of selfishness and self-love. What imagination does for us is to find a means of stimulating these motive forces, and it does so by providing a supply of objects strong enough to stimulate them.[37]

Not only is it doubtful whether we could view emotion and volition as distinct. We cannot conceive the imagination by abstracting it from somaticity. For sure, the imagination is something tied to hope and fear, likes and dislikes, appetite, passion, impulse, and so on. For this reason, Descartes and Pascal regarded the imagination as the source of error. The imagination is tied to emotion and produces images from out of it. Emotions, by means of the imagination, can be transformed into something objective, strengthened as such, and made permanent. We do not support the mystical romanticism and irrational voluntarism of Sorel's theory of direct action. There is a logic even within emotion. It is not that there is volition at the root of the imagination, but rather the imagination is at the root of the will. While on the one hand we cannot consent to the irrationalism of voluntarism, on the other hand, we cannot consent to the determinism of intellectualism that places reason at the root of the will. The issue of the freedom of the will can be solved neither by mere rationalism nor by mere irrationalism. The philosophy of the imagination, transcending both rationalism and irrationalism, can provide the key to solving even the issue of the freedom of will. As in the case of myth, the imagination is already active in the genesis of utopia as well. Utopia, too, is a product of the imagination. And if we are to think of the difference between myth and utopia in relation to the imagination, following the distinction of the imagination in Kant, we can probably view myth as belonging to the productive imagination (*Produktive Einbildungskraft*) and utopia as belonging to the reproductive imagination (*Reproduktive Einbildungskraft*).[38] Kant, with deep insight, reduces anticipation (*Vorhersehung*), as in recollection (*Erinnerung*), to the function of reproductive imagination. But one might take this to coincide with the Bergsonian-Sorelian view concerning utopias. In the historical world, myth precedes utopia, utopia precedes science, and the imagination is more originary than reason. Utopian socialism preceded scientific socialism. And if we take Sorel's myth such as of the general strike in his theory of direct action, in reverse, to be what dramatically expresses in concentration already given theories of socialism, one important issue is here presented concerning the function of the imagination when theory is transferred to the standpoint of practice. The faculty of practical thought is the ability to transform universal theory into concrete form, and in this way, the ability to transform *Theorie* (theory) into *Form* (form) belongs to the imagination. Theory becomes form by means of the activist's imagination.

In order, however, for theory to manifest by transfiguring into an image of intuition by means of the activist's imagination, the imagination must somehow already be active at the root of theory. As concerns Sorel, he mentions three rules as fundamental for the scientific research of social phenomena:[39] 1. The modalities that appear at the base of every classification erected among phenomena, every relationship and [all given] facts depend on the practical goals that are pursued. It is prudent to always make these goals clear. In sociology or economics, it is, therefore, necessary from the beginning to search for a simple subjective procedure and to know what one is attempting to accomplish and accordingly subordinate the entirety of the investigation to the kind of solution that one approves. For instance, socialism places significant value in grasping every issue with an extremely well-defined spirit and knowing where it wants to arrive—at least to the extent that the labor movement adds sufficient pressure upon itself. 2. The method of cognition by means of concepts was created in ancient times in order to investigate immovable, geometrical entities. Accordingly, it cannot be applied to social facts that should be compared to clouds that alter its position, aspect, and spread at every moment. To grasp the moving, we must abandon Greek methods. What is effective in the investigation of social phenomena is what we might refer to as stylized projections (*projections stylisées*). Experts endeavor to comprehend social phenomena by means of image [form-image] systems (*systèmes d'images*) whereby their knowledge would not miss whatever characteristic is seen as useful for the undertaken investigation. "If sociology often ended up being sterile, it was for the reason that it was mainly being studied by people without a creative imagination (*imagination créatrice*)."[40] According to Sorel, Marx was someone who exhibited extraordinary ingenuity in the organization of stylized projections. From ancient times calligraphers and sculptors, on the basis of stylization, succeeded in raising clear ideas concerning what moves by means of the strain of the unmoving. Philosophy must learn from aesthetics. These two activities are still closely related. The expression of the moving through the strain of the unmoving means that change is even more regular, even more communicated to the reader, thus more suited to suggesting to him the idea of the existence of laws. In other words, the more rhythmical it is, the more successful it should be. Marx's dialectic works in this way. 3. Ideological constructions are, of course, necessary, but they are also the most frequent causes of our errors. We must, therefore, reject everything that is not a product of reflection, that is active on the basis of institutions, customs, and empirical rules that have acquired a well-determined form in practice. Vico stated that in history before reflective thought theoretically grasps thing-events, there first exists popular wisdom that perceives thing-events and moreover poetically expresses them. However, this thesis is significant for Marxists as well. And one important proposition stated by Marx is connected to this rule; namely, that what appears later in history gives the key for explaining what precedes. For example, the concept of industrial capital makes for the first time the character of usurer's capital or commercial capital completely comprehensible. An ideologically foundational principle only appears when a given society has achieved its complete development. Those who wish to construct the future with ideas by anticipating it, ultimately end with nothing but phantasy. It is impossible to formulate principles of a future society and deduce from them some elements of practice; for such principles can be clearly known only when a present society ceases and yields its place to a new organization. At best what we can hope to discern within present society is nothing more than a partial becoming. Sorel makes an additional remark: "I wonder if it is possible to provide an intelligible exposition of the passage from principles to action without using myths."[41] According to him, the idea of the collapse of capitalist society in Marx was presented as a myth for concretizing class war and social revolution. Sorel's thesis, that without the use of myth we cannot explain the transfer from principle to action, plainly suggests the function of the imagination in the relationship between theory and practice. We will, however, not enter here into a critique of Sorel's above-mentioned view in regard to the method of social science which ought to form the title of our later investigations. What is relevant for us here is that in his own way he acknowledges the important significance of the imagination in his investigation of the social sciences; thus, what he refers to as myth is also nothing more than a product of the imagination or something that theory, from the standpoint of practice, transforms into myth by means of the imagination. Myth, preceding theory, originally emerges from within a definite social national substance [*shakai kokutai*, 社会国体]. It is the "poetic wisdom," the originality of which, Vico asserted in opposition to Cartesian rationalism. The originariness of the imagination vis-à-vis the intellect must be acknowledged. From the standpoint of practice, theory also becomes myth by means of the imagination. Even if Ziegler's project to comprehend the history of human thought, including the scientific worldview and even atheism, as the vicissitudes of myth,[42] is excessively overly poetic, the products of the intellect are somehow mythologized in the historical world. Within that possibility, we can recognize the existence of the imagination at the root of the intellect. The relationship between dialectic and the logic of imagination, which Sorel's theory leads us to consider, will almost certainly eventually become the most important issue for us as well.

6.

[55] If we enter the world of history, it is possible to come to think of everything as a myth, just as it is already possible even in theory. Thus, the concept of myth can no longer be limited to that which has a particular linguistic expression which is usually called myths but must express a certain mode of being of all beings. (In this case, we cannot employ the term *mythologie*, but ought to speak only of *mythe*. According to Toutain, the word *mythologie* contains two distinct meanings. It signifies, on the one hand, "the ensemble of myths and legends" (*l'ensemble des mythes et des legends*) as in the cases of *mythologie grecque, mythologie égyptienne*, and so on. And it signifies, on the other, all research, investigations, and systems concerning such myths and legends, or in other words, "the science of myths" (*science des mythes*). In either case, in contrast to the relation of the concept of *mythologie* to *logos*, we may be permitted to use the concept of *mythe* in an ontological sense by extending its meaning to a certain way of being of all beings, in addition to transforming it from its ordinarily used meaning of myth.) Of course, all beings can possess the mythical mode of being because the foundation for the establishment of society, as Aristotle believed, stems from the fact that the human being is an animal possessing *logos* (language). What is more, that a certain thing amounts to a mythical existence does not mean that it was created from the start with myth as its intention, but only indicates that the world of history at its root is established by means of the logic of imagination. This latter point is a fundamental issue for us.

Sorel recognized myth as a historical force. What Sorel calls myth primarily has to do with the creation of the future. Bertram however conceived myth primarily as the form of the transmission of the past.[43] Bertram first states that everything that was is nothing more than a symbol (*Gleichnis*).[44] No historical method can help us to see the actual, concrete reality in its original form, as naive historical realism of the nineteenth century believed. History does not entail the conceptual re-composition of that which existed in some way. Instead, history is the stripping away of the actuality of an earlier actuality and bringing it into "an utterly distinct category of existence [*sonzai*, 存在]." The picture produced by historical narration is an actuality, so to speak, of an even higher degree. When we look at it historically, we are not making past life present but rather stripping it of its present-ness, and bringing it into our own time, we are rather rendering it atemporal. What continues to exist in past lives, no matter how we try to clarify, scrutinize, and experience it, it is never a life, but always an explanation and a story. Of all events what survives as history is always ultimately a legend. A legend is the most life-like form of a historical transmission, its most primitive form as well as its final form, its most ancient form, and at the same time its deepest form. It is only legend, operating no matter when that connects the past with the present in a real way. The personage [*jin'butsu*, 人物] of the past lives on only as images [像; pictures, portraits], merely as figures [形態], only as myths. No matter what kind of philology, no matter the method of analysis, it can neither shape this portrait nor hinder or accelerate the transformation in accordance with its internal laws and inherent impulses. This image never ceases to change, and never ceases to manifest ever more rarified and thicker outlines. It is a prototype, but at the same time, it also becomes something that occurs only once. The operation of laws defining this process of the formation of legends is likewise recognizable in various kinds of legends. For example, there is no fundamental difference between the myths of ancient heroes and the legends of medieval saints. And the intensity of the formation of legends does not depend on the primitive state of mental cultivation at all. In the consciously analytical period as well, legends are neither removed nor pushed to the background. The entirety of self-awareness, self-management, philological knowledge, etc. that continue to increase has only an extremely limited effect on the genesis of legends; and its influence, whether as constraining or as facilitating, is inessential. In cases where myth attempts to realize itself, today just as much as in the past, the awakened surveying intellect encounters a limit about which it can do nothing. For individuality to continue living and acting beyond the bounds of the individual person's life would be, to borrow Burckhardt's words, magic, a religious process, and as such something escaping all mechanistic and rational influence.

There is a certain truth contained in the view that myth or legend is the living form of the transmission of history. History, however, as myth does not render history as science impossible or meaningless. We cannot accept Bertram's view of the history of myth simply as it is. Its romanticism, aestheticism, and the organicism (in analogy with the bio-organism) related to them, and so on, contain elements that would probably invite criticism. The philosophy of the imagination, in the same way that it does not consent to abstract rationalism, neither coincides with romantic irrationalism. The formation of myth pertains to the imagination. Historical facts as well as their cognition are formed into myths on the basis of the imagination, and this is possible because the logic of imagination exists at the root of history itself. Bertram says that the "law of accumulation" is operative in the formation of legends. Here as well, those who have been given more (people lend money only to the rich). Human memory is ungrateful but when it does give thanks, it gives thanks without limit and, taking every little altar of the past, decorates it with the largest memorial statue. There exists at the root of Bertram's law of accumulation something like the "process of crystallization" that Stendhal spoke of in his theory of [romantic] love, or rather it must be something identical to it. Stendhal analyzes the psychology of [romantic] love in the following manner. First comes admiration and this initial stage is purely emotional. Next, one is awakened to the traction of pleasure, namely, to desire in every possible form. And next comes "hope," and it is here that the imagination begins to operate, and along with the imagination appears, according to Ribot's interpretation, the judgment of merit. In this way [romantic] love is born. Next, the first process of crystallization begins. The process of crystallization is the discovery in all things manifest something that would enhance the love object's ceaselessly renewed perfection. By means of this, the love object is formed into someone ideal and perfect. However, there arises after this, "doubt" that for the moment confuses the process. And as one eventually conquers this, the second process of crystallization takes place. According to Ribot's notes, this process is not only peculiar to love alone, it exists at the root of every passion that is gently incubated.[45] And Delacroix states that the doctrine of the process of crystallization shows that the imagination plays a very large role in love. Love is, in effect, the work of the imagination as the movement of the heart. We love the fanciful being that we had created, but we created it because we love it.⁴⁶ We can accordingly say that the object of love becomes mythologized by means of the crystallization process. Love and the imagination do not work apart from one another. The imagination is originally representational and emotive. Ribot explains that in cases where love is idealized, or put differently, where it is relieved of its bodily and the instinctive, impulsive elements by means of the functions of exclusion and abstraction akin to the act of extracting a concept from sensation, emotional inferences disappear and, in its place, a partially emotional and partially intellectual, and hence compounded inferences, appear. We are not, however, satisfied with this sort of mechanistic explanation. The logic of imagination does not involve such mixture of inferences; rather, it is originally at once *pathos* and *logos*, bodily and mental. Generally speaking, Ribot's "logic of emotions" is dominated by even more mechanistic views. While this is based upon the limits of his psychology, it also indicates that even as he attempted to conceive in particular something like a logic of emotions, he remained under the influence of formal logic. What Bertram called the law of accumulation signifies the functions of purification and completion, namely, idealization, and we can view this as something like the process of crystallization. To the extent that love and the process of crystallization are tied together, the logic of imagination is a logic of love. *Eros* itself is what is mythical. Nevertheless, we are not simply taking Plato's, or the Platonists', cosmological myth or metaphysics of *eros* that comes to mind here simply as it is. Instead, we seek to conceive the imagination at the root of the historical world. We will, however, be unable to clarify the foundation of the imagination's logic with the immanentism of Bertram's nature mysticism. Even if we take it as a logic of love, we will have to raise it from a logic of *eros* to a logic of *agape*.

To exist historically, according to Bertram, signifies the formation of myths, the raising of things from the ground to the heavens, namely, raising them from the world of facts (*matter of fact*) to the world of form-images [*keizō*] (*image*). We may recognize therein something akin to what Ribot calls the functions of exclusion and abstraction in cases where a concept arises from sensation. But it may be thought, as logicians argue time and again, that for a concept to be formed out of something sensed by means of abstraction, there must be something universal already included within the sensible thing, or put in Platonist terms, things already share in the *ideas*. Form-images are something like the *ideas*. Yet they are not fixed but possess development within themselves. As Ribot states, *images* contain a kinetic element (*l'element moteur*) that objectifies and externalizes them, projecting them outside of ourselves. The alteration of form (*metamorphose*) belonging to the fundamental phenomena of history is conceivable not by means of the logic of the *idée* but by means of the logic of the *image*. Form-images [*keizō*] are not pure *ideas* but, so to speak, *ideas* with bodies. The myth of the *Mütter* (mothers) in Goethe speaks of this. Instead of viewing the form-image (*image*) as a symbol of the idea (*idée*), we should probably view the *idée* as the symbol of the *image*. The *image* is not an *idée*, the reflection of which had become rarefied, but rather the *idée* is something abstracted from the *image*. The *image* is not a copy of a thing. Even Sartre states that naïve metaphysics or ontology that takes the *image* as the reproduction of a thing and thinks as if it exists like a thing has hindered us from understanding the essence of the imagination. If we compare the thing with its *image*, we might recognize therein an identity of essence (*l'identité d'essence*), namely, the identity of the *idea*. But the identity of existence [being] [*sonzai*, 存在] will not follow from this. Existence [*sonzai*] as a thing and existence as a form-image are distinct in the mode of existence (*le mode d'existence*). Sartre writes that we need to sweep away, more than anything else, our almost insurmountable habit of constructing every mode of existence in accordance with the modal type of physical existence;[47] otherwise the logic of expression would be inconceivable. And we need to stop seeing the images of the imagination as simply illustrative, as Husserl does, by persisting in the standpoint of the identity of the *idea*. Furthermore, if we were also compelled to take the *ideas* as logically preceding facts, we might as well be permitted to say with greater reason that form-images precede facts. The content of logic, according to Hegel is "the description of God in his eternal essence prior to the creation of nature and the finite spirit," but this logic would have to pertain to the imagination rather than to pure thought as he claims. As Goethe stated, the imagination is "a priori to reason." The logic of imagination does not precede creation, it is the logic of creation itself. What is more, the logic of creation must possess a transcendental [*chōetsuronteki* 超越論的][48] character. Without transcendence creation is inconceivable. And we can see first such transcendence in the form-images of myths.

7.

[63] We ordinarily think of myths as relating to events of the distant past. Yet according to research on the psychology of primitive peoples, they have no idea of the past as a period within time that unfolds in the process of succession, nor do they distinguish myth and history as distinct epochs within an identical time. They lack any notion of the world's evolution. They do not think of the world of myth to be at the beginning of a historical development. They do not think of that period as part of the same time wherein beings and facts of today are in motion. Rather, the mythic past is thought to pertain to "the time of a period when time did not yet exist." The period of myths is, so to speak, pre-temporal or extra-temporal (*prétemporel ou extratemporel*). They feel the mode of being of the mythical world and the mode of being of the world of actuality to be utterly distinct in quality. "The period of myths must be conceived, not merely as a time of the past, but as a single state equivalent throughout present and future, namely, as a single period." Accordingly, when primitive peoples say that the mythical world is at the beginning of all things, they do not mean that this world belongs, so to speak, to a transcendental or trans-historical (*métahistorique*) antiquity, but rather mean that all beings are born from there or that this period is "creative." In that sense, their myths are a kind of "Book of Genesis." Malinowski writes that "[t]his myth is to the savage what, to a fully believing Christian, is the Biblical story of Creation, of the Fall, of the Redemption by Christ's Sacrifice on the Cross."[49] Preuss as well states that primitive peoples had no notion of the length of time and that myth pertains to originary time (*Urzeit*).[50] We can probably say that it pertains to originary history (*Urgeschichte*). The reality of myth and the reality of actuality are essentially distinct. For example, the word "ancestor" [*sosen* 祖先] is often used indiscriminately to express, on the one hand, a mythical existence and, on the other hand, ancestors [*senzo* 先祖]

of the present generation; but the meanings in these two cases are not the same. Ancestor in the latter sense is also important to primitive peoples. They think of their lives and felicity as depending on the goodwill of their ancestors and regard these ancestors as gods. Yet they understand these ancestors like themselves as having been born at a certain time in the past and having died. But the ancestors spoken of in myths are clearly distinguished from the above sense and also have no cord of history whatsoever that ties them to the various generations preceding the present generation. They belong to a period "outside of time," a "time when time did not yet exist." And there they "created" and "produced" what exists today. Whether this production has physiological meaning or not is not an issue for mythical thinking. Mythical thinking is indifferent to the mechanism of causal connection and focuses the mind on what we call "creation" or "metamorphosis" (*metamorphose*).[51]

Thus, what we need to pay attention to is that for primitive man the world of myth is not the events of the past in history but rather thought of as pertaining to an originary time or an originary history. Myths possess "transcendental value." Myth does not aim at "explanation," it merely reflects "the supernatural."[52] Originary time does not signify a portion of time in its succession through past, present, and future, but rather is synchronically past, present, and future, and as such it is transcendental in relation to successive time. What is more, originary history does not signify a portion of history that courses through time, but rather is the transcendental root of all history. Myth and what we ordinarily call history are of completely distinct orders. The distinction between myth and utopia in Sorel must also be understood as having as its foundation distinct orders; and therein is also the ground to be sought when Bertram, who conceives historical narration as mythical formation, says that to transmit via history is not to rescue past lives by bringing them into our time but to make them non-temporal. Transmission is also a creation. For the primitive human, the mythical world is the supernatural and reality in a noteworthy sense. It is the root of nature. The primitive human views the ancestors, heroes, of the mythical period, as having produced, and created, beings of the present. The creation of the world and the generation of the human make up the main content of myth. Creation would be inconceivable without some sort of transcendence. The characteristic of myth is found in the point that it represents this transcendence, for all that, in myths. That is to say, we can think of mythical beings on the one hand as the transcendental root of the created, to be that which creates without being created; and on the other hand, we can think of them either as animals or as hybrid beings that are half-animal and half-human or even humans just like us. For primitive peoples, the mythical world is supernatural but neither a gap nor a wall intervenes between this world and the world of actuality in any way. The supernatural and nature are not in opposition to one other as two realities that are clearly distinguished or in contention. The beings of the mythical world are, of course, very different from the beings corresponding to them in our world. The former possesses many magical powers lacking in the latter, and the former enjoy capacities to the most heightened degree of which the beings of today possess only dim traces. But these differences are, in short, mere differences in volume or quantity. Put differently, the true meaning of transcendence is not grasped by way of myth. The reason why myth is easily carried over into mere history, in cases where it has lost its mystical quality, lies in the fact that the supernatural and nature become carelessly mixed up in this way. Here we also discern the reason why primitives are not troubled by the intervention of supernatural powers in the processes of nature and furthermore regard it as natural. The supernatural and nature are thus intermingled to the extent that even such intervention is not something that inflicts violence upon nature nor imperils its order.⁵³ As long as we do not correctly understand the meaning of transcendence, we will probably also fail to correctly grasp the meaning of nature.

The examination of how the creation of the world is represented in various myths is not our concern here. As Aristotle said, the lover of myth (*philomythos*) is in a certain sense a lover of wisdom (*philosophos*, the philosopher) (διὸ καὶ ὁ φιλόμυθος φιλόσοφός πώς ἐστιν).⁵⁴ But above all Greek mythology has been an object of philosophical speculation from time immemorial. Of such speculations, let us take up just one interpretation concerning the deities of Samothrace by Schelling who possessed a deep interest in that philosophy of myth.⁵⁵ Samothrace was famous for the cult of the Kabeiroi, taken to be the most ancient of the Greek cults. The Kabeiroi consists of a group of four deities: Axieros, Axiokersa, Axiokersos, and Kadmilos. The names of these deities are not of Greek origin. According to Schelling, the first god, Axieros, who is the primary nature that is the beginning of all things, in Phoenician means first of all hunger, poverty, and furthermore yearning, seeking, or longing. This thought translates to the mythical idea that the most ancient of all nature is the night. The essence of night is lack, poverty, and longing. This night is not darkness, namely, not something hostile to light, but rather possesses light as the night that yearns and seeks to receive. In the same way, even the mythical idea that takes primary nature to be a fire that consumes everything includes the sense that its entire essence is thirst and longing. This fire is, so to speak, the nothing [*mu*, 無], and manifests the hunger for being that cannot but drag everything into itself. Schelling states that what lies below it at the deepest bottom where there no longer is anything can only be mere thirst, not something that is but something that only seeks to be. Longing (*Sehnsucht*) is the beginning of all things and the primordial source of creation. Historians of antiquity identified Axieros with Demeter. The second deity Axiokersa is equal to Persephone and means magic (*Zauber*). Moreover, the daughter is no other than the mother in a different form, namely, the most inner essence of the entire nature is hunger for being, and by means of the unceasing traction of this motive power, things are brought furthermore—as if by magic—from an initial indeterminacy to actuality or formation, but the deities who primordially have no form take form through Persephone and this deity essentially becomes the first living magic. Axiokersa and Axiokersos are tied together through the common notion of magic. This third deity Axiokersos is Dionysus but, according to the historians of Greece, is Hades. Hades and Dionysus are identical and there is a secret meaning concealed in the fact that the lord of the land of the dead is at the same time a deeply compassionate deity. Thus, the first three deities of Samothrace entail the same order and relationships as found between Demeter, Persephone, and Dionysus. The fourth deity, Kadmilos means servant and corresponds to Hermes. He does not, however, serve the first three deities but rather serves a higher deity distinct from them. If he were to serve both the lower deities and the higher deities at the same time, he would have to serve the former only to the extent that, as someone higher than these, he is the mediator between the lower ones and the higher ones, and in this way, the original concept of Hermes is to be the knot of guidance between the higher deities and the lower deities. Kadmilos signifies the one who precedes the former deities and thus serves not the deities preceding him but the deities of the future as the announcer, the messenger, of the coming deities. Axieros is the first but not the supreme, and Kadmilos is the last of the four but higher than them. For these reasons, Schelling states that the idea of emanation does not appear to be compatible with the explanation of the myths of antiquity in general and with the explanation of the myths of Samothrace in particular. For Kadmilos does not stand below in relation to the first three deities, but rather stands above them. If this is so, then who is the god that all these deities [indirectly] and Kadmilos directly serve? These deities are all forces whereby the entire world, the cosmos, exists on the basis of their activities. Accordingly, the god is of the entire world, the cosmos. His creation is the world of necessity. Nevertheless, the god whom the deities, and above all Kadmilos, serves is a supra-worldly god, a god that governs them by means of being the lord of the world, the creator (*demiourgos*) or, in its supreme sense, Zeus. Accordingly, at the deepest place where an ascending series is recognizable, there is Ceres (Demeter) who takes thirst as his essence. It is the primal and most distant beginning of all actual, manifest beings. Next are Persephone, who is the essence or ground of the entirety of visible nature, and Dionysos, who is the lord of the other world. And then there is Kadmilos or Hermes, who reciprocally mediates between nature and the other world reciprocally and, further, with the supra-worldly beyond them. And above everything is god, the creator, who is free in relation to the world. In this way, the doctrines of the Kabeiroi form a system that ascends from the lower deities of nature to the supra-worldly god that governs them.

What concerns us now is not whether Schelling's above interpretation concerning the deities of Samothrace is correct when viewed philologically, but rather its philosophical content. First, we must point to the fact that Schelling states that the idea of "emanation" is not compatible with the explanation of ancient myths. The idea of emanation and the idea of creation are incompatible. Emanationism is a single grand metaphysical form-image but, in the end, it is an immanentism. Next, we must say that the cosmogony (*Kosmogonie*) that views "primary nature," the first ground of creation, as longing or thirst is an exceedingly Schellingian and interesting idea. At the root of creation, there is great *pathos*. Moreover, this *pathos* is a night that possesses light, the hunger for being or essence (*der Hunger nach Wesen*). Stated differently, while itself remaining indeterminate as *pathos* it contains within itself an unbearable demand for determination. This sort of formless *pathos* takes form as magic. Although all things are brought forth to actuality and formation by the power of magic, mere *pathos* is not magic; rather for *pathos* to become magic, *logos*, *idea*, must presumably be added. Magic is something like technology [*gijutsu* 技術]. And so, Hermes tells of and awaits the coming god. This god is the supreme deity Zeus and, as a supra-worldly god, is the maker of the world. The deity preceding him as a whole is none other than Hephaestus, namely, the son of Zeus. If this is so, then the world is formed through *logos* and *pathos*, and even if *logos* itself is supra-worldly, as something worldly we can think of *logos* as tied to *pathos* and as acting formatively like magic. And not only that, primary nature, longing at the ground of creation, is in a certain sense one with the creator and hence must possess a certain transcendental significance. As Schelling states in his essay on human freedom, it would presumably have to be "nature in God" (*Natur in Gott*). According to Schelling, this is what is distinguished from God without being separated from God, the ground of his being. God possesses the inner ground of His being within Himself, and to the extent that God exists the ground precedes God. But because the ground cannot exist unless God actually exists, God is that which precedes the ground. Here as well the concept of immanence is pushed aside. Although the concept of becoming is the only thing compatible with the essence of things, because things are infinitely distinct from God, they cannot be generated within God, viewed as the absolute. Because they are separated from God, things have to be generated from a ground that is distinct from God. However, if no thing can be outside of God, this contradiction can only be resolved if we take things to have their ground within that which is within God Himself but not God Himself, namely, within that which is where the ground of His being is. Here as well Schelling designates this ground as, precisely, longing.[56] In the same way that God's being and the ground of His being are distinct yet one, transcendence must be at the same time immanence. Absolute *logos* and absolute *pathos* must immediately be one. By taking form as magic, formless *pathos* becomes world-formative. If magic also has some sort of logic, it must presumably be something like a logic of imagination. The world, of course, is not formed by mere magic. The world is being formed by means of technology. We can recognize the limits of mythical form-images in regard to the formation of the world where magic and technology must be distinguished. However, as we will investigate shortly, there is a logic of imagination within technology itself.

8.

[74] As we already stated, history includes myth, whether as creation or as transmission. Creation and transmission, or tradition, are tied together. Transmission itself is a single [act of] creation, and creation itself would be impossible without tradition. Presumably the deep connection between culture and myth becomes conceivable where a Schellingian nature lies at the root of creation. Nietzsche writes in *The Birth of Tragedy*: "Without myth, every culture loses its healthy creative natural force. Only a horizon surrounded by myths can gather and unify a whole cultural movement."[57] At the root of the creation of culture, there is something that has the character of *pathos*. Of course, culture is not engendered from mere *pathos*. The *pathos* of creation must be a longing, a hunger for essence, namely, *eros* in relation to the *idea*, and as such must be something mythical. Myth does not merely have the character of *pathos* but is related to what has the character of the *idea*. Only as containing the *ideas* can myth gather together the movements of the entirety of culture into a unity. Liebert states that the historical becomes truly historical by being related to the trans-historical, and the metaphysical; and he attempted to understand the universal significance of myth vis-à-vis culture by seeking the source of myth in the turning of life towards transcendental meaning.[58] The essence of myth, as he states, is not in the mythologization of the absolute. Rather, we ought to say, conversely, that the absolute provides the presupposition of myth.

However, if, as he thinks, this absolute is nothing but a transcendental meaning, an *idea*, then how are we to conceive of myth? Myths are to be conceived not from the *idée* but from the *image* and the *image* becomes conceivable from the unity of *logos* and *pathos*. The *image* is not a reflection of the *idée* but rather is born of something higher than the *idée*. In Plato as well myth has its origin where he had to transcend this doctrine of the *ideas*.

Karl Reinhardt writes: "Plato's myths are myths of the soul, that is, myths of an internal, no longer external, or indivisible world. For this reason, they are meager in [form-]images [*gestaltenärmer*] and nevertheless veil no doctrine or theory of the soul within a transparent vestment; the soul itself and its self-movement is their source, and its [the soul's] self-formation in the internal world is their aim in order to penetrate anew the external world that has become soulless by means of the internal world."[59] The content of the myth Plato depicted, of course, was not limited to the soul but includes society and, further, the entirety of the world, but even these myths, for him, are ultimately tied to the myth of the soul and in it arrives at, so to speak, their summit.

It is not our aim to exhaustively deal with Plato's myths as an independent topic. Let us limit ourselves here to simply indicating the following points in connection to our discussion.

1. In Plato myth is first related to the issue of becoming. What possesses becoming (γένεσις [*genesis*]) cannot become an object of rational thought. That which can be grasped by pure thought is only that which always remains identical, the eternal *idea*. The creator (δημιουργός [*demiourgos*]) shapes the cosmos or the world by taking this *idea* as a paradigm, and the world is a copy or form-image (εἰκών [*eikōn*]) of the eternal. This sort of a world contains an inner kinship with μῦθος (myth), whereby it itself is a single εἰκών.[60] The world as what possesses becoming presupposes a space (χώρα [*chōra*]) or fundamental matter that is the cause of its complex movements. That is to say that the world's becoming takes not only the *idea* as a cause but space too and this must necessarily be mythical. It may be said that the world, not merely the world of *ideas* but also the spatial or material world, is not generated in accordance with the logic of mere reason. Nevertheless, becoming is a movement and movement is temporal. What is time? According to Plato, time is the εἰκών of eternity; it is a copy of eternity that advances by means of number.[61] We may thus say that time in that it is the εἰκών, again, does not have the character of *logos* but of *mythos*.

2. Plato conceived of the world's becoming as directed towards the good and that it ought to be directed towards the good. The good is endowed with the nature of immanence, and on this point the good and the *ideas* are distinguished. In contrast to the *ideas*, which are transcendent and have no direct relation to the life force that makes and nurtures organisms, the good is immanent; thus, everything empirical possesses, so to speak, a good by which it is enlivened and equipped, whereby it is maintained through its enhancement. That which has become, according to Plato, is something mixed, but it is by means of the power of the good that it can exist without being destroyed. Whether on the side of the object or the side of the subject, the good signifies the being of truth that ought

to be, and hence the good is that which produces the necessary affinity between the subject and the object. In contrast to the *idea* that is transcendent to the subject, the good is what first provides the being of truth to the subject. The good is, however, not something merely subjective but that which mediates the affinity between subject and object, for example, the good is the medium that correlates cognition and the being corresponding to it. Accordingly, in the sense of its synthetic function [*sayō*, 作用], the essence of the good is productive and the good alone is creative. And, of course, the fact that the good is not only immanent is indicated by the notion of the *idea* of the good. Not only can the good dwell in the world of the *ideas* just like it dwells in the world of experience in various figures, but it also originally possesses its home there. Transcending the good that is immanent in the world of experience, the pure being of the good in itself exists in the world of *ideas*. In this world as well, the function of the good is equal to that in the previous case: it is nothing other than the good itself, the *idea* of the good, that expresses the affinity between pure reason and its objects, namely, between *ideas*. Moreover, just as in the world of perception the sun faces the seeing eye and the seen object, and both are made by the sun to be sun-like (*sonnenhaft*) and act productively, pure reason and pure *idea* are placed in a reciprocal relationship by the force of a third something that is even higher [than either], whereby reason possesses the capacity to think purely and the *ideas* possess the capacity to be thought purely. In relation to this affinity, what gives rise to the synthetic, productive, power that overcomes every kind of dualistic estrangement is the good. The good in the ideal realm is represented as something like the sun in the world visible to the eye. In this way, we can think of the good as both immanent and transcendent, possessing the sense of subsuming the visible world of experience and the intelligible world of the *ideas*. The *idea* of the good transcends the *ideas*, and it would appear that the mere transcendence of the *ideas* is torn by means of the concept of the good.[62]

3. Now as for the soul, Plato also regards it as the cause of becoming.[63] As constituting self-movement, the soul is the origin of movement, and everything that becomes becomes from this origin. The soul's essence lies in being the mediator between the *ideas* and phenomena. That which becomes are copies of the eternal through participation in the *ideas*, but this participation signifies the soul's activity of similitude (ὁμοίωσις [*homoiōsis*, likeness, resemblance]) with, or imitation (μίμησις [*mimēsis*]) of, the *ideas*, which constitutes the cause of movement in becoming. The soul, distinguished from bodies as something with self-movement, is also something akin to the *idea*. And this sort of inclination towards similitude or imitation is nothing other than *eros*. If we take the soul to be the cause of becoming, becoming is that which desires, that which loves, while in contrast being (*idea*) is that which is desired, that which is loved. Nevertheless, to the extent that becoming is the becoming of the world possessing a beautiful order, namely, a becoming towards the good, the soul that is the cause of this movement must be that which is endowed with the character of the good. We may think of the *demiourgos* in Plato's myth of the world's creation and the becoming of the human being as the supremely good soul.

In this way the locus of myth in Plato is limited. In general, we can recognize this where becoming is an issue. It thus appears where we see that mere solitary existence and transcendence of the *ideas* must be shattered. The cause of becoming is not only the *ideas* but space, the cause of movement in becoming is the soul, such becoming is originally becoming towards the good, the good is not only transcendent but also immanent, the soul that is good is *erotic*, and becoming signifies desire or love. Myth in Plato is the myth of becoming, in particular the myth of the soul and of *eros*. And yet Plato did not attempt to abandon the pre-existence and transcendence of the *ideas*. He thus conceived the world as the εἰκών [image] (*Gleichnis* [allegory, simile, analogy])—this word first possessed a rhetorical and grammatical meaning, and then came to possess a metaphysical meaning in the Neo-Platonist school—of the *ideas*, yet it still did not possess in him the sense of a true symbol (we read this as the sense of what symbolizes and not as what is symbolized) and possessed nothing more than the sense of imitation of the *ideas*. The imagination cannot become an important issue when there is belief in the pre-existence of the *ideas*. Plato related the doctrine of recollection (ἀνάμνησις) concerning the cognition of the *ideas*. Recollection is always dealt with as a kind of imagination. The theory of cognition as recollection in Plato is founded upon the theory of the pre-existence of the *ideas* as well, but it itself bears the character of myth. Of course, to the extent that we are convinced of the pre-existence of the *ideas*, no creativity whatsoever would be admissible for the act of recollection. Nevertheless, if we must conceive, still more internally, the relationship between *anamnesis* and *idea*, and if we must, so to speak, positively ascertain the thought that genesis is *eros*, then presumably the issue of the imagination and its logic would necessarily have to emerge therein. The problem of the logic of imagination concerning the issue of becoming, putting this first of all ontologically in regard to Plato's philosophy, is a problem of the logic of mixture; for what becomes according to the *Timaios* [*Timaeus*] is constituted from form and space, and according to the *Philebus* is constituted from the unlimited [infinite, indeterminate] and the limited [finite, determinate] and is the mixed (τὸ μικτόν). And secondly, we can probably say that, epistemologically, it is the issue of the logic of recollection. It seems that the logic of mixture or the logic of recollection can be developed simply as the logic of imagination.

Nevertheless, those who discern the beginnings of the issue of the logic of imagination already in Plato's doctrine of recollection would probably admit that the doctrine of memory (*memoria*) in the later Platonist, Augustine, possesses an even more significant relationship to this issue. Memory is something that has been treated, since ancient times, as the imagination. According to Augustine memory is, first of all, a treasury of innumerable form-images (*imagines*) brought about by sensory thing-events. Therein is stored what had been given to the sense organs and which we had processed through thought either by increasing, decreasing, or altering it in some other way.[64] What enters memory is not the thing itself but the thing's form-image. And through its recollection, it is applied in the service of thought. And in memory I encounter myself. I recollect what I did, where and when I did it, and what emotions I had on the occasion. Whether I obtained it through my own experience or through believing another person, everything I recollect is retained in memory. Therein I associate things of today with things of yesterday, and on that basis think of my future acts along with their desired effects as if they were present. They are all present (*praesentia*) in memory. What enters memory is not only the thing's form-image but the thing itself also enters memory. For example, when I hear that I must distinguish three kinds of questions, namely, "does it exist?," "what is it?," "what is its quality?" (*an sit, quid sit, quale sit*), I retain the form-images of sounds constituting these words despite the sounds no longer existing, having disappeared into the wind; even though I had grasped what was expressed by means of these sounds not through some sense organ. In this case, therefore, it is not the form-image but rather the thing itself that becomes stored in my memory. Moreover, when I learned it [from another person], I did not simply believe the other person but recognized it in my mind and acknowledged its truth. Accordingly, it must have been existent within my own mind even before I learned of it. In this way, Augustine expresses a Platonist notion that we do not cognize it unless we recollect it.[65] Even if it had faded from our eyes, it was retained in our memory. It appears that Plato's theory of the *ideas* has been furnished here with a subjective foundation. My memory includes not only a number of factors like relationships or laws besides the sorts of affairs mentioned above, but in particular I also recollect my own recollection (*meminisse me memini*). If I later recollect the fact that I had now recollected this, this recollection is due to my memory as well. What is more, memory enfolds my emotions (*affections*). And because of this, I can recall all of my joys without being joyful, recall my past sorrows without sorrow, fears of former times without fear, and former desires without desire. In these examples, memory contains not the things themselves, nor their form-images, but their ideas or signs (*notions vel notations*) [notions or notations]. Furthermore, where can I discover even God other than from my own memory? Augustine writes: "And how shall I find Thee if I remember Thee not?" (*et quomodo iam inveniam te, si memor non sum tui?*)

In this way, Augustine thought of memory as enveloping all sorts of things. When I say memory, and I understand what I say, where do I understand it other than in memory? And when I speak of forgetting, and know what I speak of, how could I know of this matter unless I recollect it? In cases where I recollect memory, memory itself is present to myself by means of myself. In cases where I think of forgetting, memory and forgetting are both present, namely, the memory by which I recollect and its forgetting that I recollect are both present.[66] Forgetting is nothing other than the lack of memory. Hence if we follow Augustine, memory is the present. Memory itself is present to the self by means of the self and forgetting too becomes present by means of memory. Past and future are also present in memory. The present of memory is not the present conceived as succeeding through past-present-future, but rather must be a present wherein the latter present is synchronically existent with past and future. The concept of the imagination and the concept of time are intimately related, but we cannot take the issue of time in this case as an issue of time that simply proceeds in a straight line. In this way, the memory Augustine discusses is a present that transcends time. It may be said that in the myths of primitive man the ancestor as a mythical being, distinguished from the ancestor as a historical being, is thus placed in memory. Even if the present in memory is nothing other than an eternity, it must also imply an internal relationship to time where it is tied in particular to memory. Even if we could conceive some sort of eternity with the Hegelian *Idee*, we would be unable to conceive of time or would conceive of it as something superficial. We can say that the problem of time, more than anything else, is the problem of the imagination and that the problem of the imagination fundamentally is the problem of time. Furthermore, the logic of imagination does not conceive of time merely as time but demands at the same time the conception of time in its relationship to eternity. As Plato said, time is the [form-]image (εἰκών), or symbol, of eternity. The true meaning of a symbol is the act of symbolizing without there being something symbolized. Time, as it is, is the symbol of eternity, and it is not that there is an eternity apart from time as that which is separately symbolized. Eternity appears in time by nullifying itself or, inversely, time symbolizes eternity by nullifying itself. The imagination, as related to this sort of time and to eternity, cannot be defined simply as memory—Augustine's theory of memory is tied to a Platonist premise—and, instead, we must view memory as a symbol within a finite factor belonging to the originary imagination.

As already recognized in Plato, time is something mythical. As Valéry stated, "time is the myth of myths, the infinite of myths." And we can presumably conceive of the fundamental relationship between myth and history where the historical is temporal. Mythical time is different from physical time. The events of myth are carried out outside of time or, stated differently, in the expanse of the whole of time; or rather, in that which envelops the whole of time where all of time is compresently tied together. But every kind of myth makes the effort to position this sort of eternity within a series of periods. For this reason, every myth is a myth of origin (*mythes d'origine*) or an eschatological myth (*mythes eschatologiques*). "It explains the origin or the end of things, not because that would be the essential function of myth, but rather because myth is within time."[67] Ordinarily time is represented as a successive homogeneous continuity and the ideas of point and interval constitute the calendar. But for mythical time, the calendar is not for measuring time but for rendering time into a rhythm. Hubert and Mauss state that for magic and religion, the various successive parts of time are not homogeneous but even the parts that look equal on the basis of their volume are not necessarily equal nor of equal value, and that the parts deemed the same are equal and of equal value [only] because of their position in the calendar. The time in which events of myth occur is thus discontinuous and there is a sudden change within its progression. The continuity of time is suspended by a period of crisis (*dates critiques*). We can probably say that all myths are products of the consciousness of crisis.[68] The time that constitutes the period of crisis is different from any sort of time that precedes it or continues it, and the continuity separated by periods of crisis are mutually distinct. On the other hand, the various intermediary times included between two connected periods of crisis are each continuous and undivided. Stated differently, the concrete duration of the continuity is completely assimilated to that of the corresponding period (*période*). Rather, the concept of *period* itself is generated by the complete assimilation of the periods of crisis and their intermediary time, hence by the mutual reduction between the intermediary time and the moments, and thus also by the fact that it is temporal qua spatial. Mythical time is not quantitative but placed upon *periods* that are each qualitatively distinguished. Therefore, mythical time manifests a historical time that is distinct from physical time, and we can conceive therein a fundamental connection between history and myth.

9.

[88] Many scholars recognize the fact that myth is a product of phantasy [*sōzō*, 想像] or the imagination [*kōsōryoku*, 構想力]. For example, those like Ribot state that myth reveals the golden age in the history of the imagination, its peak of development, and that the flower of the imagination fully blooms through of the creation of myths.[69] Nevertheless people also often compare such imagination to dreams. We can think of dreams themselves as products of the imagination as well. For this reason, it is clear that to throw light upon the formation of dreams in general would furnish the key necessary to understanding the essence of the imagination, and in particular the essence of the imagination in myths. If we take dreaming to be an exception in man's conscious life, even the exception would here verify the laws.

We ordinarily view dreams to be of a completely distinct character from that of consciousness when awake. Yet Bergson opposes this view, arguing that the formation of dreams has nothing mystical about it, our dreams are made in nearly the same way as our visual perceptions of the actual world, and the mechanism of consciousness in the two cases is identical.[70] What plays the most significant role here is memory. First, the material for dreams is always sensations of the actual. Without this material, a dream would be unable to produce anything. Without any sense of sound given to the person dreaming, it would be impossible for sounds to appear in the person's dreams. What becomes the material for dreams are obscure sensations that have not yet been determined or defined. The form of their determination is memory. In that sense dreams are for the most part an utter restoration of the past, and it is only that this past is a past that is difficult for us to recognize. Even in periods of being awake we possess a multitude of memories that demand our attention as it goes on changing while fading. These memories are intimately tied to our situation as well as our activity. Although memory in human beings is not bound to action as much as it is for animals, it is still attached to action. At a given moment, our memory or, so to speak, its ceaselessly moving apex point coincides with our present and, together with it, forms a pyramid where it pierces the future. And yet behind the memory sitting upon our present concerns, at its bottom, beneath the scene illuminated by consciousness, there exist innumerable other memories. Therein our past life, in its utmost detail, is preserved. To the extent that we are acting, it is impossible for these innumerable memories to emerge on the surface. But of the specters of the memory of when we rise and leap, those that can be assimilated to the obscure sensations given to us or those that can be harmonized with our general affective situation produced according to the state of our various bodily organs when we become indifferent to our actions in tension with the present circumstances or, put differently, when we are asleep, succeed in taking on colors, sounds, or, even materiality. In this way, a dream is generated when a connection is made between memory and sensation. This is the same mechanism as in cases when we are awake. For example, when a person reads a book, that person does not thoroughly look at each printed character and often fails to notice a misprint or omission. In such cases, the characters actually seen rouse a memory, and this memory is projected outward in the form of a hallucination (*hallucination*) so that what the reader sees is this memory to a degree equal to, or greater than, the characters themselves. Bergson states, "when we look at things, what we give to ourselves is a certain kind of hallucination inserted into the frame of actuality." Memory awaits in the depths of consciousness for the opportunity to go outside, and as soon as the condition for this is furnished, it actualizes itself by connecting to sensation. The difference between dreaming and being awake is nothing other than this; when awake our lives involve action, effort, and concentration, when dreaming we are, by contrast, withdrawn from such life and in a state of indifference.

Hence, according to Bergson, memory is inserted into—and bonded with—sensation as a kind of hallucination, when dreaming or awake. What provides form to sensation is memory. From this fact, we can also think of sensation as also already included in the logical form of the imagination in our own sense. This form, according to us, is, for example, particular qua universal, subjective qua objective, real qua ideal, and so on. By means of the so-called hallucinatory activity of memory, a particular sensation possesses at the same time a universality. And by means of the insertion of memory into sensation, a subjective sensation becomes at the same time objective and, conversely, the objectivity of the sensation receives at the same time a subjectivity. And furthermore, by means of that, a material sensation comes to exist as a form-image by bearing an ideality. Bergson relates that in the combination of sensation and memory the past coincides with the present and, together with it [that combination], thrusts into the future. But memory is not simply in the past, but rather, as Augustine conceived, memory would have to be the present wherein both past and future are present. Consciousness of actuality not only flows endlessly, containing the past and pregnant with the future, as Bergson states. We must think of both past and future as coexisting in the present. And although Bergson theorizes that dreams in general are not creative this is because he relates memory merely to the past and to [the act of] seeing. However, if we take memory to be the true present, we can conceive of the function of such memory that is the true present—we would no longer be able to call this memory, and indeed would have to speak of it as the imagination—to be creative. The limits of Bergsonian philosophy lie in this immanentism. He talks about creative evolution, but in its standpoint of immanentism, even if we can speak of evolution, we cannot speak of creation. We are, of course, not saying that dreams are truly creative. What is truly creative, by contrast, is actuality itself, and it is within the actual itself that we recognize the imagination.

Now, among people who viewed dreams to be products of phantasy [*sōzō*], moreover of a certain creative imagination [*kōsōryoku*], there are those like Volkelt.[71] Dreams are ordinarily seen in sleep, but Volkelt states that if we take the essence of the mind [*seishin*, 精神] to consist in the fact that it remains ceaselessly conscious and if we take sleep to be a simple interruption of consciousness generated only in the somatic disturbance of that mind, then sleep must be something completely different from what practically exists for us. That is to say that in such cases, sleep signifies a hostile intervention, violence of an external force, undertaken by the body against the most inner essence of the mind, and hence, as in cases when we are robbed of freedom or assaulted by illness, sleep ought to be something we experience as hostile, oppressive, unstable, or even filled with pain. However, the sweetness brought by sleep even for a mind that is strongest and self-aware to the highest degree, proves that to periodically become unconscious, and thus to not have the power to keep the self ceaselessly conscious, belongs to the mind's essence itself. When awake the mind pulls itself apart from the ground of Mother Nature, stands sharply opposed to the entire world, and takes its unnatural, reflected interiority as its center. In sleep, the mind again descends and intimately dissolves into simple nature that quietly creates and, for the moment, into the nature of its body, and hence the essence of the mind approaches the fulfilling and satiating life of nature. What was logically separated in the conscious mind and diluted by the fine sieve of abstractions are, so to speak, fused into a dense sap and flows into the agglutination of intuition. Without conceiving of the state of mind that has approached nature's concrete creation where it contrasts to that sharp tension between subject and object in waking consciousness, we cannot understand how the mind in sleep attains that powerful exhilaration of every faculty it feels when waking up. It is quite distinctive that what is given after complete sleep is the feeling of a certain satisfaction, fulfillment, or ripening. Thus, according to Volkelt, dreams must involve the positive aspect of the sleeping mind, and involve certain elements of its unconscious, concrete, and natural being. Put differently, the fundamental and principle force in cases generated by dreams is, indeed, the unconsciously creating imagination.

Dreams are not simply products of an act of the association [of ideas] but belong to the imagination's creation. What we see in dreams are not hallucinations like ghosts, but embodied actualities that we can grasp with our hands. And many items in them are symbolic. Although it is said that in dreams the sharp tension between subject and object disappears, the most remarkable characteristic of dreams is that one's own self, conceived as subject, also enters and acts within the dream world, and yet we are seeing this world. As subject, I am not somewhere outside of the world and confronting it, but rather I myself who is acting has already entered the world. Accordingly, even if the imagination is something like creative nature, this nature is no mere fusion of subject and object, or identity of subject and object; rather to the contrary, it is something transcending the subjective and the objective. In the dream world, I myself, as the one who acts, has entered into this world, and yet this world is being seen. Therein we can observe the true countenance of the transcendentality of imagination. As Volkelt believed that in sleep we approach the nature that creates without consciousness, we probably would be unable to understand the imagination without this sort of nature, the sort of nature Schelling had in mind. Of course, as Volkelt stated, we approach the inner depths of the world in dreams not by means of what we experience through dream images but by means of things that are formed and exist without consciousness in the process of our dream production. It is not that the world is a dream, but that at the root of the world's creation we must think of the imagination. An important suggestion is provided for solving the well-known issue of the reality of the external world in this point that in dreams the acting self has entered into this world and yet this world is being seen.

The imagination is tied to a certain nature, nature in the subjective sense, and hence to *pathos*. The problem must be what this nature is and how this *pathos* is related to *logos*. For the present, this nature means not only our body but also the social body. The connection between the social body and the imagination is especially clear in myths. Ribot asks whether the mythical activities of antiquity still exist among civilized peoples. He answers affirmatively as follows: Even when putting aside something like literature regarded as myths that have been altered and adapted to the altered conditions of civilization, the mythical activity performed, not individually, but collectively, anonymously, and unconsciously, in its pure form, still currently survives in the production of legends (*légende*). While myths relate to the phenomena of nature, legends relate to persons and historical events. However, Ribot states that in this case if we are to consider the position of the productive imagination, the relationship of myth to legend is analogous to the relationship between illusion (*illusion*) and hallucination (*hallucination*). In other words, he means that illusions and legends are partial imagination [*sōzō*], and hallucinations and myths are holistic imagination.[72] This theory aside, the fact that legends concerning human beings and history are ceaselessly produced, even where myths about nature have disappeared as a result of the progress in objective knowledge, is because the human and history are not at all things that can simply be grasped objectively; rather to the contrary, they are thoroughly subjective. We can probably recognize a deep significance also in the fact that Plato's myths were fundamentally myths of the soul. Ribot states that in the creation of myths the faculty of imagination [*sōzōryoku*] emerges in complete spontaneity and can create, free of any sort of imitation or tradition, without being fettered by any sort of established form. But as Lévy-Bruhl states, the psychology of primitive man is, to the contrary, completely governed by collective representations, and their livelihood is shackled by conventions, institutions, and traditions, and myths themselves are products of collective representations that attempt to maintain such conventions, institutions, and traditions. The complete expression of the imagination and its logic is recognizable not in myths but in other cultures of a higher order.

Now myths are not originally something that aim at artistic expression or logical explanation, but rather, they possess practical meaning. The essence of myths is not something comprehensible merely through the *text* of their stories. We need to attend to their sociological relationships. The *text* is, of course, still important, but separated from its *context* it is without life. The story's interest is conspicuously strengthened and given its peculiar character by the method of its narration. Malinowski states:

> The whole nature of the performance, the voice and the mimicry, the stimulus and the response of the audience mean as much to the natives as the text; and the sociologist should take his cue from the natives. And the performance, again, has to be placed in its proper time-setting—the hour of the day, and the season, with the background of the sprouting gardens awaiting future work, and slightly influenced by the magic of the fairy tales. We must also bear in mind the sociological context of private ownership, the sociable function and the cultural role of amusing fiction. All these elements are equally relevant, and all must be studied as well as the text. The stories live in native life and not on paper, and when a scholar jots them down without being able to evoke the atmosphere in which they flourish he has given us but a mutilated bit of reality.[73]

In this way myths are not merely ideas but rather possess the significance of an institution [*seido*, 制度]. Those who view myths as akin to artistic or theoretical products are unable to comprehend the institutional character of myths. Indeed, it may be said that myths are conceivable as institutional in relation to their *contexts*, but their *texts* themselves are thoroughly ideal. This ideal element is not rational, it lacks objectivity, and is only subjective [*shukanteki*, 主観的]. Accordingly, to view history as myth possesses the danger of making history subjective. If the logic of imagination is merely a logic of the *image* and if this *image* is something merely *imaginary* as in myths or dreams, it cannot be the logic of history. History is not something ideal, not something subjective, but the most actual and the most objective. The logic of imagination is not a logic of mere *image* but rather it is a logic of *form*. And the institution is what is initially conceivable as objective historical *form* in this way. Therein we must advance to investigate the relationship between institution and the imagination.

2

Institution

1.

[99] Valéry states:

> The effects of society, languages, laws, "mores," arts, politics, everything that is fiduciary in the world, every effect that is unequal in its cause, requires conventions [*kanshū*, 慣習] (*convention*), or put differently, relays—through which a second reality (*une réalité seconde*) is configured and composed, along with a sensory and instantaneous reality, and covers it, dominates it—sometimes tears it apart to reveal the terrifying simplicity of elementary life.[1]

For instance, the world of politics is an "other world" (*un autre monde*) nowhere visible even while functioning in every place, reducible to the totality of conventions. Politics can be reduced to a combination of conventional substances, and these substances are exchanged among people even without knowing how they were made and how they produce effects whose extent and reverberation are immeasurable. Valéry calls these conventions fiction (*fiction*) and even writes that every social situation requires fiction. Conventions are a kind of magic or spell and can also be thought of as myth. In this way, instincts are subjugated by conventions. The movement of society towards civilization is a movement towards the domination of symbols and signs, and this is a progression from an "epoch of facts" to the "land of fiction." Every society lies upon the primary and most important convention, language and character [writing]. Society is supported by magic and is a "building of spells." Everything is maintained by the force of form-images [*keizō*]. If people do not trust in these form-images, eventually everything would collapse.[2] Accordingly, it is quite interesting that the two most characteristic thinkers of today, Sorel the Pascalian, discussed above, and Valéry, the Cartesian, each recognized the importance of myth through their mutually distinct thought. Valéry states: "in reality, it is almost impossible to clearly separate out something that is not myth since so many myths exist within ourselves and are familiar in this way."[3] He also writes in his letters concerning myth that "myths are the souls of our actions and our loves. We can only act by moving ourselves toward phantoms. We can only love what we ourselves create."[4] In history, myths are realistic; and in history, anything realistic can have the significance of myth. Valéry, however, would presumably not agree to understand what he calls convention as simply myth. For him, conventions are fictions, agreements, and products of the intellect [*chisei*, 知性]. However, even if what Valéry calls convention is a product of the intellect, as Sorel's view which attempts to altogether remove the intellectual elements from myth altogether is one-dimensional, it controls human actions not as mere fiction but, so to speak, as myth, and hence it must possess its basis in something *pathos*-like [パトス的なもの]. Myth has a nature that can be explained neither by Pascalian irrationalism nor by Cartesian rationalism. We would have to see in it the originary-form [原始形態] of the logic of imagination. Convention, of course, is not identical to myth, and their distinction is important. Moreover, we can think of them as manifesting a distinction of categories in the logic of imagination.

Incidentally, what Valéry designates as *convention* includes not only what is ordinarily regarded as customary but also morality or manners, law, politics, language, art, and society itself. Considered from the point of possessing a comprehensive meaning, we will adopt, in place of Valéry's term *convention*, the term *institution* [*seido*, 制度] that is even closer to the usual term.⁵ However, perhaps it would be fitting to use the Greek word νόμος [*nomos*, law, custom] in opposition to the word μῦθος [myth] which we have been using. What we name here institution is, needless to say, also not limited to what are ordinarily called institutions, because language, convention, morality, law, art, and so on are also to be considered as institutions. In other words, just as myth signifies one category, namely, a certain mode of being of the historical, institution signifies another category, namely, another mode of being of the historical. We can say that anything historical, including myth itself, exists as *nomos*. Moreover, in terms of our use of the term institution here, there are three meanings of institution that need to be distinguished for the moment. First, an institution is a *convention* in Valéry's sense of *fiction*. There are no institutions that do not possess some fictional character. And as the word *convention* (from *convenio* = *to come together, assemble*) suggests, it also signifies a consensus, consent or agreement, among a multitude of human beings and thus always has something of a social character. Second, what we generally called convention is normally expressed with the word *coutume* (*custom*); thus, it is not only something simply habitual but also something traditional. This is, of course, distinguished from the habit of an individual person, namely, *habitude* (*habit*). As such it always has something of a social character (the term derives from the Latin word *con-suesco*) and to that extent, it presumably must have the significance of *convention*. However, while *convention*, in the sense of fiction, is seen as something arbitrary, free, and belonging to *logos*, *coutume* is seen as something natural, necessary, and belonging to *pathos*. As such, an institution possesses a certain habitual or traditional character. We can think of *convention* in the sense of fiction as something external to us. But *coutume* (*consuetudo*) is related to the Latin word *suesco*, which in turn relates to *suum* (*sien*), and so we can think of it as having the sense of "noticing something as one's own" so that we can conceive it as something internal. Third, as the word convention [*kanshū*] (*mos, mores, consuetudo*) was, however, formerly used without distinction even in the sense of common law [*kanshūhō*, 慣習法; *Gewohnheitsrecht*],⁶ institution bears a certain lawful quality, the quality of *nomos*. As for *convention*, it confronts an individual, not simply as something for convenience, but as something that is lawful possessing coercion and authority. Institutions form what

Valéry calls a certain secondary reality, not only in the sense of fiction but also in the sense of *nomos*. The challenge is to further develop substantively the above three meanings that are included in the concept of institution in such a way as to further clarify their mutual relationships.

Every institution possesses, first, a fictional character. Here we can distinguish between mythical being and institutional being.[7] Mythical being is, to start, not something actual but indeed something mythical. Nevertheless, it is not something we ought to call fiction but rather something mystical, religious, and sacred. It is possible for institutions as well to be mythologized from the beginning and exist as a single myth, and in fact, there is no shortage of examples of this. In antiquity institutions were included within religion. For example, for the Greeks and Romans, in the same way as for the Indians, law was first a part of religion. Fustel de Coulanges writes: "Law was born not of the idea of justice but of religion and was unthinkable outside of religion. For there to be a relationship of law between two human beings, there had to already exist between them a religious relationship ... Law was nothing but one aspect of religion, there was no common law without a common religion."[8] Not only law but even something like art was a part of religion; what is more, religion was consanguineous. The public festivals, where theater and art within these festivals were developed in all their forms until the last period of the Roman empire, formed a part of the religious rituals. Nevertheless, we are not thinking of the distinction between myth and institution necessarily in terms of a temporal ordering. It is also possible to view myths as being made for the maintenance and preservation of certain institutions. And, of course, it is possible for us to consider the distinction between myth and institution where institutions remain after myths in general are thought to have perished. But our problem is a logical one. And we can admit the logical distinction between myth and institutions are, for the present, from the fictional nature of the latter. Fiction is not something that instinct can make; rather, it is a product of the intellect. While myths are something mystical, by contrast institutions are more intellectual, and we can raise the intellectual nature of institutions in contrast to the mystical nature of myths. What is at issue here is determining what sort of a thing we call in this way the intellect [*chisei*] really is.

If we are to take institutions here as fictional, then we can presumably already conceive of the intellect behind institutions as imagining [構想的]. Or, in general, the fact that it can work in fiction or hypothetically is an important characteristic of the intellect. And already, at this point, the intellect can be tied to the imagination, and in that case, we can indeed consider the intellect as tied to the imagination. Behind institutions, at the root of the intellect, lies the imagination. Institutions cannot develop without the imagination. For example, the scope of the viability of morality is limited to the scope of blood relations. Evidently, in order for established morality to expand its domain, it must be something rational. This alone, however, is not sufficient. According to Tarde, there was a time during primitive periods when blood relationships were necessary for people to be [considered] socially and morally as belonging to the same country. Artificial blood relations were created by all sorts of fictions, making it possible to extend the interests of natural blood relations to them.[9] Among many savages, there is the custom of fortifying an alliance by mixing the blood of several enemies, entering a covenant, to thus become, so to speak, of the same blood. This signifies the invention of a solemn means for extending the duties and love of fraternity beyond the narrow confines of kin. However, in order for such fictions to be invented and, moreover, be efficacious, fancy, phantasy, imagination would presumably have to be at work. Adoption, having truly manifold and also truly strange forms, was another means for the same purpose as the above. Furthermore, based on a similar idea, hospitality towards foreigners was also deemed to be a fictional union of kin, where entering the home is comparable indeed to fostering a child or mixing shed blood. Fictions of this sort are, of course, not only intellectual but cannot even be thought without the imagination based upon *pathos*. The most miraculous of this sort would be Christ's words that all human beings are your brothers and sisters, that all of you are God's children. It is the myth of the brotherhood of the world. We can say that there can be no morality without myth, or rather that the imagination is at the root of all morality.

We bow when we meet people, for example. Greetings are a fiction and institution. Are such greetings rational? The methods of greeting vary, differing among distinct peoples. Whereas we bow, Westerners shake hands. That is to say that the method of greeting does not possess any universality that we might conceive as the nature of something rational. And it is not that there exists an abstract greeting in general but that a greeting has the meaning of a greeting only as a certain concrete expression. And what is expressed in greetings, instead of something intellectual, is something emotive, namely, the volition or emotion of obedience, affection, and so on. Nevertheless, that does not mean that the institution of greeting is something completely irrational. As fiction, it must be the product of the intellect. If it was something utterly irrational, it would be impossible to be socially propagated and endure. While we may think of greetings as something instinctive, as etiquette greetings they have rather the sense of substituting instinct with fiction. Simply put, the various forms of greeting are neither merely rational nor merely irrational. As such things, they indeed belong to the imagination. In practice, the principal parts of our lives move within innumerable institutions of various sizes that cannot be said to be simply rational or simply irrational. In the same way that it would be an error to think of this as a mere irrationalism, to explain this as a mere rationalism would also be an error. We may conceive of forms of greeting, such as bowing or shaking hands, as being defined by social relations like status and class, and as expressing such social relations. This would be the intellect's way of rationally explaining institutions of greeting. Even if this is certainly the case, this still does not explain how a certain particular form of greeting was formed. Greetings are different from numerical formulas that express universal laws of nature; this is why it becomes reduced to instinct. But, from the start, it is not something instinctive but something fictional. Moreover, greetings that possess a definite concrete form are not mere products of the intellect but rather products of the imagination. Tarde states, "No matter how they appear simple for those who have been performing various duties for a long time, in their development, they were all individual original inventions, like other inventions they are inventions that appeared one after the other and spread one after the other."[10] But even something like a greeting is a single more (*Sitte* [ethos]), and mores bear the character of duty, and moreover originally it was an invention. And if we stipulate that it was indeed originally an invention, it presumably would have to belong to the imagination rather than to the intellect. As Bergson also states, our intellect is unable to grasp invention either "in its upspringing, that is to say, where it possesses something indivisible, or in its genius, that is to say, where it possesses something creative."[11] Bergson states that "creation signifies, more than anything else, emotion."[12] Yet creation is no mere emotion. Creation is conceivable only from the imagination whereby elements of *logos* and of *pathos* are one. Moreover, the sense that mores [*shūzoku*, 習俗] such as greetings are inventions is presumably restricted in comparison to the fact that things like literature or art are creations. Let us then pursue the nature of mores, or institutions in general, from the previously raised secondary significance.

2.

[110] Although it is unthinkable that institutions are things merely made by the intellect, they are frequently reduced to instinct. William McDougall and other scholars attempted to discern the source of the civilized lifestyle for human society within instinct, deriving society from individuals' instincts. Instinct and intellect are said to be opposites. According to Bergson, these are two mutually distinct developments of the same principle, that is, in the one case life remains internal to itself while in the other case it externalizes itself and loses itself for the employment of inorganic material. The fact that intellect is unable to absorb instinct is based on this oppositional nature, and within instinct there remains something essential that cannot be expressed in the language of the intellect and hence cannot be analyzed. In contrast to how intellect handles all things mechanistically, instinct takes, so to speak, an organic path by means of which life continues the work of organizing matter. The instinctive knowledge of a particular point that one species possesses concerning another species has its root in the unity of life itself. And in that juncture life is completely sympathetic in relation to itself.[13] Thus, according to Bergson, the essence of instinct is a kind of sympathy (*sympathie*), and in accordance with the meaning of the word, it means to be with *pathos*. In this way, even if instinct and intellect are opposites, are they not at some point conjoined and in accord? We see Bergson's standpoint of irrationalism and intuitionism in his considering them as thoroughly exclusive. We thus find it difficult to simply agree to this standpoint of his. James says that instinct is not always blind nor unchanging, and states as follows:[14] "[M]an possesses all the impulses that [the lower animals] have, and a great many more besides. In other words, there is no material antagonism between instinct and reason. Reason, *per se*, can inhibit no impulses; the only thing that can neutralize an impulse is an impulse the other way. Reason may, however, make an inference which will excite the imagination [*sōzō*] so as to set loose the impulse the other way."[15] If it is such a thing we ought to say that *imagination* [*sōzō*] is the middle between reason and instinct and reason can move instinct by means of a particular deduction that mediates imagination [*sōzō*]. The imagination [*kōsōryoku*] is such a thing in that at the same time that it is essentially of *logos*, it is of *pathos*. Bergson says that intellect and instinct are the poles of two principal lines of development of life, but in the imagination, they are one. The institutions of society, and society itself,

are founded not upon mere instinct, nor do they follow the logic of mere reason, as they are made according to the logic of imagination. We would have to think of the logic of reason instead as something abstracted from the logic of imagination that ought to be regarded as the originary-logic (*Urlogik*).

As stated earlier, instinct cannot explain institutions. This would turn something social into something biological. Institutions are rather what changes into instinct. Nevertheless, habit is also seen as what changes into instinct in this way. James says that instinct is also not unchanging and writes as follows: "The natural conclusion to draw from this transiency of instincts is that most instincts are implanted for the sake of giving rise to habits, and that, once this purpose is accomplished, the instincts themselves, as such, have no *raison d'être* in the psychical economy, and consequently fades away."[16] Social scientists define instinct as the mode of behavior transmitted through the inheritance of somatic structure, or as a disposition inherited in relation to behavior; but put simply, we can say that it is hereditary nature. As "second nature," habit changes into this first nature. Institutions are not simply something of *logos* but at the same time something of *pathos*, and rather than being instinctive it is something habitual.

Although habit can be thought of as nature, this must be in the sense put by Ravaisson in his theory on habit that the world of inorganic matter is the empire of destiny (*l'empire du Destin*) and that the world of organic life is the empire of nature (*l'empire du la Nature*).[17] An object that is utterly mechanistic and controlled only by external necessity does not possess what we mean by habit. What can possess habit would have to be that which can alter. But this change cannot mean something like a mere change of place. Even if we were to throw a single stone a hundred times in a row in the same direction with the same velocity, the stone will not form a habit as a result. The mechanistic view that explains habit from repetition would have to be countered. Aristotle had already stated that habit begins with the initiating act. Unless there is a change in each execution of an act, change will not be engendered no matter how much the act is repeated. At most repetition produces only a sum total of results, whether manifest or hidden. The number of repetitions and the fact of repetition itself are contingent. We may consider every act as a habit in the process of beginning. But it will be said that unless the results are accumulated they will not be visible to the eye. Of course, that is often the case. Yet it is doubtful whether repetition is always necessary, and we cannot say that a single act cannot at times create a new habit in one stroke. Even in cases where one learns through repetition, it is still possible that the various repetitions do not possess the same value or that the number of repetitions is something that cannot be reduced.[18] In either case, habit is not something that can be explained mechanistically. A habit is not simply a single state but instead a single tendency. For a change, no longer existing and not yet existing, namely, possible change, it is one continuous tendency. Habit not only includes variability but assumes a change in tendency or inner capacity. Accordingly, we can form a habit by taking the distinction, such as between possibility and actuality, inner and outer, as pertaining to the essential structure of that thing. Habit cannot exist in the world of immediacy and homogeneity, the world of inorganic order. Only that which possesses inner spontaneity can form a habit. On the other hand, however, that which is absolutely spontaneous, active, or absolutely free, could presumably not form a habit. As Ravaisson states, habit is the proportional mean of volition and nature. On one hand, nature encroaches upon consciousness, and on the other hand, freedom flows into nature. And as we can see freedom in the depths of nature, we can see nature in the depths of consciousness. In habit nature and freedom are one, and passivity and activity are one. In that sense, habit is a natural spontaneity (*la spontanéité naturelle*).[19] Habit is at-work not only in our will but within our thoughts, and we can recognize the laws of habit also in the higher realms of mental operations, such as morality, art, science, and so on. Habit is the originary-form [*genkeishiki*, 原形式] of life, of consciousness. Habit, as natured nature (*la nature naturée*), is the product and, moreover, the manifestation of naturing nature (*la nature naturante*).[20] Now, instinct is for Bergson something belonging to the form of memory, but it should be said that instead it is habit that is such a thing. Ravaisson states that between habit and instinct, between habit and nature, there is only a difference in degree, and this difference can be endlessly reduced. On the other hand, if we take habit as belonging to a form of memory, could we not conceive of everything within which we recognize the function of habit as following the logic of imagination? We would have to think this way if we were to conceive of biological nature within historical nature instead of seeing life as something merely biological. As already discussed in the chapter on myth, the problem of memory is a problem of the imagination. What had been called φαντασία [phantasy] or *imago* since ancient times are mainly memory images. The problem of the imagination is not only a problem of creation, it is also a problem of memory, and hence of tradition. Furthermore, we cannot abstractly separate creation and tradition. According to Ravaisson, "the understanding and the will only determine that which is discrete and distinct. Nature makes continuity concrete, as the plenitude of reality."[21] What the will determines by defining its limits is the ceaseless flux of involuntary spontaneity flowing without sound at the bottom of the mind. And as an immediacy preceding this, reflective thought contains an intuition where the idea and the subject thinking it are not distinguished. The understanding and the will are related only at the extremities, at the poles, at both poles. Their interval includes an endlessly divisible continuity of the middle. The continuity contains an indivisible middle term and there at every possible extension of the middle, no matter what the distance from one pole or the other pole, the two poles are in contact, and the opposites become one. As divided extremities, the intellect of an extremity includes the intellect of the middle, and the will for the end includes the will for the means. This will and this intellect now can only be mediated things, and thus as such advance endlessly. A person can never exhaust the endlessly divisible middle and thus can never re-integrate it. The mediated intellect and will must therefore contain the unmediated intellect and will of the middle. The unmediated intellect and will are something like the middle term of movement in every kind of extension of the middle. There the two poles are everywhere in contact and there the beginning and the end become one. This unmediated intellect is concrete thought wherein the idea is fused into being, and this unmediated will is love where one desires (*désir*) or rather desires at the same time as one possesses. This thought and this desire, this idea substantialized in the movement of love, this is nature. Can we not, therefore, conceive of what Ravaisson calls in these ways, "concrete thought where the idea is fused into being" (*la pensée concrete, où l'idée est confondue dans l'être*), "love, which possesses and desires at the same time" (*l'amour, qui possède et qui desire en même temps*), "the idea substantiated in the movement of love" (*l'idée substantialisée dans le movement de l'amour*), and finally "nature," the imagination?[22] Ravaisson as well states that every sort of function of the understanding contains the imagination [*kōsōryoku*] (*imagination*) with a movement.[23] The imagination lies at the root of the understanding and the will. Just as we can conceive the imagination where we can think of it neither as simply rational nor as simply irrational, we can conceive the imagination where freedom and nature are one, movement and situation are one. Habit phantasizes [*sōzō*] change and can only form a habit by making it changeable. Yet change is unthinkable apart from time. Inorganic beings do not possess any determinate relationship to time. Only that which has life contains an internal relationship to time. Habit is, however, no mere change and instead signifies continuance. And while change is temporal, the fundamental form of continuance is by contrast spatial. We can say that everything alive is temporal and at the same time spatial and that habit is the originary-form of life. Forms are engendered where time and space are one. We can also probably say that without anything habitual, forms will not be engendered. The logic of imagination is indeed nothing other than a logic of forms, and this logic manifests the fact of time qua space, space qua time. Everything in life is something with form and as such is an individual body. An individual body begins with life. We can thus also say that what can possess habit is an individual body.

Now what is habit in an individual person is convention [*kan'shū*, 慣習; also custom] in society. We must distinguish the concept of habit from the concept of convention (*custom*). And yet this is only a conceptual distinction, and the two words are frequently diverted in one another. Pascal, for example, states that "habit [custom] is our nature."[24] "Habit [Custom] is a second nature that destroys the former. But what is nature? Why is habit [custom] not natural? I am much afraid that nature is itself only a first habit [custom], as habit [custom] is a second nature."[25] And he states, "when we see the same effect always recur, we infer a natural necessity in it...."[26] "What are our natural principles but principles of habit [custom]? ...A different habit [custom] would cause different natural principles. This is seen in experience."[27] "The most important affair in life is the choice of a calling; chance decides it. Habit [Custom] makes men masons, soldiers, slaters ... We choose our calling according as we hear this or that praised or despised in our childhood.... So great is the force of habit [custom]."[28] In all these cases, the word *coutume* is used ceaselessly, but we may be permitted to render it as habit. In these words of Pascal, we can see the forerunner to the ideas of Boutroux[29] who says that "the laws of nature are its habits," and, like habit, they contain certain accidents. Aristotle has said that "*ethos* (habit) is indeed something like nature" (ὥσπερ γὰρ φύσις ἤδη τὸ ἔθος),[30] but with Pascal we can presumably invert this to say that nature is in fact something like habit. And in the words of Pascal above, we can also probably recognize a forerunner to the empiricism of those like Hume who had asserted the significance of habit and, in general, the imagination in relation to cognition, in particular the cognition of causality. Now, it is no accident that the term *coutume* is used to mean individual habit as well as to mean social habit and therein is contained a significant issue concerning the relationship between the individual person and society that we will touch upon later. For the time being, however, we cannot say that institutions are habits of the individual person but rather are social habits. Even if conventions in society are comparable to habits in the individual person, what sort of a thing, in its particulars, is a convention?

3.

[120] Pascal writes: "Nature imitates herself. A seed grown in good ground brings forth fruit. A principle instilled into a good mind brings forth fruit. Numbers imitate space, which is of a different nature.[31] Everything, root, branch, fruit, the beginning and the end, is made and guided by the same lord."[32] Just as principles of nature are imitations, principles of habit and of convention are also imitations. We can see that the reason why nature and habit or convention can easily be mutually interchanged is because they both emerge from the same principle. Only, "nature diversifies and imitates; art imitates and diversifies." (*Nature diversifie et imite, artifice imite et diversifie.*)[33] Habits, as well as conventions, are not mere nature, but things made by man. While in habit the individual body imitates itself, in contrast, in convention innumerable individual bodies reciprocally imitate each other. In the former case, the individual body copies itself within itself without limit, and in the latter case, innumerable individual bodies copy each other without limit. We can say that the former is linear and the latter is circular.

Now Tarde postulated that the essence of not only convention but society itself is imitation. As to the question "what is society?," he replied that "society is imitation" (*La société, c'est l'imitation*).[34] According to him, we can discern a universal repetition within the cosmos. Accordingly, in physical phenomena this would be undulations or periodic motion in general in physical phenomena, heredity or habit in biological phenomena (habit being interiorized heredity and heredity being exteriorized habit), and imitation in social phenomena. These are the three most conspicuous principal forms of universal repetition. A science of society is possible due to this fact as well that there exists the phenomenon of repetition within it. What we call science is the ordering of phenomena observed from the side of repetition. Society is established by means of mimetic repetition. Imitation spreads, but for imitation to occur, there must be something imitated. What contrasts with imitation is invention (*invention*). Even that which passes among us today as so to speak self-evident, once we trace their origin, were all inventions. And Tarde, who unraveled imitation as repetition (*répétition*), unpacks invention as adaptation (*adaptation*). In particular, what we ought to take note of in Tarde's theory of imitation is probably its monadological foundation. For example, he theorizes as follows:[35] We say that people do what they do. In this case, "people" means the world, and we understand here a collective impersonal as well as an unconscious model. However, before speaking, thinking, and doing as people speak, as people think, and as people do, we must first start by speaking, thinking, and doing as he or she speaks, thinks, and does. This he or she is so and so of our close relations. When we thoroughly search for the roots of "people," we always discover only a certain number of hes and shes, and therein the number of human beings become but jumbled by their increase. Despite the fact that this distinction is extremely simple, it is forgotten by those people who are convinced that it is sufficient as an explanation to say that language, religion, and so on are collective products without acknowledging the creative role of the individuals in certain institutions or social products. Such an explanation, in fact, is illusory; for, by assuming a similitude at the basis of collective force, and hence of certain relationships of innumerable human beings, it avoids the greater problem, namely, the problem of how such a general assimilation was engendered. We can respond to this problem only by advancing to an analysis of the relationships between the brains of two human beings. In cases where similitude and assimilation are formed by imitation and its propagation and, after they are formed, are made to last by tradition or, put differently, by the imitation of ancestors, they often become despotically acting forces in relation to the individual person. What has been designated the spirit or genius of a people is nothing more than a convenient cipher, nothing more than the anonymous synthesis of the originality of various individual persons. Only this originality of the individual is what is real and continues to be effectively active at every moment. And this innumerable originality is in a state of ceaseless fermentation due to the constant borrowing and exchange of models undertaken between neighboring societies and within each society. What we regard as the collective and impersonal genius is the function of the genius of infinitely many individuals and not its coefficient. Every individual person is a certain genius and a certain originality. According to Tarde, invention is adaptation, but this means the harmony of ideas and it is the mother of all harmony of human beings. At the root of every association among human beings, there originally lies the association of ideas of one individual human being. That is to say, the genius of an individual person is the real source of every social harmony. Tarde thus argues that everything in its origin is of individual persons. Basic social repetition is the initial imitator's individual fact, and this becomes the starting point of an enormous contagion. And social adaptation that is fundamental is an individual person's invention established so as to be imitated or, put differently, initially the felicitous intersection of two imitations within the mind of a single human being. On this basis, the utterly interior tendency of harmony not only manifests itself outside through expansion, but it also becomes tied to other inventions through the circulation of imitation, and ultimately the collective products of the human mind, grammar, theology, legal codes, the organization of labor, morality, and so on, are formed through the continuous complications [complexifications] of harmony and [their] harmonization. Everything comes from the infinitesimal, and everything probably returns to the infinitesimal. It was thought that everything that constitutes the visible cosmos starts from what is invisible to the eye, that which at first sight seems to be nothing, and every reality inexhaustibly comes out of there.

We should not censure this view of Tarde as simply an individualism. The innumerable individuals shape the monadological world. According to Tarde, each person is marked by their own obvious features that distinguish them from everyone, as each person is something peculiar (*sui generis*), something original, something like Leibniz's monad. And as in Leibniz innumerable monads constitute the world by mutually copying one another, in Tarde society is made as innumerable individuals mutually imitate each other. The human, as a social being, is a mimetic being. And just as there is a preestablished harmony in Leibniz's monadology, in Tarde as well, imitation, of course, and even invention, were seen as that which makes harmony among human beings by making harmony among ideas. He considered the phenomenon of opposition to be midway between repetition and adaptation; this was for him, however, something secondary, and something merely for the sake of rousing the tension of a hostile force to stimulate the inventive and hence harmonious genius. Nonetheless, Tarde's theory of imitation had to tear asunder Leibniz's intellectualism and appears to have done so. Imitation cannot be simply an intellectual process. Rather than knowing and then imitating afterward, people know by imitating. Tarde states that imitation is the function of inspiration (*suggestion*). And he states that imitation is one kind of somnambulism (*somnambulisme*), and also writes that the human as a social being that is a mimetic being is something like a true sleepwalker. He also views that the state of society, identical to a hypnotic state, is nothing but one form of dreaming. It would be a hallucination peculiar to the sleepwalker to have no ideas but those that are implicit and believe them to be spontaneous. But this can be recognized among the social human being as well. On the other hand, for such hallucinations to be engendered, the existence of sympathy (*sympathie*) would be necessary. Tarde initially had placed, not sympathy, but prestige (*prestige*) at the foundation of imitation and hence at the root of society, but eventually he corrected this view and wrote,[36] "It is sympathy that is the primary source of sociality and that is the soul, manifest or hidden, of every species of imitation, even of desirous or calculative imitation, or the imitation of the enemy. But it is certain that sympathy itself begins unilaterally before it is reciprocal." In any case there can be no imitation without sympathy. As Ribot says, sympathy and imitation are two faces of the same phenomenon; sympathy merely manifests, in particular, the passive side of the phenomenon, and imitation manifests only its active side.[37] We can probably also say that imitation manifests its intellectual face and sympathy manifests its emotive face. Imitation and sympathy correspond to the two faces of the imagination. In comparing Tarde's theory of imitation and Leibniz's monadology, we are reminded of the idea of *petites* perceptions (*petites perceptions*). *Petites* perception constitutes an important foundation for Leibniz's theory of harmony, and he also thought about the issue of beauty by its means. And if Baumgarten's so-called logic of imagination [*kōsōryoku*] also had its starting point there, it would not be impossible to conceive the logic of imagination at the root of imitation. We do not know and then imitate afterwards but know by imitating. Instead of imitating what we see, we imitate what we phantasise [*sōzō*]. Or, to put this more accurately, we imitate what we see according to what we phantasise. What is fundamental to imitation is not *perception* but rather *image*. For example, just as we mean *imitation* when we say that man is the *image* of God, *imitation* and *imagination* are intimately related.[38]

Now what we know on the one hand by means of imitation is that which is common among ourselves and others. We cannot imitate anything in the other except that which is common with the other. In order for the relationship of imitation to exist there must be something in common between two human beings. Imitation is made possible by means of our being defined by something in common, something universal at its root. On the other hand, however, we recognize in imitation ourselves as distinct from others even at the moment when we appear to conform to others to the point of identification. This is because we simply do not imitate anything besides other human beings or other things. Heterogeneity is affirmed in the movement toward homogeneity. Although Tarde's monadological sociology clarifies this latter aspect of imitation, we do not think that it can clarify this former aspect. Even assuming each original inventive human being mutually imitates the other with one another, it probably cannot explain how a single fixed form can arise from there. Tarde states that a ray of imitation (*rayon imitative*) radiates from each human being and that social life is an intricate intersection of these rays of imitation. But how does a single unified form come together from such an intersection? Tarde only says that the interference between these rays of imitation is innumerable.[39] Society thus possesses a unified form. Institutions signify these forms that society possesses. Society is inconceivable without such forms. This is also why there are those who attempt to conceive the unity of a people's spirit at the root of institutions. Concerning ancient law, in contrast to Tarde's view, Fustel de Coulanges[40] says that it is not one human being who invents it; while Solon, Lykourgos, Minos, and Numa[41] codified the laws of their countries they had not created them; and if we were to understand a single human being who creates the legal code by means of the power of his genius as the basis of the legislator and who levies this upon other human beings, there existed no such legislator among ancient peoples.[42] The condition for imitation is sympathy, namely, to share *pathos*. For such sympathy to be possible, at the root of the individual person there must exist a certain something that is of *pathos* and yet is universal. Something like the so-called ethnos [ethnicity, a people] would be that thing. But the individual person's independence would be inconceivable if we merely took that element of *pathos*, the Dionysian, as the foundation. We presumably would have to conceive the combination of the innumerable independent individuals and that which is universal like the ethnos based on the logic of imagination that is intellectual and at the same time emotive. As mentioned earlier, Pascal stated that "nature diversifies and imitates." And he also wrote, "All is one, all is different" (*Tout est un, tout est divers*).[43] If we are to take nature as following the logic of imitation as Pascal also thought, then logic would have to be a logic where the one is many, and the many are one. In developing this logic, we would also have to conceive the ethnos as well as the world.

4.

[129] Everything institutional is something conventional. But we cannot deny that this alone is inadequate as a definition of institution. As stated in the beginning, the third quality of an institution is that of *nomos*, that is, institutions possess a legal, normative, character, and it must be said that it is rather this that essentially defines institutions instead. Or rather, convention itself is already one institution and carries the character of a certain norm or imperative in the sense of *Sitte*—from which the word *sittlich* (moral [ethical]) derives. Distinguishing the concept of *Gewohnheit* (this can be used in the sense of an individual person's habit as well in the sense of social convention) and the concept of *Sitte* (mores [ethos or ethics]), Jhering states that in contrast to the former, which refers to the purely external without containing any normative element, the latter is something normative and obligatory.[44] But this distinction is only based on

concepts. If there was nothing legal or normative already existing in *Gewohnheit* itself, the so-called *Gewohnheitsrecht* (customary law) would probably be inconceivable. Puchta[45] distinguished the two by taking *Gewohnheit* as the mode of behavior of an individual person qua individual and taking *Sitte* as the mode of behavior of an individual person as a member of an ethnos. This distinction corresponds instead to the conceptual distinction made above between habit (*habit*) and convention (*custom*). Furthermore, as we have also noted in this regard, Arnold by contrast argues that Puchta's distinction is only partially correct and that the individual person is always a member of an ethnos; all of the individuals' actions depend on the inclination and mode of behavior of the ethnos; and that even their most trifling habit is inconceivable apart from their ethnos. He takes customary law (*Gewohnheitsrecht*) to mean *Recht der Sitte*.[46] Habits and conventions both contain the sense of mores, namely, norms. As Arnold states, we can probably view mores as the genus and customary law as its species. According to us, they all have the character of *nomos* and are institutional. The purely external can possess no habit; only that which has life, namely, that which contains within itself the structural connection between inside and outside, can form habits. And yet conceptually, if we follow Jhering, it is also not impossible to distinguish habit as purely external and mores as something internal. But in that case, we need to take note that the fact mores are internal means they should have the character of norms, imperatives, and as we shall eventually discuss this means that they have the significance of transcendence while habit by contrast is an immanent concept. That is to say that we would have to conceive habit, said to be external, as thus something immanent and conceive mores, viewed to be internal, as instead external in the sense of transcendence. Their normative nature is given shape in this transcendence.

Everything institutional is something with the character of *nomos*. Nevertheless, the word νόμος, meaning law, also possesses the meaning of convention (*Brauch, Herkommen, Sitte*). *Nomos* is always conceived in relation to *themis* (θέμις) and, further, *dikē* (δίκη).[47] *Themis* was originally a mythological character but meant judgment or law. *Themis* has to do with the etiquette or otherwise conventions demanded by society (primarily of the clan) and society not simply as an organization but society as a force or, so to speak, spirit. *Themis*, for those who worshiped her, was seen as the manifestation of justice in the sense of instilling what ought to be done in order to act or what is suitable for doing in accord with formed customs and conventions so that the order of society as a whole would not be disturbed. *Dikē* was also originally a mythological being but first meant convention and also meant judgment or adjudication. But if we compare *dikē* and *themis*, although *themis* also had the sense of judgment, the one that gained force from the development of such legal life was rather *dikē*. More than anything else *dikē* had to do with the equitable and fair distribution of property. It manifests legality (*légalité*) rather than morality (*moralité*). *Themis* occupied an important position in worship when the individual person had immediate and emotional contact with social coercion. By contrast, the reality and role of *dikē* were recognized in response to the collapse of the old clan and the decline of ancient worship, and when only a few traces of the rites were continued. As a result of the collapse of clan society, *Themis* took on an even more universal and yet moral character. While the mythological personality on the one hand continued in the old form, manifesting as the goddess of good counsel, it was now but incompletely suited for the new idea of justice, which instead became developed in the idea of *dikē*. Now *nomos* was first the idea of the distribution of property among human beings and then later the allotment of things in the world. On the one hand, this was in opposition to the possession of property by means of βία, namely, violence, and on the other hand it was in opposition to φύσις, namely, what exists on its own, not what is desired by man. But eventually, as *thesmoi* (θεσμοί) (meaning social conventions, in particular conventions in agriculture) and *nomoi* became connected, the social organization also came to be seen as something natural, and on the other hand, nature also came to be thought of as being ordered by laws. The opposition between *physis* and *nomos* is a well-known issue that had already appeared in Heraclitus, and we can grasp in that opposition one moment of the development of the concept of natural law.[48] Nevertheless, we ought not to view them as merely separate and in opposition. As conceivable from the combination of *thesmoi* and *nomoi*, nature is also something habitual and habit is also something natural. We can say that *physis* also has the character of *nomos* and *nomos* also has the character of *physis*. In such a way, we can conceive the issue of the imagination [*kōsōryoku*] from where nature and history are one.

There are several theories among legal scholars on the enjoyment of the legality of conventions. We do not intend here to enter into such issues of jurisprudence;[49] for laws, in particular customary law, are not the problem for us. We regard the establishment of conventions and the enjoyment of legality, in a certain sense, to be simultaneous. It is not that there was originally the problem of the enjoyment of legality, but only there being the problem of the conventional forms of law [*hō*, 法]. Conventions were originally legal matters. Or, at least institutions, in the sense that what I am here analyzing contain as a moment the fact that they are conventional, but on the other hand possess as an essential character the fact that they are at the same time legal [*hōteki*, 法的]. In this case, what I mean by law [*hō*] is not so-called law [*hōritsu* 法律], but on the contrary, indicates the sense of norms or imperatives that everything institutional is endowed with. Accordingly, we do not necessarily assent to the opinions of the school of historical law concerning the place of customary law in law [*hōritsu*]. And it would probably be inconceivable that conventions are immediately customary laws. Between convention and law [*hōritsu*], we would presumably have to think of a distinction and relationship like what obtains between mores (*Sitte*) and morality (*Sittlichkeit*). But on the other hand, any kind of law [*hōritsu*] has the meaning of an institution. And not only laws [*hōritsu*] but anything institutional possesses the sense of *nomos*. We can even view something like art as an institution. For instance, what is a classic in the arts? A classic is what becomes the standard for our tastes and what becomes the norm for our productions. Put differently, it is something with the character of *nomos*. As such, a classic must be clearly a work high in value as a thing. Moreover, one feature of a classic is that the value it possesses is fixed by tradition and hence conventional. The value whereby a classic is called a classic is not something that was first established based on our own individual criticism; rather, we educate our tastes on the basis of the classics to set its standard. Even specialist historians of literature do not examine, one by one, every work handed down as a classic in order to then recognize them as classics. Classics take reputation as their basis. A classic is something traditional and mythological. Borrowing Valéry's terms, it is fiction. It is not only that it has value. Unless it had something mythological about it, it cannot pass for a classic. Needless to say, this is not mere *mythos*. It must possess value to thoroughly endure criticism. In that sense, it must have the character of *logos*. *Logos* must, however, at the same time possess the character of *mythos* and take convention as its foundation. In short, a classic must be something with the character of *nomos*. *Nomos* is not something merely having the character of *logos*, but along with the character of *logos* it simultaneously has the character of *mythos*.[50] If we were to add to this, we may presumably say that according to our definition, what is ordinarily thought of as myth, would instead be something institutional, and myths in the original sense must be myths as the source of becoming and creation. Traditional myths are transformed into something institutional, something having the character of *nomos*, by somehow being rationalized after the fact as moral, legal, and so on, that is, to some degree adding to them the characteristics of *logos*. Valéry saw that order is made by fiction (*fiction*). This indeed is the case. But the fiction that becomes the foundation for order is no mere fiction but would have to be something with the character of *nomos*. The classics erect a certain order in the world of literature. Moreover, if the classics were to be fixed only after each person gauges their value with his/her own judgment, the world of literature would probably have to constantly end in disorder. A classic is a fiction, a convention, and a *nomos*. *Nomos* indicates one fundamental mode of being possessed by anything historical. And *nomos* is founded not on mere *logos* but on the imagination [*kōsōryoku*] having the character of *pathos* along with that of *logos*. We observe the imagination at the root of history. Of course, we do not regard everything historical to always be something institutional. As Bergson states, aside from habitual or obligatory morals, there are creative morals, in cases of art, no doubt, but in cases of morality as well. Nevertheless, we are not satisfied simply to understand them as the "two sources" of morality, but we want to consider them as originally one in the imagination. Morality is also something historical, but the logic of imagination is active at the root of everything historical. We must clarify this now in regard to institutions and especially in relation to its characteristic of *nomos*.

5.

[137] What is the nature of the norms or imperatives that are inherent in all institutional things, and how do they arise? Let us first examine twelve definitions of institution. For example, Park and Burgess write:

> An institution, according to Sumner, consists of a concept and a structure. The concept defines the purpose, interest or function of the institution. The structure embodies the idea of the institution and furnishes the instrumentalities through which the idea is put into action. The process by which purposes, whether they are individual or collective, are embodied in structure is a continuous one. But the structures thus formed are not physical, at least not entirely so. Structure, in the sense that Sumner uses the term, belongs, as he says, to a category of its own. "It is

a category in which custom produces continuity, coherence, and consistency, so that the word 'structure' may properly be applied to the fabric of relations and prescribed positions with which functions are permanently connected." Just as every individual member of a community participates in the process by which custom and public opinion are made, so also he participates in the creation of the structure, that "cake of custom" which, when it embodies a definite social function, we call an institution.[51]

From a somewhat different standpoint Cooley states:

> An institution is simply a definite and established phase of the public mind, not different in its ultimate nature from public opinion, often seeming, on account of its permanence and the visible customs and symbols in which it is clothed, to have a somewhat distinct and independent existence. Thus, the political state and church, with their venerable associations, their vast and ancient power, their literature, buildings, and offices, hardly appear even to a democratic people as the mere products of human invention which, of course, they are.
>   The great institutions are the outcome of that organization which human thought naturally takes on when it is directed for age after age upon a particular subject, and so gradually crystallizes in definite forms—enduring sentiments, beliefs, customs, and symbols. And this is the case when there is some deep and abiding interest to hold the attention of men. Language, government, the church, laws, and customs of property and of the family, systems of industry and education, are institutions because they are the working out of the permanent needs of human nature.[52]

Hence the primary element of an institution is what Sumner calls the "concept." What is included in the institution is generally recognized, and what Jhering calls "end" (*Zweck*) in law would also presumably fall under this. Generally speaking, this is what we can call the *Idee*. We can regard institutions as having the character of norms on the bases of such an *Idee*. The *Idee* in this case is also called an *Ideell* (ideal) from the fact that it is normative and hence of value. We need, however, to first take note that even if we speak here of norm, value, and ideal, it is not the ought (*Sollen*) as it is conceived by the Neo-Kantian School. The ought is sharply distinguished from the real. And yet institutions are real. The "concept" of institution, borrowing Sumner's term, is something formed into a "structure." Value, rather than an ought, is a "thing," as scholars of the Durkheim school say, and would presumably have to be real. Simiand defines thing as "that which resists our individual spontaneity."[53] Stated differently, a thing is that which presses a limit and orientation upon our individual spontaneity. And Bouglé claims that conceived on the basis that value, in the same way, possesses a restrictive, imperative, character for us, we must view values as things or realities.[54] Whether it is material or ideal, we can conceive as real what is independent of our momentary impressions, what resists our spontaneity, and what surpasses our own likes and dislikes, and we can say that value, by the same character, is also real. That is to say that in contrast to how we ordinarily think that value and reality must be distinguished because value possesses an imperative character; in Bouglé it is thought that it must be seen as the same as reality or a thing precisely because value possesses an imperative character—for a thing is nothing other than what resists our spontaneity and saddles for us the self's desires. According to Bouglé, value is objective because it is imperative and yet is imperative because it is collective. Because value is something that comes out of the collective consciousness (*conscience collective*), because it is a product of society, it puts on a restraining influence, a peculiar power. This character that value possesses cannot be explained by the nature of a thing nor by the ability of an individual. Because value flows out of collective living, it is law for an individual person's living. Thus, why Durkheim conceived society as essentially the creator of an ideal. As the conclusion of his research on the originary-form of religious life, he points to the importance of ceremonies (*culte*) in religion and states that almost every great social institution was born of religion and argues further that the ideal or idea-like (*Ideal*) is a natural product of social life. For society to be conscious of itself and cherish its feelings towards itself with the necessary intensity, society must centralize itself. This centralization determines the enhancement of moral life, deciphered by the whole of ideal ideas, and therein is expressed a newly awakened life. Durkheim writes, "A society can neither create itself nor recreate itself without at the same time creating the ideal."[55] Idealist society is not outside of actual society but constitutes a part of it. Society is not constituted merely by the souls of individuals who compose it, by the land they occupy, by the things they use, or by the movements they perform. Instead, more than anything, it is constituted by the *Idee* it itself makes. Ideals are not founded upon any power belonging to individual persons. Rather, the individual learns to form ideals in the school of collective living. The individual comes to embrace ideals by assimilating the ideals produced by society into his/herself. Durkheim says that if the individual fails to acquire the capacity to form ideals, s/he presumably would not be a social being or, put differently, not a human being.

The Durkheim school above certainly contains insight that we ought to pay attention to in relation to the abstract doctrines of value and ideas concerning the ought of the Neo-Kantian School. However, there would presumably be further difficulties if we were to receive it just as it is. Bouglé first explains the reality of value based on its nature of restraint. In other words, he thinks that values and things are identical by invoking Simian's definition that things are what resist our individual spontaneity. Nevertheless, this view resembles Dilthey's idea that explains the reality of the external world as resistance to the will, and as stated earlier, has the danger of taking the real as something subjective. To begin with, even if things are values, are they not merely subjective? A thing demands that we recognize it as that thing and constrains us in that way on the basis of the thing's nature as an "object" [*taishō*, 対象]. Lipps also states that "the object is that which demands" (*Der Gegenstand ist das Fordernde*).[56] The object's demand is recognized by the process of judgment and objectivity is none other than logicity. This kind of logicity or ideality already shapes the moment of value in things and thus, in contrast to Bouglé, it is also possible to view the constraint in things not as its so-called thingly nature but rather as belonging to value. Needless to say, we presumably cannot immediately identify what Lipps calls the "demand of the object" (*Gegenstandsforderung*) and value's normative or imperative nature. A value is not simply something objective. The subjectivity of value is always raised in opposition to the objectivity of things. A value, however, cannot simply be something subjective but would have to be something objective. Otherwise, it would presumably be impossible for it to possess the nature of constraint. Moreover, value not only becomes objective through its realization in things but must itself possess some sort of objectivity/objective nature. Would the objective nature of value need to take pure *logos*—whether we call it "pure will" or "pure emotion," there is no difference in the fact that it signifies an element of *logos*—as its foundation? Next, Bouglé argues that value is objective because it is imperative, and it is imperative because it is collective. This view indeed contains a certain truth. Nevertheless, even if we take the imperative nature of value to hang on the fact that value in this way is something flowing out of collective consciousness, the issue would have to be whether or not the collective consciousness in this case becomes the ground of the imperative nature of value to the extent that it has the character of *logos*. If we already take even the nature of constraint belonging to things as founded upon the logicity or ideality in things, it would seem that in order for institutions to possess an imperative character, in cases when in particular we consider institutions, institutions would have to contain a certain *ideal* something. As this thing shapes the institution's objective meaning, we may regard the institution to belong to the so-called "objective spirit" (*Objektiver Geist*) by containing that meaning. It is presumably conceivable accordingly that for an institution to be established, what Dilthey calls the "objective apprehension" (*Gegenständliches Auffassen*) must first, before anything else, be its root. What is peculiar to this process of objective apprehension is that only the object and the object's relations are grasped in it, and no matter the experience of the psychological faculty it is not present in it. During this operation, we "completely live in the object" and the world of objects as a construction possessing complete self-sufficiency confronts us. As such a thing, objective apprehension is also called the "theoretical turn" (*Theoretische Wendung*) in ourselves. Freyer named this the "objective turn" (*Objektive Wendung*) and understands it as the first objectification in the establishment process of the objective spirit. He writes, "It is the fundamental birth of the objective spirit. It is the most interior event in the act of psychologically becoming human."[57] Now for the objective spirit to be perfected, it is necessary that the objective meaning, or meaning with the character of *logos*, discerned in that objective turn be objectified further within a material form—the third objectification according to Freyer. As Sumner states, the concept must be formed into a structure. As Park and Burgess explain, the process whereby ideas re-embodied in structures is continuous and what is called structure here is a "cake of custom." However, the misunderstanding that we must avoid in this case is to separate in abstraction concept and structure and regard only the structure to be the conventional and not the concept. Indeed, the concept there is also conventional. That even the human mind's capacity for objective apprehension is influenced by habit has been clarified, especially in French philosophy, ever since the excellent study by Maine de Biran (*Influence de l'habitude sur la faculté de penser*).[58] What we call institution would not be possible unless human mental activity itself was conventional. Unless something natural, having the character of *pathos*, flows into that which has the character of *logos*, institutions could not be engendered. The foundation of institutions cannot be pure *logos*. Moreover, an institution is not simply a conceptual being but, to the extent that it is something that has been formed amongst visible matter, it is also a sensory being. At this point, memory thus joins sensation and hence the words of Bergson, "in cases where we see things, what we give to ourselves is a kind of hallucination inserted into the frame of the actual," comes to possess a particularly deep significance. We can probably say that without this kind of hallucination neither the institution's viability nor its nature of constraint could be engendered. We can understand Valéry's statement that society is a construct of spells to have this meaning. This does not mean that an institution, to begin with, is just that [i.e., spells]. On one side, it must be what thoroughly includes moments of the character of the *Idee*. However, we recognize therein one limitation to the view that attempts to seek the foundation of the objective spirit designated there as institution in what purely has the character of *logos*. And we discern one clue as to why we must seek it instead in the imagination [*kōsōryoku*].

Now if we go further, the spirit of institutions is a kind of theological spirit. It is not simply the spirit of tradition but further the spirit of authority. It may be said that the spirit of institutions is something opposite to the scientific spirit or critical spirit, and hence that the innermost essence of institutions exists not in the so-called "theoretical turn," and thus their nature of constraint is not founded upon values that have the character of an *Idee*. Nietzsche writes: "Among the facts that perplexes intellectuals is the knowledge that the alogical is necessary for human beings. Only the overly simple can believe that the human essence can be transformed into something purely logical." It may be said that an institutional act, borrowing Pareto's words, is not "logical action" (*action logique*), but belongs to "non-logical action" (*action non-logique*). What Pareto means by logical is "logical-experimental" (*logico-expérimental*), and behavior executed under the constraint of some conviction in a doctrine cannot be said to be logical. We can [however] also say that almost every human behavior is logical when viewed apart from the logical-experimental standpoint. The reason is that people always suppose their own behavior to result from rational inference and that their own activities agree with their own objectives. But this is the subjective side of the phenomenon, and it is important to distinguish it from its objective side. What Pareto calls logical action is an action that is both subjectively and objectively logical and hence signifies the identity of the objective goal and the subjective goal. Everything else can be called non-logical action. Action directed by convention or mores is non-logical for the reason that it is an action constituted without a subjective goal in the sense just stated. Such action, however, is rare for the reason that human beings feel an irresistible impulse to explain and give reasons for their own behavior so that it thus appears to them in the end as if it has a certain reason. In practice, however, the principle ground of that action is an emotion and the logical explanation is nothing but a secondary ground. According to Pareto, non-logical action occupies a far greater position than logical action among human social actions. Non-logical actions are analyzed into two parts: 1) a constant and certainly all the more important element that corresponds to certain instincts and emotions of the human; and 2) other elements, the intent of which are directed towards the explanation of the first element and possessing an indefinite character. The latter satisfies the desire for reason or logic (in fact, pseudo-logic), but the desire for this explanation is exceedingly entrusted to various influences. By contrast, the first foundational element is unchanging. The second element is derived from the first and is named by Pareto "derivation" (*derivation*). The first element is that which remains as constant within altering phenomena and is designated as "residue" (*résidu*).⁵⁹ Residue does not signify instinct or emotion but rather that which is founded upon them and can be thought of as the irrational nucleus [*kakujitsu*, 核実] of social action, representation, and logic. By opposing logical and experimental logic, derivation descriptively disguises the residue or has rewritten or mythologized it.⁶⁰ *Dérivation* and *résidu* therefore stand upon the relationship between "ideology" and its "actual" foundation. If we now follow Pareto, actions following convention or mores belong to non-logical action and, on the other hand, everything authoritative is nothing but a derivation and its inner truth is a residue corresponding to instinct or emotion. We can presumably think of institutions as being founded upon the authority of tradition, mores, and convention, and conceive its nature of constraint as something having the quality of *pathos*. In this way one aspect of truth, of course, is included in Pareto's thought. Nevertheless, in the same way that we cannot agree to a simple rationalism concerning institutions, we cannot approve of a simple irrationalism. It is possible to say that even non-logical actions following convention or mores objectively satisfy a logical goal, and hence are identical in their logical and experimental value to logical actions. On this point Pareto's definition of logical action is too formal. And it is also possible to say that even the actions which for an individual person come from instinct or emotion or what corresponds to them, are, seen from a historical or social point of view, as Hegel spoke of "the cunning of reason," the results of the realization of *ideal* goals. On this point, Pareto's definition of logical action is abstract and pertains to individual persons. As human beings possess an irresistible impulse to logically disguise even their own non-logical actions, they are furnished, even unconsciously or counter to their own immediate motive, with the character of acting logically. If human beings, who feel a strong desire for rationality to the extent that they cannot help but logicize even non-logical actions, took institutions to be completely irrational, it would be impossible for them to accept its authority. To begin with, the merely objective cannot actually constrain us. That which possesses the power of constraint in relation to the (epistemological) subject [*shukan*] would have to be something subjective. And yet, the merely subjective would also be unable to truly constrain us. Stated differently, that which actually constrains us can be something that possesses neither simply the character of *logos* nor simply the character of *pathos*, rather it must be something that simultaneously possesses the character of *logos* and the character of *pathos*. What is more, according to Pareto, our concrete actions are synthetic, that is, they are engendered from the mixture in various proportions of the elements of logical action and non-logical action.⁶¹ But to the extent that such synthesis cannot be a mechanical combination of independent elements, they must be one in originally being of the character of *pathos* and at the same time of the character of *logos*. In this case, for example, even if we take up dialectics, to the extent that dialectics is not the unification after the fact of abstractly independent elements that are there initially, there must be anticipated at its basis the concrete material possessing the character of *logos* as well as the character of *pathos*. Therein we can conceive the originariness of the logic of imagination. The greatest defect of Pareto's irrationalism is its failure to grasp human action as an action within the environment. If we were to look at this in relation to the environment, it should become fundamentally clear how human actions, including even what are called non-logical actions, as we will later discuss, must always include something rational as an adaptation to the environment, and yet are not abstractly logical, and that therein lies the logic of imagination.

6.

[151] In this way, the "concept" we have of institutions is neither simply a thing of *logos* nor simply a thing of *pathos*, but a thing of both *logos* and *pathos* at the same time. It is neither simply subjective nor simply objective but is something subjective and objective at the same time. As such, it is called expressive value or, rather, an expressive meaning. What is simply objective and what is simply subjective are not expressive. What is expressive must be subjective-objective. Institutions are expressive in this way. That they are imperatives is also based on the fact that they are expressive. Neither what only has the character of *logos* nor what only has the character of *pathos* is truly imperative. Only by having the character of *logos* and *pathos* can something be actually imperative. It may be conceivable that in order for institutions to obtain as what are expressive, there must be something like what Simmel calls the "turn to the *Idee*" (*Wendung zur Idee*).[62] Moreover if we are to interpret the turn to the *Idee* merely in the sense of an objective turn, it would not be sufficient as a foundation for expression. The expressive is engendered not simply by a turn to the *Idee*, but rather by the completion of form or "the becoming of form" (*Formwerdung*). But as we already stated, forms are engendered where time and space are one. *Form*, however, is engendered where the *Idee* becomes habitual. Accordingly, forms are not simply of the character of *logos* but have the characters of *logos* and *pathos*. That institutions possess a normative quality is also because they are forms in this way. In his theory of mimesis, Tarde distinguished two kinds of mimesis, convention (*coutume*) and fashion (*mode*). In conventional mimesis, the model is always something of one's native land and it is ancient. By contrast, in fashionable mimesis, the model is ordinarily of a foreign country and something new. In the former case, because it is thought that "everything old is all good," it is temporal. In the latter case, because things of other lands are esteemed and distance in space functions in the same way that distance in time functioned in the previous case, it is spatial. If, however, we view this from another side where convention is overwhelming, because people become absorbed in their own country rather than their own epoch, it is spatial. And by contrast, when fashion dominates, because people think that "everything new is all good," it is temporal.[63] That is to say that both convention and fashion are temporal as well as spatial and, as such things, possess form. Now as four kinds of social imperative [*sozialen Imperativen*], Jhering mentions fashion [*die Mode*], mores [*die Sitte*], morals [*die Moral*], and law [*das Recht*], but according to him, fashion differs from habit that is without a normative character and instead coincides with mores in the point that it possesses the power of constraint.[64] However, as known from the fact that he positions mores midway between fashion and morals, if there is a difference between the constraining power of mores or convention and that of fashion,

it would be because the latter, as something all the more in flux, is immature in form. In this way form is the unity of becoming and being, the unity of flow and continuity. For *Idee* to become *Form*, the *Idee* must be realized within a thing. In the expressive, meaning and reality, ought and being are one. Form is not what Sumner calls concept nor is it the structure; rather, form is engendered where concept and structure are one. A concept does not become matter by being formed within a structure. A value, through expression, does not become a mere reality. If we understand forms, primarily, to be engendered where concept and structure are one, the structure, as Sumner states, is its own category and not something merely physical. Hence institutions, borrowing Valéry's words, are *fiction*, and shape a certain "other world." That institutions have the character of *nomos* is due more to the fact that they are *fiction* rather than the fact that they are real. Even if this may sound paradoxical, we can probably say that the constraining nature of institutions belongs to the imagination [*kōsōryoku*]. Valéry writes: "Society rises from savagery to order. Therefore, just as the epoch of facts is savage, the epoch of order is the land of fiction—for there exists no ability to build order simply above the coercion of material objects by material objects. There must be a fictional power there," and "for this reason order demands the present operation of that which is not present, and results from the balance of instincts by means of an ideal." Rather, what has the character of *pathos* is what is factual. Even if facts by necessity compel facts, they cannot constrain imperatively. Institutions are a fictional power, and we can therefore conceive them as instead having the character of *nomos*, namely, what builds order by being law-like. Such *fiction* cannot be explained by instinct or Pareto's so-called residue and is rather something intellectual. It does not, however, simply possess the character of *logos* but possesses at the same time the character of *pathos*, and at its root of *fiction* there must be found the imagination [*kōsōryoku*]. Irrationalism is that which overlooks the fictional nature of institutions to absolutize them. The logic of fiction, and the logic of forms, is the logic of imagination.

Now institutions become established as a certain "other world" and are transcendental to life. As Cooley, however, emphasizes they are thoroughly what had been formed by man and hence this transcendence must be the self-transcendence of life. In his notion of the turn to the *Idee*, Simmel is thinking of the transcendence of life. What requires our attention, however, is that the turn to the *Idee* cannot in this case be something like a mere objective turn but rather must mean becoming form. That is to say, not only is *logos* something transcendental but *pathos* too is something transcendental; or rather, that which has the character of *pathos* and *logos*, that is subjective-and-objective, as a so-called whole, must be transcendental. The fact that in general expressions, in particular institutions, possess an imperative quality fundamentally is based upon transcendence in this way. Transcendence in this sense is, however, conceivable where transcendence to the outside and transcendence to the inside are one. Unless transcendence to the outside is at the same time transcendence within, we would not be able to speak of the self-transcendence of life in an adequate sense. In transcending within we truly become (epistemological) subjects and with this the (epistemological) object indeed comes to confront us in its objective nature, that is its transcendence. In order for there to be transcendence to the outside, there must simultaneously be a transcendence within. To transcend to the outside and to transcend to the inside are one. It may be said that even Simmel who, with his idea of the turn to the *Idee*, appears to have ruptured immanentism, without clarifying the meaning of transcendence within—to be precise, transcendence to the outside qua transcendence to the inside, transcendence to the inside qua transcendence to the outside—did not completely free himself of the standpoint of immanentism peculiar to the philosophy of life. And therefore, it must mean that transcendence concerns not merely the *Idee* but concerns forms, the imagination.

Everything institutional is something conventional, traditional, and from the past. Nevertheless, an institution commands not from the past but rather commands from the future. A command is originally something from the future and we can probably say that there is no command from the past. According to Judd, institutions are that which possess "expectation."[65] Expectations are products of group life and at the same time the most forceful fact within an individual person. Once social expectations are created, they become guides for the actions of individual persons. Not fulfilling an expectation gives rise to intense pain of an analogous sort to physical pain. In this sense expectations are new forms of reality that can claim the respect of all members of a group. And Judd regards expectation to be an element of consciousness on an equal footing with habit.[66] Manners are archived within an individual person as social expectations and, with that, as habits of personal action. And laws are manifest demands for the individual person's habits to be developed in accordance with the expectations of members of the collective. But if we regard habits not as simply belonging to an individual person but as something social, we see that whereas habits command from the past, expectations command from the future. Therefore, as with habit and expectation, institutions belong to the future as well as to the past. This primarily means that past and future are in the "present" where they can be conceived to be compresent with the present. As situated in that "present," institutions are transcendental and, moreover, imperative. Expectation is the guide for action and makes foresight possible. Valéry as well states that "future and past that, in the name of foresight and tradition, are fanciful perspectives [*perspectives imaginaires*], dominate the present and even constrain it." Future and past that dominate the present and even constrain it must be situated in the "present," compresently with the present. Even the institution called tradition must be situated in that "present." This is, of course, not something eternal but rather something historical. Moreover, T.S. Eliot rightly states: "This historical sense, which is a sense of the timeless as well as of the temporal and of the timeless and of the temporal together, is what makes a writer traditional. And it is at the same time what makes a writer most acutely conscious of his place in time, of his contemporaneity."[67] Real transcendence is immanence as well as transcendence. Institutions are transcendent; however, they are not simply transcendent but simultaneously immanent. As such a thing they possess truly imperative constraining power. The German word *Sitte*, the Latin word *consuetudo*, and the Greek word ἔθος or ἦθος, all etymologically contain the meaning of "making into one's own" (*Zu-eigen-machen*). An institution would not be valid as an institution unless it becomes immanent by becoming habitual. *Nomos* must primarily mean that which is immanent and transcendent at the same time. We can also regard what Judd calls expectation as manifesting its aspect of transcendence and habit as manifesting its aspects of immanence.

But the above investigation remains formal. To comprehend the essence of institutions concretely we need to understand it on the basis of the relationship between the actions of human beings and the environment—in which case the relation between society and the individual person becomes a problem from the very beginning. By this means we can discern an even more fundamental standpoint of critique in relation to the sociological value theory of Bouglé and Durkheim, Freyer's theory of the objective spirit, Pareto's theory of derivation, and so on. And we may clarify therein the deep connection between institutions and the imagination and throw new light upon the above investigations.

7.

[158] All institutions possess a structure. Institutions [制度] can therefore usually be referred to as organizations [組織]. Institutions are always distinguished from practices [習俗] because of their structure. If we were now to simply designate this quality of institutions as the institution's structural nature, what kind of a thing is this and how is it engendered?

First, the structural nature of the institution is based upon a certain rationality. Just as the structure belonging to a single mechanism [機械] manifests its rationality, the structure of an institution also manifests its rationality. Structure is nothing other than the *mechanism* of the institution. Even if we were there to follow Sumner and say that institutions are constituted of concept and structure, that concept would not signify anything fixed, but instead must mean the social function, as explained by Burgess and Park. In cases where structure embodies a certain social function it is called institution. The *Idee* contained by the institution must be something functional and not fixed, something dynamic rather than merely static. Regretfully, Simmel's idea of the so-called turn toward the *Idee* does not stress this dynamic, functional quality of the *Idee*. And hence, second, that sort of rationality of structure is what is necessarily required where the institution is fundamentally the adaptation of the human being's behavior toward the environment. Every sort of human action is an action in the environment and institutions are inconceivable apart from the relationship to the environment. An institution is not at all something fixed, but the working adaptation of human action toward the environment. As such an institution must possess a rational quality. For something irrational would be unable to continue in relation to the environment. On the other hand, however, institution is not the human being's action but, to the contrary, has the meaning of the environment confronting the human being's action. While institutions are what man makes, they oppose man as an environment. This is related to the fact that an institution indeed possesses structure, and that this institution possesses materiality. An institution is not something within the mind but is made through the formation of a material environment. The institution's structural nature in one sense is its materiality. The distinction within institutions between concept and structure is also due to this. But third, in the same way that spirit [*seishin*] and body cannot be abstractly separated in everything with life, concept and structure cannot be abstractly separated in institutions as well. Structure is not mere matter, it has rather the meaning of a body. An institution is something spiritual-and-somatic or subjective-and-objective and as such something independent. An institution possesses its own life and we can even say that it is something autonomous. Therefore, the structural nature of an institution manifests not only an adaptation toward the environment but manifests an adaptation toward itself. Adaptation toward itself is given by means of itself imitating itself and accordingly signifies repetition. This sort of repetition would probably signify the institution's naturalness—nature repeats—or somatic nature. Moreover, not only is the institution a somatic being but its concept is also recurring. Although I stated that *Idee* must be something dynamic, at the same time it must be something recurring and fixed. In such a way structure comes to indeed signify form. Form is not something merely static; instead, true form is that which is dynamic as at the same time static, that which is static as at the same time dynamic. This is the meaning behind the idea that what has life is what has form.

It is necessary to unfold the above three definitions with greater precision and to clarify the connections between them. Sumner recognized the difference between mores and institutions at the point where the latter possess structure and at the point where it possesses a rational character.

> The element of sentiment and faith inheres in the mores. Laws and institutions have a rational and practical character and are more mechanical and utilitarian. The great difference is that institutions and laws have a positive character while mores are unformulated and undefined. There is philosophy implicit in the folkways; when it is made explicit it becomes technological philosophy. Objectively regarded, the mores are the customs which actually conduce to welfare under existing life conditions. Acts under the laws and institutions are conscious and voluntary; under the folkways they are always unconscious and involuntary, so that they have the character of natural necessity.[68]

Sumner uses the word "mores" and the word "folkways" in this passage with the same meaning, but elsewhere he distinguishes between the two concepts.[69] Folkways are the most extensive and most fundamental function that can satisfy human concerns within the collective. Human beings within a collective exist on the basis of living conditions; they possess similar desires on the basis of a certain situation of living conditions; the relations of desires vis-à-vis the conditions are concerns under the headings of hunger, love, vanity, and fear; and the simultaneous efforts of multiple people trying to satisfy the concerns produce the voluminous phenomena of folkways through uniform, recurring, and wide-ranging simultaneous occurrences. Folkways are accompanied by pleasure or pain, in response to whether it suits itself. On this point a certain popular everyday philosophy suggests an explanation and inference. By shouldering this philosophy folkways becomes *mores* (manners). Folkways thus develop into mores and, next, become something even more determinate and clearer by following regulations, fixed actions, and mechanisms that ought to be employed. Therein structure is produced and mores become institutions. In this way, the various institutions began as folkways, became conventions, developed into mores with the addition of "a philosophy of welfare" (*some philosophy of welfare*), and further came to be completed by being furnished with structure. Furthermore, aside from such institutions that arose from folkways and mores (*crescive institutions*), there are institutions that had been enacted (*enacted institutions*). These are products of rational invention and design. Nevertheless, institutions that had been purely enacted barely persist. Although banks appear to have first emerged in the higher civilizations, in actuality they are founded upon customary practices that can be traced back to very ancient periods and are institutions made through their rationalization and systematization. "All institutions, even if we cannot ascertain their origin in mores other than by historical investigation, because the rational elements in them in certain cases are exceedingly large, are what came out of mores." Property, matrimony, and religion even today, for the most part, remain completely as mores. Hence institutions, not only emerged from mores as Sumner states but always contain the elements of mores, that is, all institutions have the character of mores. There are hardly any institutions that have been purely enacted, and even if there is such a thing, it becomes an institution in its peculiar sense only by becoming conventional. Not only is it difficult to invent and create an institution for a particular purpose where there is nothing, even in such cases something different is created than what the inventor had planned as its design becomes snatched by mores. The development from mores to institutions is a development in rationality. Nevertheless, the character of *logos* belonging to institutions cannot be conceived apart from the character of *pathos* belonging to conventions. We must not forget this point when discussing the creative nature of institutions. If some elements of mores, and accordingly the "element of sentiment and faith" (Sumner) said to naturally furnish mores, are contained even in the most rational institutions, how are these elements of the character of *pathos* and those elements of the character of *logos* tied together? The creative nature essential to institutions themselves is something conceivable on the basis of the imagination [*kōsōryoku*] that is originally of the character of *logos* as well as of *pathos*. The unifying ground that ties together the three definitions raised above in regard to the creative nature of institutions must also be sought within the logic of imagination. And in that case, what is particularly important is to grasp human behavior as behavior within the environment. Of necessity, the rationality of institutions is required in the relationships of human actions towards the environment, but this rationality cannot be mere rationality but involves the imagination. How are we to discern what we call the logic of imagination in the relationship between action and environment?

8.

[164] Let us here begin our investigation anew by returning again to the concept of habit. We can compare habit to physiological functions like respiration and digestion. The latter, of course, is unintentional while, by contrast, the former is something that had been achieved. Habit, however, resembles physiological functions in many points, especially in the point that it necessitates the cooperation between organism and environment. At the same time that respiration involves the lungs, it involves air; and in the same way that digestion involves the stomach, it involves food. It is not the case

ordinarily that there is no reason an act is attributed by a person to the human being from whom it was immediately produced. But it would be an error to think that it chiefly belongs only to them as if to think of respiration or digestion as phenomena utterly belonging to the interior of the human body. Habit, like physiological function, is a means to use and combine the environment. Habit is a technology [*gijutsu*]. Technology signifies the unity of (the epistemological) subject and object, the human and environment. Just as every habit is technological [*gijutsuteki*], every technology is habitual. Mastery in technology means to become habitual and we can probably say that a technology that had not been mastered does not really have the character of a technology. Thus, as Dewey states, "habits are the working adaptations of personal capacities with environing forces."[70] Habit requires the support of the environment, and hence also of society. Society is always distributed among our acts and in that sense every kind of act is already essentially social. As continuous adaptations, habit signifies an equilibrium.

Forms are engendered from habits due to the fact that habit is an equilibrium. But in that case, it is necessary to define with greater precision the sense in which habit is an equilibrium. First, needless to say, it means an equilibrium between an individual person and the environment. But, second, we cannot think of this equilibrium in the same way that we think of the equilibrium of physical forces. It does not signify something like the equality between active and passive forces. Furthermore, it is not something that can be reached through man's passivity vis-à-vis the environment, but rather all habits are furnished with an active character. The operation of the environment is neither decisive nor conclusive, and instead, the individual body's operation is the true principle of the achieved equilibrium. All habits owe their source to the initiative coming from the individual body making the habit. The environment's operation is of a kind that calls forth the reaction of being to spontaneously adapt itself to this environment. This means, on the one hand, that an adaptation that had been mastered escapes the knowledge of the adapted being, and together with this, on the other hand, that the equilibrium achieved in this way becomes realized, henceforth, spontaneously. In the first sense, habit resembles instinct. This cannot mean, however, that habit is wanting of thought. To the extent that habit signifies an adaptation in relation to the environment, habits cannot be short of a technological [*gijutsuteki*], and hence rational, element. Therefore, that latter sense is tied to the third significant point. That is, third, habit is not merely an adaptation to the environment but, as Segond states, "an adaptation of a being to itself."[71] While harmony with the environment is something realized so-to-speak contingently, by contrast, habit is always, and more than anything else, a being's adaptation to itself. By means of this, the continuous realization of an interior equilibrium becomes possible. This equilibrium is realized as the holistic equilibrium of mind and body. While human beings in adapting to the environment imitate the environment, they imitate themselves in adapting to themselves. At the same time that it is an adaptation to the environment, habit is an adaptation to one's self. Human beings, while adapting to the environment, at the same time adapt to themselves, and in this, the active nature or autonomy of their action is maintained. In such relationships the engendering of forms through habitualization also becomes possible.

However, if we look at the above relationships schematically, we can recognize them broadly among living things in general. According to Mercier, the life and evolution of living things unfold within the relationships of three opposing elements: namely, 1) autonomous activity; 2) the restriction (heredity) of this activity coerced to follow the laws of its own development, and 3) the external environment.[72] The first element corresponds to what we stated as the second point in the above analysis of habit; the second element likewise corresponds to what we stated as the third point; and further the third element likewise corresponds to what we stated as the first point. Everything with life exists within an environment. In addition to being defined by the environment, it in turn defines the environment. Nevertheless, it would be inadequate to see the relationship between living thing and environment as a relation of mere reciprocal functions. Everything with life is an individual body and its individual nature is expressed in its structure, centering, and autonomy. An individual body not only adapts to the environment, but at the same time is an individual body by adapting to itself, or put differently, imitating itself. Such self-imitation is that which is designated heredity. Even Tarde compares imitation among social phenomena to heredity among biological phenomena. Habit is something like heredity, and memory is something like habit. They are "imitations of oneself by means of oneself" (Tarde). Thus, we can admit that an identical tendency dominates the entire realm of life. Tarde's theory of mimesis deals primarily with the imitation of individual bodies of others, hence of the environment. Nevertheless, without considering the imitation of oneself, we would be unable to maintain his monadological individualism. Now at the same time that life reacts to the operations of the environment, it makes forms by reacting to itself. As the embryologist Brachet stated, life is a "creator of form" (*créatrice de la forme*). From the same relation is explained the fact that effort (*l'effort*) belongs to the fundamental phenomenon of life. Ravaisson also states that effort is not only the first condition of consciousness but a complete type and microcosm of consciousness. Effort comprises the two elements of action [*nōdō*, 能動] and passion [*judo*, 受動]. Passion is the mode of being existing in something different from the being to which its immediate cause belongs. Action is the mode of being existing in the being itself to which its immediate cause belongs, that is in itself. Passion and action are thus in opposition, but the combination of such opposites includes every possible form of life. And according to Ravaisson, effort is the site of equilibrium where, as it were, action and passion are in balance; it is the common boundary of these opposites, the mean where these two extremities come in contact with one another.[73] Effort certainly signifies equilibrium in this way, and to conceive of an effort that does not have the meaning of equilibrium—for example, Fichtean ego-philosophy—would be to fall into the error of not grasping man as a being belonging to an environment. However, the fact that effort is indeed effort and not mere equilibrium means that this equilibrium is something active or, put differently, that it is something acquired through the autonomous activity of life. Therein the *Form* that life possesses manifests, on the one hand, an equilibrium, and on the other hand, it manifests in addition an endless tension. Moreover, the effort of an individual body is not only an effort to adapt to the environment but to adapt to itself and hence an effort to balance spirit and body, at the same time that *Form* on the one hand manifests the equilibrium of spirit and body, it manifests on the other hand the spirit's transcendence or control over this body. This *Form* is viewed as *Idee* or thought is due to the latter sense, but in that case, we of course ought not to forget at the same time the former sense.

Now the point we ought to take up from the above discussion is that habit is a technology. Dewey says that habit is *art* and Ravaisson says that effort is *tact* [touch][74] but we can interpret either case to mean technology. As the working adaptation between environmental force and human ability, habit is technological [*gijutsuteki*]. Technology in its universal essence is the unity of the subjective and the objective. According to Ravaisson, *tact* extends from the pole of passion to the pole of action, envelops in its development everything in the middle, and in that case confirms the law of reciprocal processes in all of its developments.[75] As something technological, habit must include a rational element within itself. In opposition to viewing habit as the mere force of repeating an activity without thought, Dewey states that habit lacking thought and futile thought are two sides of the same fact. Just as habit as one kind of technology includes thought, thought as well cannot be effective unless it becomes habitual, namely, technological. Nevertheless, as it is conceivable that technology cannot be perfected as technology unless it becomes habitual and thus natural, it can already be gathered that even though technology must certainly take rationality as its foundation, this rationality cannot be simple rationality. As we will eventually discuss in detail, technology belongs to the imagination [*kōsōryoku*]. Technology in its essence is invention and what we call "the logic of invention" is the logic of imagination. Invention clearly takes science as its premise and although it is impossible to oppose it, it is always something more than rational deduction from a general law. Invention is to discern form. Invention is inconceivable if we exclude the logic of forms, and hence, the logic of imagination. As the unity of the subjective and the objective, technology is something different from a science regarded as purely objective and having the character of *logos*—this point will also require comments later. In technology, the objective is subjectified and the subjective is objectified. We ought not, however, view this process as a merely reciprocal operation at all. As we can conceive technology as always belonging to the (epistemological) subject, through that reciprocal operation it ends under the domination of the subjective. That we can view technology possessing no end besides itself as still a means is based on this relationship. Accordingly, the meaning that technology is again a means ought not to be comprehended externally. This relationship furthermore resembles the relationship that habit, where on the one hand it is the equilibrium between the environment and (epistemological) subject, is on the other hand active in every way. Just as habit is an adaptation to the environment, it is an adaptation to one's own self. Because of this technology in habit, while being outer technology, must also be an inner technology. The latter, more than anything else, involves the equilibrium of spirit and body. We can discern a key for a rational explanation here in Kassner's words, full of mystery, that man's body and spirit are connected by means of the imagination.[76] That is, the human being's body and spirit are connected by means of an inner technology and this technology takes as its foundation the imagination. In Kassner, however, technology is seen as something mythological, as if magic.

We can say that every activity of life is technological. Even our bodies as adaptations to the environment, as the evolutionists have theorized, were thus generated as technological. That which has life lives and also evolves by adapting itself to the environment technologically and inventively. Nature as well is technological. Everything that has been generated through technology is furnished with a system or structure. Life and structure are inseparable. That which is most intimately tied to the organization of an organism is what is called instinct. However, even within an identical species, instinct differs in response to differences in form. Depending on whether it is male, female, or of the neutral sex, each bee possesses distinct instincts. Even among other insects we can recognize that through the various phases of transitory states, such as of the larva, chrysalis, and moth, instinct distinct for each appears successfully. In this way, instinct is inseparable from the organic structure and is a natural tool for immediate activity. Moreover, the activity of instinct realizes the two-folded adaptation of on the one hand adaptation of the species to the environment and on the other hand adaptation of the individual body to the type of species. Seen from this point, we can consider even instinct as a single *pensée* (thought) as Segond says, or as the "*idée* of nature" as Lachelier says. Nevertheless, in instinct, thought and technology completely sink into nature and are nature itself. Although we had endeavored up to this point to stress the rationality and technological nature of habit, in habit as well as in instinct, it went without saying that rationality and technological nature sink into nature and become a kind of nature, a second nature. Furthermore, technology all contain an internally necessary tendency of becoming habitual, and on this point, technology has a part that cannot be explained from mere rationality. Technology in its own sense must, however, be distinguished from instinct; it is not something that emerges from instinct. In contrast to the fact that instinct is inseparably tied to the organic organ (*Organ*), technology in its own sense is that which makes tools (*Wekrzeug*) mechanical. According to Bergson, instinct is completely "internal," and therein is life's immediate sympathy towards itself, while by contrast technological intellect, the intellect that makes, and moreover uses, tools is completely mechanistic and external. However, we need to take note that such externality is no mere externality at all but rather is founded upon transcendence. In that sense, the immanentism of Bergson's philosophy fails to comprehend the meaning of transcendence. Technology is something conceivable only upon the root of transcendence. Furthermore, technology is not only founded upon mere intellect but instead involves the imagination. An institution is essentially what was made through technology. As Judd discusses, institutions are not products of instinct.[77] Borrowing his neologism, there must be a "tool consciousness" at the foundation of an institution.

9.

[174] Institutions, originally, cannot be conceived from an individual's habit. The above account, however, can presumably help us to comprehend the essence of institutions by corresponding to the definition given earlier for the structural nature of institutions. In a certain sense, institutions emerge from all mores or conventions. They are, however, not things that simply naturally grow from convention. In order for institutions to emerge as possessing structure, in distinction from conventions, conscious technology

must be included. We can also say that institutions are the unity of convention and technology. In that case, technology presumably means rationality and convention presumably means "the elements of emotion and faith." An institution, as something that concretely seeks the synthesis of these two elements, is not something that can be made simply by a rational process. Even if the control over nature and the invention of tools to use for this control is a purely rational process, the creation of institutions requires a technology different in nature from this. This technology must have as its foundation the imagination that has the character of *pathos* at the same time it has the character of *logos*. And even if some institution was made from a purely rational thought, in order for it to be employed in practice, it would have to be made to conform to the conventions of society and thus not only is the imagination necessary for the technology of institution-employment, if an institution becomes an institution in its unique sense only by becoming conventional through such employment the imagination would always have to be conceived at the root of an institution. There is presumably a natural difference between the technology of nature and the technology of society, between scientific technology and political technology.

Institutions are conceivable not from the habits of individual persons but from social conventions. The habits of individual persons, of course, are also socially regulated. Every individual person is born into a society and forms his/her habits on the basis of the conditions fixed by existing conventions. Conventions are said to be engendered from where a multitude of individuals responds in similar ways to identical circumstances. An institution is something that rationalizes and systematizes what is conventionally practiced, and this rationalization and systematization are required to better adapt to the environment. Conventions or mores, and institutions, are influenced by the environment. Montesquieu had already been arguing that these are especially under the Influenc' of 'he natural environment. Indeed, we have a hard time agreeing with climatic historicism or geological determinism. Nature works upon man because man works upon nature. The development of technology vis-à-vis nature diminishes the nature's immediate influence upon man. Here we ought to recollect again Ravaisson's method that heightens the activity of habit and lowers its passivity. And this method is appropriate for convention as well. The environment is not only the natural environment. There are also what are called the social environment as well as the cultural environment. Institutions are made as methods of technological adaptations toward such environments. Now although it was said that conventions are engendered from where a multitude of individuals respond in similar ways to identical circumstances if we were to consider this from another direction, a reciprocal operation occurs between these individual persons acting in this way towards the environment and in order for their activity towards the environment to be powerful and effective it is demanded that they combine and collaborate in a standardized way. Conventions are engendered in this way from within reciprocal operations and by means of such conventions, individual persons are connected. Convention is thus not just what involves the relationship to the environment, but at the same time also the relationship to society's own self. As its rationalization and systematization, institutions are the structure that society gives to itself and by being furnished with such structure, a society truly becomes a society. As the work of human beings upon the environment advances from being instinctively immediate in the direction of becoming technologically [*gijutsuteki*] mediated, the organization accordingly of human beings themselves where they are that working (epistemological) subject—for example, with the development of the division of labor—becomes all the more required. Therein we can recognize the development of institutions. Institutions always take as object the human, namely, that which is subjective and cannot be seen at all as a merely objective something. For this reason, in distinction from the technology which takes nature as object, the technology of institutions would probably have to belong even more to the imagination. If something like scientific technology [*gijutsu*] is a technology in its own sense, the technology of institutions do not stop with such technology but must also contain the sense of *tact*. *Tact* is also a kind of technology, but it signifies so to speak a subjective technology vis-à-vis objective technology. Although Ravaisson stated that the effort that manifests the complete *type* of consciousness is *tact*,[78] the technology of institutions is no mere technology but must also be *tact*. This is why in its broad sense it is said to be political. Together with other meanings, politics above all contains the meaning of *tact*. We ought not to forget this point even when thinking of the scientific nature or technological nature of politics. Not only is pure rational thought required for *tact*, which is a subjective technology, but it is especially required for the imagination. Of course, I am not saying that there is no need for rational thought in the creation of institutions. At the same time that institutions signify the adaptations of society to itself, they exist on the other hand as adaptations to the environment and as such necessitate the inclusion of objective technology. But just as customs manifest themselves as if they were imitations of themselves, indeed, as we wrote already, from where they are customs, principally by themselves, without any conscious knowledge concerning the environment, institutions also, by being born of conventions or by becoming conventional, only look as if they are established as adaptations of society to itself apart from the sense of being adaptations to the environment. And therein an objective technology must already be included. If we borrow Sumner's words, something that would become a *technological philosophy* is implied in conventions when they are made manifest. The (epistemological) subject is not merely opposed to the (epistemological) object [*kyakkan*] but becomes a true (epistemological) subject by forming expression through making the (epistemological) object its own while adapting to it. This point is the same relationship as the relationship mentioned above between the *Idee* or spirit and the body. Accordingly, *tact* which is a subjective technology must also include objective technology into itself by making it its own. It is, however, necessary that *tact* include not only technological philosophy but, borrowing Sumner's words again, something like a *philosophy of welfare*. Although, as Judd states, institutions must have "tool consciousness"[79] as their basis, they cannot just end there. On the other hand, the philosophy of welfare, as it is conceived precisely in that manner by Sumner, must also be technological or rather *tactful*, and in that sense must be technological philosophy. As that which seeks the unity of the subjective and the objective, *tact* must fundamentally belong to the imagination.

In this way even if we say that institutions are made through technology, the reason can be clarified why they are distinct from things like tools or machines. If tools for controlling nature are *real* things, institutions are *fictional* things. Moreover, the world of history is that the *fictional* is the *real*. Institutions are the structure society gives to itself and without such structure society cannot subsist. As the order that the (epistemological) subject gives itself institutions mean something more than mere tools. Society is a building of *fictions*. And as already stated, as the mode of adapting to the environment advances from being instinctively immediate to becoming technologically mediated, the mode of institutionally combining and organizing human beings where they are (epistemological) subjects working thus also develops, and the control of *fiction* also develops in response. Just as we can even regard the natural environment as society's body, anything, including science as well as scientific technology, can possess the meaning of an institution in the world of history. *Fiction* does not mean *illusion*. In the world of history, what is *real* is *fictional* and what is *fictional* is *real*. Now just as we can see society as the environment for us, we can see institutions as the environment for us as well. We create for ourselves a new environment by means of institutions. We dwell in a world where not things but *fiction* is all the more important. That which was made through our actions now comes to guide our behavior and effect a new and yet powerful influence upon us. Our life itself becomes more or less something *fictional* from the fact that it is *real*. This is the meaning of the fact that life evolves from the state of being dominated by instinct. As Judd also argues, social institutions exercise a large influence, especially upon the emotions of the individual, and civilized people are endowed with the apparatus of emotions conspicuously distinct from that of animals or primitive people.[80] As historical beings, we are not simply born of nature but formed by *fictions*. Nevertheless, institutions are what are conventional, and as such a single institution is furnished with the tendency of adapting to itself without end or imitating itself endlessly. The nature of habit is affirmative, assertive, and self-continuing. To be self-affirmative is also the nature of *pathos*. Institutions become fixed on their tendency of imitating themselves by means of themselves. Institutions that have thus become fixed can no longer be adapted to societies that continue developing. Because institutions are not, however, something like a hat that one can put on or take off at will, people make an effort to adapt institutions by some method to the altered society. What we discern in such cases is a process like what Maine had designated as *legal fiction*.[81] That is, in that case, the letter of law remains as it is while its adaptation is altered, and hence the fact of the law's reception of substantial change is hidden. At that moment law becomes something with a *fictional* meaning. If an institution's becoming fixed means that it comes to bear the character of *pathos*, an activity with the character of *logos* would presumably be necessary to make the fixed institution into something *fictional*. However, if it thoroughly has the character of *logos*, there would be no alternative but for the institution to be destroyed, and to the extent that we attempt to avoid this, we use a method like legal fiction, and therein the activity of the imagination is required. In this case, as well *fiction* has the significance of the unity of the characters of *logos* and *pathos*, and this unity is always realized through technology. The imagination itself is essentially something having the character of technology. Every institutionalization means a technologization and to make something *fictional*. For example, with matrimony by the captivity of women, its captivity later came to be technologized, institutionalized, and made into something *fictional*. It can be seen in what Maine calls legal fiction that even an institution that had degenerated into a so-called "fact" by becoming fixed can maintain its life by becoming fictionalized. A definite institution, of course, has a limit to adaptations. As the critical spirit grows it eventually destroys that institution, but people immediately sense the misfortune and come to build again a new institution.

Convention has the meaning of society's adaptation to itself. The (epistemological) subject of institutions, what Jhering calls end-subject (*Zwecksubjekt*), is not the individual person but society. The individual person is instead the (epistemological) object in the technology of the institution. To begin with, a human being is not a mere (epistemological) object but a subject. It is said that just as technology, which takes the subjective-objective human being as the self's object [*taishō*], namely, the (epistemological) object [*kyakkan*], so too institutions must belong to the imagination with the character of *pathos* and *logos*. We cannot, however, conceive the individual where s/he is no mere (epistemological) object but a subject to be on the outside vis-à-vis society, and society on the contrary includes the individual person within itself. The institution is nothing merely external but an inner order that society gives to itself. The various institutions of a particular society, as such a thing, possess a tendency towards what Sumner calls *consistency* and mutually adapt to one another. That a society of a definite period as a whole possesses a definite form is also founded upon that tendency. More than the mere demand for rationality, coherence must mean a demand for form. Although the technology of institutions takes as its (epistemological) object a plurality of individual persons, in constituting the individual person who is an (epistemological) subject as also an object, we can recognize the true subjectivity of society. This kind of subjectivity would be inconceivable without transcendence. Society is not something that can be reduced to the relations of mutual operations among individual persons, but rather possesses the significance of a transcendental subject [*chōetsuteki shukan*]. That institutions possess a normative, restrictive quality for individual persons can also be considered from this point. However, the thinking of the Durkheimian school contains the defect of failing to recognize the individual's *initiative*, the individual's autonomy or independence vis-à-vis society. The individual person is not simply an (epistemological) object for society; the individual person, in reverse, is also an (epistemological) subject who can take society as an (epistemological) object as well. To the extent that institutions are also conscious technology, it must depend on such inventions of individual persons. We can say, as Tarde did, that even conventions when traced to their origins, are inventions of individual persons. But if the performance of imitation is required for these to become conventions, as Tarde states, then we would presumably have to presuppose society where it is a universal as the ground that makes possible the relations of imitation among individual persons. Institutions are created by individuals as (epistemological) subjects who can constitute even society as an (epistemological) object. We ought, however, to call society that is constituted as an object by individual persons in this way as an "institutional society" [*seidoteki shakai*, 制度的社会], and such an institutional society ought to be distinguished from a "creative society" [*sōzōteki shakai*, 創造的社会] that is thought to thoroughly envelop individual persons where they are (epistemological) subjects and from where individual persons are created. A creative society is indeed the true transcendental subject. By becoming one with that creative society, the inventive individual can thus be inventive. Without transcendence technology would also be inconceivable. Although Aristotle stated that nature is technological, society is what is indeed technological, and we can say that human beings are also created by society through technology. In such cases, we must consider the creative society at the root of institutional society. The relationship between creative society and institutional society is something like the so-called relation between nature as producing (*natura naturans*) and nature as product (*natura naturata*). Just as the (epistemological) subject and object cannot be separated in abstraction, institutional society and creative society cannot be separated in abstraction. The human being, while something made by society, in turn, as something independent, makes society. In thus discussing institutions we have run into the problem of technology. In the following we shall thus enter into a more detailed investigation of technology.

3

Technology

1.

[185] The analysis of institutions clarified the fact that institution includes the element of technology [*gijutsu*, 技術]. Let us now investigate, in particular, the relationship between technology and imagination by directing our study toward technology and pursuing our intent.

The word *technology*, when used in the broadest sense, signifies any procedure, means, combination of means, or system for achieving a certain goal. In this way people speak of, for example, the technology of discourse, of poetry, of drama, of battle, of flight, and so on, and not only that, even speak of the technology [or technics] of amour—the so-called *ars amandi* of the ancients.[1] But in an even narrower sense, technology signifies a procedure executed through physical means we call instruments in order to attain a certain goal, what Sombart called instrumental technology (*Instrumentaltechnik*).[2] If such cases may include musical instruments, it also can include instruments for war as well as instruments for surgical operations. Therein technology is determined, in a yet narrower sense, as the procedure for making these instruments or as the procedure for physical production in general. This is something called production technology (*Produktionstechnik*), and therefore, called economic technology by Sombart.[3] In this way technology is used in broad and narrow senses. However, as natural scientific thought has become dominant in modernity, on the one hand, and as we have come to recognize the critical importance of the economy, we have come to regard production technology as technology in its characteristic sense. This fact on the other hand, contains a deep significance even apart from this circumstance. Technology and production are in an inseparable relationship. In cases when we speak of nature as technological, we are thinking of nature as also productive. The concept of production is a constitutive element of the concept of technology. Production can, however, be understood in a broad or narrow sense. As the concept of production is expanded beyond the sense of economic production, the concept of technology is also correspondingly expanded, and as the concept of technology is expanded beyond the sense of economic technology, the concept of production will also presumably be expanded in response. If we are to name production in this expanded sense *poiesis* (production [*seisaku* 制作]), we would have to say that all *poiesis* is technological. Next, the concept of instruments and the concept of technology are indispensable elements. In correspondence to the meaning of technology in the broad sense, the meaning of instruments can also be understood in a broad or narrow way. In cases where we see technology in a particular sense as economic technology, the instrument is determined as a mechanical instrument. But in a broad sense, we can also conceive the various parts of the body, namely, the organs of the organism and the body itself as an instrument. And further, we can think of the whole of nature as possessing the sense of a body for human beings and thus as an instrument. In that sense technology that is not what Sombart calls instrumental technology is also instrumental. In any case we can say that the concepts of production and of instruments are defining elements of the concept of technology.

If we are to think in relation to a category we have already dealt with, technology in a certain sense is also something institutional. We can think of technology as exhibiting its sense by becoming habitual. But it is from there that technology becomes one institution. Technology is settled as an example of *convention* based on the training and discipline of habit, attains the integrity of a habit and prescription—*consistency* that Sumner regarded as the essential inclination of *mores*—and thus comes to be endowed with the character and force of an institution. Technology not only becomes a habitual self-evidence but becomes something sanctioned by social *convention* and comes to possess a normative significance through our acts. And it comes to be organized into the common sense [*jōshiki* 常識] of the period through convention. We must say, as Veblen states, that one important aspect of technology is its institutional character.[4] To divide periods by calling a certain period of prehistory the stone age or the bronze age or the iron age, or by naming a certain society in history the feudal system or the capitalist system is, fundamentally, also possible because technology becomes institutional. In order to understand the meaning of technology concretely, it is important that we be mindful of the institutional being of technology. Moreover, technology becomes institutional not merely due to external reasons, but on the basis of the inherent quality of the existence of technology itself. Russel's differentiation of the nature of scientific temperament on the one hand and that of scientific technology arising from science on the other, and claim that in contrast to the former, which is thoughtful and experimental, and wishes for freedom, the latter tends to be static and conservative, is presumably based as well on this sort of character of technology.[5] While there are very few cases of science becoming institutional, technology in every instance is endowed with the inclination of becoming institutionalized. It will be said that science becomes nature—historical nature—by becoming technology. And while science and common sense are unambiguously distinguished, the fact that technology by contrast is always transferred into the structure of common sense is also related to the institutional quality, the quality of *nomos*, belonging to common sense. Common sense, as well as technology, are both affirmative things and as such possess an institutional quality.

Yet technology exists, in particular in the form of myth. That would be what is called magic (*Magie*). In primitive societies, just as myth possesses an important significance, magic occupies a dominant position. Preuss states: "If we want to determine the origin of dress, if we want to define social relations and achievements, e.g., the origin of marriage, war, agriculture, cattle breeding, etc., if we want to make studies in the psyche of nature peoples,—we must always pass through magic and belief in magic."[6] It is said that magic itself is born in cases where it transcends the stage of instinct as the immediate result of the struggle for existence and that religion and technology emerge out of magic without any interval. Just as every technology is a working relationship between the subject and the environment, magic as something born of the struggle for existence, is also one human activity, a primitive form, that attempts to submit the environment to the self's will. Magic, therefore, contains a technological purpose and, in contrast to how technology, only in its peculiar sense, takes as its foundation objective scientific knowledge, magic believes in a certain mysterious force. Put simply, magic is the mythical form of technology. And moreover, from a certain perspective, we might also view myth itself as based upon a demand for technology. The human demand for technology, as beings living within the environment, is universal. Although it is generally said that anthropomorphism and animism are ideas characteristic of myth, according to Veblen, this sort of anthropomorphist idea is "the self-contamination of the sense of workmanship itself."[7] The essential character of anthropomorphism consists in imputing activity into a foreign object, more or less, in accord with human modes of activity. But such anthropomorphism ordinarily means "the interpretation of phenomena in the language of a craftsman."[8] That is, we can conceive therein that foreign objects make things in the same way as craftsmen. "The facts of observation are conceived as facts of workmanship, and the logic of workmanship becomes the logic of events."[9] For what Veblen means by the self-contamination of the sense of workmanship (instinct) is the human interpretation of observed phenomena by imputing into them a disposition towards handicraft, the most fundamental instinct among human beings, indeed, on the basis of the demand of the instinct for handicraft itself. And the anthropomorphism or animism that arises as a result, in turn, becomes real obstructions to the development of technology. And as such imputation into foreign objects of the disposition to handicraft is gradually pushed behind observed phenomena, the formation of myths, leaving its unsophisticated immediate stages, also become more precise by means of further completed anthropomorphic ideas. Yet the inclination to attribute the disposition of workmanship to external facts is not lost but continues. According to Veblen, this allowed, on the one hand, the modern scientist to universalize his observations with the idea of cause and effect and, on the other hand, allowed for the continuation of the idea of God as a creative workman, the great artisan. We can consider that the reason why the *propter hoc*, and hence the ideas of function or force, are included in the idea of causality is due to the anthropomorphism of workmanship. And this fact indicates that science is something originally born of the demand for technology. Pure scientific thought, of course, would endeavor to be released from such an idea. Yet can technological thinking itself be free in the thought of the idea of *propter hoc* concerning its causal relations? We can say that myth already exists at the root of technology in this extremely universal sense. Just as there is the demand for technology at the root of myth, myth is there at the root of technology. Or, put differently, we can say that there is something like magic in all technologies. But it is necessary to thoroughly determine this meaning with precision. If it would be one-sided to explain all of myth with the demand for technology—as already stated in the chapter on "Myth," the idea of myth cannot be explained merely by anthropomorphism or, what is seen as its older form, animism; and it will be explained later in the chapter on

"Experience" that what we think of as the world of imagination is a world preceding anthropomorphism or animism—to conceive technology as just magic would be even more dangerous. Technology and magic in their proper senses must be thoroughly distinguished. Magic, instead, is the middle term between myth and technology.

Brunchvicg writes that "the craftsman (*homo faber*) and the religious man (*homo religiosus*), before taking attitudes that today appear to be opposed to each other, meet one another in the magician (*homo magicus*)."[10] Seen from the side of religion, magic is to be driven away towards technology. Seen from the side of technology, magic is to be driven back toward religion. Further, just as Brunchvicg states that the magician does not cease being our contemporaries but rather probably manifests the psychology of the masses of our contemporaries in the processes of everyday life, magic does not simply belong to the past but there is instead some magic in every technology. We thus need to first consider the meaning of magic before discussing technology in its proper meaning.

2.

[192] It is said that magic is an exceedingly ambiguous and very much indeterminate phenomenon and that it is almost impossible to define it. It is, however, seen as a certain intermediary between technology and religion.[11] In the points that it has a practical purpose, the majority of its applications possess a mechanical quality, and what has its principle idea possesses experiential mimesis, magic is similar to secular technology. But in cases where it appeals to a particular user, relies on a spiritual medium, and performs ritual activities, magic departs from technology and approaches religion. It is even said that among religious ceremonies, there are almost none without items that also fall within magic to that degree. Nevertheless, therein always lie many points that do not agree with the ideas people ordinarily hold in regard to religion, and the mutual antagonism, one to the other, of religion and magic is constant. The two poles that distinguish religion and magic are sacrifice and curse. Religion always constructs a kind of ideal toward which hymns, prayers, and sacrifice ascend. Magic avoids that realm and, on the contrary, approaches curses that surround itself with magical ceremonies. In contrast to religious ceremonies that generally require broad daylight and a public quality, magical ceremonies are ordinarily conducted at night, in darkness. On the other hand, we can regard magical ceremonial activities to be creative. They are viewed to have the efficacy of making things. On this point, we must say that magic is closer to technology than religion.

As stated at the beginning, the concept of production and the concept of the instrument are defining elements of the concept of technology. Magic therefore first has this sort of purpose in production. Magic, as Hubert and Mauss state, works with the same aim that our technology, industry, medicine, chemistry, mechanics, and so on, work. "Magic essentially is the art of making [*art de faire*] and magicians have used their know-how, expertise, and manual skills ... It is the realm of pure production, production from nothing (*ex nihilo*), it makes with words and gestures what technology makes through labor."[12] The minimum of representations that are included in all magical acts are representations of effects because they possess a practical purpose. There is no magic, whatsoever, that does not consider efficiency (*efficacité*). Magic thinks of altering the given situation as its immediate essential effect. The magician always embraces the idea that magic is the "art of change" (*art des changements*).[13] The magician is a practitioner. There is no such thing as an honorary magician who is not active. A magician, for being a magician, must actually perform magic. For the most part representations of magic possess no theoretical meaning to the magician, and rarely would he render them in formulas. They possess only practical significance and are only expressed in magic by those acts. It is the philosopher, not the magician, who was the first to reduce them to a system. The esoteric philosopher was the one who offered a theory concerning the representations of magic. Magic itself could not even compose demonology. It is said that a catalog of demons was made by religion, whether in Europe or in India. In magic, there is no pure representation, and hence myths of magic end in the embryo stage. By contrast, myths and doctrines in religion are developed. And the fact that in contrast to religion that inclines towards metaphysics and is immersed in the creation of ideal figures, magic attempts to be of use to secular life by departing from the mystical life from which it scoops up its power and entering into secular life, is because the latter possesses the same kind of purpose as technology. As religion inclines towards the abstract, magic leans towards the concrete. Hence in response to its individualization and specialization in pursuing its various goals, magic inclines toward gradually resembling technology. From the point where it originally had a practical purpose, magic handles material, performs experiments, and even comes to make discoveries, without limiting itself to gesturing in the fictional world. Magic, accordingly, inclines towards positive science and amounts to its preparation. In contrast to religion which inclines towards metaphysics in its intellectual element, magic further devotes its mind to the concrete and becomes absorbed in knowing nature. It composed a kind of index of plants and minerals, phenomena, and beings in general, namely, the first outline of the various sciences of astronomy, physics, and natural history. In fact, in Greece, certain parts of magic, like astrology and alchemy, were applied natural science, and it was thus taken to be natural that the magician was given the name φύσικος (natural scientist) and that the word φυσικός was synonymous with magic.[14] Magicians, based on the nature of their work, must have known that knowledge is power (*savoir c'est pouvoir*). Accordingly, their knowledge was not limited to simply classifying, but at times they attempted to systematize their knowledge to discover its principle. Science owes a portion of its origin to the magician. And therein lies the circumstance that in primitive societies the one who had the spare time to engage in the observation of nature and reflect or fantasize about it, was alone the magician. We can also believe that they were also the ones who constituted the tradition of science and the method of intellectual education.

Magic in itself is, however, not at all identical to science. Although magic has a practical purpose, its most fundamental idea, according to Hubert and Mauss, is the idea of a magic power (*pouvoir imagique*) or mystical power called "*potentialité magique*." Just as magic is essentially not concerned with natural law, neither is it concerned with individual things. Accordingly, even if magic includes within itself personal representations adequate for developing myths, such myths remain rudimentary, and magic does not want to create stories about demons. Not only that, even when gods are included within magic, they lose their personality and, so to speak, throw off their myths. Instead of considering the individual characters of gods, magic problematizes their ability and power, arbitrarily demolishes their form, and frequently reduces them to mere names.[15] What thus remains in magic as essential is the "vague power" (*pouvoir vague*) called magic power, which in its entire nature cannot be expressed with the form of a demon. Magic power is instead the sort of power said to be variously expressed by the power of the magician, or of the ceremony, or of spiritual beings. Presumably, any of these function as an element of sorcery only to the extent that they are promoted with the character of being a single power, not mechanical but a magic power, truly, or through convention or ceremonies. Moreover the idea of magic power, from this perspective, can be completely compared to the idea of mechanical power. Just as we call the cause of movement power, magic power is the cause of magical effects, illness and death, happiness and health, and so on, their so-called *causa efficiens*. The idea of efficiency (*efficacité*) is presumably foundational even in the technology employed in mechanical power in the same way it is so in magic. Now what is extremely noteworthy in the idea of magic is that it includes the idea of the environment where the problematized power is active.[16] In this mystical environment, things take on an utterly distinct process than in the sensory world, distance does not obstruct contact, hopes are immediately realized, and all things can be spiritual. The idea of this power and the idea of this environment are inseparable, they coincide absolutely and at the same time are expressed by identical means. The various ceremonial forms that are devices aiming to create magic power are simultaneously also devices for creating the environment. This mixed idea of power and environment, according to Hubert and Mauss, escapes the abstract categories of our language and reason. However, even if, as these two and others of the Durkheimian school say, this cannot be comprehended on the basis of the intellectual psychology of individuals and can only be explained as a collective representation, the issue is presumably what sort of thing the logical quality of this psychology, the logic of what is called "the category of collective thought" (*catégorie de la pensée collective*) is. Such basic ideas of magic, as pointed out by Hubert and Mauss, are certainly related to absurd reasoning and fundamentally cannot be adequately explained by the doctrine of sympathy of Frazer and others that follows the theory of the association of ideas. And while Veblen's idea of the self-contamination of the sense of workmanship, discussed above, is important in raising the determination called the imputation of the sense of workmanship instead of the hitherto obscure explanations concerning anthropomorphism, as before it resembles, at places, the doctrine of emotional investment. However, if in magic it is power rather than personhood that is problematized and myths in magic, as Hubert and Mauss say, "aim intently at things rather than spiritual personalities, and are quite objective," it probably would be difficult to adapt Veblen's idea to the explanation of magic. Thus, it seems that the coincidence of the idea of power and the idea of the environment said to characterize magic, as we shall discuss later, must indeed be a single category of magic belonging to the logic of imagination. The logic of imagination obviously does not take as its foundation the doctrine of the association of ideas, nor does it take as its foundation, as it is often misunderstood to do so, the theory of emotional investment. Magic power is a mystical power. This mystical nature of magic is expressed with the word *mana*. The idea of *mana* in magic is of the same order as the idea of the sacred (*sacré*) in religion. The idea of *mana* is even more universal than the idea of the sacred and it is said that the former includes the latter and the latter is something that is separated from the former. Now Hubert and Mauss write that even if magic power is indeed infinite and the magical environment is truly transcendent, things within the world of magic take their course according to laws. However, these laws, as we shall eventually argue, are thought to generally manifest magical figures in the logic of imagination. Hubert and Mauss take magic as belonging to collective thought, and state that judgments in magic are "almost completely transcendental synthetic judgments." And they state that they are on the one hand emotive "judgments of value," while on the other hand always rational or intellectual judgments, and that "thanks to the idea of *mana*, magic, the domain of desire, is filled with rationality."[17] Nevertheless we can already discern that it also belongs to one figure of the productive imagination, its magical figure, in the point where judgment in magic characterized as transcendental synthetic judgment is intellectual and at the same time emotive.

Even if it is evident that magic, like technology, has production as its purpose, it is not so evident that this includes the concept of instrument. Various research on magic conducted on the primitive societies of Australia almost all agree in recognizing mystical power, namely, magic power among certain human beings, and they all take the presence of this power to possess a magical substance (*substance magique*) contained in the magician's body or at least in his medicine (*sac-médicine*) bag or, strictly speaking, his mystical behavior. This magical substance is constituted, almost everywhere, of a fragment of a rock crystal or a magical bone (usually a dead person's bone).[18] We can probably say that the sort of substance found in magic has the significance of instruments found in technology. We can also view the magician's body and its gestures to be instruments. Instead of being the subject of magic, he performs the role of the instrument in the sense of being the magician only to the extent that magic power is promoted and expressed. Magical ceremonies also possess the sense of an instrument. The reason why, in contrast to the case of religion where ceremony on the one hand and myth and doctrine on the other are autonomous, in the case of magic these elements are inseparable is because ceremony in this case is itself an expression of myth or doctrine and is an instrument in the sense that it produces the effects of magic as the recipient for the promotion of magic power. It is to be noted that words, in particular, occupy an important position in magic; in other words, it is doubtful on the one hand that there is truly anything silent in ceremonies, and on the other hand, there are many ceremonies conducted solely with words. While this is important in comprehending the nature of magic in words, words are also instruments of magic. In contrast to how instruments of technology are endowed with mechanical power, instruments in magic are endowed with magic power. In this way it cannot be disputed that even though we can tentatively regard the existence of instruments in magic, the significance of the instrument of magic on the other hand is extremely vague. Technology has the function of mediating subject and object, and we can recognize therein the meaning of instrument as well. However, as Hubert and Mauss write, in magic there is a particular "continuity" or "merging" among the actor, recipient, material, and purpose of the magical act, or put generally between subject and object. And this fact again defines the character of the ceremony itself. They write:

> Magic involves a fusion of images and without this, in our view, the ceremony ... would be inconceivable, ... now this fusion ... is in itself an object of representation. In fact, no matter how distinct the various elements of representation in magical ceremonies may be, they are included in a single synthetic representation, wherein cause and effect are fused together. It is the very idea of magic, of immediate and limitless efficacy, and of immediate creation.[19]

If in this way subject and object, and cause and effect, are always reciprocally fused in magic, the idea of an instrument in its distinct sense would probably be unable to intervene. Production is simply immediate in such cases. Nevertheless, it would be said that the fusion is indeed birthed by means of the imagination. In order to evaluate this magical merger in relation to technology by clarifying its nature and meaning, we need to clarify the relationship between magic and imagination by entering into its root.

3.

[203] It is commonly recognized that an intimate relationship subsists between magic and imagination. If some philosophy is included within magicians' gestures, we can probably say that it would be a philosophy of the imagination. What Essertier calls the "lower forms of explanation," taking magic as the principle item, have the imagination as their foundation.[20] As he understood it, in the imagination the emotional and the representational are one, and emotion (*émotion*) and image (*image*) reflect one another without end and without separation.[21] But this logic of imagination, as Essertier considers it, is a primitive logic merely in the explanation of lower forms or merely in its nascent meaning even if it always exists strongly among civilized people, and the issue is whether it is or not a primitive logic in the logical sense.

The classical theory concerning magic is Frazer's theory of sympathy.[22] He outlines the intellectual principles on which magic is based into the following two: the law of similarity and the law of contact or contagion. The former is the law that similar things engender similar things or that the effect resembles its cause, and the latter is the law that all things that were in contact with one another will continue exercising their function reciprocally at great distances even after physical contact had been cut. Accordingly magic that generally takes the law of sympathy as its foundation and is generically called sympathetic magic is distinguished from homeopathic or imitative magic founded upon the law of similarity and contagious magic founded upon the law of contact. In both of these, two kinds of magic, things act reciprocally at great distances through an intimate sympathy, and the impulse is transmitted from one to the other by relying on what we might call a kind of invisible ether—this is not unlike what had been hypothesized in modern science for the same kind of purpose to explain how objects can physically act upon one another through space that appears empty. A familiar example of the principle that similar things engender similar things is that undertaking found in many periods and among many peoples, the attempt to harm or kill enemies by harming or destroying their image. In such cases, it is believed that human beings suffer in the completely same way their image suffers and that they must die when the image is destroyed. And the most common example of contagious magic is the magical sympathy surmised to exist between the human being and some severed part of her body—such as hair or nails. It was thought that the one who obtains someone's hair or nails can work his will upon the owner of that hair or nails no matter how far a place. Hubert and Mauss objected to Frazer's reduction of all magic to sympathetic magic and his regard for sympathy as the necessary and sufficient characteristic of magic. Instead, while stressing, on the one hand, the significance of social conventions or traditions as conditions for magic, they emphasized on the other hand the concept of magic power and stated that sympathy is the path that magic power passes through and is not magic power in itself. This criticism is probably completely just. But on the basis of the restriction they themselves clarified, what they discuss as the laws of magic will probably have significant meaning.[23] The first is the law of contiguity (*loi de contiguïté*) and corresponds to Frazer's law of contact. The simplest form of this concept of sympathetic contiguity arises in the identity of part and whole. Parts possess the value of the whole, and nails or hair represent the human being as a whole. One can make the whole on the basis of the part (*totum ex parte*) without obstructing separation or continuity. Expressed in different words, the personhood of a single being cannot be partitioned and lives as a whole within each of its parts. This formula applies not only to human beings but also to things. The second law is also called the law of similarity (*loi de similarité*) as in Frazer and two of its well-known formulas are that similar things are called forth by similar things (*similia similibus evocantur*) and that similar things are healed by similar things (*similia similibus curantur*). The image's relation to the thing is the part's relation to the whole. Stated differently, this means that the image is completely representative aside from all contact and every direct transport. But contrary to this formula that expresses a general awakening, the other formula that similar things are healed by similar things is unique in confirming that categorization engenders an effect in a determinate direction. From this later form of the law of similarity, we can arrive at the third law, namely, the law of contrariety (*loi de contrariété*). In cases where similar things heal similar things, it means that they engender opposites. In order to raise up contrary things, similar things call forth similar things. The abstract idea of similarity cannot be separated from the abstract idea of contrariety. Here, sympathy (συμπάθεια) becomes equivalent to antipathy (ἀντιπάθεια). Every magic had speculated about inverted things or opposing things, such as fortune and misfortune, cold and warmth, water and fire, freedom and coercion, and so on. Strictly speaking, just as similarity cannot go on without contrariety, contrariety can also not go on without similarity. In the same way, between the laws of similarity and contiguity, one faces the other. Ordinarily magical ceremonies that rely on similarity make use of contact. If the laws of magic are related to each other in this way, what sort of a thing would logic be at its root that is clearly different from the logic of the understanding?

Even if there is a limit to explaining magic merely on the basis of sympathy, we would still have to admit that sympathy has an important significance for magic. Now

Frazer had understood this sympathy as one species of the association of ideas, following the tradition of classical psychology in England, and thought that the magician's logic is simply nothing but a misapplication of the association of ideas. Tylor also states that the foundation of magic is reasoning by analogy or mere association of ideas.[24] We must say that such views are based upon a prejudice that views magic merely as a kind of science preceding science. Not only that, as Delacroix argues, the association of ideas the English School speaks of is itself a kind of magic, an unexplained attraction of the contiguous by the contiguous and of the like by the like, let alone ever explaining magic.[25] Association presupposes the mind, and so cannot explain it. That is to say that in the same way that the various elements of a single identical psychological experience are always tied together there, without the unity of consciousness assembled in the most intimate way, even contiguity would be unable to manifest its effects. We thus cannot conceive the unity of consciousness, at least with respect to magic, as the unity of mere reason. The magical item that on the contrary constitutes the premise for the association of ideas, in fact, would have to be the imagination. In this case, sympathy cannot be just emotive but instead, the emotive and the representative must be one in it. Put differently the subjective and the objective are one in the imagination. According to Essertier, in the psychology of primitive people, their representations escape them very easily and become external to them to be endowed with an objective yet non-material reality. The *image* is immediately real. The *images* they make drag them and absorb them, and they become fused into it. But they thus cultivate the images with their substance and give it a means other than themselves, existing outside of them. The primitive human is what Jaensch calls *Eidetiker*.[26] Distinct from mere representation or mere perception, their mental image is what we ought to call *image eidétique* (Essertier)[27] and in that intuitional image (what Jaensch calls *Anschauungsbild*), ego and non-ego, inner realm and outer realm, the subjective and the objective, are condensed as one. People may say that this is a kind of hallucination, illusion, or falsehood. Although Essertier states that for primitive people such mental phenomena are engendered where the central power in their consciousness is weak, if, as Dilthey discussed the relationship between the imagination of the poet and madness, we nevertheless take that cohesion of the subjective and the objective to be engendered under the stable unity of central power in consciousness—according to Dilthey, the control of mental connections—just as we would have to distinguish between the poet's imagination and madness, it cannot simply be something like a hallucination but must be considered to possess a real significance. The basis for the logic of imagination is the identity of the subjective and the objective. As an identity of opposites, the identity of the subjective and the objective is thus also said to be the basic root of dialectics. In that sense, we can also say that the logic of imagination is dialectical. However, while what ordinarily is called dialectics is the logic of what Hegel calls after-thinking (*Nackdenken*)[28] and ought to be called reflective dialectics, the logic of imagination, by contrast, is creative dialectics. Despite the reflective dialectics, we would presumably have to surmise at its root some sort of imagination, especially the reproductive imagination—as opposed to the productive imagination. We shall later investigate this relationship in detail.

Now we ought to take note that the activity of the imagination in magic is not so free. Hubert and Mauss write:

> [I]t appears that if we reflect upon the freedom presented in the roaming of the imagination, its number ... [the number of possible symbolisms], by contrast, for a given magic, is strangely restricted ... Magical imagination is quite meager in invention and the few symbols it had designed are offered for quite a variety of purposes, [for example,] the magic of knots is used for love, rain, wind, curses, war, language, and many other things. This poverty of symbolism is not due to the individual person for whom his dreams, psychologically, should be free. But this individual is placed in the presence of ceremonies and traditional ideas, which he is not tempted to renew, for he can probably only believe in tradition and there is no faith or ceremony apart from tradition.[29] ... [T]he magician's invention is not free, and the means of his action are essentially limited.[30]

Magical ceremonies and magic as a whole, more than anything else, are facts of tradition. Acts not repeated are not magical. Activities, the efficacy of which the entire social collective refuse to believe, are not magical. The forms of society have been approved by public opinion. In this way Hubert and Mauss state that tradition possesses significance for magic, and correctly stress the social constraints on magic. We had discussed the institutional character of technology, but we can probably say that magic is something far more institutional compared to technology. It is said that magical acts are mixed with acts of law, technology, and religious ceremonies, but the fact that it is systematically tied to legal constraints shows that it is something institutional. It cannot be doubted that magic is very traditional. Nevertheless, even magic that is traditional in this way must have been invented and created by the imagination. If we were to accordingly think in advance, the invention of magic is of course founded upon the imagination, and, just as it is already clear from our discussion in the chapter on institutions, its tradition as well takes the imagination as the foundation. That is, imagination on the one hand is the root of creation and, on the other hand, is also the root of tradition. In the higher cultures that recognize the free activity of the imagination, it is through the logic of imagination that we can first adequately comprehend how the combination of opposites like creation and tradition is possible, and how it makes sense to think there is no real creation without tradition and there is no real tradition without creation. Psychologically viewed, this presumably corresponds to the fact that our imagination includes both memory and phantasy (*fantasy*). Stated philosophically, this must be explained by the fact that in the imagination the natural and the historical are one and the temporal and the spatial are one.

4.

[212] Now if we return to considering what we described above as laws of magic, we can see that they are not only limited to the cases of magic but rather are what we ought to call in general the logic of symbols. The relations of identity between part and whole, identity between copy and thing, identity between similarity and opposition, and so on, stretch across the root of all symbols. Not only that, but we would also have to recognize that what these laws express, in a certain sense, are completely dialectical ideas.

The alchemists possessed what they thought to be the complete formula of their theoretical reflections, a single universal principle that they liked to place before their book of prescriptions. It is the following: "One is all, and all are within one."[31] This principle can also be expressed as follows: "One is all and all were born through this one. One is all and if all did not include all, all would not have been born."[32] Hubert and Mauss explained this in the following manner. All that is within all is the world. Now the world is at times conceived to be a living body and its parts, no matter their distance, are necessarily linked to one another. Therein everything resembles each other, and everything therein touches one another. Presumably, this sort of a magical pantheism (*panthéisme magique*) provides the synthesis of the various laws of magic. Moreover, the alchemist probably could not adhere to this formula other than to provide a metaphysical and philosophical commentary of it. Alchemists instead adhered even more to other formulas parallel to it, such as that nature conquers nature (*natura naturam vincit*) and so on. Nature, by definition, is what can be discerned within a thing and at the same time within its parts or, put differently, that which founds the laws of contiguity. And this can be simultaneously discerned in all beings of the same species as what founds, thereby, the laws of similarity. And further in enabling one thing to act upon a thing opposing it but of the same species, it founds the law of contrariety.[33] As we already wrote, we may recall that in Greece, the magician received the name of the physicist (φύσικος). Nature (φύσις) can be determined as one kind of material, non-individual, changeable spirit, or a kind of unconscious wisdom of a thing. In a word, it was something very close to *mana*. According to Hubert and Mauss, *brahman* as the basic idea of Indian pantheism is also something like *mana*, similar to magic power.[34]

The laws of magic are thus synthesized into a species of pantheism, so-called magical pantheism, and take this as its root. The logic of magic arises together with and falls with pantheism. And we can presumably say that all pantheistic thought, no matter how dialectical it appears, is essentially magical. Magical pantheism or magical idealism (*Magischer Idealismus*) is based, as can be seen in its representative Novalis, on "the magic of imagination" (*Magie der Einbildungskraft*).[35] And we should add that in discussing the logic of imagination we are not attempting to support pantheism philosophically. Even if the logic of pantheism belongs to the imagination, it is not a pure and essential figure of the logic of imagination but rather a degraded figure of it. Just as magic had to be replaced by technology, the philosophy of magic has to be replaced by the philosophy of technology. We cannot even say that the true logic of symbols is magical or pantheistic. And even what is called dialectics in its pantheistic roots is not truly dialectical but an organism theory that must instead be adequately distinguished from dialectics. We think that clarifying the fundamental concept of magic will be helpful in clarifying the essence of pantheism and its limits. So let us now consider the foundation of magic, especially from this perspective.

What is conceivable first is that the concept of nature [自然] is the fundamental concept of such pantheism. It is said that the concept of nature itself originally signified something magical. Therein the imagination is sunk within nature. Every pantheism essentially is a "natural philosophy." Joel states that natural philosophy was born of the spirit of the *mystic*,[36] but we must regard this *mystic* to be the imagination sunk within nature. To the extent that we want to avoid pantheism, the philosophy of imagination would have to be thought of as a philosophy of history, and not a philosophy of nature, for that reason. But in that case, nature and history are not abstractly opposed to one another; rather the logic of imagination is instead conceivable, fundamentally, where nature and history are one. It is not that history is seen as nature but must instead be that nature is seen within history. Next, the fundamental concept of magical pantheism is the concept of magic power (*pouvoir magique*) (here again we ought to recollect the relationship between the two ideas of φύσις and δύναμις). Magic power is an "impersonal power," but it is a mystical power rather than a mechanical power. Just as magic does not concern laws, it also does not concern individual things. Therein the particular is not something that opposes the universal at all, but instead is classified within the whole as a part and constitutes mutually a mystical connection. The scientific spirit distinguishes between a moment of contingency and a relation of necessity. Yet "for primitive human beings, there is and can be no accident. Accident signifies an undecided separation between two terms, the deference of affirmation. The consciousness of primitive people dislikes this in the same way it dislikes doubt. Accident is nothing other than another figure of doubt."[37] For their psychology, which refuses to recognize chance,[38] is not skeptical, and is extremely affirmative rather than critical, there is no opposition between the individual thing and the universal, and the independence of the individual is not acceptable. Everything is necessarily continuous. Not admitting the individual thing's independence in this way is a feature of pantheism. Although people usually say that science seeks abstract universal laws and does not admit the independence of individual things, in fact, science starts from where it admits the independence of individuals. The laws scientists posit are always prepared for alteration, taking it as an opportunity once they discover individual phenomena, not in harmony with it. We can say that the particular standing in opposition vis-à-vis the universal is the motive power for scientific research. Considered in this way, concreteness that appears to belong to pantheism, to the extent that it ends in the negation of the individual's independence, is instead abstract; and science that is said to be abstract is instead concrete. The principle of universal connection lies at the root of magic, but it does not reach particular connections as in science. And magic did not become scientific in response to estimating the particular. In short, magic in becoming particularized approached, on the one hand, technology, but on the other hand, it came to approach science as it came to speculate on and observe concrete "properties" (*proprietas*)—so-called secret power (*virtus occulta*). Magic is not to be compared with science for the reason it contains abstract laws of sympathy. Rather we can admit a scientific character in magic for having inquired into the concrete qualities of things. Magic was enabled to arrive, due to the concept of property, at the origin of scientific laws, in other words, the real origins of necessary positive relations believed to exist among determined things. The logic of imagination, as it becomes purified from its magical figures, becomes the logic of individual things. Even if we view magic itself sociologically, individual consciousness in magic becomes absorbed into the collective consciousness. In order for science to be established, the independence of individual consciousness had to have been necessary.

Of course, science did not develop directly from magic. Science is tied to technology rather than to magic. It would, however, probably be erroneous to think there exists a linear relation of development between technology and science. Moreover, we already had to take note here that imagination holds a significant meaning for the development of science. According to Essertier, science is established under three conditions.[39] The first condition is the preliminary elaboration and analysis of experience by means of the activity of the intellect. The second condition is "the leap of the imagination [*saltus de l'imagination*] which liberated the human being from raw empiricism [*empirisme brut*]." And the third condition is the independence of individual and personal thought from impersonal collective thought. We will probably investigate each of these points gradually. Magic was something like technology. It was thus something made so that the human being can go on living by adapting to the environment. But in magic this adaptation, borrowing Delacroix's words, is a kind of hyperadaptation (*hyperadaptation*).[40] Desire coerces the world for the means of ceremony believed to possess the efficacy of omnipotence. The subject gets ahead of reality and this anticipatory attention produces a hallucinatory *image*. This can explain the coincidence between the ideas of power and the environment that we previously asserted to be a characteristic of magic. In this way there is an extensive "anticipation of experience" (*anticipation de l'expérience*) within magic and, as an excess of subjectivity beyond objectivity, it is called hyperadaptation. Yet, the imagination's anticipation of experience is always required not only in the case of magic but in the everyday lives of civilized man. Above all, in cases where sudden change occurs in the social environment we inhabit, we require the anticipation of experience that adjusts to this environment. When that happens by means of the anticipation of experience the environment indeed occurs not as the environment itself but rather as its *image* and the means of adaptation in relation to the environment more or less becomes magic. And the anticipation of the environment has an important significance, not only for magic but for science as well. We can say that for the sake of the *image* engendered as the anticipation of experience by means of imagination, magic can approach science. Therein lies the imagination's leap from raw empiricism and the *Idee* can be born there. Man's superiority lies in his ability to roam among the fanciful and the absurd. Perhaps this is humanity's greatest superiority in relation to animals. Imagination rather than reason shapes the first difference between the human being and animal. Animals primarily live amidst the immediate impressions of their senses. The memory images of these sensations are weak and easily extinguished and do not possess importance in their lives. Human beings, however, live not only in the narrow world of present sensations but in their own broad world where the mind is ceaselessly visited by clusters of vivid figures of past sense impressions. It is within this broad and mysterious land of waking dreams that human beings begin their human career. These waking dreams probably owe much of their content to sleep dreams. It appears that some of the lower animals also have dreams in their sleep, like human beings. But human beings are different from the lower animals, probably, in being able to remember their dreams. And by retelling it human beings can add improvements to it. Whether sleep dreams or waking dreams, they are much too vivid to not tell. And further, to retell them gives certain emotions a so-called second impression and relief. In the case of animals only the primary expressions of emotions are discovered amongst their actions in the world of sense impressions. In the case of human beings, not only are the primary expressions of trust, anger, love, hate, curiosity, wonder, and so on, discerned amongst their actions occurring within the world of sense impressions, but their secondary, and dramatic, expressions are discerned in adventures and actions within the world of dreams. The human being at first owes a lot to such love of stories. By retelling, and also listening to, stories about the world of dreams, human beings learn to think. In the world of dreams, they escape the solid facts of the world of sense experience to freely move, can behave without obstruction by their abilities, can call forth figures and tie them together as they wish, and thus in this so-called amusement they discipline the ability that later manifests as the faculty of constitutive thought in its application to the world of sense experience. "It is better to have an erroneous *idée* than to not have any at all."[41] A craftsman, to the extent that he is a craftsman, does not arrive at the *Idee*. Essertier states: "The creation of the gods was an event more decisive for the development of thought than the manufacture of instruments. The true opening of the intellect, myth made the arrival of science possible."[42] Nevertheless, what includes science is not only magic but rather we may consider technology as essentially tied to science. If so, is it only magic, only this mythical technology, that relates to the imagination while technology itself possesses no relationship to the imagination? We must now investigate the relationship of technology to the imagination by entering into technology in its original meaning.

5.

[221] It is certain that there is an intimate relationship between science and technology. Needless to say, technology has science as its foundation, but science also has developed by being stimulated by technological themes. As the progress of science made the progress of technology possible, the progress of technology also made the progress of science possible. But no matter how intimate the relationship is between the two, it would be inconceivable that they are tied in a linear fashion. The thinking human (*homo sapiens*) is not something that directly comes out of the craftsman (*homo faber*). Between science and technology there is the same sort of opposition that generally occurs between theory and practice. What generally mediates opposites like theory and practice is the imagination. Just as the mediation of the imagination is required to move from technology to science, the mediation of the imagination is required to move from science to technology. Imagination is required at the root where a dialectical relationship that is the unity of opposing things can be considered. There must be the logic of imagination at the root of what is ordinarily called dialectics and the latter is a reconsideration of the former. There must be an intuition at the root of logic. And this intuition, instead of being something merely irrational, must in itself be something containing an intelligible, logical meaning.

To move from technology to science there presumably needs to be the leap of the imagination, just as Essertier argues. It is not that workers who use instruments seek to construct a theory by comprehending its mechanism. Espinas states:

> Surprisingly, neither the tool nor even the machine always obliges the worker to be clearly aware of the ends realized by their means, or of the ability of man to

indefinitely vary his procedure ... The tool is one with the worker, a continuity of the body's organ, its projection to the outside. While using it like extended limbs, the worker almost never attends to its structure or ever considers how its various parts are well adapted to that purpose. The labor achieved by its help hence can be seen as even more natural.[43]

For the worker the instrument is an "unconscious projection" (*projection inconsciente*) of organs and a continuation of the body. The machine, of course, is not the projection of the very tip point of the limbs but is a "projection of the joints that permits the execution of a certain movement with the exclusion of other movements by combining the limbs to one another and to the torso and reciprocally operating them." The craftsman was a technological expert who used instruments as extensions of his body without reflecting on their structure or dynamics and who for a very long time had no knowledge of mechanics. Without comprehending the gigantic trajectory of his invention, neither did he think of admiring it. The human race used that first machine for a long time without holding a trifling of pride concerning it and without thinking of inventing other things from it. The inventor of the machine remained anonymous or rapidly sunk into the abyss of oblivion. It was thought that the means they employed to realize their work, in many cases, did not deserve to be remembered. Myths about the heroes of cultural development appeared late and it was not the case that all inventions received the honor of becoming myths. Essertier writes: "Technology implicitly contains science but cannot engender it to the extent that it adheres to sense experience. Magic deliberately escapes this experience, but the arbitrary connections it establishes between phenomena can never yield any truly positive knowledge regarding the phenomena. In a word, the former is within truth, but it is not free, while the latter is free but perpetually in error."[44] Just as for magic to become science it must be restrained by experience, for technology to become science it must be freed from the restraints of experience. We will probably especially examine the relationship between experience and the imagination which will become an issue here later in the chapter on "experience." Through leaps of the imagination, an instrument becomes an *Idee*.

However, even if it is certain that technology is not free nor conscious, is it because, as Essertier thinks, technology adheres to sense experience and ends with the immediate satisfaction of desires? Even if it is certain that the craftsman employs instruments as extensions of his body and that the labor making use of instruments is thought to be "natural," in order for instruments to be used in this way, the instruments had to have been invented and given. And the invention itself of the instruments clearly cannot arise from sense experience [alone]. This invention requires imagination. Even in cases where natural things are utilized as they are as instruments, such discoveries presumably already require a leap of imagination. And the fact that the invented instrument is used unconsciously is fundamentally based on the institutional quality of technology rather than being based on the empiricism of technology. Technology comes to possess its meaning by becoming habitual and the instrument becomes a part of the body, and its labor can be natural by becoming habitual in this way. It is noted that the progress of technology is discontinuous. "What is conspicuous in the order of positivist inventions is its discontinuity, its sporadic emergence in a certain period, separated by long intervals of non-activity, standstill, and even retreat."[45] It is conceivable that the progress of science is discontinuous—although to think so requires the addition of a limitation—but in contrast, the fact that the progress of technology is conspicuously discontinuous is due to its habitual, traditional, and institutional qualities essential to technology. It is also noted that there existed a certain kind of relationship between technology and religion. It is said the first machines were often offered to the gods and were sanctified in ceremonies prior to being used for their utility. This fact speaks to the *demonisch* quality of the technological inventions of human beings, and at the same time shows that this combination with religion secured the institutionalization of technology. In order for science to become technology it has to rely on the mediation of the imagination, but as science becomes technology it also becomes natural. The *Idee* is generated within nature by means of the imagination, and so-to-speak returns to nature by means of the imagination. Imagination is what ties together nature and history. This is the reason why genius is said to be something like nature.

Now, as Espinas states, the instrument belongs to the subject as an unconscious projection of the organ, an extension of the body. But, needless to say, it is not simply subjective but on the other hand thoroughly belongs to the object. That is, the instrument is subjective and at the same time objective. As Noiré clearly analyzes, "the peculiarity of the tool [instrument] and its utterly immense significance is in the fact that it is a part of the subject and at the same time still an object."[46] If the fundamental meaning of technology is that it makes instruments, the essence of technology must therefore be to mediate between subject and object. In technology, the human becomes a thing, and the thing is made human. While activity through the body's organs is immediate, by contrast, activity through instruments is something mediated. As something subjective and objective, the instrument can mediate everything subjective and objective in technology. We can say that if we are to consider that in order to mediate the subjective and the objective in technology, an instrument that is already subjective and objective is necessary, for such an instrument itself to be made as something mediated between the subjective and the objective, there must already be at its root a subjective and objective imagination. This point is the issue we need to enter and investigate.

The single fundamental concept in every technology is the concept of form (形). Everything made by technology possesses form and technological activity itself is endowed with form. To the extent that we see form, we can see technology. We may consider nature as also technological because all things with life possess form. We can view the form of living things, as evolutionists say, as an adaptation of living things to the environment and for that reason as engendered unities of the subjective and the objective. To that extent we can see therein the technology of nature. And according to us, wherever we can see forms, we can see the activity of the imagination, and the logic of imagination is a logic of form. The philosophy of the imagination is not something that tries to cultivate a path through an undetermined fantasy, but instead has its center of gravity in form, the most determined thing. The difference between science and technology primarily returns to this point as well even if it is untrue that form is not problematized in science at all. In technology, scientific knowledge must become forms. This discovery of form is founded upon imagination. It is said that technology anticipates science. Even if that is certainly so, science cannot enter technology unless knowledge becomes form. It is said that technology presupposes the subjective aims of human beings along with presupposing the objective knowledge of science. Technology is something that endows human volition with a thingly form. It conjoins the thing's objective causal relations to human subjective aims. However, if man's desires or will were something merely subjective, how can it be combined with the thing's objective relations? In that case, what is called the purpose would presumably already have to contain an objective determination. The purposive cause in technology, as Aristotle thought, must be εἶδος (form). Unless desire or will becomes form, it cannot enter into technology. In this way imagination is indeed desire or will that becomes form. In the imagination the subjective slips out of the subject by becoming form. While animals are slaves to the organs of the body, human beings can control instruments and, through this, be masters of bodily desires. If the principle of science is causality, the principle of the will is teleology. We can probably say, as Engelhardt argues, that the essence of technology is the unity of the doctrines of causality and teleology, taking technology as what synthesizes the objective causal relations of things and the subjective aims of human beings.[47] The philosophical issue of how to harmonize causality and teleology, taken to be the most difficult since ancient times, has actually been solved in technology. Moreover, that which solves this is neither the understanding nor the will but instead the imagination. Teleology is not simply the reverse of causality. The aim in technology would have to be *eidos* (form). Besides, *eidos* is not something objectively given as Aristotle thought but born of the inventor's imagination. Technology is creative and through it, the world achieves new form. We can recognize the imagination's transcendence where its free product possesses objectivity. The transcendence of human existence is not something mystical. Rather the transcendence of human existence lies in the clear fact that what is produced by the human is utterly objective. Imagination is not simply something subjective at all. Rather, what is subjective in the imagination's free operation goes beyond the subject by becoming form. We can recognize the logic of imagination in the very technological acts of human beings, activities that do not end with phenomena within consciousness. If we take human freedom to actually exist within the unity of causality and teleology, and moreover where this unity is creative, the issue of freedom apart from the imagination would be inconceivable. The issue of freedom is not real apart from the issue of creation and creation is not something that occurs merely within consciousness. In order to clarify such relationships further, we need to consider here what we mean by form in greater detail.

6.

[230] The logic ordinarily called formal logic today originally was not simply formal at all but rather one species of what we call the logic of form. It is something that was established by taking as the foundation Greek ontology that saw *idea* or *eidos*, meaning form, to be reality. This sort of logic of form had to become so-called formal logic due

to its restriction to a certain philosophical view concerning form along with the fact that it was moved to an ontological foundation distinct from that of Greek ontology. Consequently, we are now able to consider a logic of form different from formal logic, due to the fact that there must be a perspective on form different from that of Greek philosophy.

In Greek philosophy, form was thought to be unchanging and eternal. According to Plato, *idea* neither arises nor ceases but is always "one and the same" (ἕν τε καὶ ταὐτόν). In this way the ontology of the eternally self-identical form constitutes the root of the principle of identity or the principle of contradiction in formal logic. But how is this if we take form to be historical and changing? Modern evolutionary theory, by illustrating the alteration of species, has already overturned the thought that takes form to be eternally unchanging. *Species* originally meant form. The fundamental concept of history is the alteration of form, namely, *transformation* (*Metamorphose*). Without the genesis, development, and vanishing of form, history is inconceivable. Aristotle saw things in their movement but did not think that forms themselves are generated and disappear. If we take form to be what changes, Aristotelian logic cannot but reach an impasse.

Form, on the one hand, is form that is settled, unmoving. Form is thoroughly spatial and without its spatiality form would be inconceivable. But on the other hand, form is temporal as what becomes and develops. Of course, there can be no form where there is only movement and no rest. Rather form is the unity of becoming and being, *Idee* and flow. Form is temporal and at the same time spatial, spatial and at the same time temporal, movement qua stillness, stillness qua movement. As such a thing, form is a living form and is historical. If formal logic is a logic of form, we can say that dialectics is also a logic of form. The conversion of categories in dialectics manifests the conversion of form. Dialectics is a logic of historical form and historical form, in the sense of being temporal qua spatial and spatial qua temporal, is dialectical. Even if we say that formal logic is a logic of form, it is abstract. Every living form, as something dialectical, manifests endless tension and this tension is nothing but life. Form manifests the tension of life and the tension of life cannot be sought other than in form. Bergson also states that life is tension, but a defect in his philosophy lies in the point of viewing life as pure flux[48] while not considering what we call form.

Now if we take form to be dialectical and changing, form presumably would not be something like a mere *Idee*. Even if we take the *Idee* as a single form, he provides no explanation of how, in that case, one form is dialectically generated and develops from another form. Form as something dialectical must be that which is born of matter or nature rather than from an *Idee*. However, form, originally, is no mere matter, but is the unity of matter and spirit, the *pathos*-element and the *logos*-element. As such a thing, form is not involved in pure thought, but rather involved in imagination. Form is essentially *image* rather than *idée*. It will be said that the *idée* is something abstracted and fixed out of an *image* by thought. At its source, the logic of form must be a logic of imagination rather than a logic of thought. Greek philosophy that saw form as eternally unchanging conceived the *idea* as an object of pure thought. However, this way of thinking in classical philosophy was itself in fact something of an intuitional and plastic quality.[49] It would be impossible for the thinking of form to not be intuitional in some way. Thought was something intuitional even for Descartes, who is considered the founder of modern rationalism. It was under the influence of the philosophy of *Aufklärung* that thought, and intuition came to be violently separated. We shall deal with Kant in detail later. But while in his first *Critique* he considered the unity of the imagination as what synthesizes intuition and thought, eventually in his third *Critique* he expanded what the Wolffian school called the logic of imagination into a critique of the faculty of judgment, and this had a great impact on the development of German idealism. Hegel's dialectic is something we ought to call a logic of historical form, but the intuitional character of this dialectic is also noted.[50] That dialectics in this way contains an intuitional character suggests that, at its root, it is not a mere logic of thought but a logic of imagination, that dialectics ordinarily considered is a retrospective dialectics—the importance of reconsideration [retrospection] will probably be again made an issue—and not a creative dialectics. In this point there is much that we can learn from Goethe's thought that was a philosophy of form. Although the classical logic of Greece was a logic of form, as shown in Plato's doctrine that the cognition of the *idea* is recollection, it was not a logic of creation. Hegel's dialectics, by regarding form as historical, developed the Greek logic of form, but it was also limited by remaining in the standpoint of contemplation and not taking the standpoint of practice or creative action. The fact that the logic of form up to now was not seen as a logic of imagination is related to the fact that philosophy had taken the standpoint of contemplation and not the standpoint of action. In art as well it is in relation to creation, not contemplation, that the imagination became a real issue. If every act possesses the meaning of production and hence of expression, and form is what is formed in such acts, then the logic of form would have to be a logic of imagination.

Dilthey and others have clarified that Hegel's dialectics was not a logic of mere thought but a logic of life. More than anything dialectics is a logic of life. Nevertheless, even if dialectics is a logic of life, it would presumably be inconceivable if life was mere flux and not something that makes form. As something that makes form, life is technical. To the extent that not only human beings but nature makes form, we can view it as technological. We can probably also say that human beings only continue what nature accomplishes. In discussing genius in art, Séailles states that genius is not something mystical but rather nature itself is the genius.[51] "Thought continues life [*la pensée continue la vie*], it has the tendency of assimilating and organizing everything it soaks up within. We can correctly define it qua life of the body as 'creation.'"[52] In order to comprehend genius, it would be good to study this creative power in all of its stages.

> A fundamental law ties thought to life, that is, the tendency to organize and bring the many to one and diversify the unity by gathering together elements it can arrange around it; the rebirth of sensations within the *image*, and the intimate relationship of the *image* to movements realizing this. Nothing more is needed to explain genius. Art is the necessary consequence of the life of *images* in the spirit.[53]

Séailles writes that genius, far from being a miracle, is the most universal fact of inner life. We can probably say that this sort of creative power that can continue nature within spirit is imagination. Ribot considered the inventor's imagination and instinct as analogous and, according to him, instinct "is one equivalent form of the creative faculty" (*une forme équivalente de la faculté créatrice*). Moreover, he regarded this creative faculty as manifesting in 1) the physiological process (the development of the embryo), 2) the psycho-physical process (instinct), and 3) the psychological process (the creative imagination).[54] Ribot states:

> In the higher level, which is properly psychological, the starting point is the guiding *idée*, the ideal of the artist, the scholar, and the mechanic. The mechanism of development is identical to that of the embryo or instinct. Whether the mother *idée* [*idée mère*] appears at once or is the result of latent labor, the primitive elements are always somehow analogous to the embryo or instincts.[55]

I do not completely agree with Ribot and Séailles. However, even in their views, we can recognize the creative logic of imagination already working within nature as well. To the extent that natural life can be viewed as technological and as making form, it follows the logic of imagination. Everything with life is in an environment and life makes form from its technological adaptation vis-à-vis the environment. Just as we already discussed before instinct is also one way that life adapts to the environment. To the extent that technology is something that makes form, we presumably cannot view technology as a mere means. Form is what life gives to itself and through this life is life. While life is regulated by the environment, the point that it makes form on its own even while being regulated by the environment proves life's autonomy. We can also interpret the basic concepts of Aristotle's ontology as being elucidated from what has been made by technology, which he had conceived of form as pre-existing and did not view them as being born from within the process of technology itself.

As already mentioned, nature is also technological as something that makes form. We can say that the history of nature is a history of the *transformation* of form. The form possessed by living nature is made by relations of adaptation between subject and environment. Human technology as well basically means adaptation between subject and environment. Through technology, human beings make their own, society's, and culture's forms, and by altering these forms they go on making new forms. The forms [形式], needless to say, of culture, of human acts, and the various institutions of society as well, are all form [形]. Human history is also the history of *transformation* (the alteration of form). Natural history and human history are united in the concept of *transformation*. What is conceivable at their ground is technology. Pacotte writes: "Technology continues the work of nature" (*La technique continue l'oeuvre de la nature*).[56] Aristotle as well already said, "technology on the one hand completes what nature could not accomplish, and on the other hand imitates nature" (ὅλως τε ἡ τέχνη τὰ μὲν ἐπιτελεῖ ἃ ἡ φύσις ἀδυνατεῖ ἀπεργάσασθαι, τὰ δὲ μιμεῖται).[57] Technology appends to the body's organ an instrument similar to the body but independent of it. Technology takes up the construction of the cosmos again at the point where nature abandoned it. Moreover, the foundation for all technology is the motions of our body and this body itself was also originally something technologically formed. If we take human technology as continuing the technology of nature in this way, human history and natural history must be grasped in a unified manner in contrast to their abstract distinction made by the humanist way of thinking.

7.

[238] It is said that the essence of technology is invention. Any technology, if we return to its origin, was an invention. "Invention" is distinguished from "discovery." As expressed in the words *discover, entdecken, découvrir*, discovery means to take out what has been covered, to find out what was hidden, not known. Even if what is discovered is said to be new, essentially it has to be something that was already there. It was only that we could not see it prior to discovering it as it was covered. By contrast, invention means to produce something new, something that had not existed. Although both speak of the new, there is the distinction that while invention makes a thing exist, discovery instead makes a thing known. That is, invention is creation and discovery is revelation.[58] "Discovery adds to our knowledge, and it belongs to the domain of science. Invention gives us a new relief, and new resources, and it belongs to the domain of technology."[59] Moreover the two words are ceaselessly employed with confusion, and this is not something utterly without reason. Discovery and invention not only mutually anticipate one another, but there are many cases where a single occurrence has the meaning of discovery as well as of invention, and invention at a certain point is also discovery and discovery is also at a certain point invention. Nonetheless, akin to how science and technology are distinguished, the two can be logically distinguished. While we consider what has been discovered to originally be something that was already there, to "already be there" in this way entirely is the fundamental character of what is objective, and hence we can speak of discovery as objective cognition [客観的認識] or cognition of an object [対象的認識]. However, invention is involved in production. There is no invention without cognition, and although it is certain that invention is accompanied by cognition, at its basis invention is something belonging to production or creation. For that reason, we must say that invention demands that we grasp it as itself from the standpoint of action or practice. What sort of thing is the "logic of invention" that Leibniz once dreamed of and that has been much ignored until today?

What is called formal logic is the logic of the cognition of objects. As such a thing, already we can probably not regard it as a logic of invention. If we borrow Le Roy's words, "classical precepts primarily teach us how to go about verifying the accuracy and rigor of a demonstration once completed and to control the experimental or theoretical commodity after it comes out of the factory, where it was manufactured . . ." and nothing more.[60] It only offers a standard after the fact. One must grasp this in the movement of that process itself. Put differently, discursive-thought (*pensée-discours*) is not the issue but rather active-thought (*pensée-action*). A certain critical-thought (*pensée-critique*) is not the issue, but creative-thought (*pensée-créatrice*) is the issue. But active thought or creative thought is intuitional but not separated from sensibility. Though we can say that any kind of invention always possesses the character of an artwork, neither its psychology nor its logic can be grasped from the standpoint of mere enjoyment. "Every inventor is a man of action, a practitioner. His thinking hardly resembles that of a passively contemplative aesthete or an ideological critic except in fleeting episodes."[61] He thinks like a man of action. Though like a man of action, his position is thoroughly that of a scientist. But how is it possible for someone who is a thinker to think like a man of action? In order for opposites like thought and action to be tied together, mediation by imagination is required. For a thinker to think by taking the standpoint of an actor while remaining a thinker, and for an actor to act by taking the standpoint of a thinker while remaining an actor, is possible through the mediation of imagination. Le Roy also claims that imaginative intuition is required for all cases and that the intuitional *image* is the *idée* that is the mother of all inventions. "People discern it [the intuitional *image*], as the dynamic principle of analysis or as the completion of synthesis, in every true root and end of creation. Only that is actually feasible."[62] No matter how much a relatively significant thought must enter into a pathway to invention, imagination is there at its beginning and end. Needless to say, I cannot agree with the entirety of Le Roy's Bergsonism. Imagination, as something mediating between *pathos* and *logos*, stands at the root of invention. And imagination, as producing form, stands at the end of invention.

We can distinguish between three moments concerning technology in a particular sense, namely, the technology of mechanical instruments. First the cognition of natural laws must be expected. People cannot engage in technology while violating natural law. No matter how nature moves according to that law, it does not engender instruments from within itself. Thus, with a glance, we can distinguish between what naturally exists and what was made by technology. Technology is the synthesis of objective laws and subjective aims. But furthermore, such a synthesis would have to be realized by real changes in things. Technology produces a certain technological form by actually changing things. If, among these three moments, we take the first to be the objective, the *logos*-element, and take the second to be the subjective, the *pathos*-element, technology searches for the synthesis of the objective and the subjective, the *logos*-element and the *pathos*-element. This synthesis, reaching the third point, is realized in a certain technological form. Therefore, as stated before, the issue of technology is an issue of form. Nevertheless, form is not an item of mere *Idee* (*logos*). Instead, as known from its source, we can say it is the unity of the *pathos*-element and the *logos*-element, the unity of the subjective and the objective, and hence is essentially something dialectical. We can presumably understand this dialectical character of form from the next point. The cognition of natural laws that we anticipate as the first moment of technology is by nature something logical and thus, in its essence, universal. But the human setting of ends, as the second moment, has a practical meaning. In practice or action, there is no such thing as universal practice or universal action but always only individual, concrete, particular practices or actions. Hence in the sense that technological form manifests the unity of the logical and the practical, unity of the universal and the individual, we can regard them as dialectical.

Desauer saw that philosophically the issue of technology is an issue of form. And from there he arrives at the idea of the "transcendental essence of technology."[63] According to Dessauer, it is an extremely significant fact that there exists only a single best solution to each primary problem in technology. For example, bicycles first appeared as a variety of shapes, but as they became perfected, they were consequently unified in a single form. When the technological construction for the same end appears to be various, the main reason is in the fact that the aim, at a glance, was not as singular in meaning, or the solution was still incomplete. The various models of automobiles all have the same main purpose but differ in their secondary purposes. There are one-seater cars and there are multi-person cars, there are cars to ride within town and there are long-distance cars, there are open ones and ones not open. And yet if we were to settle on a unified end for all these particular constructions, the number of solutions would by far be determined. In fact, as this sort of effort is made, setting into types or standardization would diminish the diversity of ends and means in technology. If we think hard here, it means that only a singular best solution exists for a single completely cognized and hence determinate end. Perhaps it is because for one end, there does not exist multiple material of equal value, nor do multiple forms of equal value exist. Such singularity of the best solution for all roughly possible unique technological problems means that the solution already exists in its possibility and thus is pre-established. It is not that we constitute the solution but only that we discern that existing thing already prestabilized (*prästabiliert*). The technological human only changes the possible being of form given in advance to the actuality of the empirical world. According to Dessauer, it is there that we can recognize the transcendental essence of technology. Therefore, he states that technological form is something prestabilized by the creator (God) and that exist by transcending experience. In this way he calls the world of unique form planned a priori, "the fourth empire." He is claiming that, in contrast to the world of theoretical reason, the world of practical reason and the world of judgment that Kant attempted to establish in his three *Critiques*, it shapes a distinct fourth empire. Now I do not think that we can support Dessauer's theory like this even if we must admit that the issue of technology involves the issue of form and that in some sense it includes the issue of transcendentality. If technological form exists as planned and inventors merely find them out instead of producing them anew, how is Dessauer able to conceive the essence of technology as especially "invention" and even call it "creation." Every creation must have the meaning of "creation from nothing." There must be some place where the *Idee*-like form comes out from within matter or nature, where the *logos*-element is engendered from within the *pathos*-element. And if we take technology as only trans-empirically discerning the form pre-existing as prestabilized, technology could not be conceived to be something historical. Form does not exist by preceding technological actions; it must be formed by these acts themselves. The idea that technology shapes the fourth empire is also abstract. It is instead important to first focus on the fact that not only artistic activity but even actions we call theoretical and practical, thus all of our activities, have the sense of expressive functions. In short, Dessauer does not understand the fact that technology is something historical and that technological form is also historical and dialectical items. In order to remove such misunderstanding and furthermore understand the transcendental nature of technology, we need to think by starting afresh.

The starting point of the study is always the fact that everything that possesses life is within an environment. Every living body, in all cases, lives within an environment. Even someone like the biologist Haldane considers, not only the external environment, but what he calls the internal environment.[64] Even the likes of sociologist Durkheim speaks of what he calls the inner social environment.[65] As Haldane argues, there exists a relationship where the environment is expressed within the structure of the living body and in turn the living body is expressed within the environment. All technology is birthed from the working relationships between the subject and the environment and, in this way, what we call form is made through technology. Even constructive, mechanical technologies, fundamentally, do not go beyond that relationship. Everything with life is technological, but only human beings possess mechanical technology or put differently, technology not with bodily organs but with what we regard as instruments as the mediation in its proper sense. Human peculiarity is in possessing not only the technology of organs (*Organtechnik*) but instrumental technology (*Instrumentaltechnik*). By means of this, human beings can be intellectual instead of being slaves to desire. The particularity of human technology must be founded upon a certain particularity of the being of the human. According to Plessner, the particularity of human existence is in being eccentric (*exzentrisch*).[66] This means that human beings can stand in a relationship of distance to their environment and even to themselves. While always within the environment, human beings transcend the environment instead of living in coordination with the environment, and at the same time, the environment transcends human beings. As subject the human being transcends the environment and as object the environment becomes something that had transcended man. Transcendence towards the subject is simultaneously the object's transcendence. We need here to focus on the dialectical character of transcendence. The human being is able to look at things objectively only by becoming subjective. Sociologists say that the individual person all the more feels that society, in his/her relationship to the self, is "transcendent"—by contrast, each member of the small tribes of Australia bears the entirety of his/her tribal culture upon him/herself. The civilized human reflects upon this transcendent society and gradually cognizes it more clearly as an "object." We can come to know a thing objectively because the thing is transcendent to us, and things are transcendent to us because as a subject we transcend things. Viewed historically, the reason the independence of individual persons became the cause for the development of science is due to this. To begin with, human beings cannot go on living apart from the environment. For human beings to go on living, who had been separated from the environment, they need to be connected to the environment again. Nevertheless, this connection can no longer be directly executed for human beings. This is where technology is born as the mediator between subject and object. Human technology is thus defined by the transcendence of human existence in the above manner.

But what we must not forget on this occasion is that the transcendence of human existence must be understood in the entirety of its being. That human beings stand in a relationship of distance to the environment originally holds an intellectual significance. Therein the intellect is given its ground. On the basis of the environment's transcendence to us, we can cognize the environment objectively and as an object, and the human is of *logos*. Nevertheless, the object's transcendence is simultaneously the transcendence of human beings towards the subject; and the transcendence is dialectical. The subjective transcendence of human existence fixes even the human quality of *pathos*. Man is transcendent not only in the so-called spirit but also in the body. Human beings are *demonisch*. A *demonisch* being is an emotive being bearing the character of infinity and transcendence. It is needless to say that technology is founded upon the intellectual character of human beings, but this in turn is founded upon a certain character of man's *pathos*, its *demonisch* character. Socrates' intellectual technology would probably be unthinkable without his *demonisch* character. Human living is technological in its every activity and is not limited to the realm of empirical technology. The human demand for technology is universal. The myth of Prometheus presumably speaks of the *demonisch* character of technology. The fact that human *pathos* is *demonisch* indicates the limitless poverty of human existence, and this poverty is derived from the fact that this being, no longer living in harmony with the environment, is subjectively alienated from the environment. This *pathos* that is originary for the human being is what Nietzsche calls the *pathos* of distance. More than anything else the *pathos* of distance is the heart of the warrior. The human being who, as subject, became independent of the environment must live by fighting. Therefore, technology possesses the meaning of tactics for human beings. That Spengler regarded technology as the "tactics of living" is also not without reason. But Spengler erred in one-dimensionally stressing the *pathos*-character of technology or the *pathos*-character of *logos*. Instead, it is necessary to understand the *logos*-character of *pathos*. Technology is something that unifies *pathos* and *logos*. Along with its *demonisch* character, the transcendence of human existence defines its intellectual character. And what unifies *pathos* and *logos* is imagination, and imagination completes this unity in form with the victory of *logos*, the victory of the *Idee*. Imagination is what draws out *logos* from *pathos*. The *Idee* is drawn out of *pathos* by means of the imagination's *Zauberkraft* (magical power). Both *pathos* and *logos* indicate the transcendence of human existence, and the imagination must also do the same. It would be mistaken to think of imagination as merely immanent. Form is something thoroughly transcendent. *Pathos* and *logos* are reconciled in the envisioned [imagined] form, but this reconciliation is something historically dialectical. Form itself is something thoroughly dialectical and historical. History is change from form to form, namely, to *metamorphose*.

8.

[250] As already stated, we can take natural history and human history to be unified in the concept of the alteration of form (*transformation*) as the root of technology. Nevertheless, if we are to look from the standpoint of the alteration of form, we would have to recognize an important significance in descriptive science that had been unfairly disregarded in relation to mathematical natural science. In modernity, mathematical natural science has been taken to be the ideal of scientific cognition and it was thought that we ought to progress towards a mathematically explanatory science while descriptive science remains at a low stage. The claim "to raise history to science" was also made in the same direction. But now if we view natural history and human history as unified with the concept of *transformation* at the root, we can understand the importance of descriptive science itself. Description is originally concerned with the alteration of form. If we consider how technology continues the work of nature, even natural science cannot permit the overestimation of the method of mathematical natural science. Technology is related to the alteration of form. The overestimation of mathematical natural science is based on the separation of the idea of science from technology and that it lacked in general a practical and historical perspective. Technology, originally, takes as its foundation the cognition of natural laws, hence, mathematical natural science. The development of modern technology would be

inconceivable without the development of modern science. However, technology and science are not immediately the same, and technology is what makes things external by converting the abstract universal laws of science into concrete forms. The concept of form is the guide in technology. But, on the other hand, we cannot forget that form is made through the mediation of the cognition of laws. Hegel's logic continues the Greek logic of form and incorporated the concept of history into this, but the mediation of science in his dialectic is insufficient. We can say that Hegel's logic would become actual by taking as mediation Kant's logic tied to mathematical natural science. Just as technological form takes the cognition of natural laws as mediation, the logic of imagination must also take the logic of modern science as mediation. Moreover, the logic of imagination as a logic of form follows the idea of technology rather than science that takes law as its idea. And there is a reason for this. In contrast to how the laws of science are said to be abstract, technological form is always something concrete. What is more, they are not mere particulars but unities of the universal and the particular, things sublating law and science within themselves. And it is thought that the realm of technology is broader than the realm of science, and the human in every activity is technological and is technological even in realms that are at least today not dealt with scientifically. Furthermore, the human race has always been living by means of technology even before the appearance of the idea of science in its proper sense, that is, modern science as technology is older than science and is ancient alongside the human race. Modern science itself was also originally born of technological demands and is technologically utilized. In this way, we can say that the logic of imagination as a logic of form, taking its orientation in technology rather than in science, is an even broader and even more fundamental logic for human culture.

Now technology is born as war against the environment, the war of human beings transcending towards subjectivity. As Spengler says, technology is the tactics of living. However, it would be incorrect to one-dimensionally emphasize merely the combative sense of technology. Technology is not merely a method of combat but rather a method of reconciliation. The human, who has been estranged from nature, joins nature again through technology and returns to nature. Therein we probably ought to understand the dialectical quality of the imagination itself.

The human dominates nature by means of technology. We may say that the desire for such domination or so-called will-to-power is founded on the *pathos* of distance, hence also the subjective distress of human beings. However, domination at the same time signifies cooperation. We cannot even dominate nature without cooperating with nature. The one who attempts to dominate nature must submit to nature. *Pathos* must become *logos*. Furthermore, technology is nothing other than the method of human adaptation to nature. In the sense that technology is adaptation, it is not merely a method of tactics but at the same time a method of reconciliation. Fighting is for the sake of reconciliation. According to Tarde, every invention signifies the adaptation of phenomena: "Invention—what I mean is that which destined to be imitated, because that which remains closed within the author's mind has no significance socially—invention is a harmony among ideas, which is the mother of all human harmony."[67] He says that the true source of all social harmony is in the genius of individual persons. Even viewed sociologically, inventions and thus technology signify adaptation and, for that reason, harmony. However, inventions are also born of contradiction rather than from within harmony. As already stated, Ribot says that the inventor's imagination resembles instinct, but concerning this Paulhan argues that although invention thus continues instinct, on the other hand, it opposes instinct.[68] Invention is, of course, an expression of the harmonious inclination of spirit, but it is not just that. It, more or less, almost always results from a dark struggle of skill. Therein we can, of course, always see the spirit's essential activity of organization. In addition to this, we can see in general the elements that are clearly opposed to instinct and organic life, and for that reason, the invention emerging from there can be characterized as a new state. That is, those elements are mutually opposed and universal harmony results from some sort of strife. Paulhan states that this is the reason why genius or the inventive temperament is compared to imbalance or confusion, or psychotic conditions.[69] Le Roy also stresses the dynamic quality of inventive thought and states that contradiction is the natural environment for invention.[70] Invention operates only in the midst of contradiction. The law of contradiction is, without a doubt, the first principle of logic for any kind of controversy, but he regarded this to not be the case in the logic of invention. But invention, if we borrow Bergson's words, is born from the necessity to stop in the application of the intellect "at the precise point where an all-too brutal logic smashes the subtlety of reality" from the need for "ever new adjustments to ever new situations."[71] In this way, invention must be something dialectical. Invention is the dialectical harmony of contradiction and, at the same time that it is strife, it is reconciliation.

We must, however, be willing to understand the dialectical property of technology by advancing from the dialectical property of the imagination itself. As stated earlier, along with technology being engendered through the estrangement of human beings from nature, human beings reconnect to nature by means of technology and, in a certain sense, return to nature. Tarde talks about imitation and invention as fundamental laws of society, but invention and imitation belong to the nature of technology and, moreover, to the nature of imagination itself. Technology, needless to say, is invention. But not only that, technology is endowed with the inclination to always imitate itself or, put differently, technology is repetitive. Technology comes to possess its meaning by becoming habitual. We already spoke of the institutional quality of technology. And we have also already discussed concerning the relationship between institution and imagination in the chapter on "institution." In this way technology involves imagination, whether as invention or as habit. Furthermore, to become habitual is to become natural. Technology that manifests as an invention returns to nature by becoming habitual. The fact that technology involves imagination both as invention and as habit is founded on the fact that what is called imagination remembers along with being creative. (Just as Tarde considered, memory is also one form of imitation.) For this reason, if, as Tarde argues, invention and imitation are the roots of society, we can presumably say that the logic of society is the logic of imagination. It is necessary to grasp this fact, dialectically and in unity, that the imagination remembers along with being creative. In antiquity, imagination was mainly understood in the sense of memory. By contrast, today especially the creative nature of the imagination is stressed. Many scholars, starting with Ribot, thus mainly discuss the creative imagination. However, we ought to grasp the imagination in the twofold sense, and in its dialectical unity, that it remembers as well as being creative. The nature of technology indeed demands this.

Human activity in its every direction is technological. Not only technology in the merely narrow sense nor only in art as well, but further also in science and politics, needless to say, but even morality is technological. I hope to consider each of these, in each case, later. It is not only that all of so-called culture is technological but man's formation itself is technological. A true person of culture is not simply someone who makes culture but must mean someone whose being-human itself is culture. Paulhan writes that "we invent our personality little by little; we invent ourselves in the same way that we create an artwork or a science."[72] But the personality cannot be formed where there is only invention without imitation. Thus, Paulhan had to continue writing that "each of us is a kind of work, and in the same way as in the development of a fragment of a play or a poem, the *routine*, imitation and invention of its formation is quite unequal among individuals but occupy their respective positions."[73] Moreover imitation cannot be limited to just imitating others but must mean imitation of one's self (to become habitual). If invention is temporal, imitation is spatial. Form is originally something temporal and spatial and personality is also formed by imitation together with invention as one form. What we can think of as merely spatial is not a living form but a dead form. A living form is spatial as well as temporal, that is, it is something dialectical. Now Paulhan says that people not only invent *Idee* but also invent impressions and emotions.[74] If we thus take everything to be inventions, is not only technology but nature in relation to technology or "experience" in Kant's sense also invented? If we can say that experience is also invented, in what sense is this the case? Here we must turn to consider the relationship between experience and imagination. We would like to further clarify here the nature of philosophical logic and the logic of imagination by initiating our study from a new starting point by entering into this problem while reflecting on the meaning of the imagination in Kant's critique of experience and Fichte's science of knowledge.

4

Experience

1.

[258] The word *experience* [*keiken*, 経験] contains a double meaning. First, it signifies something objective. When we speak of experience, we mean something we actually encounter, something objectively given. If we are permitted to speak of illusions and hallucinations as also experience, the fact that something is experienced, even if it is an illusion or a hallucination, would have to be an objective fact. But on the other hand, when we speak of experience it is always related to the (epistemological) subject.[1] Experience is the experience of someone who experiences and would be inconceivable without the experiencing subject. Hence it has the meaning of something subjective. Experience is accordingly something subjective and objective, objective and subjective. What does it essentially mean to say that experience is something subjective and objective? What are the subjective and the objective in this case tied to?

The orthodox theory concerning experience, namely, England's philosophy of empiricism, viewed experience as something psychological and belonging to consciousness. To the extent that every experience is experience related to a subject, this naturally has its reason. But if experience was only of consciousness, it would be something subjective. Nevertheless, the proper impetus of empiricism would have to be where it presumably is positive and empirical. Empiricism would thus probably look for its foundation in sensation. While sensation belongs to consciousness, we regard it as immediately related to things. It is said that the principle of empiricism is the proposition that "there is nothing in the intellect that was not first in the senses" (*Nihil est in intellectu, quod non prius fuerit in sensu*). And yet how can we confirm the objectivity of sensation or ideas? Locke thought that ideas are signs or representations of things. This so-called *representationism* presupposes the simplistic realism of common sense and this premise, more than anything, requires examination. If ideas were the only objects that directly appear to the mind, how can we compare our ideas with their originals and accordingly confirm the agreement between our ideas and the reality of things? What ground do we possess to roughly suppose such an independent world of things? Instead as Hume said, "the mind has never anything present to it but the perceptions and cannot possibly reach any experience of their connexion with objects."[2] "[W]e never really advance a step beyond ourselves, nor can conceive any kind of existence, but those perceptions, which have appear'd in that narrow compass."[3] If experience is something belonging only to consciousness, then for empiricism

Berkeley's proposition that "to be is to be perceived" (*esse est percipi*) would have to be the conclusion. Berkeley writes:

> It is indeed an opinion strangely prevailing amongst men, that houses, mountains, rivers, and in a word all sensible objects, have an existence, natural or real, distinct from their being perceived by the understanding ... yet whoever shall find in his heart to call it in question may, if I mistake not, perceive it to involve a manifest contradiction. For, what are the forementioned objects but the things we perceive by sense? and what do we perceive besides our own ideas or sensations? ... In truth, the object and the sensation are the same thing.[4]

In this way, despite the fact that its original motive was to be positively empirical, in its conclusion it fell into subjectivism and idealism.

Empiricism subjectified the thing called experience. Experience for empiricism becomes a mental state completely permeated with subjectivity. Now, this subjectification is connected to the fact that the philosophy of empiricism took experience to be primarily an issue of knowledge. From the standpoint of knowledge, it is possible that experience is merely a matter of consciousness. In that case, we can probably regard the subject of experience, namely, the knower, to be the mind or consciousness, the so-called subject, and experience to be what is utterly manifest to consciousness or the subject. But once we take the standpoint of action, the subject of experience can no longer simply be consciousness nor can experience simply be phenomena of consciousness. In that case, the subject of experience, namely the actor, must be one with its own body [*jitai*, 自体], and experience, without stopping at being phenomena of consciousness, would have to be events in the objective world. To start, experience always contains the meaning of knowledge. To experience is to know in a certain way. Hence, we cannot take the standpoint of action as something abstractly opposed to the standpoint of knowledge. Instead, the original meaning of the concept of experience must consist where we consider the issue of knowledge also from the standpoint of action. The philosophy of empiricism, indeed, was unable to solve the issue of knowledge by regarding experience merely as something psychological. To see the idea, just as it is, as sufficient, is to take away any cognitive value from it. The impossibility of this perspective is shown by the fact that Berkeley had no choice but himself to withdraw his thesis that identified things with sensation. By simplistically regarding the idea as an idea of a thing and by thinking that ideas are always related to things, Locke admitted the reality of the world of things outside the mind. But from the standpoint of empiricism, we have to say this was incomplete. In either case, to consider things as simply things outside the mind is only possible from the standpoint that regards the subject of experience as merely the knower, namely, the so-called subject of cognition. From the standpoint of knowledge, we can think of the subject as consciousness and things as things outside of consciousness. In this point, materialism, with its claim that the criterion for distinguishing materialism from idealism is whether it admits or not admits beings outside of consciousness, in fact, remains in the standpoint of knowledge analogous to the idealism it rejects, and does not truly take the standpoint of action. From the standpoint of action, the subject is furnished with a body, and the fact that things are outside the subject does not mean that they are simply outside of consciousness but rather must mean that they are outside the self's body. Only as such can we say that the thing is independent. The subject is not simply consciousness but an independent being. That which is the subject of action and the thing related to this subject are together situated in a single world and are each independent beings within this world. Hence experience is a *relationship* between independent beings. As a relationship between independent beings, it is a real relation, and these beings can be related by being situated in a single world.[5] Experience is a so-called encounter between independent beings. The reason why experience was thought to be something merely passive in empiricism was because it remained seen from the standpoint of knowledge. Experience, as a dynamic and active relation, has the significance of an *event*, and in this original sense, it is *historical*. Knowledge as well ought to be conceived not simply as the relationship between consciousness and thing, namely, between the so-called subject and object, but instead as a certain specified relationship between beings. What we call empirical knowledge should not be conceived as the passive state of a conscious self but rather on the basis of the relationship of action between the acting self and the environment. The importance of sensation is also something that we first come to comprehend sufficiently from the standpoint of the acting self. As the apex of the somatic and acting self, sensation is the apex of experience. We ordinarily think of experience and experiment to be somehow distinct, but the word *experience* and the word *experiment* properly have the same etymology and both emerged from *experiri*, the word meaning *to try*.[6] Every activity of man is essentially technological and experience is already a certain experiment. Like experiment, experience means trial through action, and the knowledge attained through acting—by trying and erring, erring and trying—is nothing other than experience.

English empiricism was developed critically in American pragmatism. Critiquing empiricism, Dewey states the following. First of all, in the orthodox view, experience is regarded primarily as a knowledge-affair. But to eyes not looking through ancient spectacles, experience clearly looks like an affair of intercourse involving a living being with its physical and social environment. Secondly, according to tradition, experience is (at least primarily) a psychical thing, infected by "subjectivity." However, what experience suggests about itself is a genuinely objective world that enters into the actions and sufferings of human beings and undergoes modifications through their responses.[7] What we stated above in this way agrees with Dewey's views. Experience is no mere phenomenon of consciousness but an occurrence in the world. It obtains in the active negotiation between ourselves and the environment. On the basis of viewing experience generally in the above way, what kind of relationship would it have with the imagination?

2.

[265] If we easily formulate experience as the relationship between the environment and man, we can probably regard it to be the relationship psychologists speak of

between stimulus and response. This is also the relation between object and subject. Roughly speaking, reality is in the fact of relating, within the "activity of relating" (*activity-between*).[8] Subject and object are equally important in the single process of action, and reality is in their relationship, within the endless development of this relationship. The relation of stimulus and response actively develops and is not mechanical. Every behavior is a behavior within the environment and the environment is a constitutive element for behavior. Although behavior is a response to stimuli from the environment, even when we speak of stimulus it is not at all something merely receptive. Every response is something we ought to call a *recurring response* and is a movement that comes out of and returns to oneself. According to Holt (B.E. Holt), the contraction of the muscles is caused, only in a certain sense, by mere stimulus, and in fact, this muscular activity itself produces in one part the stimulus that causes its muscular activity. That is, when muscles contract, the sense organs in those muscles are stimulated. As a result, there is a nerve impulse transmitted almost simultaneously from the muscles back to the center, thus establishing a recurring response. According to Bok (S.T. Bok), "[t]he reflex arc is the path of stimulations in consequence of a function of the individual itself . . ." Vis-à-vis visual stimulus the animal reacts with a movement that alters its visual stimuli. "Reflex-reaction must alter the perception of the reflex-stimulus."[9] A response arises by means of the stimulus but at the same time the stimulus is altered by this response and hence the response is also simultaneously altered in order to respond to the altered stimulus. The activity of an individual object is aroused only in a certain sense by the stimulus of the environment, for that activity itself helps to produce the environment that causes the individual object's activity. In this way, even the objective circumstance is in fact not merely objective but simultaneously subjective. It is something being made through the reciprocal operations of environment and subject and, as circumstances developing in this way, we ought to call it a holistic situation. Behavior is also something not simply subjective but at the same time objective. It is nothing other than the environment's function. Behavior is not a mere receptive response but at the same time a dynamic activity. The living body responds not only to the environment but instead, responds to the environment *plus* the living body. Every response is a recurring response. The nature of reality is neither in mere subjectivity nor in mere objectivity but where it is subjective and objective. Therein must we conceive the reality of experience as well.

Action and environment are inseparably related in the above manner. The environment makes the action, and the action makes the environment and the two are tied as one. In this way we call our acts *integrative behavior*. Integration is the conjunction that occurs in the relationship between two activities, namely the activity of the subject and the activity of the environment. This conjunction is not a mechanistic synthesis but rather a creative one and, with its occurrence, creates value. Behavior is not merely subjective but is this integrative behavior as holistic behavior. The function of *integration* is a creative principle. Although the environment and behavior reciprocally influence each other, this relationship does not remain a mere reciprocal function but instead, as it is called a recurring response, the behavior as one holistic behavior synthesizes within itself the two activities into one whole. As Bok states, the reflex arc is the path of stimulus received as the effect of an individual object's activity.

The environment operates on man because man operates on the environment. We can here discern the limits of geographical determinism or the climatological-historical view.[10] As a recurring response, action possesses a self-creative coherence. And as a holistic, integrated, behavior it is endowed with form. All of our actions have form. Form signifies wholeness. The fact that actions possess form first means, primarily, that actions arise where they are the activity between subject and environment. If actions were merely subjective, the form of action would be inconceivable. Form is the unification of the subjective and the objective. But the fact that actions possess form means, secondarily, that the synthesis among the activity of subject and environment, on the side of the subject, is indeed engendered where it is integrated in the action itself. Action, in the sense of a recurring response, is something of that nature. The autonomy of action would have to be conceived here as well. The form of action is the expression of its autonomy and if action is not autonomous it would be unable to possess form. To conceive the autonomy of action merely from the subject apart from the environment, as in the philosophy of subjectivism, would be abstract and meaningless. The autonomy of action is nothing other than the self-creative coherence that action possesses as a recurring response. Action, in that sense, in being autonomous possesses form. The action's form is the integrated unity it possesses as an integrated behavior. As such it always includes a relationship to the environment and hence the action's form manifests a functional whole. Now, as already mentioned, experience pertains to action, and experience as such shapes the forms of action. The action's form, more than anything, is first made in experience. As the environment changes, the integrating operation proceeds one step at a time and the so-called *behavior pattern* is formed.[11] Experience, more than anything, is what makes behavior patterns. If we can conceive the relationship between experience and forms in this way, we can go on to conceive from this basis the relationship between experience and imagination. The logic of imagination is the logic of forms. We thus need to analyze the relationship between experience and forms by entering further into it.

The relationship between subject and environment is called adaptation, and anything that has life lives by adapting to the environment. Our actions are behaviors of adaptation. This adaptation, when it is not instinctive or reflexive, is undertaken through a process of *trial and error*.[12] Experience is nothing other than this process of trial and error. Therefore, experience is originally dynamic and, even when we speak of adaptation, it is not at all a merely static relationship. But, on the other hand, if it was only dynamic with nothing static about it, action would be without form and it would also be inconceivable for living things to be furnished with form. The form of living things was actively engendered as the form of adaptation and hence it is functional and not simply substantial.[13] As an equilibrium or so-called *complacency* (harmony), form is engendered where there is something static. Raup sees *complacency* as the foundation of human behavior and states that at its root it is the same as the tendency among physical phenomena towards equilibrium.[14] The fact that adaptation means equilibrium reveals how our acts are not simply active but are passive at the same time they are active and are active at the same time they are passive. Stated differently, this means that our acts must be regarded not just on the basis of the subject but on the basis of the environment as well at the same time as of the subject. The form of action is something subjective and objective. And even when we speak of equilibrium, it is not merely passive but passive by being active and active by being passive, and form displays passivity qua activity and activity qua passivity. We must avoid thinking of a mechanical relation in the word adaptation. The thinking of the psychology of so-called behaviorism is still mechanistic. By regarding the environment as simply objectively fixed and viewing behavior as an adaptation to that environment, it overlooks the fact that my response changes the environment, or rather that the environment plus my response changes the environment, and hence overlooks the fact that adaptation is not an adaptation to the mere environment but rather an adaptation to the environment plus the living body. Bok says that "following reflex and range, reflex and response is the function that actualizes and changes the perception of stimuli." The perception of stimuli is something that is altered by the response itself and response is the response to that perception of stimuli. The action's form is the form of the holistic behavior by corresponding to the holistic environment. As such, form manifests *meaning*. Meaning is the intrinsic functional relation of whole and part. Behavior is its constitutive part when viewed as a holistic environment, and the environment is its constitutive part when viewed as holistic behavior. Adaptation is not a mechanical equilibrium, and we must regard even what Raup calls *complacency* as the integration of behavior. An individual body and the environment reciprocally make each other anew and their relationship is also made anew. The behavior's process of integration is creative. It is said that we adapt to the environment through experience, but this experience is creative and, as Follett states, it is originally a creative experience. The subject's adaptation to the environment is invention rather than adaptation. The action's form belongs to such inventions. When I say that the logic of action is a logic of imagination, I do not mean that one thinks up the form of action in advance with imagination and then acts in accordance with it. I mean rather that action itself follows the logic of imagination. The forms of action are made from within the acts themselves and indeed experience shows this fact. Experience is creation, invention, more than a process of verification. We do not test behavior with thoughts existing in advance. Behavior contains its own test within itself and that behavior is nothing other than experience. Concretely speaking, now, how is this fact that experience is creative in this way related to the issue of imagination?

Ordinarily, we think of experience as belonging to the past. This was also the understanding of the philosophy of empiricism. Regarding this, Dewey states the following as the third point of his critique of empiricism. So far as anything beyond a bare present is recognized by the established doctrine, the past exclusively counts. Registration of what has taken place, a reference to the precedent, is believed to be the essence of experience. Empiricism is conceived of as tied up to what has been or is "given." But experience in its vital form is experimental, an effort to change the given. It is characterized by projection, by reaching forward into the unknown. Connection with the future is its salient trait.[15] It is certainly an error to view experience as simply a connection with the past. But neither would thinking of it as simply a connection with the future escape being one-sided. Experience includes the connection with the past and this is why we call it experience. Experience is what we accumulate and the accumulated is experience. To accumulate experience means to add on to the process of trial and error. Habit is generated from the accumulation of experience. Experience is what Guillaume calls adaptation by trial and error (*l'adaptation par "essais et erreurs"*), and this is a principle form of habit.[16] Habit is a form of equilibrium and according to Raup manifests *complacency*.[17] That form can emerge from experience means that habits are generated from experience. The action's form is made as it becomes habitual. For experience to become habitual is for it to enter the form of memory. But memory belongs to imagination. As seen in Hume's philosophy empiricism recognized an important significance in habit. Moreover, its theory of habit is based on the mechanistic explanation of the association of ideas. Habit is the link or association raised between perception and behavior and is made and intensified by means of repetition. But the linked terms, perception and behavior, are in themselves unchanging, and the doctrine of the association of ideas in empiricism, seeing unchanging "elements" within mental facts, regarded these elements as only gradually composed in a mechanistic manner. But in this it missed an important fact, namely, that perception and behavior are changed through habit. We perceive things completely differently in our intimate environment than when we first encountered that environment. The perception necessary for a behavioral performance is extremely different between the very beginning and very end of its rehearsal. Namely, as Guillaume states, habit engenders a transformation of perception (*les transformations de la perception*).[18] It is usually said that through habit things are made "unconscious," but with these vague words, one neglects an accurate analysis of that transformation. It is not simply that things become unconscious through habit but that, strictly speaking, it generates a change in perception. Everyone says that behavior is changed through habit. But the reason why the important fact concerning the transformation of perception in habit is missed is because one regards them by separating the habit of perception and the habit of behavior and thus fails to comprehend the situation as a holistic situation and the behavior as a holistic behavior. Bok says that reflex and response actualizes and changes the perception of stimuli, but even in the case of habit through condition and reflex, the habit alters perception. Experience does not disappear as something utterly of the past by passing into forms of memory. Instead, the past acts upon the present and memories of the past are alive within the perception of the present. As Bergson states, sensation is tied to memory. Put differently, imagination works within perception and gives it form. We can probably say that recurring responses are memorable ones. Perception also enters into the forms of imagination. Distinguishing organic adaptation and real habit in the relationship between the living being and its environment, in contrast to how organic adaptation is a direct response to biological value, Guillaume states that real habit is the individual's response to the value of a thing's "meaning" (*signification*) resulting from his/her relationship to the thing and from its organization within the field of perception. But that meaning is engendered where memory is active within perception and arises from the conjunction of perception and memory. As Dewey originally stated, experience is not simply a connection with the past but rather with the future. Experience is something active and every act faces the future. Accordingly, what is more primary in experience is anticipation rather than recollection, projection to the future rather than summoning of the past.[19] Experience includes the anticipation of experience. Dewey states that by including an *imaginative forecast of the future*, experience is useful for guidance in the present.[20] Unless it thus contains an imaginative forecast of the future we cannot speak of experience as being creative. But as Dewey recognizes the *imaginative recovery of the bygone* is indispensable in a successful invasion of the future.[21] There is no creation apart from tradition and without creation tradition cannot be born as tradition. Since ancient times, *memory* and *fancy*[22] have been thought to belong to the imagination, but they live within experience by being connected as operations of imagination. The imaginative forecast of the future is active within the imaginative recovery of the bygone and the imaginative recovery of the bygone is active within the imaginative forecast of the future. The essence of experience lies instead where it transcends raw empiricism by means of the imagination. What we call holistic behavior contains the connection of past to future, and the holistic situation must also be likewise.

The essence of imagination is to synthesize and unite and thus to make forms. As Coleridge skillfully expressed, *imagination* is an *esemplastic power*, it is an *esemplastic* (ἐσ *into* + ἓν *one* + πλαστικός *molded, formed*) power, namely, a power that forms into one, brings about the unity of form.[23] Forms of acts are made in experience. But experience in particular means knowledge as well. Action and knowledge are tied together in what we call experience. As we shall discuss later, we can understand this conjunction through the concept of technology. As trial and error, experience is experimental and technological. What we call empirical knowledge is essentially experimental, technological knowledge. Forms are also conceived in knowledge and its most fundamental form is what we call categories. Categories must be forms of reality, not merely forms of knowledge or forms of thought. What we call experience as well means reality and not simply knowledge. It is thought that forms of experience are forms of reality in addition to being forms of knowledge. If the concept of experience is tied to the concept of form in this way, it must be tied to the imagination. It is thought that forms of experience are forms of understanding. In practice, if experience is not just reflexive or instinctive, it must be something related to understanding. If that is the case, what sort of relationship do understanding and imagination have? Spaier writes: "However the deep conviction from which all their works (of Locke, Hume, and their successors) proceed, namely, the conviction that the understanding is identical with the imagination, expresses the very truth."[24] Let us then consider this issue first within the philosophy of empiricism.

3.

[277] The empiricists had deep and firm feelings about the concrete character of thought. They knew that understanding is nothing without sensation. We need to accept this as empiricism's enduring value. But beginning with Hume, the empiricists have taken the stance of atomism. They regarded sensations and ideas as independent elements akin to atoms. What pragmatism as a new development of classical empiricism tries to overcome is this atomism. According to James, to the extent that empiricism attempts to be "radical," we need to consider that we also experience the relationship itself of conjoining parts of experience. For what he calls radical empiricism, the basic

assertion is that the relationship conjoining an experience is itself an experienced relationship, and whatever species of relationship that had been experienced is "real," analogous to anything within the system. As the fourth point of his critique of empiricism, Dewey states the following. The empirical tradition is committed to *particularism*[25] (which is the same as saying *atomism*). Connections and continuities are thought to be foreign to experience, to be by-products of this dubious validity. However, in addition to being an undergoing of the environment, actual experience that is a striving for its control in new directions is pregnant with connections.[26] Certainly experience is not something atomistic and we need to think of relations or conjunctions as themselves also experienced. We need to reject Humean atomism. But on the other hand, as James says that his radical empiricism "... is essentially a mosaic philosophy, a philosophy of plural facts, like that of Hume and his descendants ...," we need to admit a certain plurality belonging to experience.[27] But for him that relationship itself that conjoins the many can be thought to be within experience. Now what posits relations among facts is, more than anything, inference. Accordingly, we would probably need to regard inference as also included within experience. As the fifth point of his critique of empiricism Dewey states the following. In the traditional notion, inference, so far as it is other than a revival of what has been given in the past, goes beyond experience and hence is invalid. But experience itself is full of inferences. There is no conscious experience without inference.[28] If it is as he says, we would have to say that logic is within experience and not something outside of it.[29]

If we follow empiricism, what is given in experience are individual particulars. Hume writes, "'tis a principle generally receiv'd in philosophy, that every thing in nature is individual ..."[30] Accordingly the important issues raised for empiricism are, first, How can universal ideas exist?; and second, How are individual sensations and ideas conjoined in a single relationship? The former is the issue of abstract ideas, and the latter is the issue of categories like substance and causality. Concerning these issues, let us try to examine Hume's theory.

First, how can the issue of abstract ideas be considered? Berkeley claimed that every universal idea is nothing but a particular idea tied to a certain term and that this term, in response to necessity, calls to mind other individual things resembling it by giving this idea a broader meaning. Hume recognized this discovery as extremely valuable and developed it in his own manner. Abstract ideas are thought either to represent every possible particular degree of quantity or quality, or to not represent any particular degree of them. Hume rejected the latter view. It is completely impossible to conceive some quantity or quality without forming a precise concept of its degree. The precise length of a certain line is not different from that line itself and is indistinguishable from it. And the precise degree of a certain quality is not different from that quality itself and is indistinguishable from it. But the former theory, that abstract ideas represent every possible particular degree of quantity and quality, is only possible in cases where the capacity of the mind is infinite, yet it would be absurd for the human mind to be infinite. By altering what we consider here to be absurd, Hume's intention was to show that—even if the mind's ability is not infinite—we can instantly make concepts of any possible degree of quantity or quality no matter how incomplete, at least in a manner suitable to any purpose of reflection or discourse. This theory can be summarized in the following five points: 1. The repeated experience of perceptions of resemblance forms a habit within imagination and, by means of this habit, the occurrence of perceptions of resemblance possesses the propensity to call-forth composite ideas of the past. 2. When perceptions discover resemblance in regard to a certain point, we apply the same term to them despite clear differences in other points. 3. As the consequence of repeatedly using the same term to qualitatively similar perceptions in regard to a certain point, other associations are engendered, that is, associations in the habit of imagination this time associating the abstract term employed in that way and the perception's image named in that way. 4. Once this kind of habit is attained, hearing that term revives a single idea among those objects and makes imagination regard it together with all of its particular circumstances and proportions. In this way, as a consequence of this second association or habit, simply hearing that term is enough to form an image of a certain quality of the present perception by instigating the initial habit. 5. Now the same word has probably been often employed in this way with other perceptions differing in many points from the idea called forth. But this word cannot revive ideas of every individual thing and only, so to speak, touches the mind to revive that habit that we had attained by surveying those things. In cases when the initial habit and the habit of association between that initial habit and the term are both not completely perfect, the mind will probably look over the meaning it conceives and several things in order to understand the range of collection intended to express the general term, unsatisfied with forming an idea of a single individual thing. As these two habits become perfected, however, the consequence of hearing that term calls forth neither all nor even a majority of the images associated with the first habit, but instead only one is called forth together with an "instant *readiness*" or "potency" (*power*) of the imagination to supply the other. In this way, for example when we use the abstract term, *human being*, we do not distinctly depict all of them [human beings] in the imagination. Instead, we are prepared to instantly think of any one of them when prompted in response to present purposes or necessities. To hear a certain word calls forth not only a single individual idea but simultaneously a certain habit, and that habit, in response to the needs of the time, produces any of the other individual ideas. In short, even what we call abstract ideas are in themselves individual, and it is only by means of habit that they become universal in their representation.

In this way the issue of abstract ideas was placed in an intimate relationship with the imagination. It became settled by the imagination and its habits. Hume writes:

> '[T]is certain *that* we form the idea of individuals, whenever we use any general term; *that* we seldom or never can exhaust these individuals; and *that* those, which remain, are only represented by means of that habit, by which we recall them, whenever any present occasion requires it. This then is the nature of our abstract ideas and general terms; and 'tis after this manner we account for the foregoing paradox, *that some ideas are particular in their nature, but general in their representation.* A particular idea becomes general by being annex'd to a general term; that is, to a term, which from a customary conjunction has a relation to many other particular ideas, and readily recalls them in the imagination.[31]

And he says that "there is nothing more amazing than the imagination's instant readiness to suggest those ideas." This "kind of magical faculty in the soul" is "always most perfect in the greatest geniuses, and is properly what we call a genius, [and] ... is however inexplicable by the utmost efforts of human understanding."[32] The *genius* of the understanding is neither in impressions nor in ideas but in the imagination.

Now Hume explained habit as the association of ideas. But as Ravaisson said, it is not the association of ideas that explains habit, rather it is the principle of habit that explains the association of ideas.[33] The law of habit is not mechanical but rather organically alive. According to Hume abstract ideas are nothing but particular ideas tied to a general term, and they become universals in their representation by means of habit. Nevertheless, our language is also originally a product of the imagination and as such our language always signifies particulars at the same time as universals, and on the other hand the imagination is always at work even at the root of our constitution of concepts. Therefore, our concepts are originally universal as well as particular, and particular as well as universal. It is not that the idea and the universal term initially exist separately and then become associated by means of habit. Rather concepts and ideas are originally tied together from the start. Sensations are already included in the forms of imagination. The simple impressions that Hume thought to be elemental are probably nothing more than abstract entities. He considered sense impressions to be "original" in a twofold sense. First, they always precede the ideas corresponding to them. Initially, the impression exists, and then as the impression is *copied* the idea is engendered. One fundamental thesis of his philosophy is that "all of our ideas are copied from our impressions." Second, the impression is complete in itself without containing any "*reference*" to something transcending the self. Accordingly, it is not expressive. What are called reflective impressions in distinction from sense impressions, such as feelings, desires, emotions, are derived from our ideas, and thus even though they are not original in the first sense, they were regarded as original facts in the sense that "they are complete in themselves and do not contain any reference at all to other feelings, volitions, actions." In this way, the self-sufficiency of impressions was one of the features of Hume's atomism. Nevertheless, as Bergson said that memory is included even within sensation, nothing like pure impression exists, and we must say that sensations are already perceptual and hence expressive. The doctrine of sensation on which empiricism is based is an abstract theory. But it is worth taking note that Hume's theory of abstract ideas recognizes the important significance of the *image*. According to him, our ideas are all copies of our impressions, but the capacity to "repeat" impressions in this way is memory and fancy, through which ideas are engendered. An idea is thus the image of an impression. And our thinking and reasoning are founded upon such images. Aristotle had already stated that "the mind cannot think at all without images" (οὐδέποτε νοεῖ ἄνευ φαντάσματος ἡ ψθχή).[34] Concrete thought is always tied to images. This concrete thought was the problem of empiricism in Hume, who attempted to approach life with its philosophy.[35]

But what we call sensation may not be just intellectual and representational. The word *sensible* [*sensory*] in everyday terminology, in addition to depicting something intellectual on the one hand, already manifests something affective on the other hand. Sensation, in addition to containing the meaning of something intellectual and objective, contains the meaning of something affective and subjective. Descartes thought that our sense organs fail to instruct us about the true nature of things and only convey in what regard they may be useful or harmful to us.[36] Instead of occupying the position of a gateway to knowledge, the senses occupy the position of stimuli to action. They constitute a clue in regard to behavior and are a leading element in the subject's adaptation to the environment. The issue of sensation does not belong under the heading of knowledge but instead belongs under the heading of immediate stimulus and response.[37] We can probably say that sensation is the apex of the somatic-active self. Sensation, from the start, is not at all something simply subjective and affective but simultaneously something intellectual and objective. As such we may consider sensation as having the significance of "signs." What we call sensation is already expressive. Therefore, the fact that sensation is symbolic or expressive in this way must be due to the fact that what we call sensation is not merely sensation and that the imagination is active within it.

4.

[287] Above we clarified how Hume's theory of abstract ideas is intimately related to the imagination. This problem was primarily the question of: How can there be universal ideas in empiricism when according to its standpoint everything existing is an individual? Now the next issue concerns how individual sensations and ideas can be conjoined in a single relation. In regard to this issue what is especially important in Hume is the idea of cause and effect. As he himself believed, a critical analysis of the idea of causality belongs to the definitive and most original work of his philosophy.

The idea of causality is but one of what Hume calls the "*philosophical relation.*" He raised seven universal and basic philosophical relations that we can view as "the source of all philosophical relations": resemblance, identity, position in time and space, proportion of quantity or number, degree of quality, contrariety, and cause and effect.[38] Among them cause and effect, first of all, has the quality of being a "*natural relation*" in addition to being a philosophical relation.[39] Hume discerned that the word *relation* is ordinarily used in two very distinct senses. On the one hand, it means "that quality, by which two ideas are connected in the imagination, and the one naturally introduces the other"; and on the other, it means "that particular circumstance, in which, even upon the arbitrary union of two ideas in the fancy, we may think proper to compare them."[40] Put differently, a relation is either a *relation of association* or a *relation of comparison*.[41] And in common terminology, relation is always the former, and "'tis only in philosophy, that we extend it to mean any particular subject of comparison, without a connecting principle."[42] Therefore what is called a philosophical relation is the relation of comparison and what is purported a natural relation is the relation of association. For Hume, the quality that conjoins or associates ideas in the imagination are three, resemblance, proximity in time or place, and cause and effect, and these are natural relations. They become characterized as natural, in the sense that without them the habits constituting understanding cannot exist, presumably because they are natural to the mind.[43] The principle of association is active universally, and "[i]ts effects are every where conspicuous; but as to its causes, they are mostly unknown, and must be resolv'd into *original* qualities of human nature, which I pretend not to explain."[44] The force that associates ideas is not something derivative but an "original" law of human nature. Hume considered this to be a kind of gravitational force in the mental realm comparable to gravity in the natural realm. Moreover, this fundamental principle of association for him was essentially a law of the imagination.

The characteristics of causality may be discerned, secondly, in the following manner. Of the seven species of philosophical relations given above, the four relations of resemblance, proportions in quantity or number, degrees in quality, and contrariety "depend solely on ideas..." which we can compare to one another.[45] For example, from the idea of triangle, we discover the relationship that the three angles of a triangle are equal to two straight angles and that this relationship is unchanging as long as our ideas remain the same. By contrast, the relation of contiguity or distance between two things can be changed simply by altering its place without any kind of change in the things themselves or their ideas. No matter how utterly similar they are to each other or even if they appear in the same place at different times, we can differentiate two things in terms of number. And we can never discover, simply from their ideas, the force whereby one thing produces another thing. In this way, the three relations of identity, time and place, and cause and effect, are endowed with the character of "changeability without any kind of change in their ideas."

But third, we may conceive the most characteristic quality of causality in the following manner. According to Hume, the four relations that depend on mere ideas, namely, resemblance, opposition, degree of quality, and proportion in quantity or number, are "*objects of knowledge and certainty.*" We can discover these relations at a glance, and it is appropriate to say that they belong to the realm of intuition rather than demonstration. In cases where things resemble each other, the resemblance immediately strikes the eye or rather the mind and almost never requires any further investigation. The same goes for opposition or degrees of quality. No one doubts that being and non-being are opposites that are mutually destructive and utterly incompatible. And even when it is impossible to judge precisely concerning the degree of qualities like color, taste, warmth, and cold, when their difference is very small, it is still easy to determine whether one of them is higher or lower than the other in cases where their difference is conspicuous. We give that discernment always at the first glance without examination or inference. When we determine the proportion of quantity or number as well, we can know at a glance the higher or lower between them with the same method. It is especially so when the difference is very large and conspicuous. Now how is it with the other kinds of relations, in particular relations that do not rely on ideas and can be present or not present even when the idea remains identical, namely, the three relations of identity, position in time or space, and causality? According to Hume, any kind of inference is nothing but a comparison and discovery of a constant or inconstant relation carried by two or more things in relation to each other. In this comparison, there are cases when two things are both present to the sense-organs, or when one is present and one is not present, when only one of either is present. When two things are both present in the sense-organs accompanying their relation, we call this perception rather than inference. Conceived in this way, we cannot regard as inference any kind of observation we make concerning relations of identity or time and place. The reason is that, in any of them, the mind never transcends what is immediately present to the sense-organs to discover the thing's actual being or relation. The relation of cause and effect is the only relation that can be compared to ideas that a single impression presented by them cannot present but is anticipated in imagination. "'Tis only *causation*, which produces such a connexion, as to give us assurance from the existence or action of one object, that 'twas follow'd or preceded by any other existence or action..."[46] The other two relations (identity and the relation of time and space), aside from the extent to which they influence or are influenced by causality, cannot be used in inference. And the substantial identity of things present here in this place can be compared in immediate perception. But the continuous being of things beyond perception can be inferred only on the assumption that the cause of their being does not change. And even if time and place themselves allow comparison without inference, immutability or change can be inferred only as the effect of causality. Thus, among the three relations not existing in mere ideas, "the only one, that can be trac'd beyond our senses, and informs us of existence and objects, which we do not see or feel, is *causation*."[47] The relation of causality is the principle of inference for everything concerning facts.

Originally Hume's research started from the distinction between knowledge of ideas and knowledge of facts. We can find this distinction already in Hobbes and in Locke, but Hume provided a clearer definition than Hobbes and, in regard to its application, was more thorough than Locke. Our objects of knowledge are divided into two kinds, *relations of ideas* and *matters of fact*. Geometry, algebra, arithmetic, in general any proposition that is intuitively or demonstratively certain belongs to the first kind of objects. For example, the proposition that three times five is equal to half of thirty displays the relation between these numbers. "Propositions of this kind are discoverable by the mere operation of thought, without dependence on what is any where existent in the universe. Though there never were a circle or triangle in nature, the truths, demonstrated by Euclid, would for ever retain their certainty and evidence."[48] With the same method, we are unable to confirm knowledge of the second kind of objects, matters of fact. Their certainty, no matter how great, is not of the same quality as objects of the first kind. The opposite of every fact is still possible. For we can always easily and clearly understand it as if it were in harmony with reality without containing any contradiction. That the sun may not rise tomorrow morning is something we can comprehend, just as much as how it may rise, and contains no contradiction. Therefore, even if we attempt to demonstrate its falsehood, it would be futile. And if it were demonstratively false, it would contain a contradiction and we would be unable to clearly understand it. When thought in a purely conceptual way that which exists may also not exist. The non-existence of a certain fact means that it contains no contradiction and hence neither can we at all explain the existence of a certain fact from a mere concept. We cannot make the inference of being demonstratively certain. But this does not mean that it therefore must be uncertain; rather, this certainty just means that it differs in kind from the certainty of a proposition concerning the relation of ideas. Hume states that the report in a single letter from Burton that Caesar really existed or that the island of Sicily exists, for someone who had never visited the island, is properly an assertion without any proof or intuitive ground for cognition, but that it does not, however, mean that it is not true or not certain.[49] Therein we can think of a different kind of certainty. The feature of *intuitive and demonstrative knowledge* is that its opposite is incomprehensible. According to Hume, every proposition whose truth is independent of actual being is analytic. By contrast, every synthetic proposition is empirical. Experience becomes an issue with this kind of distinction and opposition between conceptual knowledge and knowledge of facts. "It may, therefore, be a subject worthy of curiosity, to enquire what is the nature of that evidence, which assures us of any real existence and matter of fact, beyond the present testimony of our sense, or the records of our memory."[50] Indeed this word "*beyond*" signifies experience. Inference from experience takes us beyond our memory and sense organs. Therein we can conceive the synthetic nature of experience as well. The examination of experience as knowledge was the task Hume assigned to himself. His contribution was in seeing the problem within experience instead of seeking the solution to experience and this shows his status in the history of philosophy. Empiricism, the philosophy of experience, became critical in Hume. Even the inquiry into the principle of causality was directly related to the general issue concerning the cognitive value of experience, and he determined with greater clarity the problem concerning this value by altering its form instead into an issue concerning the meaning of that principle. "All reasonings concerning matter of fact seem to be founded on the relation of *Cause* and *Effect*. By means of that relation alone we can go beyond the evidence of our memory and senses."[51] What is the ground of that principle of causality?

5.

[295] We need to consider here the origin from which the idea of causality derives. According to Hume, no matter what the idea, it would be impossible to completely understand it unless we investigate the original impression from which it emerged by tracing it back to its origin. For every idea is a copy of an impression. We will now try to investigate from every possible direction by focusing on those two things, whatever they are, called cause and effect, in order to discover the impressions that produce these ideas. We immediately notice in this case that we are unable to discover them even within whatever particular qualities of things. For we can discern a thing that may be designated as cause or effect but without possessing that quality, no matter which one we take up. Indeed, whether outer realm or inner realm, although there is not one being that cannot be conceived as cause or effect, there is also no single quality that universally belongs to every being and gives them the qualification to be designated as cause or effect.

If the idea of causality is thus not founded on some quality of things it must be derived from a certain relationship between things. What we then first discover is that things conceivable as cause and effect are contiguous [to each other]. Even in cases where distant things operate on each other, if we investigate them closely, we find that they are tied by a chain of mutually contiguous causes. Accordingly, the relation of *contiguity* is essential to the relation of causality. Next, the second relation that we can conceive as essential to causal relations is that the cause precedes the effect in time.

Stated differently, the relation of *succession* is essential to causal relations. Nevertheless, contiguity and succession alone do not give a complete idea of causality. There is something that, even while contiguous to and preceding a certain thing, cannot be conceived to be its cause. When we speak of a cause, it must mean that it produces other things; cause is a *productive principle*. In this way, between cause and effect we can conceive a *necessary connection*. And this relationship, for the idea of causality, is by far more significant and decisive than either of the other two relations discussed above. Therefore, we shall now endeavor to discover the impression from which that idea derives, again by examining things from every direction, in order to discover the essence of this necessary connection. In this case, if we were to focus on the known qualities of a thing, we immediately discover that such qualities do not depend at all on the relation of cause and effect. And if we were to consider the relation of things, we cannot discern anything other than the relations of contiguity and succession. But then, as already mentioned, it would be incomplete and insufficient.

Thus, Hume divided the issue in two in order to break through the difficulty we are confronted with. First, for what reason do we assert that everything with a beginning to its existence necessarily has a cause? Second, why do we conclude that a specific cause must necessarily have a specific effect, and what is the inference that divides one from the other, and what is the nature of the belief we place in it? We need to distinguish these two issues.[52] The first relation involves the causal relation in general. The issue is whether we can or cannot cognize *a priori* from the mere idea of change the necessity to suppose a cause for every change. The second issue involves each particular causal relation. In this case we take as the premise a certain cause given in experience and on the basis of this premise examine the essence of the inference to the effect. The issue is whether what guides us from a given cause to the effect following it is experience or whether this effect can be determined in advance from the mere consideration of the cause itself without waiting for the experience.

If we think about the first issue, the universal maxim of philosophy that whatever begins to exist must have a cause for its being, according to Hume is a content of "*belief*" rather than belonging to "*knowledge*." He demonstrates this first on the basis of his views concerning the scope of knowledge. Every certainty emerges from the comparison of ideas, from the discovery of a relation unchanging to the extent that the ideas continue to be identical. Such relations are resemblance, proportion in quantity and number, degree of quality, and opposition, and, according to Hume, these four relations are the foundations of knowledge and none of them are included in the proposition that anything with a beginning also has a cause for its being. This proposition is thus not intuitively certain. He further advances the following demonstration. The necessity of cause for a new being or for a new transfiguration of a being, no matter what the being, cannot be demonstrated unless it simultaneously shows that it cannot begin existing without some distinct principle of production. But it is completely impossible to prove this latter proposition.

> [A] all distinct ideas are separable from each other, and as the ideas of cause and effect are evidently distinct, 'twill be easy for us to conceive any object to be non-existent this moment, and existent the next, without conjoining to it the distinct

idea of a cause or productive principle. The separation, therefore, of the idea of a cause from that of a beginning of existence, is plainly possible for the imagination; and consequently the actual separation of these objects is so far possible, that it implies no contradiction nor absurdity; and is therefore incapable of being refused by any reasoning from mere ideas ...[53]

Here Hume appeals to the basic proposition of his philosophy that "What are distinguishable are separable." That every event must have some cause means that the ideas of cause and effect are necessarily connected. If so, it would be impossible to separate these ideas. They are separable, however, because they are distinguishable, and the negation of their necessary connection contains no contradiction whatsoever. The proposition that what is distinguishable is separable reveals the axiom of atomism in Hume's psychology and logic. Anything mutually different is distinguishable, and anything distinguishable can be separated by thought or imagination. And the reverse is equally true, that is, things that can be separated are distinguishable, and things distinguishable are mutually different.[54] This theory, in addition to the theory that ideas are copies of impressions, constitutes the fundamental premise of his empiricism. He says that all of our ideas are copied from our impressions, there are no two impressions that cannot be completely separated, and whenever imagination recognizes a difference among ideas, imagination can easily make a separation.[55]

Hume executed his examination in regard to the principle of causality, as shown above, first on the basis of his view concerning the scope of knowledge and next on the basis of his theory that what is distinguishable can be separated, and he held that this is neither intuitively nor demonstratively certain. Let us especially take notice of the fact that this examination is not founded on his theory that ideas are copies. Every demonstration concerning the necessity of a cause is a false demonstration and is sophistic. For example, Locke attempted to demonstrate the necessity of causality from *nihil ex nihilo*. To deny that every event has some cause is to affirm that events have themselves as cause or have nothingness as cause. In relation to this demonstration that reduces the denial of cause thus to an absurdity, Hume says that it is sufficient if we consider that when we reject every cause, we are rejecting them in practice and not supposing that nothingness or even the thing itself is the cause of being, and hence we cannot draw out a demonstration explaining the absurdity of the rejection from the absurdity of these suppositions. If we take it to be true that everything must have some kind of cause, it follows from the rejection of every other cause that an event must have itself as the cause or nothingness as the cause. However, because the truth of the law of causality is indeed the point at issue, to assert that the opposite of this law means that things are produced by nothingness is the falsehood of demanding the issue to be decided in advance. To argue from the premise that the necessity of the cause means that cause and effect are corelative terms is even more like child's play. That every husband must have a wife does not mean, in fact, that some human beings must be married. That every event that is called an effect in its proper sense must have a cause cannot even help to prove that some events are called effects in the proper sense.

If the idea of causality now is neither intuitively nor demonstratively certain, where does this idea and the conviction supporting it come from? If this idea does not derive from "knowledge or some scientific inference," it would have to be birthed from "observation and experience." It is clearly not by way of deduction from his theory of ideas as copies that we are faced with experience as the alternative left by Hume. The next problem is how experience can engender this sort of principle. Here Hume considers it convenient to immerse this problem into the issue of why we conclude that a certain specific cause must have a certain specific effect, why we infer one from the other, or put differently, to absorb this problem of the relation of causality in general into the issue of each particular relation of causality. As we shall see later, according to him, the same answer provides the solution to these two problems.

Now because inference must begin from something and cannot proceed without end, the inference of causality must begin with our memory or the direct perception of our sense organs. And in cases where only a perception called cause or effect is present, its corelative is inferred in an idea. In this way, the inference of causality includes the present perception of sense organs or memory and the idea arrived at by means of inference. We thus need to explain the following three matters. First, the original impression. Second, the transition to the connected idea of the cause or the effect. Third, that idea's essence and quality. First, speaking of sense impressions, "human reason cannot completely explain" its ultimate cause. And speaking of the impressions of memory, in practice we can distinguish them from fancy only in the points of *force and vivacity*. In regard to the second issue, the inference from impression to idea, Hume again argues the following on the basis of his theory that what is distinguishable can be separated. Unless we see the object by considering it as it is in itself beyond the ideas we form of it, there is no object that would include the being of some other thing. That inference would be equal to knowledge and would presumably include the utter contradiction and impossibility of conceiving something different. However, because everything distinguishable is separable, clearly there can be no impossibility of that sort. When we transition from a present impression to the idea of something, we can presumably separate that idea from the impression and replace it with some other idea instead. That is to say, Hume rejected the necessary connection between impression and idea on the basis of his atomism.

If we therefore take causal inference as something not based on reasoning, it would have to be empirical in its essence. The essence of this experience is the following:

> We remember to have had frequent instances of the existence of one species of objects; and also remember that the individuals of another species of objects have always attended them, and have existed in a regular order of contiguity and succession with regard to them. Thus we remember to have seen that species of object we call *flame*, and to have felt that species of sensation we call *heat*. We likewise call to mind their constant conjunction in all past instances. Without any farther ceremony, we call the one *cause* and the other *effect*, and infer the existence of the one from that of the other.[56]

In this way we came to discover a new relation between cause and effect. It is their "*constant conjunction*." Contiguity and succession are insufficient for us to declare two things as cause and effect to the extent that we do not recognize that these two relations have been maintained in many cases. It would be profitable to directly examine this relation of "constant conjunction" in order to discover the essence of "*necessary connexion*" that constitutes an essential part of causal relations. Constant conjunction is the constant repetition of impression and idea conjoined in space and time. But neither "constancy" nor "repetition" are attributes of constantly repeated impressions and ideas. Therefore, this newly found relation does not signify the discovery of some distinguishable special feature of a perception.

> For it implies no more than this, that like objects have always been plac'd in like relations of contiguity and succession; ... we can never discover any new idea, and can only multiply but not enlarge the objects of our mind.... From the mere repetition of any past impression, even to infinity, there never will arise any new original idea, such as that of a necessary connexion ...[57]

Nevertheless, after the discovery of the constant conjunction of a few things, we always engage in inference from one thing to another. It is therefore important to investigate the essence of this inference, the transition from the impression to the idea. And as if to anticipate his conclusion, Hume writes, "[p]erhaps 'twill appear in the end, that the necessary connexion depends on the inference, instead of the inference's depending on the necessary connexion."[58]

Now because it is thought that the transition from the impression, present to memory or sensation, to the idea of the thing called cause or effect is founded upon the recollection of past experiences and their constant conjunction, the next issue is whether experience produces this idea by means of *understanding* or by means of *imagination*. Stated differently, are we determined in this transition by reason or determined by a certain association and relationship? If we assume reason to determine us, it would presumably proceed on the foundation of that principle, the principle that "cases that we had not experienced must resemble cases that we had experienced and must always be uniformly identical in the process of nature." However, the fact that it is impossible to demonstrate this is shown by the fact that its contrary is conceivable. We ought to notice that Hume ceaselessly uses this method of proof. That is, we can at least conceive change within the process of nature and this fact is sufficient to prove that such change is not absolutely impossible. Because its contrary is conceivable, the *uniformity of nature* cannot be demonstratively proven. In this case, neither can we rely on probability just because certainty is lacking. Probability in itself manifests not the relation of conceived ideas but instead only the relation of things and in certain points is founded upon our memory and sensation and in other points is founded upon our ideas. That conclusion would be completely illusory without the contamination of impressions into the inference of probability. And without the contamination of ideas, the mental operation that observes relations, in its original sense, would be sensation, not inference. Therefore, it must be that in every inference of probability, we infer from a certain thing present to the mind that we see or recollect, a certain thing we cannot see or recollect but conjoin it. But because the thing's only connection or relation that can guide us beyond our immediate impressions of memory or sensation is that of cause and effect, neither can the inference of probability be taken as independent of this relation. Accordingly, although the inference of probability takes as its premise the resemblance between things we have experienced and things we have not experienced, clearly this premise in itself cannot depend on probability. In this way, if the inference of causality cannot take reason to be its foundation, we would presumably have to seek its principle within the imagination.

6.

[307] What was shown so far in Hume's analysis concerning the idea of causality is that the idea of cause and effect is the idea of certain things that had been constantly conjoined. "We cannot penetrate into the reason of the conjunction. We only observe the thing itself, and always find that from the constant conjunction the objects acquire an *union in the imagination*."[59] However the idea of causality that had been clarified so far is nothing but a single "philosophical relation." As contiguous and successive things, cause and effect cannot be compared in regard to their constant repetition. Even if contiguity and succession are both simple orders in their configuration and mode, distinguishable from such impressions and ideas, neither "constancy" nor "repetition" are attributes of constantly repeated impressions or ideas. Furthermore, according to Hume, the content that shapes the "natural relation" of cause and effect is constituted by the association of essentially contiguous, successive, and constantly conjoined impressions and ideas. "Thus tho' causation be a *philosophical* relation, as implying contiguity, succession, and constant conjunction, yet 'tis only so far as it is a *natural* relation, and produces an union among our ideas, that we are able to reason upon it, or draw any inference from it."[60] And indeed causality is something more than a philosophical relation to the extent that it is an *association*.

The answer to the problem concerning the essence of transition from impressions to ideas in the inference of causality, in this way, is that this transition is an operation of habit in association or imagination, not an operation of reason. We will here return to the beginning and inquire about the idea of necessary connection most essential for the idea of causality. What I had been seeking was its source. Essentially contiguous, successive, and constantly conjoined impressions are engendered in sense experience. Now it may be thought that because the observation of repeated impressions only repeats identical ideas, we cannot proceed. But if we investigate this even further, we find that the effect of repetition is not always the same:

> For after a frequent repetition, I find, that upon the appearance of one of the objects, the mind is *determin'd* by custom to consider its usual attendant, and to consider it in a stronger light upon account of its relation to the first object. 'Tis this impression, then, or *determination*, which affords me the idea of necessity.[61]

The original of the ideas at issue is thus discovered, not in sensory experience, but in the inner impression of an active habit.

Hume initially considers two points as certain, namely: 1) somehow there is an inference, in accordance with constant conjunction, from cause to effect; and 2) the mere repetition of impressions or ideas will not engender anything new. But because the idea of necessity in practice usually occurs by accompanying this repetition yet is not duplicated among one or several of the repeated impressions, the idea is not engendered merely from the repetition. This means instead that we need to either discover or produce something new that is the source of that idea. In that case, it is clear that repetition cannot show anything new. Moreover, it is also already clear that, on the basis of constant conjunction alone, no connection or principle can be engendered that would permit the progression of inference. Hence it is clear that the constant repetition of conjoined perceptions can neither discover nor produce anything new. However, the situation changes when "*the gentle force of association*" is added to this repetition. Hume now says that "the observation of this resemblance produces a new impression *in the mind* . . ."[62] When asserting that the idea of necessity results from the observation of resemblance, he understands on the basis of "*resemblance*" not only that philosophical relation, but that natural relation of association. For Hume, resemblance was a principle of the association of ideas. "['T]is from this resemblance, that the ideas of necessity, of power, and of efficacy, are deriv'd. These ideas, therefore, represent not any thing, that does or can belong to the objects, which are constantly conjoin'd."[63] Here "resemblance" involves the natural relation of association thus named at the same time that it involves properly resembling things that were constantly conjoined. Together these shape habits in the imagination where their felt determination is the impression of force or necessity:

> The idea of necessity arises from some impression. There is no impression convey'd by our senses, which can give rise to that idea. It must, therefore, be deriv'd from some internal impression, or impression of reflexion. There is no internal impression, which has any relation to the present business, but that propensity, which custom produces, to pass from an object to the idea of its usual attendant. This therefore is the essence of necessity.[64]

In this way, the idea of necessity arises, not from the impression of some sensation, but from the impression of reflection which is the felt determination of habit in imagination from the association of ideas of things that were constantly and repeatedly conjoined.

Hume thus attempted to solve the issue of the necessity of causality through the habit [or custom, 習慣] of imagination:

> All inferences from experience, therefore, are effects of custom, not of reasoning. Custom, then, is the great guide of human life. It is that principle alone, which renders our experience useful to us, and makes us expect, for the future, a similar train of events with those which have appeared in the past. Without the influence of custom, we should be entirely ignorant of every matter of fact, beyond what is immediately present to the memory and senses. We should never know how to adjust means to ends, or to employ our natural powers in the production of any effect. There would be an end at once of all action, as well as of the chief part of speculation.[65]

Experience is something natural rather than rational. The principle of experience is causality. The relation of cause and effect is a natural relation in addition to being a philosophical relation, and it is a natural relation because it is founded upon the habit of imagination. Here we recall the words of Pascal:

> The father [parent] fears lest the natural love of their children may fade away. What kind of nature is that which is subject to decay? Custom is second nature which destroys the former. But what is nature? For is custom not natural? I am much afraid that nature is itself only a first custom, as custom is second nature. What are our natural principles but principles of custom?[66]

Hume resolved another important category that he had analyzed, the category of substance, in the same way by means of the imagination. The issue of substance involves the continuous existence of impressions. However, because it cannot be proven by sense perceptions or by reason, "its idea must completely originate in the imagination." Every impression exists and appears as an intrinsic, disappearing, being, and the idea of that independent, continuous being, must arise from the cooperation of something with those qualities and the qualities of the imagination. Presumably because only a few impressions are believed to have a continuous existence, this belief must arise from a certain specific quality of those few impressions. The first of those qualities is the "*constancy*" of impressions, which we may believe to possess a continuous being. The mountains, houses, and trees that lie across before my eyes at present have always appeared to me in the same order, and when I lose sight of them by closing my eyes or turning my head, I find immediately afterward that they return to me without the least change. However mere repetition in the order and content of perceptions cannot explain our belief in their continuous being. For things frequently change in the order of their perceived qualities. But we might admit that they do maintain a "*coherence*" even in such changes and possess regular reciprocally dependent relations. This is the basis for a kind of inference from causality and produces the idea of its continuous being. For belief in the continuous being of things, a "kind of system," constancy, of the mental images of memory and sensation are necessary. Change or difference in perceived things, of course, cannot be clarified by constancy in the system of memories and sensations. Moreover, such change is harmonized in the imagination by means of a kind of inference from causality, with repeated memory images or sense impressions. While sitting in his room, hearing the opening of the door, and seeing the delivery man enter with letter in hand, Hume infers the continuous existence of his door and stairs. For in relation to that particular sound, the appearance of a person in his room, and the transport of a letter, the habit of inferring that causality is formed in him. The sounds heard, the delivery man and letter that appeared, and the memories accompanying them fail to give Hume the guarantee of anything beyond these things themselves. Moreover, because their appearance and memory activate the operation of habit associated with them, Hume infers that the continuous being of such cause is the condition of the repetition of their appearance. The experiences of sense and memory are thus expanded in accordance with rules existing as habits of the imagination. While present impressions resemble them in key points, it is the same when they call forth partially different memories of experience as well. We can explain change in present experience at the time by change in resemblance in the past and inference to the associated cause. When Hume returned to his study after being absent for an hour, he found that the fire had burnt. But at the time he was used to seeing in other cases the occurrence of a similar change in similar durations of time whether he was there or not. This coherence in such change is a particular quality of external things and their constancy. Change that is not constant or coherent would probably not be associated with the habit of the imagination. Moving ahead, Hume writes the following:

> ... as all reasoning concerning matters of fact arises only from custom, and custom can only be the effect of repeated perceptions, the extending of custom and reasoning beyond the perceptions can never be the direct and natural effect of the constant repetition and connexion, but must arise from the co-operation of some other principles.[67]

One such principle is the propensity of the imagination to advance in its course, without any new impulse, beyond the system of memory and sensation like a boat moved by oars. Hume focuses here on the *"transitive impulse"* of the imagination.[68] The coherence of perceptions would be quite large if it was expanded to include belief in the continuous being of these perceptions, but it is this propensity of the imagination that gives rise to this expansion. The other principles that cooperate with habit in connections is the constancy and coherence of perception. According to Hume's view, the inference of causality is transitive, namely, it goes beyond memory and sensation. Expansion of causality by inference not only arises from habit but requires the imagination's operation of transitive impulse. The habit of causal inference includes an element not present within the system of memory and sensation and irreducible to the repetition of mental images in association. This element is the transitive propensity of the imagination.

7.

[315] Thinking back, Hume's theory concerning causality began with the distinction between demonstrative knowledge and knowledge of facts. We can probably consider this distinction by comparing it with Leibniz's eternal truth (*vérité éternelle*) and truth of fact (*vérité de fait*). According to Leibniz, eternal truth is truth concerning the being of essences and its principle is the principle of contradiction. However, because contrariety in regard to actual beings does not include contradiction, he considered its principle to be the principle of sufficient reason, not the principle of contradiction. For Hume as well, intuitive demonstrative knowledge involves the relation of ideas independent of actual beings and its sign is that its opposite could not be comprehended. Accordingly, it is based on the principle of contradiction. Opposites concerning facts, however, are possible. Their opposites do not contain contradiction and hence can be understood. The principle of knowledge of such facts is the principle of causality. We can recognize an agreement to that extent between the idea of the principle of sufficient reason in Leibniz and the idea of the principle of causality in Hume. The principle of knowledge of facts in the rationalist Leibniz was thought to be the principle of sufficient

reason and in the empiricist Hume was thought to be the principle of causality. We can presumably also consider these by including the principle of causality broadly within the principle of sufficient reason.[69] In comparison to Leibniz's way of thinking, which is ontological, Hume's way of thinking is epistemological. But in contrast to how the principle of sufficient reason in Leibniz was not something fundamentally opposed to the principle of contradiction,[70] we can probably say that Hume, in relation to the principle of causality, discovered what we call the logic of imagination. But in Hume, the principle of intuitive demonstrative knowledge and the principle of knowledge of facts remained separate. Kant, who is said to have synthesized the rationalism of the continent and the empiricism of England, ascribed to imagination the role of synthesizing understanding and sensibility.

Causality, according to Hume, is the principle of all inference concerning facts. While intuitive demonstrative knowledge is analytic, every synthetic proposition is empirical. In its original meaning experience is relational. He also writes that philosophical relations are not *connections* at all, but that natural relations of association are connections and are also "*principles of union or cohesion.*" Synthesis is synthesis in imagination. Synthesis in imagination, according to Hume, is a ground of "*belief,*" namely, empirical synthetic knowledge, distinct from "*knowledge,*" namely, demonstrative analytic knowledge. This synthesis is first founded upon the imagination's transitive impulse. Inference from experience carries us beyond our memory and sensation. All causal inference is regulated by habit that transfers past experience into the future.[71] We need to understand this transitive propensity of the imagination as its original temporality. Synthesis in imagination is synthesis in time. Although causal inference is regulated by past experience, we can probably view past experience to be nothing more than a kind of accident.[72] If we consider them simply by themselves, every past experience has the same weight. That we cannot think of the idea of causality or of effect as mere accident is due to the force of association intrinsic to the habit of imagination. Belief in causality is obtained from impressions and ideas in the habit of its associations. It is also the same with belief in regard to things or substances. Thus, if we see this as a whole, it is established neither from an impression nor an idea, nor from associations without the terms, but from the synthesis of imagination. This synthesis is indicated on the one hand by the transitive impulse of the imagination and on the other hand by its habit.

Imagination, in this way, occupies a central position in Hume's empiricism. As a result, he opposes, in addition to rationalism, *sensible phenomenalism* as well. The construction of empirical knowledge or belief is supported neither by means of reason nor sensation, but rather by the imagination. According to the usual view, imagination means "*the faculty, by which we form our fainter ideas.*"[73] However, the imagination that Hume conceives as "the ultimate judge of all systems of philosophy"[74] is neither that of popular opinion nor that of ancient philosophy. Hume writes the following in the conclusion of his research concerning understanding: "The memory, senses, and understanding are therefore, all of them founded on the *imagination, or the vivacity of our ideas.*"[75] Moreover, in order to consider the imagination as the final judge for all systems of philosophy,

> I must distinguish in the imagination betwixt the principles which are permanent, irresistible, and universal; such as the customary transition from causes to effects,

and from effects to causes: And the principles, which are changeable, weak, and irregular;... The former are the foundation of all our thoughts and actions, so that upon their removal human nature must immediately perish and go to ruin."[76]

"*The understanding,*" for Hume, is "*... the general and more establish'd properties of the imagination.*"[77] And what he calls natural relation is the principle of unity and cohesion in imagination. Now if we take the felt power of the imagination as the decisive element in belief, what does it mean that we repel non-philosophical probability even when strongly felt and that we need to receive philosophical probability even when less strongly felt? Hume states that this difficulty cannot be removed other than by assuming the influence of a universal rule. By rules of the matter, he means rules by which we ought to regulate our judgments concerning causality. But these rules are formed on the basis of the essence of our understanding. Hume raises eight rules as such rules and states, "[h]ere is all the Logic I think proper to employing my reasoning; and perhaps even this was not very necessary, but might have been supply'd by the natural principles of our understanding."[78] Hume discovers the rules governing causal inference within an analysis of the essence of our understanding. Excluding the hyperbole of "our scholastic headpieces and logicians,"[79] he regarded logic to be originally constituted from the essence of understanding—to the extent that it is constituted by the habit of causal inference.

Experience takes synthesis in the imagination to be its fundamental principle, but this means on the one hand the transitive propensity of the imagination and on the other hand the habit of imagination. Moreover, we can say that habit is also transitive. For "[h]abit is another principle, which determines me to expect the same for the future."[80] Habit operates as the cooperation of recollected experience and the habit of expectation. As such, habit is truly cohesive or synthetic. That the imagination is transitive would have to mean not only that it is transitive but, at the same time, that it expects what is transitioning in one present. On this basis we can say that the imagination is truly synthetic. But to say that the imagination is transitive and at the same time embraces what transitions in a single present must mean that it is not simply temporal but, in addition to being temporal, modeled on an eternity. Therein we can conceive the transcendental nature of the imagination. Coleridge distinguished the imagination into "*the primary imagination*" and "*the secondary imagination.*" He held the primary imagination to be the living, motivating agency of all human perception and as a repetition in the finite mind of the eternal act of creation in the infinite "*I am.*" He views the secondary imagination to be an echo of the former, co-existing with the conscious will and, yet, identical with the primary imagination in its species of agency, but in a degree different only in the mode of its activity.[81] Although we recognize here a theory similar to Fichte's thought concerning imagination, Coleridge is speaking of the transcendental nature of imagination and its creativity. Needless to say, Hume's doctrine of the reproduction of experience and ideas would not permit going that far. On the other hand, however, the problem of the imagination would probably be inconceivable if we completely exclude the issue of habit that was made the foundation in Hume's theory of the understanding. According to Hume, every inference from experience is a result of habit. What guarantees the principle of the *uniformity of nature* is habit. Natural relations are based on association, but association can exhibit its meaning by means of habit. Associations undetermined by habit, accidental associations by means of resemblance or contiguity, lack the force of belief. Not every case of association of a present impression with a fresh idea is belief in an "actual being." That would require association to rely on established habit rather than the "pure caprice" of states of affairs.[82] Even if it is difficult to consider, from the basis of nature or experience in terms of natural science, that habit is the foundation of experience or nature, it would presumably possess a much deeper meaning if we understood experience as active experience and nature as historical nature. Moreover, in Hume, following his atomism and mechanism of the association of ideas, habit itself was grasped mechanistically. Hume defines it as follows: "we call everything custom, which proceeds from a past repetition, without any new reasoning or conclusion . . ."[83] But as already discussed, habit is not explained by mere repetition. It is not that habit is explained by the association of ideas, rather the association of ideas is explained by habit as well. Habit is also a result of the operation of imagination as what Coleridge calls an *"esemplastic power."*[84]

The conclusion of Hume's theory of understanding was, as Spir stated, that understanding and imagination are one.[85] He also sought the foundation for the categories, like causality and substance, in the habit of imagination. This idea in Hume, however, could not but fall into skepticism. In order to move beyond such skepticism, one must deeply grasp the transcendental nature and logical nature of the imagination. Therefore, I would like for us to further pursue the issue of the imagination in Kant, who is said to have been awoken by Hume from his dogmatic slumber and further to have overcome that skepticism.

8.

[323] The issue was experience for Kant as well. The *Critique of Pure Reason*[86] is a critique of experience. Herbart already stated that "Kant had processed the concept of experience anew."[87] According to Cohen, Kant discovered "a single new concept of experience." The critique of pure reason is a "logic of experience" and, at the same time as it is a logic of experience, it was a metaphysics of experience.[88]

In order to discuss the issue of imagination in Kant's theory of experience, we need to first glance at the history of this concept in him. Originally Kant took this concept from Baumgarten's metaphysics.[89] Baumgarten distinguished the lower cognitive faculty (*facultas cognoscitiva inferior*) from the higher cognitive faculty (*facultas cognoscitive superior*), namely, the intellect (*intellectus*). The latter was divided into sensation (*sensus*) (*Sinn*), imagination (*phantasia*) (*Einbildungskraft*), discernment (*perspicacia*) (*Unterscheidungsvermögen*), memory (*memoria*) (*Gedächtnis*), phantasy or poetizing (*facultas fingendi*) (*Dichtungsvermögen*), foresight (*praevisio*) (*Vorhersehungsvermögen*), judgment (*judicium*) (*das Vermögen zu beurteilen*), anticipation (*praesagatio*) (*das Vermögen etwas zu erwarten*), and composition (*facultas characteristica*) (*das Vermögen der Zeichenkunde*). These are discussed in sections 519–650 in Baumgarten's work but this is the major philological source for Kant's views concerning the imagination. In Baumgarten's classification of the "faculties," only the distinction between the higher cognitive faculty and the lower cognitive faculty is systematic and for the others, he merely raises the various functions in parallel to each other. Among the ones particularly related to Kant's concept of the imagination above are imagination, memory, and phantasy.[90]

Imagination is the faculty of representing a perception again that at one time was present to sensation when the object is no longer present (*Habeo facultatem imaginandi seu phantasiam. Comque imaginations meae sint perceptions rerum, quae olim praesentes fuerunt, sunt sensorium, dum imaginor, absentium*). Turning that famous formula around, Baumgarten states that "nothing is in the imagination that was not first in sensation" (*Nihil est in phantasia, quod non ante fuerit in sensu*). The image of imagination (*imaginationes*) follows the law of the association of ideas (*association idearum*) and this law is the law of, so-to-speak, the totality (*percepta idea partiali recurrit eius totalis*).[91] Memory is taken up completely independently of this (reproductive) imagination. It is the faculty of recognizing representations reproduced by the imagination all as what was present within consciousness. When involving the recognition of sense representations, it is called sense memory (*memoria sensitive*), and when involving the recognition of conceptual content it is called intellectual memory (*memoria intellectualis*). The power to represent what is common, the universal, is active within memory (*Repraesentatis pluribus perceptionibus successivis, usque ad praesentem, partialem commune habentibus, partialis communis repraesentur, ut contenta in antecedente et sequente*). Phantasy, according to Baumgarten, is the particular faculty that analyzes the reproduced content of consciousness and recombines the parts into a new independent construct. This faculty also follows certain laws of totality (*Phantasmatum partes percipiuntur ut unum totum*). He postulates poetic phantasy [poetizing] (*facultas fingendi poetica*) as one species of it.

It is thought that Kant often lectured on Baumgarten's theory, but by relying on it he attempted to clarify the concept of the imagination. In Kant's lectures on metaphysics, as transmitted by Pölitz, imagination or, according to what was called there the formative power (*die "bildende" Kraft*), manifests in the following three forms:[92] 1. As the faculty of present formation (*Abbildung*) where it relates to present representations; 2. As the faculty of re-formation [or: reproduction] (*Nachbildung*) where it takes up representations from the past and conjoins them with those of the present (by means of association); and 3. As the faculty of pre-formation (*Vorbildung*) where it forms future representations out of present ones by following their relation to the past. What we ought to notice in this classification is that it proceeds by following a purely formal principle relying on the temporal directions of present, past, and future. While we can recognize in the faculty of present formation Baumgarten's sensation (*sensus*), in the faculty of reproduction Baumgarten's memory (*memoria*), and in the faculty of preformation Baumgarten's foresight (*praevisio*), the imagination (*Einbildungskraft*) in Kant, in distinction from Baumgarten, constitutes the higher concept. Where this classificatory schema takes time as the principle, we can recognize the germ of the theory that the proper domain of *a priori*[93] imagination in the *Critique of Pure Reason* is time. Parallel to this classification other classifications appear in the lectures on metaphysics, showing the same three functions of the imagination: 1. The faculty of

Einbildung: the faculty of producing images from itself independently of the object's actuality; 2. The faculty of *Gegenbildung*: The object (*Gegenbild*) is useful in producing images of other things, and language is such an object for depicting representations of things; 3. The faculty of *Ausbildung*: This constitutes the idea of the whole and endeavors to compare the object to the idea of the whole. We can recognize Baumgarten's *facultas fingendi* (productive imagination) and *facultas characteristica* (composition) respectively in the first two faculties, but they are all reduced to one item called imagination. In contrast to the first classification that is temporal, this classification has a spatial nuance. The prefixes "*Ein*," "*Gegen*," and "*Aus*" are items of spatial qualities. Here we see the first stages of the theory of transcendental philosophy that takes space as also a domain of the imagination. Now in the lectures on metaphysics, formative power or imagination, at times, is considered from the viewpoint of the meaningfulness and arbitrariness (*Willkürlichkeit*)[94] of the methods of its operation. In those cases, the arbitrary operations of the imagination are assigned to sensibility as the lower faculty of cognition, and its meaningful operations are assigned to the higher faculty of cognition, hence the understanding. In connection with the position of the imagination in the *Critique of Pure Reason*, therefore, we ought to take note of this fact that the domain of the imagination was broadened beyond the limits of sensibility to the realm of understanding. Not only that, but it also appears that the imagination is already related to reason as well. That is to say that while imagination as the faculty of *Ausbildung* in the second classification can be compared to Baumgarten's *phantasia*, as something involving the idea of the whole, as written above, we can presumably relate this to reason conceived as the faculty of ideas or the faculty of the whole. In other words, Baumgarten's schema has been transformed in various directions and the characteristics in him of Kant's concept of imagination have already appeared decisively.

In contrast to how the concept of the imagination in the *Lectures on Metaphysics* clearly reveals its origin in Baumgarten's psychology, Kant in his *Anthropology* (*Anthropologie in pragmatischer Hinsicht*, 1798) provides far more independent perspectives. In contrast to how the classification in the former is somewhat external, the schema of classification in the latter is taken from the structure itself of the so-called faculties. Here the characterization of some aspects of this faculty clearly show an influence of transcendental philosophy. Here the imagination, before anything else, is divided into productive (*produktiv*) and reproductive (*reproduktiv*). The imagination (*facultas imaginandi*) is defined as "a faculty of intuitions even when the object is not present" (*Vermögen der Anschauungen auch ohne Gegenwart des Gegenstandes*).[95] And the productive imagination is the object's original exhibition (*exhibition originaria*) and thus the faculty of exhibition preceding experience, and reproductive imagination is derivative exhibition (*exhibition derivative*), namely, the faculty of exhibition that recalls to the mind previously held empirical intuitions. "Pure intuitions of space and time are original exhibitions, and all others presuppose empirical intuition, which is called experience when connected with the concept of the object so that it becomes empirical cognition."[96] We eventually will need to take note of the fact that, in comparison to his discussion in the *Critique of Pure Reason*, he attributes the intuitions of pure space and time to the original exhibitions of the productive imagination. Now we cannot interpret the productive nature of imagination to mean that it can produce sensible representations that previously were not at all given to our sensible faculty. No matter how great an artist, or even enchantress, imagination may be, it is not "creative" in that sense and instead must get the material for its formations from the senses. Thus, the formations of imagination are not universally communicable as the concepts of understanding are.[97] In that case it is interesting that Kant takes note of the particular meaning of the word "sensation [sense]" (*Sinn*) (always in the singular). That is, the receptivity of the imagination to representations in their communication is called sense [sensation]. One says, "this man has no sense for it." In this case, what is meant is not the incapacity of the senses but rather, partially, the incapacity of the understanding to apprehend the representations communicated to him and unite them in thought.[98] The word sensation, quite ordinary in everyday terms, is in this way related to the imagination. Even when we speak of nonsense (*Unsinn*), or of there being full or profound *Sinn* within it [a remark], or call *der gesunde Menschenverstand* [sound human understanding] as *Gemeinsinn* [common sense], we would probably likewise be unable to conceive the word *Sinn* without relation to the imagination.[99] Furthermore, we ought to take note when he defines genius and says, "the originality (non-imitative productivity) of imagination is called genius when it is in agreement with concepts,"[100] by comparing it with the issue of the imagination in the *Critique of Judgment*.

The sensible imagination [phantasy] of productive imagination is divided into three kinds. 1. Sensible imagination [phantasy] of formation (*Dichtungsvermögen des Bildung*), namely, the molding faculty (*imagination plastica*) of intuitions. Phantasy (*Phantasie*) is its arbitrary operation, and its meaningful operation is called composition or invention and is the power of artistic creation. 2. Sensible imagination [phantasy] of association (*das sinnliche Dichtungsvermögen der Beigesellung*), namely, the associative faculty (*imaginatio associans*) of intuitions in time. The law of association, the frequently succeeding empirical representations, form a habit within the mind, and when one appears the other also appears. This is nothing but the law of contiguity. 3. Sensible imagination [phantasy] of affinity (*das sinnliche Dichtungsvermögen der Verwandtschaft*), namely, the faculty of affinity (*affinitas*) through the common origin of representations from one another. Affinity means cohesion of various things through derivation from a single foundation. The play of imagination, in this case, follows the law of sensibility that provides it with material, and its association accords with rules even without the consciousness of rules and proceeds in accordance with the understanding even if not derived from (*aus*) the understanding. In the above view, even if a detailed explanation is lacking in Kant's attribution of association founded on habit to the productive imagination, in contrast to Hume's still mechanistic idea, it implies a profound suggestion. But what especially possesses an important relation to the theory of the imagination in transcendental philosophy is the doctrine of the sensible imagination [phantasy] of affinity. He writes here, "[u]nderstanding and sensibility, for all their dissimilarity, join together with affinity spontaneously to produce cognition, as if one had its source in the other, or both originated from a common root." Furthermore, this state of affairs "is . . ., at least, to us incomprehensible" and if we try to investigate it human reason cannot but get lost in the dark.[101]

Next reproductive imagination is handled on the basis of the heading as "a faculty that makes present by means of imagination things of the past and of the future."[102]

Here we must take note that Kant attributes foresight (*Vorhersehungsvermögen*), namely, the faculty of representing something as that of the future, to the reproductive imagination.[103] When the faculty of making present things of the past (the power of recollection) (*Erinnerungsvermögen, Vermögen der Respicienz*) is acting arbitrarily, it's merely called reproductive imagination. By contrast, when it acts meaningfully it is called memory (*Gedächtnis*). Foresight (*praevisio*) is also called *Divinationsvermögen* (*Vermögen der Prospicienz*) and is "the necessary condition of all practical activity and of the ends to which man directs the use of our powers."[104] Any desire implies a foresight of what is possible in one's powers. Kant writes that our recollection of the past is undertaken only so that we can foresee the future. On such occasions, we look at our surroundings, from the standpoint of the present, in order to decide on something or prepare ourselves for it. As in Baumgarten, he sees foresight as ascending in special cases to the level of prophetic talent (*Wahrsagergabe*) (*facultas divinatrix*). Just around the middle point between the powers of recollection and foresight is the power of composition (*Bezeichnungsvermögen*). It is the faculty of cognition of what is present as a means of cohesion between the representation of what had been foreseen and the representation of what is past. Here Kant discusses the cognition of symbols (*Symbole*) and characters (*Charaktere*).[105]

Kant's posthumous works show how he constantly made new efforts to unfold the concept of the imagination. In his attempts to anthropologically determine the position of the imagination in the system of faculties, we can recognize a general tendency to try to raise this concept, more or less, to the position of the central concept of the full range of sensibility, nay, of the whole of mental activities. The fluctuations in his solutions are signs that he was not satisfied with classifying the functions in isolation as fixed and in parallel to each other. His incentive for ceaselessly attributing new capacities to the imagination, manifest here from a variety of angles, appears to be this "creative principle," as the original power of the mind, as if a presentiment of something like a unifying basis from out of which they all emerge or in which they are synthesized.

The standpoint of the *Anthropology* and the standpoint of transcendental philosophy presumably are not immediately identical. In contrast to the standpoint of transcendental philosophy, which is transcendental in a distinct sense, the standpoint of the human being is empirical. But we have seen that Kant's *Anthropology* already includes something equivalent to the idea of transcendental philosophy. On the other hand, we can say that the issue of Kant's transcendental philosophy or critical philosophy, in a distinct sense, is anthropological. In the transcendental methodology of the *Critique of Pure Reason*, he says that all the interests of one's reason, the speculative as well as the practical, can be combined in the following three questions: 1. What can I know?, 2. What ought I to do?, and 3. What may I hope?[106] But these same questions reappear in his *Logic* and furthermore, it is here stated that the three questions can be reduced to a fourth, the question of "What is the human being?," and that all of these are problems of anthropology (*Anthropologie*).[107] Hume said, "as *the science of man* is the only solid foundation for the other sciences, the only solid foundation we can give to this science itself must be founded on experience and observation."[108] Although Kant's issue was also anthropology, we can presumably say that in contrast to how Hume's anthropology was empirical, his had to be heightened to what might be called transcendental anthropology. This transcendental anthropology was made possible through the presentation of the completely new and unique issue of transcendental philosophy that made Kant's name great.

But in either case, it might be raised that the standpoint of anthropology is psychology. The standpoint of transcendental philosophy, in opposition to this, is purely logical. The issue here is the logical *a priori* that founds the validity of our cognition. We need to strictly distinguish between the problem of the *a priori* in the logical sense and the problem of psychological occurrences. Riehl thus designates psychological elucidations and deductions that are included within critique as "the improper" (*das Ungehörige*).[109] If it is something that merely belongs to empirical psychology, it certainly would be something without a place. But in cognition, the object of cognition is not the only issue, but the cognition of the object is also the issue. In addition to being the issue of the object, the issue of cognition is the issue of an operation. There, along with transcendental logic, we can conceive of transcendental psychology. Kant himself in the preface to the first edition of the *Critique of Pure Reason*, says that the Deduction of the Pure Concepts of Understanding in the Transcendental Analytic, the most important part of the *Critique*, possesses "two sides," and writes the following:

> One side refers to the object of pure understanding, and is intended to expound and render intelligible the objective validity of its *a priori* concept, and indeed for that reason is essential to my purpose. The other side seeks to investigate the pure understanding itself, its possibility and the cognitive faculties on which the pure understanding rests, and hence its subjective aspect. Although this exposition is of great importance for my chief purpose, it does not form an essential part of it. For the chief issue is always: What and how much can the understanding and reason cognize apart from all experience? and not How is the faculty of thought itself possible? The latter, as it were, is the search for the cause of a given effect and is thus somewhat hypothetical (though, as I will show on another occasion, that is probably not the actual state of affairs), and in this case it may appear that I am being permitted to simply express an opinion so that that the readers can also thus be free to be express a different opinion.[110]

Here Kant states therefore that the concept of pure understanding has an objective side and a subjective side. He distinguishes the Transcendental Deduction of the categories between the "subjective deduction" (*subjective Deduktion*) and the "objective deduction" (*objective Deduktion*).[111] If the latter is transcendental-logical, the former is transcendental-psychological. Moreover, transcendental logic presumably is unable to separate from transcendental psychology. The deduction of the first edition is heavily tinged in the so-called subjective deduction, but perhaps this shows that Kant [at this point] was yet unthorough. In any case, as cited above, even there while first denying that the subjective deduction belongs essentially to the main purpose of the *Critique*, he dares to execute it. If so, perhaps it only has "an illustrative significance" (*eine illustrative Bedeutung*) to make the abstract idea of the deduction of objective logic easily comprehensible.[112] This part was rewritten in the second edition. However, to view this by taking it to mean that there was some change in Kant's standpoint would be going too far. It is impossible to see that what pertains to a transcendental psychology was wiped away in the second edition. Transcendental logic, indeed as founded upon the transcendental nature (transcendentality) of the subject, can be separated from transcendental psychology. In transcendental philosophy, borrowing Kant's terms, there is the issue of the "source" (*Quell*) or "origin" (*Ursprung*) of cognition. This issue of source or origin is none other than the issue of transcendental psychology. We might say that it resembles the issue of phenomenology in Husserl. As the basis for the possibility of experience in general and the cognition of objects, Kant raises "three subjective sources of cognition" (*drei subjective Erkenntnisquellen*) or "three original sources (faculties of the soul)" (*drei ursprüngliche Quellen (Fähigkeiten oder Vermögen der Seele)*), sensation, imagination, and apperception.[113] And he states that these faculties have at the same time as they have an empirical application, a transcendental application. That transcendental application is none other than the issue of transcendental psychology. Transcendental logic must be tied to transcendental psychology and in turn transcendental psychology must be tied to transcendental logic. Logic and psyche need to be united. Subjective deduction and objective deduction must be united. Even though the transcendental deduction, as Kant stated, possesses in itself something "belonging to the hypothetical" for indeed being subjective, it can escape this subjective nature by becoming tied to objective deduction. Kant tried to harmonize that psychological hypothesis to its epistemological result. And in this way anthropology can presumably be tied to transcendental philosophy through the issue of so-called transcendental psychology. That Kant's *Anthropology* is heading towards the unification of the lineage of the faculties and the investigation of the "creative" functions of the mind by transcending the empirical to become profound, shows that it is rushing in this way towards the transcendental.

9.

[340] As already stated, the issue of the *Critique of Pure Reason* was experience. Kant's transcendental logic is a logic of experience. The logic of experience is transcendental logic because experience is not merely empirical but rather the unity of the empirical and the transcendental. The logic of experience is a logic of content and the logic of objects. The imagination would presumably fail to find a place on the basis of mere formal logic. The logic of imagination cannot be formal logic. Transcendental logic is related to the imagination where it is the logic of objects. Of course, as long as it is a logic, it is clear that it cannot be only about the content and that there must be some formal aspect there. Put differently, it is related to pure content. Kant is saying that transcendental logic is related to certain content, that is, it is limited merely to that of pure transcendental cognition.[114] Formal logic abstracted from all content of cognition, Kant's so-called general logic, is nothing but the negative touchstone of truth and does not decide truth in terms of content (objective truth). In contrast, transcendental logic is the "logic of truth" (*Logik der Wahrheit*).[115] This is because no matter what the cognition, it cannot oppose this logic without losing every content, namely, every

relation to the object, and hence every truth. Imagination will probably have no position on the basis of a logic of mere *Richtigkeit* (correctness). It is on the basis of the logic of *Wahrheit* (truth) that the imagination becomes an issue. Although transcendental logic is a logic of truth, of course as logic it does not deal with individual concrete empirical truths. Instead, it is the consideration of "transcendental truth" (*transzendentale Wahrheit*) that makes them possible. Kant writes, "all our cognition falls within the bounds of possible experience, and only in this universal relation to those experiences consists that transcendental truth which precedes all empirical truth and makes it possible."[116]

The basic concept of transcendental logic is synthesis. Without such a thing as synthesis, what was given to us would remain a chaotic manifold. Synthesis belongs to the subject's productive or spontaneous faculty. If the subject was to remain in a state of inactive passivity, the given would only blur our consciousness as a "throng" of phenomena or "capriccio." In regard to the problem of synthesis Kant had focused on the imagination. Empirical psychology already emphasizes the productive nature or spontaneity of the imagination in recollection, poetry, and dreams. If psychology before Kant had seen its activity mainly in the reproductive, in the output of false images, in illusions, fabrications, and feverish dreams, Kant's *Anthropology*, as already shown, had recognized its activity in far broader and normal processes of perception or representation. This idea had to be even further deepened in his transcendental philosophy. Kant thus says,

> Synthesis in general [*die Synthesis überhaupt*], as we shall hereafter see, is the mere result of the power of the imagination. The imagination is a blind but indispensable function of the soul, without which we should have no cognition whatsoever, but of which we are scarcely ever conscious.[117]

As we already touched upon, Kant speaks of the three sources of cognition at the beginning and end of the deduction of the pure concepts of understanding in the first edition of the *Critique of Pure Reason*, and explains that in each of these there exists, aside from its empirical employment, the transcendental employment:

> There are three original sources (faculties of the soul) which contain the possibility of all experience, and cannot in themselves be derived from any other faculty of the mind, namely, sensation, imagination, and apperception.... All of these faculties have a transcendental as well as an empirical employment which concerns the form alone, and is possible *a priori*.[118]
>
> There are three subjective sources of cognition upon which rests the possibility of experience in general and the cognition of its objects—sensation, imagination, and apperception. Each of these can be viewed as empirical, that is, in its application to given appearances, but all of them are likewise *a priori* elements or foundations, which make this empirical employment itself possible.[119]

And on the basis of these three original sources of cognition, Kant recognized three modes of synthesis. These are: 1. The synthesis of apprehension in intuition (*die*

Synthesis der Apprehension in der Anschauung). 2. The synthesis of reproduction in the imagination (*die Synthesis der Reproduktion in der Einbildung*). 3. The synthesis of recognition in the concept (*die Synthesis der Rekognition im Begriffe*). These are also described as: 1. The transcendental synopsis (*Synopsis*) of the manifold through sensation; 2. The synthesis (*Synthesis*) of the manifold through imagination; and 3. The unity (*Einheit*) of this synthesis through original apperception. In any of these syntheses, in correspondence with the empirical employment and the *a priori* employment of these faculties, there is an empirical synthesis and a pure or *a priori* synthesis. Moreover, the pure synthesis constitutes the limitations of the possibility of that empirical synthesis.

Now in explaining the above three modes of synthesis in order, Kant at the start noted the following. Our representations, whatever their origin, whether due to the influence of outer things or produced through inner causes, whether they arise *a priori* or empirically, as modifications of the mind, they must belong to inner sense (*der innere Sinn*) and as such all our cognitions are ultimately subordinate to the formal condition of inner sense, namely, time. They must be all ordered, connected, and brought into relation in time. And "[t]his is a general observation which, throughout what follows, must be borne in mind as being quite fundamental."[120] Therefore the above three modes of synthesis are always established on the ground of time and time is their common character. This general caution provided by Kant is important in understanding the relationship between their syntheses and imagination. For imagination is properly related to time. As we have already seen, having analyzed in his *Lectures on Metaphysics* the imagination or what is described there as the formative power (*die bildende Kraft*), Kant states there that this faculty produces either representations of present time, or representations of past time, or representations of future time. The formative power is, therefore, constituted from 1. the faculty of present-formation (*Abbildung*) (*facultas formandi*) of representations of present time, 2. the faculty of re-formation (*Nachbildung*) (*facultas imaginandi*) of representations of past time, and 3. the faculty of pre-formation (*Vorbildung*) (*facultas praevidendi*) of representations of future time.[121] In this way the *Bildung* (formation) of *Einbildung* (imagination) is related to time. Accordingly, if any of the above three modes of synthesis is established on the ground of time, we can regard them in common as involving the imagination.

1. The synthesis of apprehension in intuition: Every intuition implies a manifold and is the unity of the manifold. In order for that unity to be a unity in accordance with the manifold, the mind must distinguish between before and after in accordance with the succession of impressions, for "each representation, in so far as it is contained in a single moment, can never be anything but absolute unity."[122] For the unity of intuition to obtain from this manifold, first there is the survey of the manifold nature, next its cohesion is necessary, and this process involving intuition is what is called the synthesis of apprehension. Although intuition provides the manifold, when it does so but without the activity of synthesis it cannot be contained in a single representation even if it is a manifold. This synthesis is no mere *now* but a *Synopsis* (synopsis) that sees the succeeding *now, now, now* . . . in a single present and can be regarded as corresponding to what is called *Abbildung* in the *Lectures on Metaphysics*. (In this case, *Abbildung* does

not have the meaning of imitation but is formation in the sense of direct observation of the form of the object itself.) This synthesis of apprehension without being limited to empirical intuition should also be applicable to pure intuition. Without that, neither would we possess the transcendental representations of space or of time. For these representations are only produced in the synthesis of the manifold offered by sensibility "in their original receptivity" (*in ihrer ursprünglichen Rezeptivität*). Herein lies the pure synthesis of apprehension. However, if every intuition is given in the forms of space and time, the pure synthesis of apprehension would have to be the basis of the possibility of their empirical synthesis.

Now, what then is the relationship like between that synthesis of apprehension and imagination? Kant says that every phenomenon [appearance][123] contains a manifold and hence although that synthesis is required because we are conscious of the perceptions in themselves as individually dispersed, perceptions cannot have this combination in the sensations themselves. Kant then writes the following:

> There must therefore exist in us an active faculty for synthesis of this manifold, and I name this the imagination, and I name its immediate operation on perceptions {*deren unmittelbar an den Wahrnehmungen ausgeübte Handlung*}, apprehension {*Apprehension*}. Since imagination has to bring the manifold of intuition into the form of an image {*in ein Bild*},[124] it must previously have taken the impressions up into its activity, that is, have apprehended them.[125]

In the note to the same passage, Kant says that "[p]sychologists have hitherto failed to realize that imagination is a necessary ingredient of perception itself {*ein notwendiges Ingredienz der Wahrnehmung selbst*},"[126] and, proud of his unique view, raises as a cause of their negligence the fact that the imagination had been limited to something merely reproductive. The pure synthesis of apprehension must therefore be one mode of productive imagination or *a priori* imagination. And so in the second edition of the *Critique of Pure Reason* he only discusses empirical apprehension and, instead of pure apprehension, speaks of "the successive synthesis of the productive imagination."[127] And as we had already noted, in the *Anthropology*, the pure intuitions of space and time are attributed to original exhibitions (*exhibition originaria*) of productive imagination.

2. The synthesis of reproduction in imagination: In this case as well Kant starts from the reproductive synthesis in the operation of empirical representation. Representations that had often succeeded or accompanied [one another] in the end become associated and thereby connected, and when one of those representations is given, the other representation is reproduced according to a certain rule even when the object is not present. It is clear that this reproduction belongs to the imagination. Imagination, according to the definition, is "the faculty of representing in intuition an object even when it is not present" (*das Vermögen einen Gegenstand auch ohne dessen Gegenwart in der Anschauung vorzustellen*).[128] If representations were indiscriminately reproduced as they were encountered by chance, what appears would not be any determinate relation but the disorderly collection of representations and so would not engender any cognition. Thus the reproduction of representations must have rules. But these rules of reproduction are premised on the fact that phenomena themselves

actually follow these rules and that within this manifold of representations, there occurs rule-abiding accompaniment or succession. Otherwise, our empirical imagination would be unable to do anything suited to its faculty and would probably be buried in the mind as a dead faculty unknown to us. If a cinnabar is red or black, light or heavy, my empirical imagination would still be unable to remember the heavy cinnabar with the representation of the color red. On this point without any rule that phenomena themselves already follow, no empirical synthesis of reproduction could be established. And so Kant states, "there must then be something, which as the *a priori* ground of a necessary synthetic unity of appearances, makes possible in this way even the reproduction of appearances."[129] There must be the *a priori* imagination's pure synthesis of pure reproduction as the ground of the possibility of the empirical imagination's empirical synthesis of empirical reproduction. "However, if we reflect that appearances are not things in themselves, but the mere play of our representations, and representations are ultimately reduced to the determinations of inner sense, we would immediately come to discover this something."[130] It is clear that the pure synthesis of pure reproduction is related to time as the formal condition of the intuition of phenomena.

> If we can show that even our purest *a priori* intuitions yield no cognition, save insofar as they contain a combination of the manifold such as renders a thoroughgoing synthesis of reproduction possible, then this synthesis of imagination is likewise grounded, antecedently to all experience, upon *a priori* principles. And we must assume a pure transcendental synthesis of imagination as conditioning the very possibility of all experience (which is to say that the possibility of experience necessarily presupposes the reproducibility of appearances).[131]

If I were now to draw a line in my head or think of the time from one day to another day or attempt to represent a certain number, I would necessarily have to grasp these manifold representations in thought, one by one, in order. But if I always forget the preceding representation (the beginning portion of the line, the preceding part of time, the unit of time represented in order) and do not reproduce it when moving to the next representation, the representation of the whole would not happen at all, nay, "not even the purest and most primordial fundamental representations of space and time would arise."[132] This means it is not lost in the synthesis of reproduction, or put differently, it is preserved. But in order for what had been experienced before to be preserved, the mind must "distinguish time," and on that occasion it must see things like "before" and "at that time." What had been experienced before, unless it is preservable in general, would utterly be lost ceaselessly with the *now* of each occasion. Thus, in order for the empirical synthesis of reproduction to be possible, the "no longer now" already in advance must be reproduced as itself prior to every experience and be made one with each *now*. This occurs in pure reproduction, and pure reproduction is the pure synthesis of pure imagination. But if we take pure imagination to be essentially productive (*produktiv*), would it not be a contradiction to say that reproductive (*reproduktiv*) synthesis belongs to productive imagination? In response to this question, we can answer that pure reproduction in advance forms the possibility of reproduction in general by making the "before" manifest as itself. That is, this pure synthesis forms pastness itself and is equivalent to what is called *Nachbildung* in the *Lectures on Metaphysics*. So then where does this pure synthetic nature reside in this formation? The primordial formative preservation of the "at that time" is the formation preserving the "no longer now" and this formation is united with each *now*. Pure reproduction as formative of the present is essentially united with the pure synthesis of intuition. Kant says, "[t]he synthesis of apprehension is thus inseparably bound up with the synthesis of reproduction."[133] Every now is now already "just now." In order for the synthesis of apprehension to synopsize *now, now, now* ... in a single present, it must be able to preserve the present manifold surveyed each time as that thing. Accordingly, it must simultaneously be the pure synthesis of reproduction.

3. The synthesis of recognition in the concept: Just as the synthesis of apprehension is tied to the synthesis of reproduction and anticipates it, the synthesis of reproduction—and hence also the synthesis of apprehension—is tied to the synthesis of recognition and anticipates it. Kant first writes, "[i]f we were not conscious that what we think is the same as what we thought a moment before, all reproduction in the series of representations would be useless."[134] For our present thought is a new representation in the current state and this representation would accordingly not in any way belong to the act whereby it was to be gradually generated, and the manifold of representation would never, therefore, form a whole, since it would lack that unity that only consciousness can impart to it. For example, when counting numbers, if I were to forget that the units, hovering now before my mind, were added in succession by myself, I should never be able to produce the quantity through the successive addition of units, and so also be unable to cognize the number. The concept of number is obtained on the basis of the consciousness of the unity of such synthesis. Synthesis aiming at unity or identity thus lies at the root of the synthesis of apprehension and of the synthesis of reproduction to guide them. Kant designated this synthesis, synthesis "in a concept." This is because the concept is the representation of a unity appropriate as something identical for the many. "For this unitary consciousness is what combines the manifold, successively intuited, and thereupon also reproduced, into one representation."[135] Lacking this consciousness concepts would be impossible and then the cognition of objects would be utterly impossible. What then is an object? The object is said to correspond to cognition and hence is also something thus distinguished from cognition. But primarily we have nothing aside from our cognition that we can set over against it as something corresponding to this cognition. However, our thought recognizes that a certain necessity accompanies every cognition's relation to its object. That is to say, our cognition considers the object as something to be determined a priori in some manner instead of its unreliable haphazard determination. Because it has to be related to an object, our cognition must be necessarily and, in relation to this object, mutually consistent.[136] Put differently, it must possess a unity where it shapes the concept of a single object. But because what is related to us is only the manifold of our representations, the unity necessary for the object is nothing other than the formal unity of consciousness in the synthesis of the manifold of representations. Hence,

only when we have thus produced synthetic unity in the manifold of intuition ..., we are in a position to say that we cognize the object. But this synthetic unity is impossible unless the intuition is produced by the function of synthesis in accordance with a rule whereby the reproduction of the manifold *a priori* is made necessary and renders possible a concept in which this manifold is connected.[137]

For example, we think of a triangle as an object whereby we are conscious of the combination of three straight lines according to a rule by which the intuition of a triangle can always be exhibited. This unity of rule determines all the manifold and limits it to the conditions which make the unity of apperception possible. And the concept of this unity is the representation of the object.[138] Now all necessity is grounded in a transcendental [*a priori*] condition. There must, therefore, be a transcendental ground of the unity of consciousness in the synthesis of the manifold of all of our intuitions, and also in the synthesis of concepts of objects [客観] in general and also in the synthesis of all objects [対象] of experience. Without this it would be impossible to think of any object for our intuitions. For the object is nothing more than something, the concept of which expresses the necessity of synthesis in regard to it. This original and transcendental condition is nothing other than transcendental apperception.[139] In this way Kant introduces here the concept of transcendental apperception (*die transzendentale Apperzeption*). There can be in us neither cognition nor even the mutual connection or unity of cognitions without the unity of consciousness which precedes all data of intuitions, and by relation to which representation of objects is alone possible. This "pure original unchangeable consciousness" is what he calls transcendental apperception. That it deserves this name is already made evident by the fact that even the purest objective unity, namely, that of *a priori* concepts (space and time), is only possible through a relation of the intuitions to such consciousness.[140]

And so, the issue for us is this third synthesis, essentially the relation of the first synthesis and imagination that acts rather by guiding the earlier two syntheses. We should be able to solve this issue by first clarifying the relation between this synthesis of recognition and time. As we already stated, if we regard pure apprehension as equivalent to present-formative *Abbildung* and pure reproduction as equivalent to past-formative *Nachbildung*, can we not conceive pure recognition as corresponding to what in the *Lectures on Metaphysics* is called future-formative *Vorbildung*? In fact, Heidegger for example thought in this way and explained this in the following manner.[141] The synthesis of recognition is engendered by, so-to-speak, preceding the other two syntheses. It was appropriate that Kant gave the name recognition (*Rekognoszieren*) to this synthesis of identification. It is a prior reconnaissance (*erkunden, rekognoszieren*), a search (*durchspähen*) for that which must be grasped in advance as identical.[142] By means of this the syntheses of apprehension and of reproduction can pre-discover the complete domain of beings, within which it can work upon them in general. This reconnoitering synthesis of identification as something empirical, however, necessarily presupposes a pure identification. If we put this differently, as pure reproduction forms the possibility of reproduction, pure recognition provides the possibility of identification. When this pure synthesis reconnoiters, it does not reconnoiter beings it can pre-preserve as identical but instead reconnoiters the horizon of pre-preservability in general (*den Horizont von Vorhaltbarkeit überhaupt*). This reconnaissance as pure reconnaissance is the originary formation of the precedent (*das Vorhafte*), namely, the future. Therefore, the third synthesis is essentially time-formative as well. It is a pure *Vorbildung* (preformation) and an operation of pure imagination. Furthermore, the intrinsic structural predominance of this pure preformation over the other two, while being alongside them, reveals the most originary essence of time—that it primarily temporizes from the future. Thus, according to Heidegger, pure apprehension, pure reproduction, and pure recognition each belong to the transcendental imagination and are nothing but the "three modes" of its pure synthesis and reveals the unity of three aspects of time as present, past, future. As a pure formative faculty, the transcendental imagination is time-formative or enables the revelation of time. This is the inner essence of pure, namely, productive transcendental imagination and, in a word, we can say that transcendental imagination is originary time.

What becomes an issue now in this original interpretation, as we described above, is the transcendental apperception Kant raised as the ground of the synthesis of recognition. Transcendental apperception means "I think" (*Ich denke*).[143] Is it possible for this *I* and time to coincide? Kant says, "the abiding and unchanging 'I' (of pure apperception) {*das stehende und bleibende Ich (der reinen Apperzeption)*} forms the correlate of all our representations..."[144] He also calls this *I* "the standing or remaining self" (*das stehende oder bleibende Selbst*)[145] and defines transcendental apperception as "pure original unchangeable consciousness" (*das reine, ursprüngliche, unwandelbare Bewusstsein*).[146] If so, would not transcendental apperception or transcendental ego be something transtemporal, eternal? In response to this question, Heidegger first shows that the essence of both time and the "I think" is indicated by the same predicate. In other words, just as the *I* of pure apperception is said to be "*das stehende und bleibende Ich*," in the chapter on the schematism that clarifies the transcendental essence of time, Kant says the same concerning time. He says, "time does not pass {*die Zeit verläuft sich nicht*}. What are transitory in time are passing. Among appearances, the non-transitory, namely, substance, corresponds to time, which itself is non-transitory and abiding {*die Zeit, die selbst unwandelbar und bleibend ist*}."[147] The coinciding of predicates that manifest the essence of time and the transcendental ego, therefore, does not mean that they are together "in time" (*in der Zeit*). But, according to Heidegger, neither does this mean that the *I* is not "temporal" (*zeitlich*). Staying or remaining are not ontological definitions concerning the immutability of the *I*, but rather *a priori* definitions, and means the following. Only to the extent that the *I* itself maintains in advance the nature of staying and remaining in general, does it form the horizon of self-identity, within which an object can be experienced as something identical that changes. What is called "*stehend*" means that the *I* as "I think" pre-preserves "*Stand und Bestand*" (constancy) and as such the *I* forms the correlate of constancy in general. However, this pure production of pure phenomena of the present in general is the essence of time itself as pure intuition. The staying and remaining *I*, in my originary formation of time, put differently as originary time, is nothing other than the objectification (*Gegenstehenlassen*, namely, letting-stand-in-opposition) of the object (*Gegenstand*, namely, what stands-opposed) and the formation of its horizon. Nevertheless, is Heidegger's interpretation thus really valid as an interpretation of Kant? We need to pursue the issue of the imagination in Kant further from the schematism to the third *Critique*.

10.

[359] The issue was the synthesis of recognition in concepts and the relation between transcendental apperception and the imagination. In regard to the other two syntheses, namely the synthesis of apprehension and the synthesis of reproduction, it is clear from where we discussed earlier that they belong to the imagination. Thus, if the issue of experience is something that can be settled at this point, as Hume said, the understanding is "... the general and more establish'd properties of the imagination,"[148] and it would be conceivable that the understanding and the imagination are one. By further raising the concepts of transcendental apperception or pure apperception, Kant moved beyond Hume's standpoint of empiricism. It is, accordingly, important for understanding Kant's theory of experience to clarify the relationship between transcendental apperception, or understanding, and the imagination.

In the first edition of the *Critique of Pure Reason*, the Transcendental Deduction possesses two paths. One is the path from above (A116–120) and the other is the path from below (A120–128). The path from above starts from pure apperception. It is the point where all representations become one possible experience by being consolidated there and attaining a unity of cognition for the first time. Every intuition, unless it is taken into consciousness in either case whether by directly flowing into consciousness or by mediation, is nothing to us, without relations, and cognition is only possible by our being conscious of it. In regard to all representations belonging to our cognition, we are conscious *a priori* of the thoroughgoing unity of our self as the necessary condition for the possibility of every representation. This consciousness is self-consciousness or self-awareness (*Selbstbewusstsein*) as original apperception, and it is the transcendental principle of the unity of every manifold of our representations (and hence in intuition). Self-awareness in Kant, expressed as "I think" (*Ich denke*), namely, the consciousness of the thoroughgoing identity of the self itself (*die durchgängige Identität unserer selbst*),[149] is a synthetic unity, not an analytic unity. It is not an abstract self-identity as when we say "I am I" but instead a synthetic unity established in accord with the manifold. Kant states that "the unity of the manifold in the subject is synthetic and therefore transcendental apperception supplies the principle of the synthetic unity of the manifold to all possible intuition."[150] But what must be there for transcendental apperception to be a synthetic unity in this way. Kant follows the above by saying, "This synthetic unity, however, presupposes or includes a synthesis {*Diese synthetische Einheit setzt aber eine Synthesis voraus oder schliesst sie ein*}. And if the former is to be *a priori* necessary, the latter must also be *a priori*."[151] In order for transcendental apperception to be a synthetic unity instead of an analytic unity or, borrowing Heidegger's words,[152] for it to be a veritative synthesis (*die veritative (Wahr-machende) Synthesis*) instead of a predicative synthesis (*die prädikative Synthesis*), it must presuppose a single original synthesis or subsume it. We might say that transcendental apperception in itself is the capacity to unite and not the capacity of synthesis.[153] "Synthesis in general ... is the mere result of the power of imagination."[154] Kant follows this by further saying,

> Therefore, the transcendental unity of apperception relates to the pure synthesis of imagination, as an *a priori* condition of the possibility of all combination of the manifold in a cognition. But only the productive synthesis of the imagination can take place *a priori*, for reproductive synthesis rests upon conditions of experience. Thus, the principle of the necessary unity of pure (productive) synthesis of imagination, prior to {*vor*} apperception, is the ground of [the possibility of all] cognition, especially of experience.[155]

That is, from the perspective of synthesis, the synthesis of the imagination is the most originary and as such "precedes" apperception, and apperception must also "presuppose" it as the unity of synthesis. Put differently, apperception must face the pure synthesis of the imagination and work upon it. We can probably say that the unity of apperception in a certain sense is something coming after in relation to the synthesis of the imagination. Kant states, "the unity of apperception in relation to the synthesis of imagination is the understanding; and this same unity [the unity of apperception], with reference to the transcendental synthesis of the imagination, is the pure understanding."[156] In other words, apperception, to the extent that it presupposes pure imagination, is mere understanding. In relation to the originary synthesis of the imagination, apperception functions as mere understanding. Now because pure synthesis must combine *a priori*, that which it combines must be given *a priori*. Pure imagination, therefore, must be related to time, and in this way is the mediator between transcendental apperception and time, or between the understanding and sensibility. The imagination, as nothing but its own power, in this way occupies the rank of mediator. This was indicated by the first path.

The second path has its start at the bottom, namely, the empirical. That which is given to us initially is phenomenon [appearance] and when this becomes tied to consciousness it is called perception. Because each phenomenon contains a manifold, and we thus become conscious of perception of all kinds as it is dispersed individually in itself, its combination is necessary. But perception cannot have this in sensation itself. The active power for the synthesis of this manifold is the imagination and, as we stated before, the function it exercises immediately upon perception is named apprehension. Imagination must bring the manifold of intuitions into a single form-image [*keizō*]. However, with just this alone, even this manifold of perception would presumably be unable to produce any form-image, or even any of connection of impressions. For this there must exist some further additional subjective ground. More specifically, the reproductive power of the imagination that recalls previous perceptions in relation to later perceptions when the mind transitions from one perception to another and in this way exhibits an entire series, is necessary. Nevertheless, if representations were mutually reproduced just as they were accidentally encountered, only their disordered heap without any determinate representation would be produced and accordingly no cognition would arise. Thus, the reproduction of representations must have rules and representations must be combined in the imagination according to those rules. The subjective empirical ground of reproduction following these rules is designated the association (*Assoziation*) of representations. Nevertheless, unless the unity of such association also possesses an objective ground and it becomes impossible to apprehend the phenomenon apart from its founding upon the condition of the possible synthetic unity of this apprehension by means of imagination, the conformity of the phenomenon to a certain connection in human cognition would presumably be utterly accidental. For even if we possess the capacity to associate perceptions, by this alone it would be completely uncertain whether these perceptions are associable (*assoziabel*) or not. And if the perceptions were not associable, a group of perceptions such as many empirical consciousnesses nonetheless dispersed in my mind, without them belonging to the individual consciousness of my self, not only that, all sensations, would presumably become possible. But that is impossible. For we can say that for every perception I am conscious of it only by inserting it into the individual consciousness of an original apperception. For that reason, there must be an objective ground that constitutes the necessity of only the possibility of laws covering all phenomena or, put differently, a ground that can be recognized *a priori* and preceding every empirical law of the imagination, where all phenomena can be seen as in themselves associable and in their reproduction given by sense-organs according to universal laws of thoroughgoing connection. Kant called this objective ground of every association of phenomena [appearances], the affinity of appearances (*die Affinität der Erscheinungen*). Now we cannot discern this ground anywhere apart from the fundamental principle of the unity of apperception in relation to every cognition that ought to belong to us. In accordance with this fundamental principle all phenomena must be apprehended as if in agreement with the unity of apperception. Yet this would be impossible without the phenomena's own, and objectively necessary, synthetic unity in their connections. That is to say that the fact that phenomena "conform to the unity of apperception" (*zur Einheit der Apperzeption zusammenstimmen*)[157] means that the synthesis of imagination vis-a-vis apperception makes the latter possible by producing a synthetic unity in the connection of phenomena and thus the affinity of phenomena. Kant therefore states,

> For this reason, the objective unity of all (empirical) consciousness in one consciousness (of original apperception) is thus the necessary condition of all possible perception; and the affinity of all appearances (near or remote) is the necessary consequence of a synthesis in imagination which is grounded *a priori* on rules.[158]

Although the unity of apperception is a necessary condition of all phenomena, the synthesis of imagination precedes it and through it, phenomena can accord with the unity of apperception. And in this way apperception as well can relate to phenomena by means of the synthesis of the imagination. Kant, therefore, states elsewhere the following. Originally all phenomena [appearances], as representations, belong to self-consciousness, but self-consciousness is the numerical identity (*die numerische Identität*), and nothing can be cognized save in terms of this original apperception. Now this identity, to the extent that it is supposed to be an empirical cognition, must necessarily enter the synthesis of all the manifold of phenomena [appearances].

Phenomena, therefore, are subject to *a priori* conditions, with which their synthesis (in apprehension) must be in complete accordance. Thus, all phenomena [appearances] stand in a thoroughgoing connection according to necessary laws, or, in other words, stand in a transcendental affinity, of which empirical affinity is a mere effect.[159] Affinity is the affinity of the manifold (*die Affinität des Mannigfaltigen*). Thus, for the unity of apperception to enter phenomena in this way the synthesis of the imagination is presupposed, and by means of this, apperception as the numerical identity or numerical unity (*die numerische Einheit*) becomes a synthetic unity. Now the necessary unity in the synthesis of phenomena belongs to the transcendental function of the imagination.

> Therefore, although at a glance it may seem strange, but nonetheless an obvious consequence of the preceding argument, only by means of this transcendental function of the imagination can the affinity of appearances be possible, and with it their association be possible, and through this association finally their reproduction according to laws be possible, and so experience itself be possible. For without this ... function, no concepts of objects would together make up a single experience.[160]

In this way the *a priori* function of imagination is something original of its own. But if so, what significance does pure apperception, by contrast, possess? Kant says, "[i]t is this apperception which must be added to pure imagination, in order to render its function intellectual. {*Diese Apperzeption ist es nun, welche zu der reinen Einbildungskraft hinzukommen muss, um ihre Function intellektuell zu machen.*}"[161] The synthesis of the imagination is its own original synthesis. Apperception, by contrast, is added to it in order to make its function intellectual. "If the synthesis of the imagination, even if it is undertaken *a priori*, combines the manifold only as it appears in intuition—for example, in the shape of a triangle—it is always in itself sensible."[162] To say that it is sensible means that the synthesis of the imagination is something intuitional and involves (form-)images (*Bild, Gestalt, Bezeichnung*). In the language of the second edition, this synthesis is a synthesis of (form-)images (*synthesis speciosa*) as opposed to intellectual synthesis (*synthesis intellectualis*).[163] "Concepts can arise only by relationship of the manifold to the unity of apperception. While concepts belong to the understanding, they can be related to sensible intuition only by means of the imagination."[164] As already stated, "the unity of apperception in relation to the synthesis of the imagination is the understanding,"[165] and concepts related to sense intuition are only established through the mediation of the imagination. Kant writes,

> We thus possess pure imagination as a fundamental faculty {*ein Grundvermögen*} of the human soul, where it lies *a priori* at the root of all cognition. By its means we connect the manifold of intuition on the one side to the condition of the necessary unity of pure apperception on the other side. Both ends of sensibility and understanding therefore must stand in necessary connection through the mediation of this transcendental function of imagination. {*Beide äusserste Enden, nämlich Sinnlichkeit und Verstand, müssen vermittelst dieser transzendentalen Funktion der Einbildungskraft notwendig zusammenhängen.*}"[166]

From what was stated above, it cannot be doubted, first of all, that Kant conceived the imagination as an independent primal power. Its unique fundamental function is synthesis. Apperception as well, to the extent that it involves synthesis, must presuppose the imagination. To begin with, this synthesis is not an intellectual synthesis, and the unity of apperception must be added to intellectualize the function of the imagination, but this is rather a secondary relationship vis-à-vis the function of the imagination itself. Next, Kant recognized in the synthesis of the imagination the significant duty of mediating sensibility and understanding. It is the mediator for apperception and time. By taking the synthesis of the imagination as mediation, phenomena on the one hand match the unity of apperception, and the unity of apperception on the other hand enter into phenomena. When this happens the imagination works not in the manner of mechanically linking sensibility and understanding after the fact, but instead works in a manner that makes their synthesis possible, to begin with. It is originally cohesive and, as its own power, forms the unity of the other two. Relying on Heidegger's words, it is *die bildende Mitte* (the formative center).[167] The synthesis of the imagination is a veritative synthesis, not a predicative synthesis because it is involved in this way in the unity of intuition and thought. In this sense, the imagination possesses a fundamental relation to "the logic of truth." Now in the discussions and conclusion of the *Critique of Pure Reason* Kant further makes the following noteworthy statements. He says,

> There are two stems {*zwei Stämme*} of human cognition, which perhaps arose from a single common, but to us unknown, root {*au seiner gemeinschaftlichen, aber uns unbekannten Wurzel*}. They are sensibility and understanding. By means of the former objects are given to us, and by means of the latter they are thought.[168]

He says,

> We shall content ourselves here with the completion of our task, namely, to complete the task of merely to outline the architectonic of all cognition arising from mere pure reason. And we shall begin from the point where the common root of our faculty of cognition {*die allgemeine Wurzel unserer Erkenntniskraft*} divides and throws out two stems. One of those stems is reason. By reason here I understand the entire higher faculty of cognition. Thus I am contrasting the rational to the empirical.[169]

It is clear that the empirical here is sensibility itself. What is designated the "fountainhead" of cognition in other cases is seen here in these passages as a "stem" arising from a single common root. And in contrast to how the former passage described the "common root" with the word "perhaps," in the later passage, the "common root" is described as something existing. Furthermore, in both passages, this root is only suggested and even stated to be "unknown to us." Ought we to understand this common root of sensibility and understanding to be the imagination? We are reminded here of what Kant said in the *Anthropology* in regard to the imagination of affinity.[170] Therein he defines affinity as "the connection of the manifold by virtue of its origin from one ground" (*die Vereinigung aus der Abstammung des Mannigfaltigen von einem Grunde*).[171]

> The play of the imagination {*das Spiel der Einbildungskraft*} in this case follows the laws of sensibility, which provides the material, and this is associated without consciousness of the rule but still in keeping with it. So the association is carried out in conformity with {*gemäss*} understanding, though it is not derived from {*aus*} understanding.[172]

The *Critique of Pure Reason* also states that the synthesis of the imagination is sensible, as we have already seen. However, it is not just sensible. Even if it does not arise from the understanding, it conforms to the understanding, and even if we are not conscious of this, it conforms to laws and thus is at the same time intelligible. This is so not because it is forced by the understanding but rather it is so on its own. This is why it is called the play of the imagination. And in this case Kant brings the concept of affinity into the relationship between understanding and sensibility:

> Understanding and sensibility, for all their dissimilarity {*Ungleichartigkeit*}, join together with affinity spontaneously to produce cognition, as if one had its source in the other, or both originated from a common root {*als wenn eine von der anderen, oder beide von einem gemeinschaftlichen Stamme ihren Ursprung hätten*}. But that is impossible or, at least, to us incomprehensible how heterogeneous things could spring from one and the same root {*au seiner und derselben Wurzel*}."[173]

In the note for this passage, he further asks, "[i]n what darkness human reason gets lost when it tries to probe the source {*Abstamm*}, or even merely guess what it is!"[174] "The imagination is a blind but indispensable function of the soul, without which we should have no cognition whatsoever, but of which we are scarcely ever conscious."[175] Kant thus confronted the issue of the imagination in the most significant part of the *Critique of Pure Reason*, namely, the Transcendental Deduction. And in regard to the imagination, he recognized its status as mediator between sensibility and understanding. Construction [*kōzō*, 構造], through sensibility and understanding and their connection, is grounded in the structure of the imagination. The latter occupies a fundamental position in the founding of human cognition to the extent that the former two are thought to be derived through differentiation from it. We must say that Heidegger's contribution in his Kant reading was in clarifying the significance of the imagination in this way.

Nevertheless, would not the admission to an underlying status for the imagination in this way contradict the many passages in the *Critique of Pure Reason* where a central position is attributed to apperception? There are various problems requiring us to enter into and investigate. This is not simply the formal issue of "predominance" concerning apperception and imagination but the more essential issue of "structure" [*kōzō*, 構造].

First, Kant raised sensibility, imagination, and apperception as three sources of cognition, but in other places he only considered two sources. He says, "our cognition springs from two fundamental sources of the mind. The first is the capacity of receiving representations (receptivity for impressions), and the second is the power of cognizing an object through these representations (spontaneity of concepts)."[176] And further, more pointedly, he says, "we have no source of cognition besides these two (sensibility and understanding)."[177] And yet, despite this, if we accept that "cognition arises only through their combination," there would have to be something that mediates sensibility and understanding, and we can say that that is indeed what the imagination is. Moreover, if we consider that this combination is not made after the fact but instead unites them and that this "synthesis" originates them in their connection and unity, we may have to view the imagination rather as the origin, the original unity, of these sources. But a counter argument can be made to this view that what combines sensibility and understanding is none other than original apperception. But if we accept this to be the case, the imagination as an original source would be eliminated and its significance would have to be taken as utterly secondary.

Second, in the second edition the status of the imagination, in fact, is conspicuously demoted and almost eliminated. He says,

> since all our intuition is sensible, the imagination, owing to the subjective condition under which alone it can give to the concepts of understanding a corresponding intuition, belongs to sensibility. But inasmuch as its synthesis is determinative and an expression of spontaneity and not, like sense, determinable merely, and which is therefore able to determine sense *a priori* in respect of its form in accordance with the unity of apperception, imagination is to that extent a faculty which determines the sensibility *a priori*. And its synthesis of intuitions, in accordance with the categories, must be the transcendental synthesis of imagination. This is an action of the understanding on the sensibility {*eine Wirkung des Verstandes auf die Sinnlichkeit*}, and its first application to the objects of our possible intuition (and thereby it is the ground of all other applications above)."[178]

That is, the imagination here is admitted to be spontaneous, in distinction from mere sensibility, at the same time that it is sensible, but this spontaneous synthesis, in fact, can be thought to be the work of the understanding in relation to sensibility. Because it is the application of the understanding in relation to the objects of intuition, we can think of it to be in accordance (*gemäss*) with the unity of apperception or the categories. It is said to be "the transcendental act of imagination (the synthetic influence of the understanding upon inner sense)" (*die transzendentale Handlung der Einbildungskraft (synthetischer Einfluss des Verstandes auf den inneren Sinn*); and apperception is viewed as "the source of all combination" (*der Quelle aller Verbindung*).[179] Now if we look back to the passage in the *Anthropology* previously mentioned, the imagination there as well pertains to understanding at the same time as being sensible, spontaneous at the same time that it is receptive. It is also written in the above passage from the second edition of the *Critique of Pure Reason* that its synthesis belongs to spontaneity and that, to that extent, the imagination is said to be productive. However, in the *Anthropology* the association of the imagination accords to rules without the consciousness of rules, accords (*gemäss*) to the understanding even if it is not derived from (*aus*) the understanding, and is seen as the "play" (*Spiel*) of the imagination. In such a way the imagination, indeed, essentially pertains to the understanding at the same time as pertaining to sensibility. Kant thus started to think that the original affinity in the imagination between sensibility and understanding may mean that the imagination is their common root. And he says that "the originality... of imagination is called genius when it is in agreement with concepts" (*Die Originalität der Einbildungskraft, wenn sie zu Begriffen zusammenstimmt, heist Genie*).[180] The imagination is essentially something of genius. It does not belong merely to a small number of geniuses; it is the capacity for genius that primordially belongs to human beings.

Third, we thus need to view the issue of the imagination in Kant in a double relationship. On the one hand the imagination, as a fundamental capacity (*ein Grundvermögen*), possesses its own peculiar function. Kant, as we already stated, is also known to have admitted this essential activity of the imagination. Heidegger's contribution was mainly in attempting to grasp the primary form of the synthesis of the imagination. But on the other hand, the synthesis of the imagination secondarily has a reflected, intellectualized form.[181] "Apperception is that which must be added to pure imagination, in order to render its function intellectual."[182] Transcendental apperception renders the imagination intellectual. When this occurs the imagination thoroughly stands under the condition of transcendental apperception. Nevertheless, we can also say that it is able to be rendered intellectual in this fashion because it is essentially not only of sensibility but at the same time also of the understanding. The twofold mode of being of the synthesis of the imagination, in the above manner, constitutes a relationship of two sides of the same coin, and this is the reason why, so to speak, the balance between apperception and imagination is recognized in the first edition of the *Critique of Pure Reason*. But in the second edition, the essential form of the synthesis of the imagination is hidden and its secondary form forcefully appears at the forefront. What is the reason for this? Here we need to recall that what Kant calls experience has a particular definition. That is, it signifies experience in natural science, following laws. It was experience as it pertains to objects. And he conceived transcendental apperception, indeed, as the "correlate" (*Korrelatum*) of such an "object" (*Gegenstand*). "The unity of apperception is the transcendental ground of the necessary conformity to law of all appearances in one experience. This unity of apperception in respect to a manifold of representations... is indeed the rule, and the faculty of these rules is the understanding."[183] In this way apperception, in regard to the cognition of objects, is identified with the understanding. "The synthetic unity of apperception is that highest point to which we must ascribe all employment of the understanding, even the whole of logic, and hence transcendental philosophy. Indeed, this faculty is the understanding itself."[184] In this way, by reason, it is natural that the transcendental function of the imagination was grasped one-sidedly from the standpoint of the understanding and that its synthesis was thus viewed as a work of the understanding confronted with sensibility. And here Kant, in connection to his critique of Hume, states that this principle of affinity also "has its seat in the understanding."[185] Kant designated the transcendental apperception as "*Radikalvermögen*" [radical faculty].[186] The understanding's radicalism has amounted to almost obliterating the imagination. This radicalism is quite natural from the standpoint of the understanding. Nevertheless, experience is most likely not something that can be limited to experience as the lawful object of natural science. The second edition of the *Critique of Pure Reason*, as a theory of experience in this determined sense, may be more radical than the first edition. But even so, if we are to read what we call experience even more broadly, or in a more ordinary sense, or a more original sense, we need to recognize an even more fundamental significance in regard to the imagination as will be shown later. But, in the first place, are apperception and understanding the same at all? To the extent that we are dealing with the cognition of objects we can say that in Kant apperception and understanding are viewed to be the same. But on the other hand, apperception and understanding are not necessarily viewed to be the same even in Kant. The fourth point of the issue is what kind of distinction can be conceived there. The issue we raised concerning Heidegger's Kant reading at the end of section 9 can probably be completely solved only by discovering other possible meanings of this apperception and by problematizing its relationship to the imagination and hence, again, to time. Therein we must next discuss this issue by connecting it to the issue of the schematism.

11.

[378] The problem of Kant's schematism is the application of the pure concepts or categories of the understanding to phenomena. He deals with this issue at first somewhat superficially. He discusses the idea of subsumption (*Subsumtion*) in traditional logic as the guiding thread. That is, the application of the categories to phenomena is presented as a problem of the subsumption of sensible intuitions to the pure concepts of the understanding in accordance with experience. Now, in order to subsume a certain object under a concept the former's representation must always be of the same kind as the latter. But when speaking of the subsumption of empirical intuitions to pure concepts of the understanding, one is sensible and the other is intellectual and hence they are distinct in character. How is subsumption in this case possible? Kant states,

> Obviously there must be some third thing {*ein Drittes*}, which is homogeneous on the one hand with the category, and on the other hand with the appearance [phenomenon], and which thus makes the application of the former to the latter possible. This mediating representation must be pure (without anything empirical at all), and yet at the same time, while it must in one respect be intellectual, it must in another be sensible. Such a thing is the transcendental schema {*transzendentale Schema*}.[187]

Now the transcendental determination of time is universal and, to the extent that it is founded on an *a priori* rule, is of the same kind as the category. But time, on the other hand, to the extent that it is implied in every empirical representation of the manifold, is of the same kind as the phenomenon. The application of the category to the phenomenon, as a schema of a concept of understanding, therefore is presumably made possible through transcendental time-determination that mediates the latter's subsumption under the former. But such schema-time (*Schema-Zeit*) is a product of the productive imagination [*seisanteki kōsōryoku*, 生産的構想力]. We can thus say that the understanding and sensibility are tied through the imagination as the mediation.

In order to clarify what this schematism means we need to clarify what sort of a thing the schema is. "The schema in itself is always a product of imagination. Since, however, the synthesis of imagination aims at no special intuition, but only at unity in the determination of sensibility, the schema {*Schema*} has to be distinguished from the [form-]image [*keizō*] {*Bild*}."¹⁸⁸ The imagination (*Einbildungskraft*) presumably involves (form-)images. The schema also signifies σχῆμα = *Gestalt*, *Form*, and can be thought to be a (form-)image. How are (form-)images and schemas distinguished and how are they related? The (form-)image is the thing's form or its *look* (εἶδος, ἰδέα). When I look at a dog, the dog's form is the (form-)image and is the *look* of that which is there. That which is there is a single dog, but its (form-)image, without ceasing to be what is there, is not merely that one dog. At the same time, we cannot avoid seeing that thing's single manifoldness there. In other words, this perceived dog presents how the dog is seen universally. Hence, we can say that therein lies the rendering-sensible of the concept as it presents that which we represent in the concept of dog. To begin with, that dog possesses in-itself its definite *look*. But at the same time because it is a dog, it is presented as that which does not have to be viewed in the way that the dog is seen. It shows us simply how a dog approximately can be seen. That is, it presents the range of a dog's possible *look*, or more strictly speaking, it presents that which regulates (*regeln*) how something in general must be seen in order for it to manifest a *look* corresponding to dog. The representation of this rule is the schema. Kant states,

> The concept 'dog' signifies a rule according to which my imagination can delineate the figure of a four-footed animal in a general manner. In this case it is not limited to any single determinate figure such as experience, or any possible image that I can represent *in conreto*, actually presents.¹⁸⁹

In this way the concept is not something transcending the representation of the regulative unity of rules. What is called concept in logic is grounded in the schema. Immediately preceding the above cited sentence, Kant writes as follows: "The object of experience or its image is never adequate to the empirical concept. Therefore, this concept always stands in immediate relation to the schema of the imagination, as a rule for the determination of our intuition, in accordance with some specific universal concept."¹⁹⁰ Kant's idea that concepts are always related immediately to the schemas of the imagination is quite an astounding perspective in regard to the logical issue of the establishment of concepts. Logicians like Sigwart have already shown that the common view that concepts are made through abstraction cannot but lapse into *aporia*.¹⁹¹ But Kant's view that concepts are grounded in schemas can be seen as a stunning solution to that *aporia*. What can be said about empirical sensible concepts can also be said about pure sensible concepts. Here as well we need to distinguish (form-)images and schemas. For example, if I successively hit five points, they are the (form-)image of the number five. By contrast when I merely think of numbers in general—where it can be five or a hundred—this thought is instead the representation of a method (*die*

Vorstellung einer Methode), in accordance with a certain concept, that represents a single collective amount (for example, a thousand) in (form-)images, and not the (form-)image itself. In the case of a number like a thousand, the (form-)image overlooking it would presumably be incomparable with its concept. "This representation of a universal procedure of the imagination {*diese Vorstellung von einem allgemeinen Verfahren der Einbildungskraft*} in providing an image for a concept, I entitle the schema of this concept."[192] But it's not that the concept is first there and then the imagination forms this into a (form-)image [*keizōka* 形像化]. Instead, the schema of the imagination is at the root of the concept. The concept is not made, for example, through abstraction from the (form-)image but rather is grounded within the schema. By means of this it is also possible to abstract the concept from the (form-)image. [Kant writes:] "Indeed, it is the schemata, not images of objects, which lie at the ground {*zum Grunde liegen*} of our pure sensible concepts."[193] The concept of a triangle in general and the (form-)image of a triangle would never adequately match. This is because the concept of triangle possesses a universality valid for all triangles regardless of whether a triangle is right-angled or obtuse-angled, while it would be impossible for a (form-)image to attain such universality as it is always limited to a portion of this range. "The schema of the triangle can exist nowhere but in thought and signifies a rule of synthesis of the imagination {*ein Regel der Synthesis der Einbildungskraft*}, in respect to pure figures in space."[194] At the root of the concept is the schema and in it the concept is rendered sensible while the concept is instead something abstracted from it. The schematism is indeed the original concept formation itself. Kant says:

> This schematism of our understanding, in its application to appearances and their mere form, is an art concealed in the depths of the human soul {*eine verborgene Kunst in den Tiefen der menschlichen Seele*}, whose real modes of activity nature is hardly likely ever to allow us to discover, and to present to our gaze.[195]

These noteworthy words agree with Kant's words in another passage, dealing with the admirable quality of the imagination we raised in the previous section. It is clear from this that he recognized an originary function in the imagination.

Imagination for Kant was originally that which synthesizes sensibility and understanding. It appears in the *Critique of Pure Reason* indeed where the synthesis of sensibility and the understanding became an issue. This synthesis is originary to the extent that he regarded it as the hidden common origin of sensibility and the understanding. But would this admission to the originary nature of the imagination not contradict other statements in Kant elsewhere? Kant therefore says in a passage we already cited, A124: "[T]he synthesis of imagination, even if it is undertaken *a priori*, combines the manifold only as it *appears* {*erscheint*} in intuition—for example, in the shape {*Gestalt*} of a triangle—it is always in itself sensible."[196] But the fact that the imagination is sensible in this way would presumably not mean that it is *only* sensible. The imagination *must* instead be thoroughly sensible in one aspect. Otherwise, it would be unable to be that which synthesizes the understanding and sensibility and hence be unable to make possible the application of the categories to phenomena. The imagination belongs to sensibility to the extent that it pertains to intuition. But to the extent that its synthesis is spontaneous the imagination instead pertains to the understanding. For this reason, if we again cite B151, Kant says,

> ... since all our intuition is sensible, the imagination, owing to the subjective condition under which alone it can give to the concepts of understanding a corresponding intuition, belongs to sensibility. But inasmuch as its synthesis is determinative and an expression of spontaneity, and not, like sense, determinable merely, and which is therefore able to determine sense *a priori* in respect of its form in accordance with the unity of apperception, imagination is to that extent a faculty which determines the sensibility *a priori*. And its synthesis of intuitions, in accordance with the categories, must be the transcendental synthesis of imagination. This is an action of the understanding on the sensibility, and its first application to objects of our possible intuition (and thereby it is the ground of all other applications above).[197]

We can say therefore that the imagination, on the one hand, is sensible to the extent that it is seen as "belonging to sensibility," but on the other hand pertains to the understanding to the extent that it is seen as "an action of the understanding on the sensibility."[198] Moreover, as we already stated, we can interpret this passage as denying the originary nature of the imagination by assigning the imagination merely to sensibility and seeing the *a priori* synthesis of the imagination in fact as an act of understanding in sensibility. Therein we conceived the radicalism of the understanding. And in this case, we need to take note of the fact that [the phrases] "in accordance with the unity of apperception" (*der Einheit der Apperzeption gemäss*) and "in accordance with the categories" (*den Kategorien gemäss*) were used in an identical sense and hence that apperception and understanding are seen as identical, by relating it to what we discussed in the previous section. But we have been stating that there is already in Kant the recognition of the unique origin of the imagination. The synthesis of the imagination accords with the categories because it does so naturally on the basis of the function of the imagination itself and not because it is coerced by the understanding. Therefore, as Kant states in the *Anthropology*, the play of the imagination accords with (*gemäss*) the understanding even if it does not emerge from (*aus*) the understanding and is hence intellectual. Imagination is originally sensible and pertains to the understanding. We can presumably recognize this clearly in the schemas. After speaking of "an art concealed in the depths of the human soul," Kant writes as follows:

> This much only we can assert: the *image* [form-image] is a product of the empirical faculty of the productive imagination,[199] the *schema* of sensible concepts (such as figures in space) is a product and, is as it were, a monogram, *a priori* of pure imagination, through which, and in accordance with which, images themselves first become possible. The images can be connected with the concept only by

means of the schema it depicts {*bezeichnen*}, and in themselves are never completely congruent with the concept."²⁰⁰

Imagination as that which involves only (form-)images is sensible, but the (form-)image itself is possible also by depending on, and following, the schema. And the (form-)image can be tied to the concept because at its root it takes the schema as its mediation. Kant further follows this by writing the following:

> On the other hand, the schema of a pure concept of understanding can never be brought into any [form-]image whatsoever {*etwas, was in gar kein Bild gebracht warden kann*}. It is simply the pure synthesis, determined by a rule of that unity, in accordance with concepts, to which the category gives expression, and is the transcendental product of imagination, a product which concerns the determination of inner sense in general according to conditions of its form (time), in respect of all representations, so far as these representations are to be connected *a priori* in one concept in conformity with the unity of apperception.²⁰¹

Thus, the schema of a pure concept of the understanding, distinct from the pure concept of the understanding, namely, an empirical sensible concept such as dog or a pure sensible concept such as triangle, is time. This schema, in the point that it "can never be brought into any image," is different from other schemas. We may say that therein lies the superior character of the understanding belonging to the schema or time. Otherwise, time would not be what can never be brought into any (form-)image whatsoever. Instead, we would have to think the character of what Kant calls time to be this, namely, time as the schema of pure concepts of the understanding and hence time involved in the cognition of objects. But the act of the imagination that forms the schema, according to Kant, is in "providing an image for a concept" (*einem Begriff sein Bild verschaffen*).²⁰² It is thus clear that in cases where we say that there is no (form-)image in a schema, time, that (form-)image must have a particular meaning. In other words, it does not mean that there are universally no (form-)images in schemas, time. It only means that it cannot be taken out of the range of what can be empirically intuited. This (form-)image is given in pure intuition and as such it is called "the pure [form-]image" (*das reine Bild*). Kant says that "the pure [form-]image ... of all objects of the senses in general is time."²⁰³ We can discern the same words in cases where he defines the concept of understanding or *Notion*. He thus says, "[t]he pure concept, insofar as it has its origin in the understanding alone (not in the pure [form-]image of sensibility {*nicht im reinen Bilde der Sinnlichkeit*}), is called a concept of the understanding (*notio*)."²⁰⁴ Time, as "pure (form-)image" is the schema-(form-)image (*Schema-Bild*) and is not merely nothing but a form of intuition vis-a-vis the pure concept of the understanding. Concepts of the understanding thus possess their own unique character and it is hence clear that we can recognize in the imagination its own function. Now just as concepts in general are grounded on schemas, categories as originary concepts (*Urbegriffe*) are grounded on schemas or time. Therefore, just as

Heidegger states, we can say that "the Transcendental Schematism is the originary, essential concept formation in general."[205]

12.

[389] Nevertheless, one point we ought to take note of here is that the schematism is placed within the section called "Transcendental Judgement." A theory emerges from this that Kant's schematism initially is something that concerns judgement and not the imagination. Hence it denies the uniqueness and originary nature of the imagination. How was Kant's schematism brought to the basis of the faculty of judgment? What is the relationship between the imagination and judgment? I think it is evident from our discussion above that in recognizing the proper function of the imagination, he is thinking of the problem of the synthesis of the understanding and sensibility. But as we already touched upon, Kant is at the same time treating the issue of the schematism as an issue of subsumption (*Subsumtion*). On this basis schematism and judgement are tied together. For judgement (*Urteilskraft*), according to Kant, is "the faculty of subsuming under rules {*das Vermögen, unter Regeln zu subsumieren*}, that is, of distinguishing whether something does or does not stand under a given rule."[206] In this way by presenting what initially was an issue of *synthesis* as an issue of *subsumption*, Kant removed the imagination, the principle of synthesis, from the forefront, to allow judgement to make its appearance. More specifically, the issue of the synthesis of the understanding and sensibility was replaced by the issue of "how the *subsumption* of empirical (not only, but also universal sensible) intuitions under pure concepts of the understanding, hence the *application* {*Anwendung*} of categories to appearances are possible,"[207] and the schematism was discussed as the relationship of subsumption by judgment. The issue of synthesis was formalized, conceptualized, and hence also externalized as the issue of subsumption. In this case, the pure concepts of the understanding or the categories were presupposed to be already given, and the issue was their *application* to phenomena, or to discriminate whether empirical intuition "does or does not stand under a given rule (*casus datae legis*)."[208] Now Kant had asserted that in subsuming objects to concepts, the representation of the former must always be of the same kind (*gleichartig*) as the latter and, thus thought, that in order for phenomena to be subsumed under the categories, the mediation of a certain third that in one aspect is intelligible and in another aspect is sensible is necessary, and took the Transcendental Schematism to be the third that possesses such a character. But as long as we are conceiving this on the basis of the relationship of subsumption, even if Transcendental Schematism can constitute a certain mediating synthesis, it would be active, borrowing Heidegger's words, as nothing but the secondary predicative synthesis (*die prädikative Synthesis*) and we cannot say that it is acting as an essential synthesis, namely the veritative synthesis (*die veritative Synthesis*).

How did the formalization of the Transcendental Schematism, its conceptualization or externalization, arise in this way? We can consider this issue by tracing it back to the external nature of the procedure whereby Kant derived the categories from the table of judgments. The categories were thus assumed to be "given rules" and, even in the Transcendental Deduction of pure concepts of the understanding that discusses the most fundamental issue of the *Critique of Pure Reason*, appear in the external formula whereby the issue of the deduction of the categories is the application of the categories to phenomena. Despite this we have seen therein that the issue of synthesis is dealt with in an original manner in relation to the imagination. If we appropriate Heineman's words, we can also say that "the Transcendental Deduction is the genuine battleground of two opposing tendencies."[209] And the reason why the issue of the imagination was pushed away from the forefront, as already stated, was due to the radicalism of the understanding and was also related to the fact that what Kant problematized was the experience *of objects* and that this experience was the experience of the lawful objects of natural science. In this case the fact that transcendental apperception and the understanding were identified is just as we had already mentioned. We can interpret the treatment of the Transcendental Schematism as a relationship of subsumption through judgment as being tied to its externalization, conceptualization, or formalization. The relationship between the understanding and sensibility is essentially an issue of synthesis and not only an issue of subsumption. It is probably more appropriate to consider the issue of synthesis as rather relating to apperception than to such judgment. In fact, in regard to the standpoint of the *Critique of Pure Reason* that discusses the issue of the cognition *of objects*, Kant identifies apperception with understanding. But, on the other hand, it can be thought that he distinguishes the two. That is, while on the one hand he says, "this faculty (the faculty of the synthetic unity of apperception) is the understanding itself,"[210] he says on the other hand that "even the possibility of understanding rests on the unity of consciousness."[211] We probably ought to say that the understanding and apperception are not identical but that the understanding does no more than manifest the object-logical aspect of transcendental apperception. Apperception is not just something intellectual. Instead, we can consider it as something holistic that sums up the intellectual and the sensible. Kant, in fact, also speaks of it as "an all-comprehensive pure apperception" (*eine allbefassende reine Apperzeption*)[212] or "the totality of a possible self-consciousness" (*das ganze mögliche Selbstbewußtsein*).[213] Thought in this way, can we not view apperception as not only "assuming" the synthesis of imagination as a synthetic unity as Kant states but, in turn, as maintaining this within itself or maintaining apperception instead in its original form as the imagination? We can thus arrive at the idea of the "imagination" in the sense Humboldt had in mind.[214] In this case the imagination is nothing but aesthetic apperception (*die künstlerische Apperzeption*). To begin with, although this is not something merely sensible but rather idealist or rational, this *idea* or reason is not something abstract at all. According to Humboldt, *ideas* are "the original [or: root] point" of the totality or "of all relations" (*der Wurzelpunkt aller Relationen*), and only the imagination in its original unity is allowed to synthesize relations. Interpreted in this way, even something like the schemas as Humboldt thought, as expressions in the history of the basic idea (*Grundidee*), would have to be something like ideal forms (*die idealischen Formen*). They would have to be schemas in the historical formation of the world. To begin with this is not how Kant thought of the matter. Yet was not such an idea already prepared in this manner within Kant? Here we need to reflect upon Kant's work that exerted the deepest influence upon later German philosophy, beginning with Humboldt, the *Critique of Judgment*.

It becomes quite interesting when we notice the treatment of the schematism in the *Critique of Pure Reason* as an issue of judgment and see how, as already stated, this externalizes the issue on the one hand but on the other hand also suggests an intimate relationship between judgment and imagination. Indeed, Kant's third *Critique* was called "*The Critique of Judgment*." But according to Cassirer this was something tied to what Baumgarten, and his pupil Meier as well as Tetens, called "the logic of imagination [構想力]" or "the logic of phantasy [想像]."[215] We can also probably see a deepening in the third *Critique* of the logic of judgment or imagination that appeared in the first *Critique* as the schematism. Judgment in the first *Critique* was first defined as "the faculty of subsuming under rules."[216] We can discern the same sort of definition in the third *Critique* as well. It is defined as "the ability to think the particular as contained under the universal."[217] Otherwise it is also said to be the faculty of "the subsumption of the empirical intuition … under the concept.…"[218] Furthermore Kant writes as follows: "When the concept of an object is given, the task of judgment, in using that concept for cognition, is its exhibition (*Darstellung*) (*exhibitio*), that is, in reference to the concept to consider an intuition corresponding to it."[219] Would not the task of judgment, seen in this way, agree with what the first *Critique* spoke of as "the universal operation of imagination that endows concepts with their (form-)images"? This thing called "*Darstellung (exhibition)*" was called "*bezeichnen*" in another passage and in the *Anthropology* the productive imagination was said to be the power of *exhibitio originaria* (original exhibition) of objects and *exhibitio derivativa* (derivative exhibition) of objects.[220] Indeed even in the third *Critique*, following the above quoted sentence, it is written as follows:

> There are cases where it is the imagination by means of which we realize a concept that we hold in advance concerning an object as an end, as happens in art, or where (as in the case of organisms) it is by nature, in its technic, when we assume at the ground of our judgment concerning its product, the concept of an end.[221]

The relationship between judgment and imagination is thus apparent. Kant also says that judgment is "the faculty that makes the imagination conform to the understanding."[222] However, as already stated in the *Anthropology*, the imagination in its proper freedom is in conformity with the understanding and therein lies its so-called genius. And as we will eventually argue, the concept of genius in the third *Critique* also agrees with that view. Therefore, judgement is identical with the imagination—in this case the imagination will presumably become something like the aesthetic apperception conceived by Humboldt by including something intellectual; or, it is an aspect of logical reflection vis-à-vis the original function of the imagination—in this case judgment is the faculty that makes the imagination conform to the understanding or the faculty to subsume it under rules as stated in the first *Critique*. Incidentally, as we already saw in the passage cited above, the technology [or: technics] of nature (*die Technik der Natur*)[223] is made to correspond to the imagination in art. As we can perceive from the fact that the idea of "technology of nature" is derived from

Shaftesbury, it is intimately related to the imagination.[224] At the root of every technology we need to conceive the imagination. The imagination is technological [technical]. In the *Critique of Pure Reason*, it says that the schematism is "an art {*Kunst*} concealed in the depths of the human soul."[225] The imagination is at work not only in the depths of the human soul but also at work in the interiority of nature. There is an intimate relationship between art and technology. Rather than a lawful nature of the kind discussed in the *Critique of Pure Reason*—abstract nature in natural science—the technology of nature involves concrete nature, namely, the forms of nature.

Now the issue of the third *Critique* is the issue of teleology. It is related to aesthetic teleology and to nature's teleology. The issue of judgment that was viewed formally and externally in the Transcendental Schematism as dealing with the relationship of mere subsumption between the understanding and intuition is here viewed intrinsically as a teleological (*teleologisch*) relationship obtaining between the understanding and intuition or between universal and particular. Looking back, could we not see the relationship in the *Critique of Pure Reason* between intuition and understanding as also something teleological, involving the *Kunst* of schematism? In this book Kant speaks about the architechtonic (*Architektonik*) of pure reason. Architechtonic means "the art of systems" (*die Kunst der Systeme*), and by means of this our knowledge attains a scientific quality.[226] System means "the unity of the manifold cognitions under one idea" and idea means "the concept of reason of the form of a whole {*ein Ganzes*}."[227] By means of this concept, the scope of its manifold and the positions of the reciprocity of its parts are determined *a priori*. Accordingly, the scientific concept of reason contains the end and the whole that is congruent with this end. We can say that the art of systems is teleological. And Kant, further, states that, "[t]he idea requires for its realization the schema {*Schema*}, that is, an essential manifold and order of its parts, both which must be determined *a priori* from the principle of the end."[228] In this case he distinguishes the technological [or: technical] unity (*die technische Einheit*) and the architechtonic unity (*die architektonische Einheit*). He states, there is

> ... the schema, ... not devised in accordance with an idea, that is, in terms of the ultimate aim of reason, but empirically in accordance with purposes accidentally occasioned (the number of which one cannot know in advance); and the schema which originates from an idea (where reason assigns the ends *a priori* and does not wait for them to be given empirically) ...

and states that the former yields technological [technical] unity and the latter grounds architectonic unity.[229] To begin with, it is clear that what we call technology [technics] in general is not something merely empirical, as we will argue later from the ideas of technology in art and nature in the third *Critique*. We can view the architectonic of reason as itself a technology. We can say that the necessity of schemas in such cases indicates that the imagination must be at the root of this technology as well. Kant conceived a teleology in regard to the systematic unity of cognition, but we can conceive that teleology is even more broadly and deeply included within our cognition or experience. Preceding our entrance into this issue, we need to examine the issue of the third *Critique* in even greater detail by relating it to the logic of imagination.

13.

[398] In order to understand the third *Critique*, namely, the *Critique of Judgment*, by relating it to the logic of imagination, we first need to clarify what sort of position it occupies in Kant's system of critical philosophy. Time and again this issue has been discussed, but its interpretation has been one-sided or formal and inadequate both historically and logically.[230] The *Critique of Judgment* is treated, before anything else, as a theory of aesthetics (*Aesthetik*) and, furthermore, as a theory of taste (*Geschmack*). This kind of presentation of the issue belongs to the eighteenth century or modernity. There were in Greece or the Middle Ages as well the beginning of aesthetics and theories of technology, attempts at a psychology or metaphysics of beauty, but aesthetics in the modern sense did not exist. By being defined as a theory of taste, modern aesthetics is distinguished from traditional ones. Here the specifically aesthetic subject (*das spezifisch aesthetische Subjekt*) is presupposed. The origin of the issue of the aesthetic subject was the Renaissance. It is said that the Renaissance discovered "the human being," but the human that appeared there, before anything else, was the artist, the freest personality, the genius. What was thus experienced in the Renaissance was also brought into self-awareness during the eighteenth century. The issue of the aesthetic subject was discussed as an issue of taste from the aspect of enjoyment and as an issue of genius from the aspect of production. This issue of the time also became the heart of aesthetics in Kant as well. The aesthetic subject is always a living individual and concrete human being. As the subject of science, in particular of lawful natural science, the human being is no longer a living individual concrete human being but instead conceivable as an abstract logical essence. Kant's "consciousness in general" in his *Critique of Pure Reason* was, as-it-were, such a thing. Logic appears to grasp the human in its utterly concrete nature, but logic moreover brings the norm that dissolves individuality to the forefront and has the danger of losing the concrete human for the sake of an unconditioned law. The concept of personhood in Kant's *Critique of Practical Reason* indeed indicates this danger. The aesthetic subject, however, does not permit that sort of abstraction or ambiguity. In the aesthetic realm, the human must be recognized as human, or put differently, in its individuality, life, and concreteness. The aesthetic subject at the root of Kant's theories of taste and genius is that sort of a concrete subject. If we regard the essence of critical philosophy to exist in the philosophy of the (epistemological) subject revealed through the so-called Copernican turn of the first *Critique*, we can view the third *Critique* that took up or had to take up, the issue of the subject in the most concrete form as constituting the summit of critical philosophy. Kant discussed in this book the issue of nature along with the issue of beauty, but nature here is no longer nature reduced to universal laws as in the *Critique of Pure Reason* but nature in concrete form, in particular, lived nature, that is the organism. The lived individual and concrete subject is historical man in general. Accordingly, we can consider it a matter of course that Kant discussed the issue of historical purposiveness and narrated a philosophy of history at the end of the *Critique of Judgment*.

Next, while Kant's philosophy is characterized by critique, if we look at the word "critique" (*Kritik*) in intellectual history, it was commonly employed during the same period in the sense of the critique of taste and Kant's term is an appropriation of this. Kant's words, "our age is especially the age of critique"[231] in the preface to the first edition of the *Critique of Pure Reason* presumably speaking of this situation. The problem of critique appeared at the same time as the problem of taste, and we can say that taste is the original domain of critique. Critique presupposes the independence and freedom of the (epistemological) subject. Taste is the subjective expression of that situation where its objective expression is critique. To the extent that we can recognize objective norms, critique does not exist. But also, to the extent that each experience can be seen as the final criterion there is no critique. Where rules are still valid there is not yet any need for critique and where only experience is esteemed, there is no longer a need for critique. We can easily comprehend this relationship in the domain of beauty. In cases where there are aesthetic concepts in the sense of norms, there is no necessity for taste or critique and all that is required is only the mere application of rules. By contrast in cases where each person's taste is absolutely valid, all objectivity is lost, only experience dominates, and aesthetics is no longer a branch of philosophy but becomes, at best, statistics. Put differently, only in cases where the individual response to something aesthetic, as experience, is admitted as the final judge, can there exist any dispute requiring critical judgment. But at the same time the decision of this dispute becomes conceivable only when at the same time experience is not valid as the sole judge. This judgment, without being merely rational, however must possess objectivity. Thus, the issue of taste ought to indicate a new method for objectively cognizing.[232] If only rules and concepts were sufficient, a "doctrine" (*Doktrin*) of beauty would exist but the "judgment" of taste would not exist. Kant's lifelong endeavor was to overcome the opposition between, on the one hand, objective doctrine and, on the other hand, an empiricism that unconditionally admits everything subjectively given, namely, the opposition between rationalism and empiricism. We can probably say that the problem of aesthetic critique was the prototype for the general issue of critique. Aesthetic critique is the model for methods of opposing rules without having to abandon principles, for methods of recognizing the right to experience without being merely empirical. The essence of every critique exists between concept and experience, between the universal and the particular, between the objective and the subjective, between the rational and the irrational. Critical cognition aims at the concrete.

We therefore can comprehend the intrinsic relationship of continuity between the *Critique of Pure Reason* and the *Critique of Judgment*. The critique of taste in the latter is the critique of experience in the former. Just as in beauty the intuitive is important, things such as sensation or intuition in experience are indispensable. And so, in emphasizing the Transcendental Analytic in an interpretation of the *Critique of Pure Reason*, perhaps we have to recognize the meaning of the Transcendental Aesthetic that was about to be erased. Here, as the word *Aesthetik* (aesthetic) shows, we can see that the *Critique of Pure Reason* is tied, by means of the Transcendental Aesthetic, to eighteenth-century intellectual history, in particular the school of Leibniz and Wolff and the aesthetics of Baumgarten and Meier. To begin with, just as we cannot rely simply on intuition even in the judgment of taste, the issue in experience is not only intuition but the synthesis of intuition and understanding. In this way, the issue of the *Critique of Pure Reason* developed into the Transcendental Deduction and then into the Transcendental Schematism, and the imagination and judgment became problematized. This, however, is an issue of the third *Critique*. But just as Stadler argued, in regard to teleology, we can interpret the hypothesis of reflective judgment in the *Critique of Judgment* as being identical to the third transcendental idea (*die dritte transzendentale Idee*) in the *Critique of Pure Reason*.[233] And thus we can furthermore presumably relate the Appendix to the Transcendental Dialectic (*Anhang zur transzendentalen Dialektik*) in the *Critique of Pure Reason* to the issue of judgment. Putting this generally, when searching for systematic key trends in the *Critique of Pure Reason* more concretely in the direction of "experience," namely, man's concrete lived experience, and leaving the inclination to place them in "science," namely, mathematical natural science, we can clearly recognize its continuous and intrinsic relationship with the third *Critique*. Just as we had discussed above, the imagination that looked as if it decisively has a significant role to play in the Transcendental Deduction was removed to the background while the abstract (epistemological) subject, called consciousness-in-general, appeared in the forefront, and, in the same relation, the issue of the imagination that ought to have an originary relation to it in the Transcendental Schematism was replaced by the issue of judgment seen in itself extrinsically and formally. However, the actual (epistemological) subject of experience, like how the aesthetic subject had to be conceived, is a personal concrete lived subject. And we can presumably consider even what we call art as experience as Dewey said.[234] Baeumler states, "[t]he Transcendental Aesthetic, Deduction, and Dialectics establishes much more than the world picture of abstract 'nature' as the existence of things under laws. However, this *more* attains its clear expression only in the third *Critique*."[235] Incidentally, if we interpret the Transcendental Deduction, constituting the summit of the *Critique of Pure Reason*, as the logic of imagination, as discussed above, we can interpret the issue of the third *Critique* in its entirety from the standpoint of the logic of imagination. And we can presumably regard the issue of historical purposiveness at the end of this book to provide the most concrete key to solving the issue of experience in the first *Critique*.

14.

[405] Now Kant took the issue of judgment of taste as an issue of (the faculty of) judgment. He defined the power of judgment as "the faculty of thinking the particular as contained within the universal"[236] and also put this as "the faculty of subsuming the empirical intuition under the concept"[237] as well as "the capacity of subsuming the particular under the universal."[238] To view the faculty of judgment as the capacity of subsumption (*Subsumtion*) agrees with the definition of judgment in the first *Critique*, namely "the capacity of subsuming under rules." And this also presumably matches the tradition of logic that generally views the essence of judgment in terms of the relation of subsumption. According to Kant here judgment is differentiated into determinant judgment and reflective judgment. "If the universal (the rule, principle, law) is given, the judgment which subsumes the particular under it is determinant ... If, however, only the particular is given and the universal has to be found for it, the judgment in relation

to it is just reflective."²³⁹ Now when distinguished in this way, even if we can regard the operation of determinant judgment as subsumptive, how can we say that the operation of reflective judgment is subsumptive? When we speak of subsumption, must not something universal, a concept or rule, always be given? As we stated earlier, when viewing the issue of the Transcendental Schematism in the *Critique of Pure Reason* as an issue of subsumption or, more precisely, as an issue of "the subsumption of empirical intuition under pure understanding," the original issue of the synthesis of intuition and understanding in the Transcendental Deduction was lost, the pure concepts of understanding or the categories became presupposed as already given, and further, their "application" to phenomena had become the issue and became formalized and abstracted. At the same time, the danger was there that the critique that was to synthesize rationalism and empiricism came to incline towards rationalism. Could reflective judgment work subsumptively? Aesthetic judgment, according to Kant, is reflective but how is it subsumptive? And even if it is subsumptive, in that case is it not reflective only in a secondary sense, in the sense of being a reflection of a certain originary act and no longer [itself] originary? If that is so, what sort of a thing is originary judgment? Kant often argued how the judgment of taste cannot presuppose concepts or rules. What is it that originally becomes connected in such judgment? Kant also says that judgment is "the capacity to adapt imagination to understanding," but this cannot mean that there is first the concept of the understanding to which the imagination is adapted. According to him beauty is the emotion of pleasure, but it is something that arises in "the free play {*das freie Spiel*} of imagination and understanding."²⁴⁰ Free play means that no matter what the specific concept, it will not fetter it to particular cognitive rules. In this case the relationship of imagination and understanding is also called "mutual accord" (*wechselseitige Zusammenstimmung*) as well as "harmony" (*Harmonie*). Because the judgment of taste does not presuppose any definite concept, understanding in this case as the capacity for the unity of concepts is the understanding as the capacity in general of just concepts or rules and the imagination as the capacity for bringing together the manifold of intuitions is the imagination in general as the capacity in general to freely compose (form-)images. And their accord is what is required of "cognition in general" (*Erkenntnis überhaupt*). Therefore, the mutual accord of imagination and understanding has the meaning of their "mutual subjective common accord" (*wechselseitige subjective Übereinstimmung*).²⁴¹ Therein lies the ground for the universality of aesthetic pleasure and this universality is none other than a subjective universality. Now in what way can this "free play," "mutual accord," "mutual subjective common accord" between imagination and understanding be a relationship of subsumption? In cases where we cannot presuppose an objective concept, reflective judgment that is to discern the universal vis-à-vis the given particular—as Kant says it is subjective—must go on seeking the universal in the subjective direction, thoroughly in the direction of acts. This universal must be thoroughly subjective, not at all an object, and must have the character of nothing. This universal, to begin with, cannot be something merely intellectual. Therein we must conceive of an utterly new meaning of subsumption. Moreover, in that standpoint of the universal, we may say that reflective judgment is determinative and that determinant judgment, in turn, is reflective. This universal will eventually have to become significant in connection with the issue of teleology.

In the *Critique of Judgment*, Kant, seeing the act of judgment in presentation or expression, writes as follows: "When the concept of an object is given, the function of judgment, in its employment of that concept for cognition, consists in presentation {*Darstellung*} (*exhibitio*), i.e., in placing beside the concept an intuition corresponding to it."[242] And in the First Introduction of the *Critique of Judgment*, he also conceives the faculty of judgment as the capacity "to exhibit {*Darstellung*} (*exhibitio*), in intuition, the object corresponding to this concept."[243] We can view judgment, as the power to combine the universal and the particular, to be expressive. Every expression is the unity of that which is universal and that which is particular. However, if the unity of the universal and the particular is nothing but a formal relationship that is merely subsumption, even if we view this as a relationship of expression, it is still abstract and we cannot really call it expressive. The faculty of judgment that "arranges in relation to concepts intuitions corresponding to them" must rather mean the faculty of the imagination. In the *Critique of Pure Reason*, there is a reference to "the operation of imagination in general that endows concepts with their images."[244] The act of presentation or expression indeed belongs to the imagination. Even if in cases where concepts are given, we take it to be some process of so-called judgment that arranges intuitions corresponding to them, in cases like art where concepts cannot be presupposed, what is even more expressive would have to be the productive imagination that Kant recognized in the *Anthropology* as the power of original exhibition (*exhibitio originaria*).[245] According to what is said there, the "play" of the imagination conforms to rules even if without the consciousness of rules and acts in conformity with the understanding and even if it is thus not derived from understanding. What we call given concepts do not exist in true expressions, and concepts instead emerge from within the process of expression as something like schemas by means of the productive imagination. Productive imagination is creative and possesses the sense of "creation from nothing." In relation to such imagination, we would probably have to regard what we call reflective judgment as something illustrative in relation to the prototypical.

The universality of judgment of taste, according to Kant, is a subjective universality. This is founded upon the free harmony required of imagination and understanding by cognition in general, and the possibility, universally communicated by pleasure on the basis of the former. Now, what is it that provides this harmony? In the essence of the judgment of taste, this cannot be given in concepts and would have to be given in intuitions. It is grasped not by concepts but by emotion or rather by sensation (*Sinn*). Moreover, because this sensation must possess universality it must be a common sense [共通感覚] (*Gemeinsinn*). Kant, therefore, states, "judgments of taste ... must have a subjective principle, which determines what pleases or displeases, not by concepts but by feeling only, and further with universal validity. Such a principle, however, could only be regarded as a common sense."[246] Common sense is essentially distinct from common understanding [共通悟性] (common sense [常識]) (*gemeiner Verstand*), also called at times common sense (*Gemeinsinn* {*sensus communis*}). The latter judges by means of concepts, not emotions. Common sense is a kind of sense (*Sinn*) that differs from any kind of outer sense. Therefore, for Kant the subjective principle determining the judgment of taste is common sense.[247] The fact that Kant brings up common sense in his argument that judgments concerning beauty belong to reflective judgments is worth noting. He sees the judgment of taste as also a judgment of common sense.[248] Common sense is the subjective principle of determination vis-à-vis reflective judgment. In this case, we can recognize the same relationship that we considered earlier in regard to presentation or expression between the imagination and judgment. We can also presumably say that so-called reflective judgment, in relation to originary common sense rather than the judgment of taste, instead takes a secondarily reflective standpoint. In this case, it is suggestive that in the *Anthropology* Kant ties the imagination and sense (*Sinn*) together.[249] That is to say that the word sense there means "receptivity in relation to representations of the imagination in communication," but more than anything that sense is fundamentally required in art.

Nevertheless, the fact that Kant grasped the problem, thought to belong originally to the imagination, as a problem of judgment, should have an important significance for us. As a consequence, the imagination was placed in an intrinsic relationship with the understanding and its logic thus unavoidably made an issue. The logic of reflective judgment is none other than the logic of purposiveness (*Zweckmässigkeit*). The purposiveness of beauty, according to Kant is subjective purposiveness. He explains this as follows:

> If the form of an object given in empirical intuition is of such a character that the apprehension, in the imagination, of the manifold of that object and the exhibition of a concept of the understanding (regardless of what kind of concept it is) are in agreement, then understanding and imagination are in mutual harmony, in mere reflection, so that it furthers their task, and the object is perceived as purposive [but] only for the judgment. Accordingly, we view the purposiveness itself as merely subjective, for it neither requires nor produces a determinate concept of the object, and the judgment itself is no cognitive judgment at all. Judgment of this kind is called an aesthetic judgment of reflection.[250]

That is, aesthetic purposiveness as subjective purposiveness is established in the mutual concordance or harmony between imagination and understanding and is purposive only for judgment. Aesthetic judgment does not rely on concepts by assuming concepts. "Beauty is the form of an object's purposiveness to the extent that purposiveness is perceived in the object apart from the representation of an end [purpose]."[251] Because the concept is not presupposed there, this purposiveness is a "purposiveness without a purpose [end]" (*Zweckmässigkeit ohne Zweck*).[252] This is the essence of beauty as subjective purposiveness. By contrast we can cognize objective purposiveness only in the relationship of the manifold to a definite end [purpose] and hence only by means of concepts: "An end is the object of a concept so far as this concept is regarded as the cause of the object."[253] Now the fact that the harmony between imagination and understanding is pertinent for the faculty of judgment must be for the reason that the function of judgment exists in joining intuition and the understanding. Furthermore, the combination of intuition and the understanding is the fundamental condition for cognition to obtain, and Kant thus regarded the harmony of imagination and understanding as requisite for cognition in general. He writes:

As the subjective universal communicability of the mode of representation in a judgment of taste is to subsist apart from the presupposition of any definite concept, it can be nothing else than the mental state present in the free play of imagination and understanding (to the extent that they are in mutual accord, as is requisite for cognition in general {*Erkenntnis überhaupt*}). When that happens, we are conscious that this subjective relation suitable for a cognition in general {*dieses zum Erkenntnis überhaupt schickliche subjective Verhältnis*} must be just as valid for everyone, and consequently as universally communicable, as is any determinate cognition, which always rests upon that relation as its subjective condition.[254]

We can thus recognize the relationship between *the Critique of Judgment* and the Transcendental Schematism of the *Critique of Pure Reason*. The issue there was the synthesis of intuition and the understanding as the condition that makes cognition possible. This issue was already the fundamental issue of the Transcendental Deduction and there the imagination was brought up for its solution. But, as we mentioned earlier, in the Transcendental Schematism despite the fact that it was taken up as an issue of the schemas of the transcendental imagination, the problem of synthesis was formalized and externalized as a problem of subsumption through judgment. He discusses the issue of the synthesis of intuition and understanding in the third *Critique*, as the condition of cognition, in relation to reflective judgment, as the harmony of imagination and understanding. It is needless to say that the imagination pertains to intuitions. The fact that the issue of "synthesis" became an issue of "harmony" means that the issue is not cognition and hence not the content of the operation, but rather the operation itself is the issue. Thus, he conceives harmony as the relationship between the general operation of the imagination and the general operation of the understanding. This purposiveness, then, is subjective purposiveness. By contrast the issue of the *Critique of Pure Reason* is objective. Kant states,

> ... if the given representation occasioning the judgment of taste were a concept which united understanding and imagination in the estimate of the object [対象] to give a cognition of the object [客観], the consciousness of this relation would be intellectual (as in the objective schematism of judgment {*der objective Schematismus der Urteilskraft*} dealt with in the *Critique* [*of Pure Reason*]).[255]

However, the judgment of taste relates not to cognition but to pleasure and displeasure. Therein Kant thought that for reflective judgments concerning beauty there is no schema. He says in the First Introduction to the *Critique of Judgment*,

> ... in the power of judgment, we can see understanding and imagination as they relate to each other. Furthermore, we can consider this relation, first objectively, as belonging to cognition (as it was in the Transcendental Schematism of judgment). However, we can also consider this same relation between the two powers of cognition merely subjectively, insofar as one facilitates or hinders the other indeed in one and the same representation and thereby affects one's mental state, and thus as a relationship that can be sensed.[256]

Kant speaks thus of the relationship between the first *Critique* and the third *Critique*. However, if we accept the interpretation that this issue of the Transcendental Schematism, in its originary sense, is an issue of the imagination and secondarily belongs to the faculty of judgment, can we not correspondingly regard the problem of reflective judgment in the third *Critique* as also originarily belonging to the imagination and secondarily belonging to judgment? Otherwise, should what Kant designates as reflective judgment not be the same as what we call the imagination? Kant attempted to purely and subjectively grasp the issue of beauty first as an issue of the judgment of taste. Nevertheless, in regard to beauty, there is also the issue of beautiful object. Can we not conceive of some purposiveness in the structure of the beautiful object as well and further that it possesses the character of purposeless purposiveness? The problem would probably not end with what Kant calls subjective purposiveness. We ought to view the issue concerning the beautiful object not only simply from the aspect of enjoyment but as an issue of the judgment of taste. Instead, we need to grasp it, in its originary sense, from the standpoint of production. This is where the issue of genius appears in the *Critique of Judgment*. Kant states that all art is a product of genius. We must next therefore enter more deeply into the problem of the purposiveness of beauty, in general the issue of teleology, by taking as a clue Kant's theory of genius. And on that occasion a new problem of the schematism will probably emerge in relation to so-called objective schematism.

15.

[416] It may be said that Kant's aesthetics, as a theory of the judgment of taste, takes the standpoint of enjoyment and not the standpoint of production. But we may consider how discussing the issue of genius had amounted to further taking the standpoint of production. According to Kant, "[f]or estimating beautiful objects, as such, what is required is taste; but for fine art, i.e., the production of such objects, one needs genius."[257] That is, while taste is what enjoys and estimates a given beautiful object as a beautiful object, the existence of that beautiful object, its production, is due to genius. He says that "the beautiful object is only possible as a product of genius." Now akin to how Kant's critique of taste shows an intimate connection to the issue in the intellectual history of the same period, his doctrine of genius also contains an intimate connection to the development of the intellectual history of the same period.[258] Furthermore his theory of the judgment of taste and his doctrine of genius, to begin—even if one is said to take the standpoint of enjoyment and the other to take the standpoint of production—must both necessarily possess, and also do possess, an intrinsic relationship with one another.

The definition Kant gave for genius is as follows:

Genius is the talent (natural endowment) which gives the rule to art. Because talent, as the innate productive faculty of the artist, belongs itself to nature, we may express the manner thus, that is, that genius is the innate mental aptitude (*ingenium*) through which nature gives the rule to art.[259]

Why do we think that fine arts are necessarily only possible as products of genius? No matter what art, to the extent that it is not a product of mere accident and must have objectivity, it must also presuppose rules at its root. But the concept of fine art is such that because it does not permit judgment concerning the beauty of its product to be derived from any rule that has a concept for its determining ground, fine art, consequently, is unable of its own to devise the rule whereby it is to bring about its product. Moreover, because a product can never be called art without some preceding rule, nature within the (epistemological) subject must give the rule to art, that is, fine art is only possible as a product of genius.[260] Genius conforms to the rule without consciousness of the rule and conforms to concepts without possessing concepts, and hence as nature provides the rule to art. When we say that genius is nature, first of all, we do not mean nature in the sense of the natural sciences. Kant calls genius, "nature in the subject" (*die Natur im Subjekte*), but this is nature in the subjective sense, not an objective nature, and is none other than historical nature. Such nature is not just necessity but rather the unity of necessity and freedom. Genius is utterly free and yet coincides with concepts and provides art with rules. This is the productive capacity of a preconceptual, and in that sense unconscious, nature, and the rule in art are first derived by reflection on that activity of genius. Genius is the "favorite of nature." Further, it is not that only particular human beings are geniuses, but that as Kant shows in his idea of the "technology of nature,"[261] nature as historical nature, in its roots, is genius. The technology of nature, like all technologies, is the unity of freedom and necessity. To begin with, art is also nothing other than a single technology. And just as genius qua nature provides the rule to art, for Kant the technology of nature, as we will eventually discuss, provides the rule to cognition in the natural sciences. And although Kant writes that "nature proves beautiful where it appears at the same time as art, but art can be called beautiful where it appears as nature even while we are conscious of its being art,"[262] just as art is beautiful indeed because it appears as nature at the same time that it is art as the product of genius, nature can also be beautiful indeed because it appears as art at the same time that it is nature as the product of the technology of nature. Just as we need to conceive of nature (genius) at the root of the beauty of art, we need to conceive of art (technology of nature) at the root of the beauty of nature. In either case they are such through their establishment in the historical world. The historical world is a unity of nature and freedom, freedom and nature. Now in the *Anthropology*, Kant says that "the originality (non-imitative production) of the imagination is called genius when it is in agreement with concepts."[263] If so, not only would we have to conceive of a logic of imagination at the root of art, necessarily viewed as a product of genius, but we would also have to consider a logic of imagination at the root of concrete nature seen in the technology of nature. There is probably a logic of imagination at the root of the historical world. Lange-Eichbaum argues that genius is not a particular type of human being but only a social relation and something that is established through social reputation, but this would have to mean that genius exists historically as what we call a "myth" and, even as such, is conceivable only by viewing the logic of imagination at work at the root of the historical world.[264] Nevertheless, would an interpretation of Kant's theory of genius, and further his teleology, as a logic of imagination, agree with his doctrine as depicted in the third *Critique* itself?

According to Kant, the first characteristic of genius is originality (*Originalität*).²⁶⁵ Genius is the talent to produce something for which no definite rule of its production can be given, and it is not a quality of skill for what can be learned according to some rule. Genius is that which is completely opposite to the spirit of imitation.²⁶⁶ Even great brains such as Newton cannot be called a genius because everything he discovered can be learned, that is, they can be achieved through the natural path of investigation and reflection according to rules and are not different in type from what can be acquired by means of diligent imitation. While in science [scholarship] the difference between the greatest discoverer and the most faithful imitator does not go beyond a difference in degree, the difference in art between genius and mediocrity is one of type.²⁶⁷ Moreover this is not to demean science [scholarship] in contrast to art. Instead, as something that anyone can learn, science possesses great merit whereby its usage is constantly perfected as its knowledge develops without end. But in art such ceaseless progression is absent, and we may discern the situation of a standstill at which we can neither pass nor broaden the limits of a certain summit that had already been previously attained. Even if we can problematize the point that Kant had recognized genius only in art and not in science,²⁶⁸ there may be no room to dispute his point that genius is originality. And originality, as Kant conceived, presumably belongs to the imagination more than anything else. But even if it is original, it can also be meaningless, so as a second characteristic of genius, its product must at the same time must serve as a model and be "exemplary" (*exemplarisch*). If we state this differently, it itself is not born of imitation and, further, it must become a criterion of artistic evaluation, and become a rule, for others. Genius in this way as nature provides rules to art, but what kind of rules are these? They cannot be something like useful norms summarized in a certain method. If so, judgement concerning beauty ought to be something definable by following concepts. The necessity belonging to judgments of beauty is not a necessity of conceptual universality but an "exemplary" (*exemplarisch*) necessity.²⁶⁹ Every work of art is unique, being one and not two and, instead of being a rule, it is an "example" (*Beispiel*). It is something thoroughly particular that at the same time thoroughly refers to something universal. What we can see there is an archetype or prototype (*Urtypus*) in the Goethean sense. It is thoroughly sensible and thoroughly ideal. In that sense we may say that the rule, genius qua nature provides, is a schema rather than a rule. As a schema it would presumably have to be a product of the productive imagination. Taking that schema as the medium, a work engenders work and genius calls forth genius. While Lessing stated that "genius is ignited only by genius," Kant also states that "[t]he artist's *Idee* [ideas] arouse like *Idee* on the part of his pupil, presuming nature to have endowed him with a like proportion of the mental powers."²⁷⁰ The work of genius is a case not for "imitation" (*Nachahmung*) but instead a case for "succession" (*Nachfolge*) by another genius, in whom "it arouses a sense of his own originality and, as a result of exercising in art freedom from the constraint of rules, a new rule is won for art, whereby it presents itself with talent as exemplary."²⁷¹ We should come to know here that genius as a concept of historical human beings needs to be philosophically founded in a concrete manner distinct from the concept of personhood in the *Critique of Practical Reason*. That is, in contrast to how we had sought the foundation of the concept of personhood here and there in universal laws, placing the uniqueness that essentially ought to belong to personhood therefore in danger, the historical uniqueness of genius is completely recognized. We would therefore presumably need to conceive of something like Leibniz's monadology as its philosophical foundation. In fact, looking at intellectual history, it is Leibniz's monadology that provided a significant foundation for the development of the theory of genius in Germany. For moral personhood as well, as a living historical human being, it cannot be something like "laws" in the *Critique of Practical Reason* but would instead have to be something that are "examples" in the sense of genius in the *Critique of Judgment* or in the sense of historical schemas. Moral personhood itself also belongs to genius and is historically creative. As Bergson states, morality itself is also creative. And as Bergson says, if we can recognize the distinction in morality between habitual or probabilistic morality and the morality of creative personhood, just as we can conceive of the productive imagination at the root of the latter, we may conceive of the reproductive imagination at the root of the former. Morality is also like that as something historical and there is the logic of imagination at the root of the entire historical world. Now third, according to Kant, because genius is at-work as nature, we cannot describe, or in other words, depict in a scholarly fashion how s/he produces his products. If we take the activity of genius in this way as a pre-conceptual or, so-to-speak, unconscious activity, we would have to say that what regulates it is neither the understanding nor reason but the imagination. As the word genius derives from *genius*, namely, a word having the meaning of a particular spirit given to a human being at the time of birth that protects and guides him/her, its original *Idee* is thought to be by means of heaven-sent revelation. S/he cannot explain the mystery of his/her creative work for others and perceives instead that what s/he had made was made by that which transcends him/her. In this way, fourth, genius is the operation of nature that defines rules, not for science [scholarship] but for art. The fact that Kant recognized genius in only art, apart from its validity or invalidity, would show the intimate relationship between genius and the imagination. As Dilthey says, the imagination is a supremely artistic capacity. The artist not only knows but makes things. Works of art are sensible material things. The logic of imagination is not merely a logic of cognition but, more than anything, the logic of producing such things. Kant recognized, in epistemology as well as in the doctrine of genius, an important significance in the imagination in relation to sensation, intuition, and material, and further in relation to the understanding in regard to them. In another passage from the *Critique of Judgment* where he explains genius, he says that genius is primarily a talent for art and not a talent for science [scholarship] where clearly known rules must precede and determine the procedure, and

> ... secondarily ... [genius], being a talent in the line of art, presupposes a definite concept of the product as its end and hence understanding, but [in addition] presupposes the representation of the material {*Stoff*} (even if indefinite), that is, the intuition, for the presentation of that concept and thus the relationship of the imagination to the understanding.[272]

But expression in art presumably cannot simply be expression in intuition of a definite concept given in advance. The *Idee* in art is born of the artist's act of expression itself. Thus,

> ... thirdly ... [genius] displays itself, not so much in the realization of a projected end in the presentation of a definite concept, as in the portrayal, or expression, of aesthetic ideas {*aesthetische Idee*} containing abundant material for effecting that intention, whereby it represents the imagination as free, emancipated from all guidance of rules.[273]

Genius truly manifests in the expression [presentation] of aesthetic ideas. If so, what kind of a thing is the aesthetic idea? What kind of relation does it have to the imagination?

What is most essential for genius, according to Kant, is "spirit" [精神] (*Geist*). The art of genius always has spirit. Spirit is none other than the "faculty of presenting aesthetic ideas." And the aesthetic idea is "that representation of the imagination, which induces much thought" (*diejenige Vorstellung der Einbildungskraft, die viel zu denken veranlasst*), and yet as no definite thought whatever, namely, a concept adequate to it, and which language can never quite arrive at it or express it. In this way, the aesthetic idea is a counterpart to the rational idea (*Vernunftidee*).[274] This is because while the rational idea is a concept to which no intuition can be adequate, the aesthetic idea is an intuition to which no concept can be adequate. The aesthetic idea is already a representation of the imagination. The reason why it is called an idea is due to the reason that while on the one side, it at least strives towards something lying across and transcending the limits of experience and thus attempts to approach the expression of a rational concept (an intellectual idea), and this fact gives it the outward appearance of an objective reality, on the other side and moreover primarily, as an internal intuition, no concept can completely conform to it. To express that aesthetic idea is essentially only the "talent (of the imagination)." In this way, the representations of the imagination are, on the one hand, thoroughly intuitional and at the same time, on the other hand, thoroughly ideal. Kant says that spirit in the aesthetic sense is "the animating principle in the mind" (*das belebende Prinzip im Gemüte*).[275] The material employed by this principle to animate the mind is "that which sets the mental powers into a purposive swing, that is, into a self-maintaining play which strengthens those powers relating to it."[276] This is none other than the aesthetic idea, and spirit is the faculty expressing that aesthetic idea. The powers of the mind fittingly stirred by the aesthetic idea are the imagination and the understanding, said to be harmonized in free play where we had already taken it to be the foundation of the judgment of taste. Thus, the theory of genius and the doctrine of judgment of taste are tied together. Kant states,

> The mental powers, therefore, whose union (in a certain relation) constitutes genius are imagination and understanding. While the imagination, in its employment for cognition, is subjected to the constraint of the understanding and submits to its restrictions to be conformable to the concept belonging to it, aesthetically the imagination is free, over and above its agreement with the concept, to furnish of its own accord, a wealth of undeveloped material for the understanding. And because the understanding, even if in its concept pays no regard to this, can make use of it not so much objectively for cognition but rather subjectively to quicken the cognitive faculties and hence also indirectly for cognition, therefore

genius can be said to consist properly in the happy relation that science [scholarship] cannot teach nor industry learn, enabling one to discover ideas for a given concept, and, besides, to hit upon the expression for these ideas. By means of this the subjective state of mind induced as the concomitant of a concept may be communicated to others.[277]

Imagination and understanding must coincide in genius but in this case the imagination does not abide by the compulsion or restriction of the understanding. Instead, the free and original activity of the imagination naturally coincides with the concept. There can be no "free play" in the understanding. It belongs to the imagination and the free play of imagination in genius spontaneously accords with rules and therein rests its nature of genius. Following his explanation of genius in the above given passage (*Kritik der Urteilskraft*, §49), Kant states,

> ... fourthly, the unsought and undesigned subjective purposiveness in the free harmonizing of imagination with the understanding's conformity to law presupposes a proportion and accord between these faculties that cannot be brought about by any observance of rules, whether of science or mechanistic imitation, but can only be produced by nature of the [epistemological] subject.[278]

Genius is the faculty of discovering ideas rather than concepts and giving these ideas expression; and these ideas are thoroughly intuitional. It must become manifest not simply in cognition but in things, in expressive things, and in the production of such things. The accord between the imagination and the understanding that is subjective and objectively indefinite attains expression as an aesthetic idea. Aesthetic ideas are historical forms in art and are given as individually determined forms. In relation to the work objectively expressing such an aesthetic idea, harmony in the free play of the operations of understanding and imagination is brought about in the subject on its receiving end. The activity of genius properly exists in expressive production and the expressed aesthetic idea is originally a representation of the imagination. In it the imagination and the understanding are united objectively and expressively. Therefore, Kant's definition in the *Anthropology* that "the originality (non-imitative production) of imagination is called genius when it is in agreement with concepts"[279] can probably be maintained even in the *Critique of Judgment*. The logic of imagination more than anything is the logic of expression. We can regard Kant's concept of "spirit" (*Geist*) in his theory of genius as corresponding to his concept of "sense" (*Sinn*) in his doctrine of the judgment of taste. What is called spirit here is something intuitive rather than pertaining to the understanding. Spirit is none other than the imagination seen as *ideal*. Spirit in that sense will eventually become the focus of the philosophies of Humboldt and others.[280] The essence of such spirit, in distinction from the understanding and reason, is in being properly expressive.

However, the concept of spirit, or the concept of the aesthetic idea, in the *Critique of Judgment*, as something ideal, appears to approach the concept of what Kant calls the "intuitive understanding" (*intuitiver Verstand*). As is well-known, philosophy following Kant was developed on the basis of the standpoint of intuitive understanding. What has been called its dialectics was also nothing other than intuitive understanding. We need to clarify the standpoint of the logic of imagination in relation to such dialectics. As already seen in the *Critique of Pure Reason*, we can consider the imagination as the synthesis of sensibility and the understanding. In the same way, we can conceive of intuitive understanding as the synthesis of intuition and the understanding. However, in contrast to how the intuitive understanding, as so-called archetypal intellect (*intellectus archetypus*), takes the standpoint of the infinite, namely God, the logic of imagination remains thoroughly in the human standpoint. There is a reason why Heidegger in his reading of Kant took up the issue of the imagination by relating it to the finitude of human existence. The logic of imagination presumably ought to be that which tries to pull the logic of intuitive understanding that had attempted to take the standpoint of God back to the original standpoint of human beings. It would have to be that which turns the trans-historical logic of intuitive understanding into an original historical standpoint. Hegel's dialectics, taking the standpoint of the intuitive understanding, stood upon an a-temporal trans-historical standpoint and in actuality remained in the standpoint of contemplation. Consequently, philosophy, as the owl of Minerva, could only speculate about the past, and his dialectics bore the fate of degenerating into something formal. How can the logic of imagination distinguish itself in opposition to this? Before touching on this issue, we will need to further consider the issue of teleology in Kant's *Critique of Judgment*.

16.

[431] Kant arranged purposiveness into various distinctions. It is clear already from what we had stated that when he did so he first considered the purposiveness of beauty. The purposiveness of beauty is a subjective purposiveness. This is established in the harmony between imagination and understanding, but the free activity of the imagination as so-called purposeless purposiveness or lawless conformity to law spontaneously coincides with the concepts of the understanding. Kant accordingly also calls this "the free conformity to the law of the imagination" (*freie Gesetzmässigkeit der Einbildungskraft*).[281] But we recognize beauty not only in art but in nature as well. There is such a thing as the beauty of nature (*Naturschönheit*) and in nature we can regard a subjective purposiveness of beauty. What kind of a thing is nature beauty? For an object to be generally enjoyed as beautiful it must be grasped intuitively, not conceptually. According to Kant's words, the object's form in this case must be grasped "in an apprehension (*apprehensio*) of the object prior to any concept."[282] Now concerning the grasp of *apprehensio* (apprehension), we recall the following that was written in the *Critique of Pure Reason* in regard to the synthesis of apprehension in intuition: He says,

> There must therefore exist in us an active faculty for synthesis of this manifold, and I name this the imagination, and I name its immediate operation on perceptions, apprehension {*Apprehensio*}. Since imagination has to bring the manifold of intuition into the form of an image {*in ein Bild*}, it must previously have taken the impressions up into its activity, that is, have apprehended them ...

And further, "the imagination is a necessary component of perception itself."[283] In this way, the form grasped in the aesthetic object must be something intuitional and figurative. According to Kant, the purposiveness in the object given to experience from a merely subjective ground is first represented "as the harmony of the form of the object—in the apprehension of the object prior to any concept—and the faculties of cognition that combine the intuition with concepts for the sake of cognition in general."[284] That is, the form apprehended in the object must be something that mutually advances and harmonizes the operation of the imagination as the faculty of intuitions and the operation of the understanding as the faculty of concepts. The judgment of taste is established where the consciousness of this harmony manifests as a feeling of pleasure that is universally valid, and the representation of subjective aesthetic purposiveness stands upon the feeling of immediate pleasure in the object's form. Nevertheless, the coincidence between the operation of the imagination and the operation of the understanding is something requisite for "cognition in general" (*Erkenntnis überhaupt*). Every cognition is a synthesis of intuition and concept. As already stated, this "cognition in general," which was raised as the ground of the universal validity of aesthetic judgment, shows the link between the *Critique of Judgment* and the *Critique of Pure Reason*, between Kant's aesthetics and his epistemology. At this point, we can recognize with greater clarity this link in what he called the formal logical purposiveness of nature. Kant said that "nature when it looks like art, is beautiful."[285] Nature is beautiful because nature is technological [technical], and there must be at the root of the beauty of nature the technology of nature. But what Kant calls the "technology of nature" (*Technik der Natur*) is the formal logical purposiveness of nature. There must be an intrinsic relationship between such logical purposiveness and the aesthetic purposiveness of nature. Furthermore, the idea of the logical finality of nature in the *Critique of Judgment* is tied to the idea of the Transcendental Dialectic in the *Critique of Pure Reason*.

What exactly is the logical purposiveness of nature? In the *Critique of Pure Reason*, nature was problematized and elucidated as "one nature" (*eine Natur*). Even while speaking of this as experience, experience was problematized and elucidated as "one experience" (*eine Erfahrung*). As such a thing, we can consider nature or experience as a system. But experience here means "possible experience in general," and nature means "nature in general" (*Natur überhaupt*). This nature was regarded as established by means of the laws of the understanding as the *a priori* conditions of possible experience in general. Accordingly, that system is none other than a "system according to *a priori* laws." But such nature in general, borrowing Kant's words, is nature viewed formally (*natura formaliter spectata*) and not nature seen in terms of its content (*natura materialiter spectata*). Incidentally, what we ordinarily experience as nature is nature seen in terms of its content. We can recognize therein various particular empirical laws. Such nature is "nature defined by the manifold of particular laws," and the experience is not experience in general but a "particular experience" (*besondere Erfahrung*). Such particular laws cannot be deduced *a priori* and are contingent for understanding. If so, are we to roam within the "labyrinth of the diversity of particular laws"?[286] Empirical laws are endlessly manifold. But our investigations of nature seek the systematic connections of these empirical laws. It demands that we "consider the aggregate

{*Aggregat*} of particular experiences as a system {*System*} of them."²⁸⁷ Not only is nature viewed formally as a system, but nature seen in terms of its content must also be a system. In contrast to the former which means a "transcendental system following transcendental concepts (categories)," the latter signifies a "system of nature following empirical laws."²⁸⁸ And our empirical cognition presupposes a system in the latter sense. However, the possibility of endlessly manifold empirical laws cannot be cognized transcendentally [*a priori*] and for the understanding is "contingent." The possibility of the unity of nature, the unity of experience, and following empirical laws is contingent. The system of nature following empirical laws is, for the understanding, "utterly irrelevant" (*ganze fremd*).²⁸⁹ According to Kant, what makes possible the empirical system of nature that is inconceivable from the standpoint of the understanding is the transcendental principle of reflective judgment. This is the principle of the specification of nature (*Spezifikation der Nature*)²⁹⁰ concerning empirical laws. Kant says that "nature specifies universal laws into empirical laws by following the forms of a logical system for the sake of judgment."²⁹¹ By means of this principle, as the more universal and the more particular are conjoined in an intrinsic relation following an order, a systematization of the diverse empirical laws takes place without the particular being seen as contingent in opposition to the universal. Empirical laws that are contingent for the understanding are made lawful according to the principle of specification, and by presupposing that principle our empirical cognition seeks the unity of nature. The "lawfulness of the contingent" (*Gesetzmässigkeit des Zufälligen*) is none other than purposiveness. This purposiveness that arranges the endlessly diverse empirical laws into a logical system is a formal and logical purposiveness. Furthermore, it is fitting for our faculties that cognize nature, and is a subjective purposiveness. In the cognition of nature there is the demand to judge the particular as something included under the universal and to subsume it under the concept of nature. Not only is judgment the faculty to subsume the particular under a given universal²⁹² but, in reverse, to discern the universal in relation to the particular. The specification of nature thus is fitting for judgment. Kant writes that "nature specifies its universal laws according to the principles of purposiveness for our cognitive faculties."²⁹³ Now discovering connections among the many different natural laws and unifying them under a comprehensive principle gives us satisfaction. Our intent to seek the unity of experience is accomplished, but on the other hand "the achievement of every intent" (*Ereichung jeder Absicht*) is tied to a feeling of pleasure. The formal logical purposiveness of nature is accompanied by a feeling of pleasure. Therein we can recognize the relationship between logical purposiveness and the purposiveness of beauty. Moreover, it would be said that the pleasant sensation of beauty, according to Kant, is the pleasant sensation of disinterestedness, and this must be distinguished from the pleasure that accompanies the achievement of intention. However, the pleasant sensation tied to the logical purposiveness of nature manifests beauty in knowledge so that as intellectual beauty or abstract beauty we can view it as a species of beauty. For such pleasant sensation is unrelated to volition. Kant says,

> ... when the condition for the attainment of design is a representation *a priori*, as it is here a principle for reflective judgment in general, the feeling of pleasure is

also determined by a ground *a priori*, thus valid for everyone. Moreover, that is merely by means of the reference of the object to the cognitive faculty. And the concept of purposiveness here having no reference at all to the faculty of desire, is hence utterly distinct in character from all practical purposiveness of nature.[294]

That is, logical purposiveness is that which becomes the principle of pure feelings and the principle of the purposiveness of beauty. The fact that beauty is suitable to judgment is due to the agreement required by "cognition in general" between the operation of imagination and the operation of understanding, but this concept of cognition in general already suggests an intrinsic relation between the purposiveness of beauty and logical purposiveness. The concept of cognition in general was conceived simply from the viewpoint of action, but in contrast to this the concept of logical purposiveness possesses an even greater significance for the logic of beauty where it includes the logical determination of the object even while being said to be subjective. We can regard the ground of judgments of beauty to be logical purposiveness in the form of the object. Nevertheless, although the agreement between the operation of the imagination and the operation of the understanding was required for cognition in general, is the imagination therefore without any relation at all to the formal logical purposiveness of nature? In order to investigate this question, we need to further consider this by entering into the logical purposiveness of nature.

17.

[438] The idea of the logical purposiveness of nature ties the *Critique of Judgment* together with the *Critique of Pure Reason*. Kant discussed the transcendental ideas in the Transcendental Dialectic of the latter book. According to him, our understanding relates only to objects of experience. The object of experience is something conditioned. Concerning all things conditioned, we can consider its *condition* and, further, consider the *condition of that thing*, and in this way consider the *whole of the condition*.[295] But the totality of such conditions transcend experience and hence transcend the understanding. It belongs to concepts of pure reason that are distinct from concepts of pure understanding. What Kant calls transcendental ideas are none other than such concepts of pure reason. Although our cognition can never arrive at them, they are necessities indispensable for our cognition, and our cognition first attains unity by means of them. As the third element in these transcendental ideas, Kant raised the "disjunctive synthesis of parts in a single system," but as Stattler says[296] we can probably see this as corresponding to the concept of logical purposiveness in the *Critique of Judgment*. The idea of system is set forth in detail in the Appendix to the Transcendental Dialectic. Reason demands the unity of cognition. Yet,

> ... this unity of reason always presupposes an idea, namely, that of the form of a whole of knowledge—a whole which is prior to the determinate cognition of the parts and which contains the conditions that determine *a priori* for every part its position and relation to the other parts. This idea accordingly postulates a complete

unity of cognition obtained by the understanding, by which this cognition is to be not a mere contingent aggregate {*Aggregat*}, but a system {*System*} connected according to necessary laws.[297]

Further, he depicts in detail the logical structure of what he calls system in this passage. In order for a system to be established, there must first be the principle of homogeneity (*Homogeneität*) (also called *Gleichartigkeit*). Systematization becomes possible only with the presupposition of homogeneity or identity among the manifold things.[298] Viewed logically, this corresponds to the principle of genera (*Prinzip der Gattungen*) that subsumes the manifold things under a genus and further under a higher genus. But a system would not be established by such a principle alone and, if that was all, the system would instead be destroyed. Confronting the logical principle of genera is the principle of species (*Prinzip der Arten*). This principle demands things possess a further diversity or difference despite their agreement on the basis of an identical genus. In other words, reason exhibits mutually contradictory interests, on the one hand, interest in the extent (universality) dealing with the genus, and, on the other hand, interest in the content (determinateness) dealing with the manifold of species. In the former case, we attempt to acquire simplicity by ascending to the genus and in the latter case we attempt to amplify the system by starting from the genus and descending to the manifold included at the base of the genus.[299] Just as there is the transcendental principle of homogeneity at the root of the logical principle of genus, there is the transcendental principle of specification (*Spezifikation*) (also called *Mannigfaltigkeit* or *Varietät*) at the root of the principle of species.[300] But in order to complete systematic unity, in addition to these two principles there must be added a third, the principle of continuity (*Kontinuität*) (also called *Affinität* or *Verwandtschaft*). This is something that arises from the union of the previous two principles and requires a seamless transition through the gradual growth of differences from each species to another species.[301] In this way we can see the concept of logical purposiveness in the *Critique of Judgment* to have its logical structure clarified in the three principles of homogeneity, specification, and continuity.

Now the specification or logical purposiveness of nature, whether we speak of genus or species, or what is spoken of in the First Introduction to the *Critique of Judgment* as the "classification of the manifold" (*Klassifikation des Mannigfaltigen*),[302] even while making us think of something formal-logical yet is nothing formal-logical at all. To begin with, we can formal-logicize even what we call a system in terms of classes in the relation of genus and species. But for this to be possible we need to anticipate a transcendental principle dealing with systems. Kant states, "the logical principle of genera, if applied to nature (by which I understand here merely objects given to us), presupposes a transcendental principle."[303] This transcendental principle is the above-mentioned principle of homogeneity. And regarding the principle of species, he writes that "this logical law would also be without meaning and application unless there lies the transcendental law of specification at its ground …"[304] The logical purposiveness of nature is the transcendental presupposition for the application of the viewpoint of formal logic to nature. In contrast to formal logic that is abstract, the logic of purposiveness is concrete. The concrete is the root of the abstract and the latter is understood on the basis of the former rather than the former being understood on the basis of the latter. If so, what sort is the logic of purposiveness? What we call system is the concept of totality. This is not something that can be conceived on the basis of the relationship of genus and species in formal logic. It must be conceived in the relationship of whole and parts. The whole is not "the analytic universal" (*das Analytisch-Allgemeine*) of the genus in formal logic, but instead "the synthetic universal" (*das Synthetisch-Allgemeine*). The universal in the analytic universal does not determine anything concerning the manifold, and the particular vis-à-vis the universal is contingent. On the contrary, the part in the synthetic universal is seen as a development in specification or differentiation and the whole does not imply the contingency of parts.[305] Here the principle of continuity is complete. Concerning this principle, Kant says that it is the continuous transition from each species to other species by means of the gradual growth (*stufenartiges Wachstum*) of diversity, and that when this happens the entire manifold "spring" (*abstammen*) from one highest genus through all degrees of gradually widely extended determination.[306] In this way the logic of purposiveness has an aspect that may remind us of Kant's so-called intuitive understanding. As we cited the passage before, he says that "the idea concerning the form of the whole of cognition precedes the fixed cognition of parts and includes the restrictions that define *a priori* the position and relation of each part vis-à-vis other parts."[307] The logic of purposiveness may have an aspect that reminds us of Hegel's logic.

But to begin with, Kant's logic is not identical with Hegel's logic. Concerning the ideas, Kant admitted only the "hypothetical use of reason" (*hypothetischer Gebrauch der Vernunft*). Therefore, the idea as a concept of pure reason is not constitutive (*konstitutive*) of our cognition but remains merely regulative (*regulative*). What is called the hypothetical use of reason in the *Critique of Pure Reason* corresponds to how purposiveness belongs to reflective judgment and not to determinant judgment. That is, as something belonging to reflective judgment, purposiveness is not a constitutive principle but a regulative principle for the cognition of nature and accordingly is only a heuristic principle (*heuristisches Prinzip*). After stating that the purposiveness of nature or the technology of nature is only a heuristic principle, Kant says, "such an investigation, as a part, belongs to the system of the *Critique of Pure Reason*."[308] It is evident that there is an intimate relation between the *Critique of Judgment* and the *Critique of Pure Reason*. Now is the purposiveness of nature really simply regulative as Kant thinks and not constitutive at all? Would not our empirical cognition instead require it to be also constitutive? As already mentioned, Kant conceived the logical principle of genus as presupposing the transcendental principle of homogeneity. To the extent that formal logic can be applied to the empirical cognition of nature, must not there be at its root purposiveness or what perhaps we ought to call the "systematicity of nature," moreover as a constitutive principle? Kant says the fact that "particular laws stand under more universal laws, their principle thus curtailed, is not only an economic principle of reason but an intrinsic law of nature."[309] No matter how the universal laws of pure understanding, the categories and the *a priori* forms of space and time, condition and constitute the object of experience, unless these concrete things further agree under the specific laws in the relations of their content, we are left within Kant's so-called "labyrinth of diversity,"[310] not knowing what to do. When that happens, we would not at all grasp nature, nay it would not be possible in general, and would presumably be, borrowing Liebmann's words,[311] an "incomprehensible confusion" (*unbegreiflicher Wirrwarr*). Helmholtz said, "it is, in any case, evident that science that aims to grasp nature must start from the presupposition of nature's conceivability {*Voraussetzung ihrer Begreiflichkeit*}."[312] However, no matter how each thing is placed under the determinations of time and space and the categories, if they were utterly unrelated to each other in content and were heterogeneous, we would be unable to grasp them. In order for nature to be something we can grasp, purposiveness must possess the significance of a constitutive principle. Lachelier, in his "Foundation of Induction," thought that the principle of induction stands upon two distinguishable laws.[313] One principle is that whereby phenomena form a series wherein the existence of what precedes determines the existence of what follows. The other principle is that this series, by means of this, forms a system and in this system the idea of the whole defines the being of the parts. Now the phenomenon that determines the other phenomena by preceding them is called the efficient cause and, according to Kant, the whole that produces the being of the parts is the final cause. If we accept what Lachelier says, for induction to be possible purposiveness, like causality, would have to have the sense of a constitutive principle. Although Kant had stated that in order for the logical principle of genus to be applied to nature a transcendental principle of homogeneity must be presupposed, for induction to be applicable to nature we must anticipate nature's systematic purposiveness. We can view the uniformity of nature (*uniformity of nature*) that Mill conceived as the fundamental requirement for induction to be an abstraction of the principle of nature's systematic purposiveness. Kant thought that the act of reflective judgment seeks something universal vis-à-vis the given particular, but induction moves in the same way from the given particular to the universal. We can say that every empirical cognition begins with comparison. By comparing what had been individually perceived we form a common empirical concept and by comparing particular empirical laws we discern an even more universal empirical law. Incidentally, taking the purposiveness of nature as premise, Kant says, "it must precede all comparison."[314] We thus have to say that purposiveness is not something that is merely a foundation of judgments of beauty or of the cognition of organisms, but is the foundation of every empirical cognition.

18.

[446] Nevertheless, an interpretation only in the above manner would be to read Kant's standpoint as identical to the standpoint of Hegel. What we have clarified so far is that the idea of a system in Kant as a concept of reason possesses the logical structure of intuitive understanding and further that it would have to possess a constitutive significance. And indeed, Hegel's logic of reason is a logic of intuitive understanding, and what in Kant was conceived to be merely regulative in Hegel becomes constitutive. Kant's standpoint of the *Critique of Judgment*, to begin with, cannot be the same as Hegel's standpoint. While on the one hand acknowledging the important meaning of teleology, Kant on the other hand tried to avoid falling into a metaphysics of intuitive

understanding by keeping the standpoint of a discursive understanding. As we shall eventually raise and discuss this, teleology implies the logic of intuitive understanding. In this way we may be able to view Kant's standpoint in the *Critique of Judgment* to stand upon the logic of understanding (intuitive understanding) and a Hegelian logic of reason (intuitive understanding). Kant stated that in the order of the cognitive faculties judgment occupies the position of a mediating link (*Mittelglied*) between the understanding and reason, but the logic of reflective judgment must as such be a logic of the middle. But this kind of logic would not be established if we think of the principle of reflective judgment as merely regulative in contrast to the principle of understanding as being constitutive as in Kant. As we already argued, in order for empirical cognition to be possible, the requirement for the purposiveness of nature is to be a constitutive principle and, further, unity is required of teleology and causality. Lachelier conceived the law of causality and the law of purposiveness to be the foundation of induction. These two laws as intrinsic laws of nature, however, do not exist as isolated from one another but must be unified. In this way I think that the logic of reflective judgment originally had to be a logic of imagination. The logic of imagination is situated in the so-called middle between the logic of understanding and the logic of reason. However rather than simply being intermediate, it is instead a logic more originary than both, and we can say that, in relation to this, the formal logic of understanding to begin with, but also the Hegelian logic of a dialectic of reason, is already formal. In what way must Kant's logic of reflective judgment develop into the logic of imagination and in what way can it be developed into the logic of imagination? We must first consider this problem.

In explaining the logical purposiveness of nature Kant often employs the word "affinity" (*Affinität*) (*Verwandtschaft*). For example, he says:

> It is a subjectively necessary transcendental presupposition that nature does not have this disturbing boundless dissimilarity of empirical laws and heterogeneity of natural forms, but that, rather, through the affinity of its particular laws under more general laws it takes on the quality of experience as an empirical system.[315]

In the *Critique of Pure Reason* this principle of continuity is also called the principle of affinity. Nevertheless, the affinity of particular laws or also the affinity of particular natural forms may remind us of that "affinity of appearances" (*Affinität der Erscheinungen*) or the "affinity of the manifold" in the Transcendental Deduction of the *Critique of Pure Reason*. And in this case, Kant thought that "the affinity of all appearances ... is a necessary consequence of a synthesis in imagination which is grounded *a priori* on rules."[316] If so, might not what is called the affinity of particular laws, or also the affinity of particular natural forms, in the *Critique of Judgment*, somehow anticipate synthesis in the imagination? Synthesis in the imagination, as a synthesis that does not ruin the diversity in content, would fit that principle of specification or diversity that the idea of a system requires along with the principle of homogeneity. The nature of the imagination cannot be satisfied unless diversity exists simultaneously with homogeneity. We can view the subjective affinity of appearances [phenomena], considered from the abstract standpoint of so-called consciousness-in-general in the *Critique of Pure*

Reason, as instead having been grasped objectively from the concrete standpoint of reflective judgment as the technology of nature. Furthermore, although we must say that in Kant the technology of nature is conceived to be something subjective as a merely regulative principle, nonetheless what is subjective from the abstract standpoint is, on the contrary, objective from the concrete standpoint, and what is objective from the concrete standpoint is, instead, subjective from the abstract standpoint. Nature's logical purposiveness, according to Kant, is the technology of nature. Kant states:

> ...thus to bring given appearances [phenomena] under empirical concepts of determinate natural things, reflective judgment deals with them technically {*technisch*}, not schematically {*schmatisch*} ..., artistically {*künstlich*}, not mechanically {*mechanisch*} like an instrument guided by the understanding and the senses, in terms of a principle that is universal but at the same time indeterminate, the principle of purposive order, for the benefit of our judgment, by which the particular laws of nature are made suitable for the possibility of experience as a system.... Hence judgment itself makes *a priori* the technic [technology] of nature into a principle for its reflection.[317]

And he says, "the power of judgment is properly technological. Nature is represented as technological only to the extent that it harmonizes with, and necessitates, that operation of judgment."[318] However, as we already discussed, the logical purposiveness of nature cannot remain simply a principle of reflection of judgment but must possess an ontological significance. Although it is said that judgment operates technologically, not schematically, judgment as such is reflective judgment and in the Transcendental Deduction of the *Critique of Pure Reason* it is clear that determinant judgment operates schematically. Kant writes in the First Introduction to the *Critique of Judgment*,

> In general, concerning the universal concepts of nature which first make possible a concept of experience (possessing the particular empirical determination), reflection has its instruction already in the concept of nature as such or, put differently, the understanding, and judgment, requiring no special principle of reflection, schematizes *a priori* and applies these schemata to each empirical synthesis. And without such synthesis, no empirical judgment would be possible. Here judgment not only reflects but also determines, and its Transcendental Schematism, at the same time, is useful by providing it with a rule under which it subsumes given empirical intuitions.[319]

In this way, according to Kant, determinant judgment is schematic and reflective judgment is technological. But as we discussed earlier, Transcendental Schematism belongs not to judgment but to the imagination. The schematism of determinant judgment is nothing other than what reflects and formalizes the original operation of the productive imagination from the abstract standpoint of consciousness-in-general. In the Transcendental Schematism, Kant calls the schematism "an art concealed in the depths of the human soul" (*eine verborgene Kunst in den Tiefen der menschlichen Seele*),[320] but we might view this hidden art as having been objectively brought to light in the technology of nature in the *Critique of Judgment*. Rather than saying that the technology of nature is not at all schematic, nature's technology is also schematic in some sense. But it is not something abstract like the transcendental schemas. Instead, it is something concrete that we conceive as *Typus* (type) as well as *Stil* (mode). And we can probably say that the technology of nature, like any other technology, or rather as the archetype of every other technology, belongs to the imagination.[321] Every technology is a synthesis of the particular and the universal, the subjective and the objective, the ideal and the material, freedom and necessity, teleology and causality. Kant conceived the technology of nature to be simply purposiveness but originally it is a synthesis of causality and purposiveness, and we would have to say that as such it belongs to the imagination. Every technology, as a productive synthesis, concretely expresses its synthesis in form. The logic of imagination is not only a logic of synthesis but also a logic of forms. Form and unity in form cannot belong to judgment seen as a faculty of subsumption. What Kant considered in the logical purposiveness of nature was not simply specific empirical laws but concrete "forms of nature" (*Naturformen*). Even what we call empirical laws are not simply formal like *a priori* laws but, as empirical laws with content, manifest the forms of nature even if they are more universal. Even what is called genus and species in the *Critique of Judgment* was conceived not simply formal-logically but as forms of nature. The logic of purposiveness should have been a logic of forms. Now Kant, in particular, conceived the organism as a figure of nature. In itself, it contains a kind of purposiveness. By thoroughly investigating this issue of the organism and, in turn further investigating the connection between the issue of aesthetic purposiveness and the technology of nature, and, advancing, and clarifying the connection to moral teleology, I would like to clarify how the issue of reflective judgment must develop into the logic of imagination and in what sense it is a logic of the middle between the logic of understanding and the logic of reason, and as such what logical structure it possesses and, further, in what point it differs from the logical structure of so-called teleology.

19.

[453] Kant styled the formal-logical purposiveness of nature, the technology of nature. Nature seen as the technology of nature, according to his words, is "nature as art" (*Natur als Kunst*). Art is one kind of technology, and we can recognize an analogy between the technology of nature and art. Kant says that to study nature according to formal-logical purposiveness is to study nature in "analogy with art" (*nach der Analogie mit einer Kunst*).[322] Furthermore, he had conceived the technology of nature, as the formal-logical purposiveness of nature, to be something subjective, and when considering nature in analogy with art, nature is "estimated, not in an objective relationship to the object, but in a subjective relationship to our faculties of cognition."[323] As something thus subjective, the technology of nature harmonizes with the purposiveness of beauty. Is the technology of nature, however, nothing but something simply subjective? Technology in art makes things objectively. Concerning organisms, Kant conceives of "organic technology" (*organische Technik*). This belongs to the

technology of nature, and he says here that this technology of nature may be called "plastic" (*plastisch*).[324] We can view organisms as products of the technology of nature. In a superior sense they are "forms of nature" (*Naturformen*). And, according to Kant, an organism is a "natural end [purpose]" (*Naturzweck*) and nature's intrinsic objective purposiveness. Thus, in a sense at least to the extent that the organism is called nature's intrinsic objective purposiveness, we can say firstly that the technology of nature, as organic technology, is intrinsic and objective. Even so, can the formal-logical purposiveness of nature and its intrinsic purposiveness originally be in agreement? Although Kant states that to view nature in terms of the technology of nature is to see nature in its analogy with art, Kant also writes that the organism ordinarily is often viewed as an "analogue of art" (*Analogon der Kunst*). Not only can the organism be considered in analogy with art, but art in reverse is also considered in analogy with organisms. What on earth is the logic of analogy? It would seem necessary to clarify this in order, in turn, to further clarify the connection between the logical purposiveness of nature and the purposiveness of beauty and, in addition, to make distinct the relationship between the logical purposiveness of nature and the objective purposiveness of nature, namely, the organism.

Analogy today is ordinarily translated as *ruisui* [類推] and is regarded as an inference founded upon a weak rationale and hence as meager in logical value. But viewed historically, it was a logic that occupied an extremely important place in the philosophy of antiquity and the medieval ages.[325] The reason why it has become denigrated in contemporary times is the result of being separated from its original ontological root and being formalized. As the word *analogia* (ἀνάλογος, ἀναλογία) indicates, analogy is originally *logos* moving from bottom to top. In the sense of a *logos* moving from bottom to top, it is similar to induction. That is also why in contemporary textbooks of logic, analogy is explained to be an inference similar to induction and yet not true induction. Now as we had already mentioned, induction agrees with reflective judgment that discerns the universal vis-à-vis given particulars, but in the same way we can regard inference by analogy as belonging to reflective judgment. In fact, Kant states in the *Logic* that induction and analogy are two methods of inference of reflective judgment.

> The power of judgment in proceeding from the particular to the general, thus draw—not *a priori* (but empirically)—general judgments from experience, either inferring from many things to all things of a kind or inferring from many determinations and properties in which things of the same kind agree to the rest insofar as they belong to the same principle. The former way of conclusion is called conclusion through induction. The latter way of conclusion is called conclusion by analogy.[326]

Now as we already discussed, if we take the formal-logical purposiveness of nature to be the basis for induction, we can also regard this to be the basis for analogy as well, or rather we would probably have to say that it has its original significance as their foundation. While analogy is the same as every other logic in that it pursues the one in the many, when it does so it does not seek the one by extinguishing or leaving the many but has its characteristic in the point that it pursues the one in the many while accepting the many as it is. The formal logic of understanding unifies by analyzing the manifold of particulars, extracting what is common, and raising it as the universal concept, but when this happens the diversity of the particular is extinguished and the universal concept is raised apart from the manifold particulars. But in analogy, the manifold is recognized in its diversity. This is why logic textbooks explain analogy today to be the inference from a definite particular case to another particular case. However, to infer from a certain particular to another particular must mean seeking the one within the many. Moreover, in this case, what is required is the recognition of the many, not its extinction. This requirement appears for beings that would not let themselves be subsumed under a single formal-logical genus concept. We can see this as evident, for example, among things of distinct orders such as God and creatures, which was an important topic of *analogia* in the Middle Ages.[327] If we are to conceive an analogy between art and the organism it must be this sort of a relationship. In contrast to unification through the logic of understanding that is the unification of things of the same kind, unification by analogy is instead unification of things of different kinds, and further in this unity, the mutual difference among different things appears in the forefront instead of being obliterated. The many is one not by quitting to be many, but they are one instead by being many. Things of different kinds not only belong to distinct orders but each in general signifies something independent. The independent, as separate wholes, are things that do not allow division, and this is what I mean by form [形]. Unity in the manifoldness of the manifold forms is not through induction but rather achieved by the logic of analogy. While induction and analogy are both *logos* that moves from bottom to top, their characteristics are distinct in the point that while the former seeks the one outside of the many by extinguishing the many, by contrast the latter seeks the one within the many while accepting the many. Rather than being an incomplete method of induction, analogy instead is a logic more concrete than the inductive method. The foundation of the logic of analogy is the technology of nature and as such the technology of nature must manifest the logic of form (*Logik der Form*). Such nature is not simply nature but historical nature. As technological, nature is historical as well. The logic of forms is originally a logic of imagination and what Kant calls nature's formal-logical purposiveness, as a logic of forms, would concretely have to be a logic of imagination. Kant says that the technology of reflective judgment is the basis for the technology of nature, but the basis for the technology of nature is instead the technology of the imagination, and, in relation to such productive judgment, reflective judgment is something already truly taking the "reflective" standpoint. The logic of imagination, to begin with, is a logic of enactive intuition [行為的直観].[328] In induction and analogy, regarded as two methods of inference for reflective judgment, we can probably view the former as more often approaching the logic of understanding and the latter as more often approaching the logic of imagination.

Kant himself was thinking of the formal-logical purposiveness of nature in the direction of the logic of form. He regarded the formal-logical purposiveness of nature or the specification of nature as a principle for the "classification of the manifold" (*Klassifikation des Mannigfaltigen*). This sort of classification, as Stattler understood it, becomes concretely an issue in morphology (*Morphologie*) in the broad sense, and in this case a natural system (*natürliches System*) is sought through natural classification (*natürliche Klassifikation*). What becomes the basis for such classification, according to Kroner, is the concept of species (*Artbegriff*) in relation to the concept of law. He writes: "Biological experience first becomes generally possible through the concepts of species. Their form is thus an indispensable instrument of thought for every biological inquiry."[329] While the concept of law is constitutive, the concept of species is by contrast classificatory. Species, moreover, as *species*, ἰδέα, that is form, becomes the basis for classification without permitting its reduction to constitutive lawfulness. What is sought by the "classification of the manifold," if we were to borrow Kroner's words, is not a "system of laws" but rather a "system of forms" (*System der Formen*). Such a system concretely becomes an issue in the classification of the organism as "forms of nature" (*Naturformen*). It is no accident that in the *Critique of Pure Reason*, in the passage discussing the idea of a system, corresponding to what the *Critique of Judgment* called the concept of the formal-logical purposiveness of nature, Kant discusses the "continuous gradation of created beings" (*kontinuierliche Stufenleiter der Geschöpfe*).[330] Such continuous gradation or, according to the First Introduction in the *Critique of Judgment*,

> ... the classification of the manifold, that is, the comparison of several classes, each under a definite concept, when they are aligned in terms of their common characteristic, with each subsumed under higher classes (genera), thus finally reaching the concept that contains the principle of the entire classification (and constituting the highest genus) within itself[331]

—this kind of system—had hitherto always been represented in the form of a tree that develops through differentiation gradually from one trunk to many branches. Put differently, the specification of nature itself was thought to be an organic system. According to Kant, teleology does not belong to "natural science" (*Naturwissenschaft*) or a "theory of nature" (*Theorie der Natur*). Here we must thoroughly seek a mechanistic explanation.

> The exposition of the ends [purposes] pursued by nature in its products, to the extent that they form a system according to teleological concepts, properly belongs only to a description of nature {*Naturbeschreibung*} drawn in accordance with a particular guideline {*nach einem besonderen Leitfaden*}.[332]

The description of nature is morphology. What is its particular guideline? It would be none other than the "analogy of forms" (*Analogie der Formen*) that unifies the diverse forms of nature in their manifold. Kant writes, "[t]his analogy of forms, which despite all their differences seem to be produced according to a common archetype {*einem gemeinschaftlichen Urbilde gemäss*}, strengthens the suspicion that they have a de facto kindship in their descent from a common primal mother {*Urmutter*}."[333] We can trace their descent from this primal mother "by gradual approximation of one animal genus to another genus."[334] But the original domain of the logic of form would presumably have to be history and not nature. The logic of imagination, to begin with, is the logic of history. The analogy of forms belongs to the description of history rather than the description of nature. Nature, as something technological, to the extent that we can view it as something historical or view it so-to-speak as "history made habitual," enters into that logic.

The relationship between nature's formal-logical purposiveness and its intrinsic objective purposiveness should become further clarified by an analysis of the structure of organisms. Although the formal-logical purposiveness of nature views the whole of nature as one system, organisms form a single system, each respectively in itself. We can view organisms, respectively, as "particular systems" (*besondere Systeme*). Organisms, according to Kant, are the end [purpose] of nature but this means that "a thing bears itself as cause and also effect."[335] For example, in a tree, first from the viewpoint of the genus, its self is the cause and also the effect of itself. A single tree was produced from a tree of the same genus and again produces a tree of the same genus. In this way, putting this from the viewpoint of the genus, it produces itself and ceaselessly, on the one hand as the effect and on the other hand as the cause, has been produced from within itself as well as is producing itself within its genus, and as genus goes on always maintaining itself. Secondly, the tree also produces itself as an individual. The material that the tree adds to itself in its growth is what it works into unique properties of the kind that cannot be supplied by mechanistic relations of nature outside of itself in advance, in short, in terms of composition it goes on forming itself with material that is the product of itself. Thirdly, the parts of the tree produce themselves also in the sense that the maintenance of one part reciprocally depends on the maintenance of other parts. The leaf is a product of the tree but in turn, the leaf maintains the tree. When one part of the tree is wounded it is assisted by the other parts, and therein we can see the "self-help of nature." In this way, with the above three points, it is clear that in the organism the self relates to itself reciprocally as cause and effect, but this alone would suffice to explain organisms as ends of nature. To the extent that they are conceived by the understanding, causal relations form a series that "ceaselessly decline" (*immer abwärts*). There are things that as effects presuppose others as causes, that cannot themselves reciprocally be at the same time the latters' causes. This sort of causal relation is called the relation of efficient cause (*nexus effectivus*). In opposition to this, we can conceive a causal connection by means of ends. If we look at this as a series, it involves a relation of dependence that is "forward and at the same time backward" (*sowohl abwärts als aufwärts*), and here what was once called effect, notwithstanding, looked at backward is named the cause of that of which it is the effect. This kind of causal connection is called the relation of the final cause (*nexus finalis*).[336] In this way, the organism can be regarded as implying the final cause, but we need to further clarify its logical structure. To begin with, "a thing to be a natural end, firstly requires that its parts (in their being and form) are possible only in relation to the whole. For this thing, itself is an end and hence is comprehended under a concept or an idea that must determine *a priori* all that is to be contained in it."[337] However this alone would be unable to determine the intrinsic purposiveness of the organism's purposiveness. "Thus, a natural end of nature, secondly, requires that its parts reciprocally become the cause and the effect of their form and that by means of this, they are combined into the unity of a whole."[338] Put simply, for the end of nature, firstly its parts become possible by the whole, and secondly its parts reciprocally become possible by other parts, and through this the whole also becomes possible. Kant writes,

> In such products of nature, not only can we consider each part as existing by means of all the other parts, but also as existing for the sake of the other parts and for the whole, that is as an instrument or organ {*Organ*}. But this alone is not sufficient,.... Rather we can conceive each part as an organ producing the other parts (and hence each reciprocally)."[339]

Here the relation between the ideas of the organism (the intrinsic objective purposiveness of nature) and the system (the formal-logical purposiveness of nature) is evident. The organism depicts the logical structure of a system in its relationship of whole and part. It first manifests the principle of the identity of form in the whole, next the principle of the specification of form in the parts, and further the principle of the continuity of form in the reciprocal production of whole and parts. In this way we can say that the principle of formal purposiveness is also an *a priori* principle for objective teleological judgments.

20.

[464] The next issue therefore is the sort of relation the purposiveness of organisms have to causality. According to Kant, causality is the fundamental principle for the cognition of nature and unless the investigation of nature takes mechanism as its basis "it fails to provide any original cognition of nature whatsoever."[340] Hence we must strive to explain nature to the best of our abilities in terms of mechanistic causality.

> It is of endless importance to reason to keep in view the mechanism of nature in its productions, in explaining them, since apart from the mechanism of nature we would be unable to attain any insight whatsoever into their essence. Even if we concede today that a supreme architect had directly created the forms of nature in their appearance just as they have from all time, or has predetermined them in their evolutionary course to continuously accord to the same prototype, our knowledge of nature would not be furthered even slightly.[341]

It is our duty in the investigation of nature,

> ... to explain all products and events of nature, even the most fitting, through its mechanism as far as possible (its limits cannot be encountered within this method of investigation).[342]
>
> To actually consider phenomena in light of the correlation of ends would achieve nothing at all for the theory of nature, that is, the mechanistic explanation of the phenomena of nature by efficient causes.[343]

We, therefore, have to say that, from the standpoint of natural science, it is a matter of course to thoroughly pursue mechanistic causal explanations even for organisms.

Nonetheless, Kant at the same time recognized that mechanism alone is insufficient for grasping the organism indeed as organism. Concerning the organism, he states that in the same way, it would be "delusional" (*schwärmerisch*) to only adopt the explanatory method of teleology, completely ignoring the mechanism of nature, to pursue only a mechanism by completely denying the purposiveness of nature is fanciful (*phantastisch*). To the extent that organisms are also products of nature, we need to discern in them mechanistic relations. Otherwise, we would be unable to say that they are products of nature. Yet while organisms are products of nature, they are ends [purposes] of nature. In this way we encounter mechanism and teleology in one and the same thing. Therein emerges the "necessity of the cohesion of the two principles." How did Kant consider the cohesion of the mechanistic principle and the teleological principle?

> The principle that permits the compatibility of these two principles in the estimation of nature by means of them, must be placed in what lies beyond both {*ausserhalb beider*} (hence beyond possible empirical representation of nature), but further in what contains the ground of that representation of nature, that is, within the supersensible, to which each of the two explanatory modes must be referred. However because we can have only an indeterminate concept of a ground that makes possible the estimate of nature according to empirical laws, beyond which we cannot determine this in greater detail no matter what the predicate, it follows that the union of the two principles cannot rest upon a ground of explanation {*Erklärung*} {*Explikation*} of the possibility of a product according to given laws for determinant judgment, but can only rest on a ground of its exposition {*Eröterung*} {*Exposition*} merely for reflective judgment.[344]
>
> Now the principle common to the mechanistic derivation, on the one hand, and teleological, on the other hand, {*das gemeinschaftliche Prinzip der mechanischen einerseits und der teleologischen Ableitung anderseits*} is the supersensible, that must be placed at the root of nature as phenomenon. But of this we are unable from the theoretical point of view to form even the least positive determinate concept. Therefore, in light of this supersensible as the principle, we cannot at all explain how nature (by means of its particular laws) constitute a system, cognized by us as possible both on the principle of the production from physical causes and that of final causes. On the contrary we can only depend on the principle of the mechanism (which has always a claim to authority over natural things). And in cases where, without relying on the teleological principle, phenomena of nature arise, whose possibility is inconceivable on the mechanistic principle, we can assume that without being disturbed by the apparent contradiction arising between the principles for estimating the products of nature, we may confidently study the laws of nature by following both principles (in response to the possibility of its product being cognizable to our understanding whether by one principle or the other). For the possibility has, at least, been confirmed of their being reconciled, even objectively, in a single principle (for they deal with phenomena presupposing a supersensible ground).[345]

Because of this, nature's mechanistic nature and its teleological (intentional) technicity, concerning one and the same product and its possibility, are subject to a common higher principle {*unter einem gemeinschaftlichen oberen Prinzip*} of nature in its particular laws. But even so since this principle is transcendent, and due to the limitation of our understanding, we are unable to reconcile the two principles in an explanation of the same natural generation, even where we can understand the intrinsic possibility of this product only by means of a causality according to ends (as in organized matter)."[346]

In this way Kant supposed a single common principle standing above causal theory (mechanism) and teleology, combining them. And he placed this principle within the supersensible, within "the supersensible substrate of nature" (*das übersinnliche Substrat der Natur*),[347] and hence in the thing itself in relation to the phenomenon. This kind of principle is that which cannot be cognized by us due to the limits of human understanding. This single principle, so to speak, splits for the standpoint of us human beings into the two principles of causal theory and teleology. The investigation of nature through these two principles is not in contradiction first because this investigation is the investigation of phenomena, and second because the coherence of these two principles is ascertained on the supersensible ground of phenomena and next because these principles are related to the power of judgment. That is to say that as the maxim of determinant judgment is the fact that all products of nature are possible by means of mechanistic laws and as the maxim of reflective judgment is the fact that certain products of nature are impossible by means of merely mechanistic laws, both are established without contradiction. And Kant regarded teleology not as a constitutive principle but as simply nothing more than a regulative principle.

Nevertheless, the issue of the coherence between causal theory and teleology harbors a reason for even further questioning. Kant stated that the single common principle that combines them lies within the supersensible and regarded it to transcend beyond our understanding, but therein appears what he calls intuitive understanding. This seems to provide an objective solution to the antinomy between causal theory and teleology and to imply a principle that can combine them. It would appear that the concept of the synthetic universal or concrete universal in intuitive understanding, as already mentioned, agrees with the idea of a system and thus also agrees with the structure of the organism.[348] The logic of intuitive understanding, like the logic of the organism, is a teleology. Hegel's dialectics, founded upon the concept of the concrete universal, is a teleological system and its logic is organological (from *Organologie*). It may be said that the teleology of intuitive understanding is not a simple teleology but the unification of causal theory and teleology. But, aside from the fact that for Kant the intuitive understanding is not our understanding, causal theory becomes something subordinate in this unity, and yet this would not suit the specific gravity causal theory possesses for him in relation to teleology. According to him, while the principle of causality is constitutive, teleology by contrast is no more than regulative. Further we can view finality as a kind of causality, namely, "causality by ends [purposes]," and the particularization of causality.[349] Thus we can also consider that we ought to pursue the unity of causal theory and teleology, not in the direction of teleology but rather, by contrast, in the direction causal theory. As we discussed above, the issue of the organism is tied to the issue of the particularization of nature, and we can view the organism as an objectification of this idea. Thus Kant writes,

> ... if we are to pursue the principle of nature in the particularization of universal laws of nature known to us, the necessity of adopting the concept of design as concealed within nature (hence within its mechanism), lying at the root of the production of organized beings is unavoidable.[350]

To explain the products of nature we ought to pursue the mechanism of nature as far as we can and even if we abandon this attempt,

> ... it does not mean that it is intrinsically impossible to encounter the purposiveness of nature along this path of mechanism, but rather only for the reason that it is impossible to us as human beings. For it would presumably necessitate an intuition other than sensible intuition, and a determinate cognition of the intelligible substrate of nature—although it would be a ground from which the very mechanism of the appearances [phenomena] governed by particular laws can be shown—and such things therefore completely surpass our capacity.[351]

These sentences should deter us from conceiving the unity of causality and teleology directly under teleology. What is here called nature's intelligible substrate, an intuition other than sensible intuition sufficiently reminds us of intellectual intuition or intuitive understanding. But it would be difficult to simply say that this principle must be a teleology rather than a mechanism. Instead, as we find in the above-cited passages, it must signify a "common higher principle" that is "beyond both." Therein lies the ground of causality together with teleology and both would have to derive from it.

Moreover, it is difficult to deny that the logic of the synthetic universal of the intuitive understanding raised by Kant is something with a teleological structure. And he also views causal theory in relation to teleology as a "subordinate" "means."[352] That is, we can conceive of natural laws as "subordinate to ends as principles,"

> ... although in cases where we can conceive of ends as the ground of the possibility of certain kinds of things, we need to also assume means. Its operational laws themselves require nothing presupposing an end and consequently is mechanical, and yet is a subordinate cause of designed effects.[353]

In order to produce organic forms, nature "utilizes" mechanistic relations themselves, and employs mechanism "so-to-speak as a tool for the cause that operates by design." It can be said that this sort of view thinks of nature in analogy with art or the technological activities of human beings, but even in such cases, we conceive what we call ends as merely subjective, and beside the danger of even personifying it, there still remains the issue of how mechanism can operate in agreement with teleology. Kant states,

> ... it is quite indeterminate and will always remain undeterminable for our reason how much the mechanism of nature can contribute as a means to the design of each end in nature. Furthermore because of the above-mentioned intelligible principle of the possibility of nature in general, we may assume that nature is possible throughout in accordance with two kinds of universally consonant laws

(physical laws and laws of final causes) {*durchgängig nach beiderlei allgemein zusammenstimmende Gesetzen (den physischen und den der Endursachen) möglich*}, although we cannot discern how this is so.[354]

In any case Kant recognized the necessity of cohesion between final cause and physical cause. And yet he thought that the principle of this cohesion cannot be cognized by our understanding for the reason that it exists within the intelligible substrate of nature. Thus, we may be able to consider how even what cannot be determined from the standpoint of quantitative understanding is determinable from the standpoint of intuitive understanding. Intuitive understanding, to begin with, is the unity of intuition and understanding, separated from the standpoint of us, human beings, on the one hand as what provides the content of cognition and on the other hand as what provides the form of cognition. According to Kant, our intuition is sensible and for our understanding the content is provided from the outside. But in intuitive understanding even the content is produced from within itself. How are we then to conceive the unity of intuition and understanding? Here I am reminded of the position the productive imagination occupies in Fichte's *Science of Knowledge*. According to Fichte, the ego posits itself in opposition to itself. The posited non-ego is therefore not the thing-in-itself but rather the object. The (epistemological) object [客観] exists only in opposition to the (epistemological) subject [主観], and the subject is possible only in distinction from the object. Therefore, this means that the ego indirectly posits the object or the subject. Subject and object are in opposition. The object is posited by negating the subject and, in turn, the subject is posited by negating the object. The ego posits the object and hence negates the subject, limits its own activity, posits receptivity within itself, and must relate this receptivity over there to the object as the ground of reality. Put differently, the representation of the reality of the non-ego, independent of the ego, must be engendered over there. And the ego posits the subject and hence negates the object, limits its activity, posits receptivity within the object, and must relate this receptivity to the subject's activity as the ground of reality. Put differently, the ego must see the activity of itself as the cause of the receptivity posited in the object. Hence, it must produce the representation of the reality of the ego, independent of the non-ego, namely, the representation of freedom. Indirect positing is thus the operation of representation or of imagining (*Einbilden*). The non-ego is not the ground of reality of receptivity posited within the ego but is only represented or imaged to be such a ground of reality, and it is this ground of reality not as thing-in-itself but as a necessary representation of the ego. The ego necessarily produces this representation from within itself, and hence indirect positing must be determined as the faculty for producing representations, namely, as the productive imagination. Without this faculty, neither the representation concerning the reality of the non-ego, the indirect positing of subject and object, the reciprocal determination of ego and non-ego, their coherence, their opposition, or what we roughly call the ego, nor what we call spirit, would exist. Fichte writes that "... without this wonderful faculty ..., nothing in the human spirit can be explained—upon which the entire mechanism of the human spirit could easily be founded."[355] The theoretical ego possesses complete spontaneity and requires the ego's activity in relation to the object; this activity is independent and at the same time limited. By saying it is independent I mean that it is not conditioned by anything, or rather even that nothing conditions it and everything is instead conditioned or posited by it. The ego's independent activity is thus necessarily productive. Everything is its product. At the same time this activity must be limited, it must have an object to which the self relates. Because the ego's activity is independent it is productive and because it is limited it is objective and has an object. At the same time, it must be both, but this is possible by the fact that the product of the ego's activity is simultaneously its object. What we mean by object [客観] is that which appears to the ego as the product of an *other*.[356] Accordingly this activity of the ego must be an activity whereby its own product appears to it as an other's product or a thing external to itself. However, my product can appear to me as such a thing when in my activity I am not reflecting on this activity and hence not conscious in my activity of this activity as mine. Put differently, only in the ego's unconscious activity of production can its own product appear as an other's product. This unconscious production is the basis of consciousness and is the condition where only by its means is consciousness possible. Consciousness presupposes an unconscious activity within itself. For because consciousness becomes possible by means of reflection upon its own activity, the activity wherein consciousness is born through its reflection in itself cannot be conscious. That unconscious production is none other than the imagination. Productive imagination is the condition of consciousness, the ego. Fichte writes,

> ... thus it is taught here that all reality—of course in the sense of reality *for us* as there is no other meaning to be understood in the system of transcendental philosophy—is produced solely by the power of imagination. One of the greatest thinkers of our age, who, as far as I can see, teaches the same, describes this as a *deception* of the imagination. But every deception must be opposed by truth, and every deception must be avoidable. But if we now show, as it is to be shown in the present system, that the possibility of our consciousness, our life, our being for us, that is, our being as the ego, is based on the act of imagination, the same cannot be denied if we are not to abstract from the ego. To abstract from the ego would be a contradiction for the reason that it would be impossible for the one abstracting to abstract from itself. Consequently, the act of imagination does not deceive and instead provides truth, the only possible truth. To suppose that it is deceiving would establish a skepticism that teaches us to doubt our own existence.[357]

The ego posits itself as determined by the non-ego, and therefore it is the productive imagination. But to say that it is the imagination is not sufficient; this imagination must also become for itself (*für sich*) or, put differently, the ego must raise this activity of the other to consciousness. Hence, we need to describe what Fichte calls, "the pragmatic history of the human spirit" (*die pragmatische Geschichte des menschlichen Geistes*). This theme was inherited and developed by Schelling's *Transcendental Idealism* and Hegel's *Phenomenology of Spirit*.[358] Kuno Fischer explains:

> In the entire scope of Fichte's teachings, in whatsoever point, there is nothing larger in trajectory than the theoretical grounding of the ego by the productive

imagination. From here the *Science of Knowledge* affected its force of traction to Novalis and Friedrich Schlegel, and for a while was thought in the spirit of the Romantic School that venerated the power of imagination as God to be a philosophy closely related to itself. The same relationship that Kant has to Fichte, through his doctrine of transcendental apperception, Fichte has to Schelling and Hegel, through his theory of imagination and its development.[359]

Intuitive understanding or intellectual intuition, it seems, would be impossible without the imagination as its foundation. However, the philosophy of intellectual intuition was essentially a teleological system. What I call the logic of imagination is not the same as the logic of intuitive understanding. It is, so-to-speak, a logic of the middle between the logic of understanding and the logic of reason, and furthermore it is instead an originary logic, and we can consider the teleology of the logic of reason in turn as formalistic in relation to that originary logic.

That there must be a unity of causal theory and teleology concerns not only organisms but, first of all and more than anything, what can be conceived concerning human technology. Kant hypothesized this unity within the supersensible, but this is an open secret given in the empirical reality of human technology. And for Kant, would not the principle that combines what exists, as causal theory and teleology—two heterogeneous things for our judgment—the one common principle from which they would be derived, be the principle of the imagination? Now I recall for the present how in the *Critique of Pure Reason* and the *Anthropology* he postulated a single common root for that which exists for us as two heterogeneous things, sensibility and understanding.[360]

> There are two stems of human cognition, which perhaps arose from a single common, but to us unknown, root. They are sensibility and understanding. By means of the former objects are given to us, and by means of the latter they are thought.[361]
>
> Understanding and sensibility, being of different kinds notwithstanding and moreover as if one came from the other or both emerged from a single trunk, are in harmony on their own in order to constitute our cognition.[362]

It may be possible to conceive of the imagination as that "common root" (*gemeinschaftliche Wurzel*) of sensibility and understanding even from where intuitive understanding takes the imagination as the foundation. And further we may think in this way of the "common principle" (*gemeinschaftliches Prinzip*) that combines mechanism and teleology to be the principle of the imagination. But what sort of thing is this principle? Above all, how can we determine its relationship with teleology? Kant conceives the common principle that combines mechanism with teleology as within nature's intelligible substrate and states that this thing cannot be cognized "in the theoretical view" (*in theoretischer Absicht*).[363] Naturally, the practical viewpoint becomes an issue here. This issue is connected to the problem of historical purposiveness that Kant dealt with at the end of the *Critique of Judgment*. Therein we need to enter into this issue further. By means of this we should be able to elucidate and solve the various problems that up to now have only been suggested or remained unsolved.

21.

[480] Organic purposiveness, like aesthetic purposiveness, is purposiveness in something particular. Just as aesthetic judgment is a singular judgment, what we conceive to be beautiful is something specific, an individual artwork or an individual thing of nature. In the same way, what was conceived to be nature's intrinsic substantial purposiveness is that which is specific, each an individual organism. But the logical purposiveness of nature, as the idea of a system, is what we can consider in regard to the whole of nature. Now if we can view the organism as an objective realization of the logical purposiveness of nature in something particular, could we not consider this realization in relation to the whole of nature? Does not the logical purposiveness of nature, as the idea of a system, require this? In this case we can view the whole of nature as so-to-speak an organism. The philosophy of intellectual intuition in fact developed in this direction in Schelling. But this cannot be Kant's standpoint that conceived the mechanism of nature as a constitutive principle, and admitted the employment of teleology only as a regulative principle concerning specified natural things that would be impossible by means of mechanistic laws alone. He says that "nature as a whole is not given to us as something organic [organized]."[364] Nevertheless would not the ability already to recognize the existence of organisms that manifest purposiveness in a segment of nature also show the possibility of conceiving the whole of nature as a system of ends?

> Once we discover a faculty in nature to produce products that we can only think in accordance with the concept of final causes, we advance one step forward. May we not justly estimate that even that which do not necessitate us to search for another principle beyond the mechanism of causes, operating blindly, belong to a system of ends {*ein System der Zwecke*}? For the initial idea already guides us, in regard to its ground, beyond the world of sense, and we must regard the unity of the supersensible principle {*die Einheit des übersinnlichen Prinzips*} as valid not only for a certain species of natural beings, but in the same way valid for the whole of nature as a system."[365]

If so, what would this system of ends be like?

It is clear from the passage we cited just now that the clue to this system of ends is in the organism. Now the theory of the organism has two sides. First, viewed purely logically, the organism is established upon a fixed logical relationship of whole and part. Its logic is the so-called logic of the synthetic universal or concrete universal. Second, purposiveness in an organism makes us think of a relation to something practical akin to how the word *end* [purpose] ordinarily does. In elucidating the organism, Kant often used the word *design*.[366] To see the organism as the end of nature is to think of "generation by design" (*Erzeugung mit Absicht*). The fact that the word *Organismus* (organism) derives from the word ὄργανον, *Organ* (instrument), will presumably guide us to think, somehow, of the organism with a practical concept. Instrument means the means in relation to the end. Thus, the purely logical relation of whole and part is translated into the relation in design between ends and means. Defining the organism, Kant writes,

> ... an organized product of nature is that in which everything in addition to being an end is reciprocally also means. Nothing in it is in vain or without an end [purpose], or to be reduced to the blind mechanism of nature.³⁶⁷

In contrast to the "blind" causality of nature, we can view the organism as if it were generated by means of "an intellectual essence" (*ein verständiges Wesen*). Now the above two aspects contained in the theory of the organism are, in Kant, expressed with unity through the concept of *Idee*. He says,

> ... an *Idee* [idea] has to lie at the ground of the possibility of nature's products. But because the *Idee* in itself is an absolute unity of representation, distinct from the plurality of that which can afford no definite unity of composition at all, if it is to serve as the *a priori* ground of determination of a natural law of the causality of such a form of composition, the end of nature must be extended beyond everything contained within its product. For once we refer to this kind of operation as a whole to a supersensible ground of determination beyond the blind mechanism of nature, we would have to thoroughly estimate it according to this principle, and there would be no reason to think that the form of such a thing as partly depending on mechanism. For in that case, due to the mixing of heterogeneous principles, any reliable rule for estimation would vanish."³⁶⁸

That is, we can see the *Idee* at the root of the organism and can regard the organism as made possible by the *Idee*. The form of the organism, its unity, its shape, manifests the *Idee*. But if the organism manifests the *Idee*, we would have to think of the *Idee* in its logical structure as a synthetic universal or concrete universal. Stated differently we would be able to conceive the *Idee* within the logic of intuitive understanding. Intuitive understanding "moves from the synthetic universal (intuition of a whole as a whole) to the particular, that is, from whole to parts. Hence that understanding or its representation of the whole does not imply within itself a contingency in the synthesis of the parts."³⁶⁹ Within the synthetic universal, everything is necessary and there is no contingency at all. For this reason, if we take the *Idee* as a synthetic universal, we can think that nothing would be futile or purposeless in the organism, even from a practical or axiological point of view. As something supersensible, we can view the *Idee* as something freely founded and practical. Not only that, but we can also conceive the *Idee* as combining the practical and the theoretical. Kant says, "The *Idee* may perhaps make possible a transition from the concepts of nature to the practical concepts, and thus may give support to the moral ideas themselves, bringing them into connection with the speculative cognition of reason."³⁷⁰ To see the organism there as something fitting would be to see freedom within nature, and in general we may interpret teleology as what unifies theoretical reason as the legislator of nature and practical reason as the legislator of morality (freedom).³⁷¹ Here however we must encounter a great problem. Is it appropriate at all that freedom belongs to the teleological structure? Hegel's philosophy of the *Idee*, the philosophy of the concrete universal, taking the standpoint of intuitive understanding, indeed grasped freedom in this way within a teleological structure. Kant defined "the lawfulness of the contingent" (*die Gesetzmässigkeit des*

Zufälligen) by calling it purposiveness.³⁷² Our understanding is comparative and its universal is an analytic universal, and therein lies a contingency between universal and particular that is difficult to overcome. If we take purposiveness as the lawfulness of the contingent, the logic of teleology would have to be a logic of the synthetic universal belonging to the intuitive understanding. Moreover, according to Kant, although intuitive understanding is "an indispensable idea of reason, for human understanding it is an unattainable problematic concept."³⁷³ But we might consider that even what cannot be attained from the theoretical point of view can be attained from the practical point of view. If we can say that the thing-in-itself that was a problematic concept in the *Critique of Pure Reason* was solved from the standpoint of practical reason, we can presumably say that the issue of the supersensible substrate thought to be the ground of the organism can also be solved from the standpoint of practical reason. Now in that case would not freedom become something teleological? If to see the organism as something fitting is to see freedom at the root of nature, freedom would have to be something of a teleological structure. But would that not, to the contrary, mean a denial of freedom? What sort of thing is it that the *Critique of Judgment* describes as moral teleology?

As we already stated, Kant thought nature as a whole, as organic, is not given to us. Therefore, to view nature in its whole as a system of ends is not to conceive of it as a single large organism. For the present, it is not to think of nature in its whole as an intrinsically substantial purposiveness in accordance with the logic of intuitive understanding. But if the clue to thinking of the whole of nature as a system of ends is contained in the ground of the organism, this perspective would have to be intrinsic to the ends-means relationship. That is to say that the system of ends is conceivable from the practical point of view. Furthermore, in this case, according to Kant, purposiveness is extrinsic purposiveness. "Extrinsic purposiveness is when one thing in nature serves another thing as a means to an end."³⁷⁴ When this happens what takes the position of an end is that which possesses its own intrinsic purposiveness as a natural end, the organism. For example, we cannot view earth, air, water, and so on, as means for the accumulation of mountains. But we can view such things that do not possess any intrinsic purposiveness as means for organisms like plants, namely, natural ends. And we can view plants as existing for the sake of herbivorous animals, herbivorous animals as existing for the sake of carnivorous animals, and all of them existing for the sake of human beings. In this way, it may be possible to systematize nature according to extrinsic purposiveness. The system of extrinsic purposiveness is possible because there are things within nature that possess an intrinsic purposiveness. But with that alone, the system of ends would be unable to be a real system. Extrinsic purposiveness is nothing but relative purposiveness. While we can think of plants as existing for the sake of herbivorous animals, herbivorous animals existing for the sake of carnivorous animals, and all of them existing for man, in reverse, we can also think of herbivorous animals as existing to regulate the overgrowth of plants, carnivorous animals as existing to limit the voracity of herbivorous animals, human beings as existing to regulate the spread of carnivorous animals, and thus think of everything existing for the sake of the appropriate growth of plants. No matter what the thing of nature is, it cannot be anything more than a relative end. Nevertheless, in order for the whole of nature to take the form of a system of ends, there must be a single "final end" toward which everything would be united. Yet although the organism is a natural end, it is not the end of nature. "To estimate a certain thing as a natural end {*Naturzweck*} due to its intrinsic form is completely different from conceiving of this thing's existence as an end of nature {*Zweck der Natur*}."[375] Kant writes that in order to assert the end of nature,

> ...we require not simply the concept of a possible end, but the cognition of the ultimate end {*Endzweck*} (*scopus*) of nature. And this requires us to refer nature to a something supersensible, far transcending any of our teleological cognitions of nature. For the end of nature itself must be sought beyond nature.[376]

The ultimate end is not something that can be made by means of nature. For it is something unconditioned while everything in nature always is conditioned. The ultimate end would have to be something that transcends nature. As an absolute end, it can no longer be conceived as a means for any other thing. In this way the ultimate end, according to Kant, is nothing other than the human being as a moral being. "Concerning man as a moral being we can no longer question for what (*quem in finem*) he exists."[377] S/he is an end to him/herself (*Selbstzweck*). To begin with we cannot conceive of even a human being—a sensible being, one thing in nature, merely a single organism—to be such a thing. The ultimate end is man as "noumenon" (*Noumenon*), the human being as a being possessing "a supersensible faculty (freedom)" (*ein übersinnliches Vermögen (die Freiheit)*), namely, as a "subject of morality" (*Subjekt der Moralität*).

> Now assuming that things in the world, as dependent for their being, are in need of a supreme cause acting in accordance with ends, man is the ultimate end of creation. For without man the chain of subordinate ends would be incompletely grounded, and only in man, as the subject of morality, do we find unconditional legislation concerning ends, which therefore alone renders man capable of being the ultimate end to which all of nature is teleologically subordinated.[378]

In this way the chain of mutually subordinate ends in nature, for the first time, is completely grounded by the cognition of the ultimate end of nature, for what completes it into a system as the final end in the chain of ends in nature is made possible by relating to the ultimate end of nature. We need to distinguish, in nature, between the concept of "final end" (*letzter Zweck*) and the concept of "ultimate end" (*Endzweck*). In contrast to the final end of nature which is immanent as the final term in the teleological chain of nature, the ultimate end is transcendent, beyond nature. Its cognition "is way beyond all of our teleological cognitions of nature."[379] Moreover the concept of the final end of nature is possible in dependence on the concept of the ultimate end. That which is transcendent is the ground for the immanent. The fact that man is the ultimate end of nature makes it possible for us to view man as the final end of nature. Even if man is conceived in both of the two cases, the ultimate end of nature is man as the subject of morality, and the final end of nature is culture in human beings. Kant says that "only culture can be the final end."[380] In this way, we can consider human beings in relation to the concept of ends in three cases. First, like other organisms, human beings as organic beings are "natural ends." However, human beings are not only an end of nature but, second, also the "final end" of nature, and "in this relation to all other things of nature forms the system of ends."³⁸¹ The final end of such nature is human culture. However, third, this fact that human beings are the final end of nature is made possible by humans being the "ultimate end" of nature. The ultimate end is something completely transcending nature, and the human being is that being as a moral being, namely, a free subject. Then what is meant by culture? Human culture is not the same as human happiness. Happiness is something that the human being, as a thing of nature, naturally seeks. It is "indeed his final end in nature (not the end of freedom) but would never at all be attained by him."³⁸² For the human desire for happiness in itself has the quality of never being able to be satisfied. On the other hand, it is not that nature chooses the human being as a special favorite in regard to happiness and makes him/her bask in its affection in excess to other animals. As those who seek happiness, human beings are "always only a link in the chain of natural ends."³⁸³ Happiness cannot be the final end of nature. In order to conceive the human being as the final end [最後の目的] of nature, we need to seek out "what nature can supply for the purpose of preparing him for what he himself must do in order to be the ultimate end [究極目的]."³⁸⁴ Now although happiness is the "content" (*Materie*) of every end of human beings on earth, when we make this their whole end, they will be unable to match this by erecting the ultimate end of their being. What can be viewed as the final end of nature within every end of the human being in nature, accordingly, is only "a formal, subjective, condition, that is, the aptitude {*Tauglichkeit*} of setting ends before himself and of employing nature as a means in accordance with the maxims of his free ends generally (independently of nature, in his determination of ends)."³⁸⁵ And "the production in a rational being of an aptitude for ends in general of his/her choosing (and hence in his/her freedom) is culture."³⁸⁶ This is where nature operates in relation to the ultimate end lying outside of itself, whereby culture is thus the final end of nature. In this way, Kant recognized in nature the purposiveness of culture. And just as it was thought that even in an organism, as it were, nothing is without purpose or is futile, it is conceivable that "everything in the world is useful for something and nothing therein is futile."³⁸⁷ Moreover the purposiveness of culture is only possible by taking morality or freedom as ground. Culture can be nature's final end only in relation to morality which is the ultimate end of nature. The end of human beings is not in culture, rather the end of culture is the human being (as a moral being). Ultimately, the purposiveness of culture is the purposiveness of morality. It is established in the moral self-awareness of human beings. Kant says,

> ... man, as the single being on earth that possesses understanding, that is, the capacity of voluntarily setting before him/herself ends, is qualified to be the lord of nature, and, viewing this nature as a teleological system, he is by destination the final end of nature. But this is always subject to the condition that he understands this and possesses the will to give to it and himself such a reference of ends, as can be self-sufficient independently of nature, and, consequently, be an ultimate end— which can never be sought within nature.³⁸⁸

Human beings, on the basis of moral self-awareness, assess nature as appropriate. Nature is judged appropriate on the conviction of one's moral self-awareness that "if you can, then you should" (*Du kannst, den du sollst*).

Incidentally, the purposiveness of culture is nothing other than the purposiveness of history. According to Kant, this is purposiveness in "the development of ... humanity."[389] Culture is the capacity for ends-in-general, and such ends are what human beings ought to foster in combination with nature. The important subjective condition of this capacity for fostering ends-in-general is on the one hand the culture of skill (*die Kultur der Geschicklichkeit*) and on the other hand the culture of discipline (*die Kultur der Zucht (Disziplin)*). The latter exists in the liberation of the will from the despotism of desires.[390] By means of this, the will is furthered in the regulation and selection of ends properly significant for the entire scope of capacities towards ends. There is, in relation to this requirement of culture, an "appropriate effort of nature" that prepares human beings for the governance of reason by gradually diminishing the tyranny of various tendencies. The misfortunes born of the various inclinations, at the same time arouse, promote, and train the powers of the spirit, so that without submitting to these inclinations, we can admit, as a consequence, a development receptive of an end higher than what nature can provide. The first culture, that of skill, develops through the inequality of human beings. That is, on the one hand there is the [social] class for the production of the necessities of life, without any free time, and on the other hand, there is the class, due to the former, with the leisure time to engage in science [scholarship] and art. Furthermore, the culture of the latter spreads into the former. But with the advancement of that culture, misfortune likewise increases on both sides—for the former through its encroachment by the other and for the latter due to an internal discontent. "Moreover this splendid misery {*das glänzende Elend*} is tied to the development of natural qualities of the human species, and the end of nature itself, even if it is not our end, is thus attained."[391] The formal condition for nature to attain its ultimate design is that there be a legislative power of a single whole called civil society (*bürgerliche Gesellschaft*) to oppose the destruction of freedom by individuals in conflict with one another. The greatest development of man's natural qualities is to be engendered only within such a civil society or nation-state. But there is the danger that nation-states encroach upon one another. Therefore to prevent this a single cosmopolitan [or: world-civil; 社会市民的] whole (*ein weltbürgerliches Ganze*), namely, a single system of all nation-states, is necessary.[392] Kant writes that even war, as what is most terrifying,

> ... while being an undersigned undertaking of men (stirred up by unbridled passions), ... is a concealed yet perhaps designed attempt of supreme wisdom, to prepare, if not found, a rule of law concerning the freedom of nation-states, thus the unity of a morally grounded system of nation-states.[393]

His idea is thus sufficient to remind us of what Hegel called the cunning of reason (*List der Vernunft*). And this idea, beyond what appeared in the *Critique of Judgment*, is clearly tied to Kant's works on the philosophy of history, namely, *Idea for a Universal History with a Cosmopolitan Purpose*, *Conjectural Beginning of Human History*,

Perpetual Peace, and so on. Here he views the history of the human race to be "the execution of the hidden plan of nature." Its standpoint is none other than a "teleological theory of nature" (*teleologische Naturlehre*).³⁹⁴ Human being, even an entire race, willfully but without knowing it, oppose each another and think they are pursuing their own intent when in fact they are unconsciously working to realize "nature's design." The means nature employs to accomplish its design is "unsocial sociability,"³⁹⁵ and from out of this contradiction there results, in the end, a legislative order. In this way, that which brings about harmony through the contradictions of human beings, even by opposing their will, is "the great artist, nature" (*die grosse Künstlerin Natur*) (*natura daedala rerum*).³⁹⁶ It is evident that this nature is completely different from nature as discussed in the *Critique of Pure Reason* and the *Prolegomena*. We ought to call it historical nature. And it is needless to say that it resembles nature in the philosophy of the Romantics.

22.

[496] Now historical nature, as argued in the *Critique of Pure Reason*, is not nature seen as an object but rather nature seen as a subject. This has to be the meaning of "the great artist, nature." Nature as organic life can presumably also be conceived as an issue of historical nature. Historical nature is formative nature, and what we call the technology of nature is originally related to this. Incidentally, Kant grasped this issue of historical nature as an issue of purposiveness. The issue of purposiveness is not simply an issue of nature but an issue of the cohesion of nature with freedom or with *Idee*. According to Kant, the organism presupposes an intelligible substrate concerning its ground, but the fact of the existence of the organism also makes us think of "a creative understanding" (*ein schaffender Verstand*) at the root of all nature. Nevertheless, would not thinking of historical nature as purposive in this way deny freedom instead? We pointed to the fact that within Kant's works on the philosophy of history and also within the *Critique of Judgment*, there is an idea similar to what Hegel called the cunning of reason. Although this might save the purposiveness of the world, man's freedom in this case would then have to become something illusory. Each human being, even entire people, without knowing it while thinking of themselves as acting with freedom, in fact would be no more than puppets for the execution of nature's design. Kant defined purposiveness as the lawfulness of the contingent. What is contingent from the standpoint of a comparative understanding, or the analytic universal can be seen as something lawful from the standpoint of the intuitive understanding or the synthetic universal, and hence necessary. The logic of teleology is a logic of intuitive understanding, a logic of the synthetic universal. But this logic comes to deny the uniqueness and freedom of the individual.³⁹⁷ Kant says, "now the concept of a thing whose existence or form we represent as possible under the condition of an end is inseparably bound to the concept of its contingency (according to the laws of nature)."³⁹⁸ The concept of purposiveness would have to be tied to the concept of contingency. Purposiveness is conceivable because from the standpoint of the understanding there is always something contingent. Spinoza viewed every form of nature as a mode inhering in substance. This hypothesis

of a substantial ground, while extinguishing every contingency, also denies purposiveness. But, with the logic of intuitive understanding, to conceive the lawfulness of the contingent in the logic of understanding in the end, likewise, extinguishes all contingency as well as negates purposiveness. In this case as well, if everything is necessary, purposiveness in a truly practical sense would be inconceivable. Put simply, with the logic of intuitive understanding even teleology could not be established. Moreover, people may say that Hegel's *Idee* is not substance (*Substanz*) but rather the (epistemological) subject (*Subjekt*). But to the extent that this logic of *Idee* is a logic of the synthetic universal, the philosophy of *Idee* cannot be a philosophy of freedom, a philosophy of history, in the most realistic sense, and cannot ground purposiveness in the sense of true action. The concept of purposiveness is inseparably tied to the concept of contingency, and therein even in the so-called teleological sense there would have to be something contingent. Purposiveness truly conceived in the sense of action is simple teleology. I thus think that even the concept of purposiveness must be founded not by the logic of intuitive understanding but by the logic of imagination.

So-called teleology takes the standpoint of immanence. This is why we can think of its logic as an organology (*Organologie*). Taking the view of the organism as an analogue of art to be insufficient, Kant writes as follows:

> For in that case, we think of an artist (a rational being) external to that thing. Instead, it organizes itself and each species of its organized products following the same pattern as a whole but with skillful deviations required for self-preservation in response to surrounding circumstances.[399]

As a thing of nature, the organism must be seen as thoroughly immanent. Organology is immanentism. But from the standpoint of mere immanentism, there is no freedom and history would be inconceivable. Notwithstanding the above words, Kant already conceived, as the ground of the organism, the "intelligible substance" or "creative understanding" or "primal ground of nature" (*Urgrund der Natur*) that transcends experience. As historical nature, the nature of organic life must also have something transcendent in its root. While the immanentist tendency is conspicuous in his works on the philosophy of history, what characterizes the *Critique of Judgment* by contrast is this transcendentalist tendency. And needless to say, this is based on the transcendentalist tendency of his concept of freedom. Hence the concept of purposiveness requires the intelligible principle as its ground, but because this utterly transcends experience he accordingly considered purposiveness to be something subjective that is only useful for reflective judgment as a regulative principle. Nevertheless, as we already discussed, reflective judgment cannot simply remain reflective. Freedom and nature must be tied together in history. The transcendent cannot simply be transcendent but must at the same time be immanent. How are we to consider this combination? Kant says:

> It is clear that it derives from the subjective character of our practical faculty that moral laws must be represented as commands (and the actions conforming to them as duties), and that reason expresses this necessity not by an *is* (being {*Sein*} (happens {*Geschehen*})) but by an *ought to be* (obligation {*Sein-Sollen*}). This could

not occur if reason, in its own causality, were considered independent of sensibility (as the subjective condition of its application to objects of nature), thus as a cause in the world, that is, an intelligible world, completely in harmony with the moral law where there is no distinction at all between ought and action, between the practical law as to what is possible for us and the theoretical law as to what is actual for us.[400]

The contrast between what is and what ought to be, between action and ought, derives from man's subjective condition whereby its intuition is sensible and hence sensibility and the understanding are thoroughly two things. In intellectual intuition or intuitive understanding, on the other hand, there is no such opposition, and being and ought, happening and freedom, are one thing, and hence theoretical reason and practical reason would also be singular. In such fashion Hegel took the standpoint of the unity of reason. Yet in this case freedom in accordance with the logic of the synthetic universal would in turn be negated. Kant did not reach that standpoint. Although intuitive understanding for him is an indispensable idea of reason, it remains a problematic concept that cannot be attained by human understanding. For history to be conceivable, however, there must be a cohesion between nature and freedom. Further, unless we think of a logic of history, not only from the standpoint of comparative understanding but also from the standpoint of intuitive understanding, from what standpoint can it be conceived?

This problem is presumably tied to the issue we submitted earlier, which is the issue of the unity of mechanism and teleology. The unity of causality and purposiveness is given in the organism. In general, it is given in the technology of nature, and in either case given as a fact in the technology of human beings. Although Kant considered the organism in terms of purposiveness, in that case he regarded mechanism as a means subordinate to teleology. Nevertheless, this viewpoint would seem to oppose the importance of causality in our natural-scientific investigations and further in our technological compositions. It would be said that a technologist thoroughly pursues causality rather than teleology. And yet, if we think of what s/he had produced, it contains a teleological structure. Herein we are reminded of the concept of a "purposeless purposiveness" that Kant spoke of concerning art. For the artist the *Idee* is not something given from the start as an end. His activity that is without any end [purpose] is free. The *Idee* is born from within his/her enactive intuition. This *Idee* is not a concept of reason but, as Kant thought, a representation of the imagination. As such it is expressive. As Kant had stated the productive imagination is the faculty of original exhibition (*exhibition originaria*). The *Idee* is originally birthed within the imagination but even the *Idee* in art, from the standpoint of reflecting on that which had once been completed, manifests a purposiveness. This is also why art works are often conceived in analogy with organisms. "Teleology without *telos*" (*Teleologie ohne Telos*) is teleology in the truly active sense. To say that aesthetic activity is without an end [*telos*] does not mean that it is completely without end and without direction. It is always being directed by the representation yielded in the artist's imagination. The *Idee* is not something provided *a priori* by reason. The so-called *Idee* instead is nothing other than what has been grasped reflectively in the originary representation of the imagination. We can also presumably conceive of this kind of relationship concerning the formative operations of historical nature. This is not to view history as art but instead to recognize the logic of imagination at the root of history. History in general is something formative and something that goes on being formed technologically. This is not moving in accordance with the *Idea* constituted *a priori* as Hegel had conceived. History is being made not in accordance with reason but in accordance with the imagination. We could also say that the reason of history is the imagination. Even if we could conceive of history as a teleological system of the development of some *Idee*, this is only possible from a standpoint that reflects on this only in regard to past history. In that sense we could also say that there is a reason why Kant reduced purposiveness to reflective judgment. As something determinative, reflective judgment must mean the imagination. To say that history is not teleologically necessary does not at all mean that we cannot know the history of tomorrow. As Ranke said, history contains "tendencies." What we mean by tendency here is not rational necessity. The historical is not simply a thing of *logos* but rather a thing of *pathos*. But again, it is not merely a thing of *pathos* but a synthesis of the element of *pathos* and the element of *logos* and as such follows the logic of imagination. Hume spoke about the "propensity" (*propensity*) of the imagination. The propensity of the imagination can be conceived as twofold in meaning, on the one hand in the direction of habit or tradition involving the reproductive imagination, and on the other hand in the direction of invention or creation involving the productive imagination. Habit is not just something necessary but can be made only on the basis of being free. As a contingency that contains necessity, we call this propensity. Nor is creation something simply contingent. In the sense that there is no creation apart from tradition, it is already necessary. Creation must also follow the tendency [propensity] of history.[401] Propensity [tendency] exists where it is an element of *logos* along with being an element of *pathos* and an element of *pathos* along with being an element of *logos*. Because history is not something teleological, it is a matter of course that historians make an effort to thoroughly cognize it in terms of causality. But when they do so the representations of their imagination are always at-work at the root of their research. In the case of technicians [technologists] as well, while thoroughly pursuing causal theory, nevertheless the representations of their imagination are ceaselessly at-work at its root. The *Idee* is originally birthed in the imagination. It is interesting in that sense that as a concept of reason Kant called the *Idee* a *focus imaginarius*, and also styled it *projektierte Einheit* [projected unity].[402] The *Idee* where it is originally a representation of the imagination can be determined as a concept. In that case, the *Idee* presumably is at-work as something like what we would call a working hypothesis (*Arbeits hypothese*) similar to how Kant conceived of purposiveness as a heuristic principle (*heuristisches Prinzip*). Our experience always contains this sort of thing. In this point it is noteworthy that in his Preface to the second edition of the *Critique of Pure Reason* he relates his transcendental method to a revolution in the methodology of natural science, namely, experiment in modern science. Experiment is experiencing by projecting into experience the *Idee*. When this happens, experience is not only receptive but active while being receptive, receptive while being active. Experiments are active and technological. However as both the word *experience* and the word *experiment* originally arose from the word *experiri* (to *try*), not only scientific experiences (experiments) but every experience is experimental, hence active. In such cases even if experience is not assembled by the *Idee*, it is always, in its originary nature, assembled by the imagination. We can also conceive of a preparatory course there for experience. Experience is not only connected to the past but is also connected to the future. Experience is established in the present where past and future are tied and originally involves enactive intuition. This enactive intuition arises where self and world are in contradiction and this unity of contradictories become the content of this intuition through the synthesis of the imagination.

Even if we grasp the representation of the imagination conceptually as an *Idee* when reflecting on the trace of its formation, there may arise the suspicion that in itself it may be something utterly indefinite. We are thus reminded of Kant's idea of the schematism. Although the operation of the imagination is not conceptual it is schematic. Kant said that reflective judgment in regard to the technology of nature is not schematic but technological. And yet in this case what is called the schematism, according to Kant's words, means "the objective schematism" (*der objective Schematismus*). If we are now to view reflective judgment *qua* determinant to be the imagination and think of the technological formative operations of history, we would have to conceive therein what we ought to call a subjective schematism in relation to the objective schematism. While the latter involves the laws of nature, the former involves forms in history. Historical forms are mediated by this to be formed in action. We can probably name these schemas as archetypes or primal phenomena of history. In the *Critique of Practical Reason*, Kant problematized one kind of schemas: "Here the issue is not the schema of a case occurring according to laws {*eines Falles nach Gesetzen*}, but with the schema ... of a law itself {*das Schema eines Gesetzes selbst*}."[403] Now for laws of freedom that the will ought to be able to determine independently of everything empirical, the schema cannot be anything sensible and thus instead of calling it a schema we ought to call it "the proto-type of moral law" (*der Typus des Sittengesetzes*). Such a prototype of moral law, according to Kant, is nothing other than the law of nature. Laws of nature, for "practical judgment" (*praktische Urteilskraft*), are the prototypes for deciding the probability of action according to moral principles. Nevertheless, can laws of freedom and nature be mediated by such prototypes for the sake of moral action? Kant says that it is only in regard to "forms of legislative nature in general" that we are permitted to use the nature of the sensible world as a prototype of intelligible nature. We can deem laws of nature, due to their universal validity, as prototypes of every legality. But by means of this, we cannot but conceive of morality only formally, we would be unable to conceive the coherence of freedom and nature, and we would be unable to determine concrete action. The schema of action is not within nature but within history. The schema of history, not the law of nature, becomes the medium for our actions. And this schema, as schema, must belong to the imagination. The imagination is not just immanent. If we say it is immanent, we can also say something like reason is immanent. In the same way that Kant speaks of the transcendental [*a priori*] imagination, we can conceive of something transcendent(al)[404] in the imagination and because there is something transcendent(al) there, we can say it is productive or creative. That which is truly creative must be transcendent(al) while being immanent, and immanent while being transcendent(al). The imagination while it is receptive as sensible on one side is also spontaneous as intellectual on the other side. It is not just temporal but is trans-temporal along with being temporal. If it is not trans-temporal, we would not be able to say it is intellectual. But just as what Kant calls schematized time happened to be spatialized time, his understanding or consciousness-in-general was, so-to-speak, a spatialized eternity. In its originary nature, the logic of imagination that manifests as the schematism is intuitive. Instead, it is the originary concept-construction itself. Logic comes out of intuition, but intuition does not come out of logic. Fichte thought that the description of the "pragmatic history of the human spirit" must begin with the imagination. According to him the category of causality manifests in the understanding initially from the imagination. He writes, "The so-called category of efficacy {*Wirksamkeit*}[405] is shown here as originating only in imagination. And so ... nothing can come into the understanding except through the imagination {*und so ist es, es kann nichts in den Verstand kommen außer durch die Einbildungskraft*}."[406] The categories of history are none other than historical forms. We can conceive them as syntheses of matter and form, or of the spatial and the temporal, or of the objective and the subjective, or of mechanism and teleology, or of the many and the one, and as such we can say they are dialectical. As dialectical, forms can be logically analyzed. But we can only grasp what sort of thing is the synthesis of dialectical opposites—the form itself of that synthesis—not by means of logic but by the intuition. Intuition, a leap of the imagination, has to be at the point where logical analysis ends. We think as if forms can be grasped by mere logic only because we are thinking of completed forms, namely, forms of the past, but that is impossible concerning forms being made or forms of the future. Concerning forms of the past as well, we would be unable to think the leaping transformations from form to form without the mediation of the imagination. The imagination has to be contained within what Hegel called the concrete universal. We can probably say that within the source and effects of dialectics there has to be the imagination.

Postscript

Because this work was written intermittently over a long period, it remained incomplete. Especially what I wrote in the final section requires a detailed discussion, but since I tentatively finished the interpretation of Kant here, I will put my pen down for the time being. Even as a reading of Kant, there may still be unsatisfactory points. I would like to mend all of these when the opportunity comes. I should be pursuing the logic of imagination itself next by seizing the issue of "language."

Notes

Translator's Introduction

1. Throughout this volume, including the translation and this introduction, I will render Japanese personal names in the traditional Japanese manner with family name first, followed by personal name. Exceptions will be Japanese authors whose primary language in their publications is English, e.g., Yoko Arisaka, Takeshi Morisato, Shigenori Nagatomo, Takushi Odagiri, and others. Their names are rendered in the Western fashion, in accordance with their publications, with personal name first and family name second.
2. See Akamatsu Tsunehiro, *Miki Kiyoshi—tetsugakuteki shisaku no kiseki* (Tokyo: Minruva shobō, 1996), 3; and "The Philosophy of Miki Kiyoshi" in *The Philosophy of the Kyoto School*, ed. Masakatsu Fujita, trans. Robert Chapeskie & John W. M. Krummel (Singapore: Springer, 2018), 65–77, 67–68.
3. Akamatsu, "The Philosophy of Miki Kiyoshi," 68.
4. Akamatsu, *Miki Kiyoshi*, 5–6, 334–35.
5. Akamatsu, *Miki Kiyoshi*, 335. Akamatsu explains the sense of "cosmopolitan humanism" that human beings are all free and equal individual beings and that such free individual persons as a whole form an ethnic culture and a national culture and ultimate form the human culture. We can add that the Taishō era (1912–26), which succeeded the Meiji era (1868–1912) when Japan rapidly modernized, was a period defined by the spread of mass consumerism, media, and production. The state mandated laws of the Meiji period gave way to a new liberalism, especially concerning family mores and the status of women. Western and American trends and ideals were idealized. This general environment of the spread of modern mass media and consumerism and Western ideals is what perhaps accounts for the "cosmopolitan" mood of Miki's "humanism."
6. On some of this biographical information, see David A. Dilworth, Valdo H. Viglielmo, and Agustin Jacinto Zavala, trans. & eds., *Sourcebook for Modern Japanese Philosophy* (Westport, CN: Greenwood Press, 1998), 290.
7. On this and the following, see Akamatsu, "The Philosophy of Miki Kiyoshi," 68–69. Also see John Krummel, "Fundamental Experience in Miki Kiyoshi" in *Tetsugaku Companion to Miki Kiyoshi*, eds. Noe Keiichi and Lam Wing Keung (Singapore: Springer, forthcoming).
8. Tosaka Jun makes this claim. See Tosaka Jun, *Tosaka Jun zenshū* vol. 5 (Tokyo: Keisō shobō, 1967), 106.
9. Akamatsu, *Miki Kiyoshi*, 334–35.
10. See ibid., 7–8.
11. Ibid., 8.
12. See Dilworth, Viglielmo, Zavala, 291.
13. Akamatsu makes this argument. See Akamatsu, *Miki Kiyoshi*, 195; and "The Philosophy of Miki Kiyoshi," 71.
14. See Akamatsu, "The Philosophy of Miki Kiyoshi," 69.
15. Ibid., 71.

16 Ibid., 71.
17 See Dilworth, Viglielmo, Zavala, 291.
18 On this, see ibid., 70–71.
19 See Akamatsu, *Miki Kiyoshi*, 195–96, 317, 335.
20 Akamatsu, "The Philosophy of Miki Kiyoshi," 70.
21 On this, see Akamatsu, *Miki Kiyoshi*, 293; and Dilworth, Viglielmo, Zavala, xiv–xv and 291–92.
22 See Akamatsu, "The Philosophy of Miki Kiyoshi," 70; Akamatsu, *Miki Kiyoshi*, 293.
23 MKZ stands for *Miki Kiyoshi zenshū* (*Collected Works of Miki Kiyoshi*) (Tokyo: Iwanami, 1966-) followed by the volume number and page number.
24 Akamatsu, "The Philosophy of Miki Kiyoshi," 74 with slight alterations in the translation from the Japanese original.
25 In Nishida, the reference to human persons as "operative elements" (作業的要素) or "creative element of the creative world" (創造的世界の創造的要素) can be found, for example, in his 1936 essay, "Logic and Life" (「論理と生命」), included in Nishida Kitarō, *Nishida Kitarō zenshū* [*Collected Works of Nishida Kitarō*] vol. 8 (Tokyo: Iwanami shoten, 2003), 51, 52.
26 Akamatsu, *Miki Kiyoshi*, 335.
27 Ibid., 320–21.
28 This is not merely the creation of history as a narrative story human beings tell themselves about their past, but the ongoing creative unfolding of the world itself.
29 Akamatsu, "The Philosophy of Miki Kiyoshi," 74, 77.
30 There are a number of other secondary sources on Miki's philosophy of the imagination that are worth consulting in both Japanese and in English. These include Fujita Masakatsu, *Kōsōryoku no ronri—Miki Kiyoshi* in *Nihon tetsugakushi* (Kyoto: Shōwadō, 2018), 313–19; Fujita Masakatsu, Muroi Michihiro, and Tanaka Kyūbun (eds.), *Saikō Miki Kiyoshi: gen'dai he no toi to shite* (Koto: Shōwadō, 2019); Fujita Masakatsu, "Logos and Pathos: Miki Kiyoshi's Logic of the Imagination," translated by Bret W. Davis with Moritsu Ryū and Takehana Yōsuke, in *Japanese and Continental Philosophy: Conversations with the Kyoto School*, Bret W. Davis, Brian Schroeder, and Jason M. Wirth (eds.) (Bloomington: Indiana University Press, 2011), 305–18; Geniusas, Saulius, "Miki Kiyoshi and the Logic of the Imagination" in *Stretching the Limits of Productive Imagination*, ed. Saulius Geniusas (NYC: RLI, 2018), 91–111; Higaki Tatsuya, *Miki Kiyoshi no gijutsuron—katachi wo nasumono toshite no kōsōryoku* in *Nihon tetsugaku gen'ron josetsu—hōsan suru Kyōto gakuha* (Kyoto: Inbun shoin, 2015), 125–46; Higaki Tatsuya, *Kōsōryoku no chii wo meguru Tanabe Hajime to Miki Kiyoshi: Nihon tetsugaku kara mita Davosu ron'sō* in *Nihon kin'dai shisō ron* (Tokyo: Seidosha, 2022), 113–35; Kosaka Kunitsugu, *Nishida Kitarō wo meguru tetsugaku gun'zō* (Kyoto: Mineruva shobō, 1997); Krummel, John, "Introduction to Miki Kiyoshi and his 'Logic of the Imagination,'" *Social Imaginaries*, vol. 2, nr. 1 (2016); Krummel, John, "Creative Imagination, *Sensus Communis*, and the Social Imaginary: Miki Kiyoshi and Nakamura Yūjirō in Dialogue with Contemporary Western Philosophy" in *Bloomsbury Research Handbook of Contemporary Japanese Philosophy*, Michiko Yusa (ed.) (London: Bloomsbury Press, 2017); Krummel, John, "Imagining and Reimagining Imagination via the Ontology of Imagination in Miki Kiyoshi," *International Journal of Social Imaginaries*, vol. 2, no. 2 (2023); Krummel, John, "Imagination and Technology in Miki Kiyoshi: Ontological Formation of/as Being-in-the-World" in *Essays on Miki Kiyoshi*, Stephen Lofts, Fernando Wirtz, and Norihito Nakamura (eds.) (Nagoya: Nanzan University Press, in print); Krummel, John, "Fundamental Experience in Miki Kiyoshi" in *The Tetsugaku*

Companion to Japanese Philosophy: Miki Kiyoshi, Noe Keiichi & Lam Wing Keung (eds.) (NYC/Singapore: Springer Pub, in print); Lam Wing Keung & Noe Keiichi (eds.), *The Tetsugaku Companion to Japanese Philosophy: Miki Kiyoshi*, (NYC/ Singapore: Springer Pub, in print); Lofts, Stephen, Fernando Wirtz, and Norihito Nakamura (eds.), *Essays on Miki Kiyoshi* (Nagoya: Nanzan University Press, in print); Odagiri Takushi, *Miki Kiyoshi to tetsugakuteki ningengaku: "ningengaku to rekishi tetsugaku" (1935) nit suite*, Kanazawa Journal of Philosophy and Philosophical Anthropology vol. 11 (2020), 15–30; Oishi, Masashi, "The Logic of Imagination: Dialectics of Objecrtification and Signification," *CARLS Series of Advanced Study of Logic and Sensibility* vol. 5 (2011), 345–60; Tanaka Kyūbun, *Nihon no "testuagku" wo yomitoku—"mu" no jidai wo ikinukutame ni* (Tokyo: Chikuma shobō, 2000); Susan C. Townsend, *Miki Kiyoshi 1897–1945: Japan's Itinerant Philosopher* (Leiden/Boston: Brill, 2009); and Yagi Kiichirō, "Quest for the Consciousness of Historicity by Kiyoshi Miki: Hermeneutical Anthropology and Philosophy of History," *Revue de philosophie économique* vol. 20, nr. 1 (2019), 159–74.

Introduction

1 This introduction was included in *Logic of Imagination* Part. 1, published in July 1939. This translation was made using the text that appears in *Miki Kiyoshi zenshū (The Collected Works of Miki Kiyoshi)* vol. 8 (Tokyo: Iwanami shoten, 1967).
2 Translator's note: Numbers in brackets at the beginning of each section and chapter will indicate the page number in the original text (1967 edition).
3 Translator's note: "Enactive intuition," sometimes translated as "active . . ." or "acting intuition," is one of the major concepts of Miki's mentor, Nishida Kitarō. Nishida means by this term a pre-epistemic (or pre-thematizing) mode of knowing through active engagement with one's environment.
4 Translator's note: "formless form" is also a reference to Nishida, who speaks of the "form of the formless" in relation to the "root of Eastern culture." See Nishida Kitarō, *Nishida Kitarō zenshū* (Collected Works of Nishida Kitarō) vol. 3 (Tokyo: Iwanami shoten, 2000), 255.
5 Translator's note: *Kage*, here rendered as "image," commonly has the sense of "shadow."

Chapter 1

1 Translator's note: Baumgarten here refers to German philosopher Alexander Gottlieb Baumgarten (1714–62).
2 Ernst Cassirer, *Die Begriffesform im mythischen Denken* (Warburg: Studien der Bibliothek, 1922), 6. [Translator's note: For an English translation, see: Cassirer, "The Form of the Concept in Mythical Thinking" in *Ernst Cassirer: The Warburg Years (1919–1933): Essays on Language, Art, Myth, and Technology*, trans. S. G. Lofts with A. Calcagno (New Haven, CT: Yale University Press, 2013). Unless otherwise stated, the references were written by Miki, as per the original text. In some instances, I was unable to include the exact sources that Miki makes broad reference to, due to the unfinished nature of the work and the difficulty of locating the specific editions and publication dates of some texts.]
3 Bronisław Malinowski, *Myth in Primitive Pscyhology* (NYC: Norton & Co., 1926).
4 Lucien Lévy-Bruhl, *La mythologie primitive*, Deuxième edition (Paris: F. Alcan, 1935).

5   Lucien Lévy-Bruhl, *Les fonctions mentales dans les sociétés inférieures*, Huitième edition (Paris: F. Alcan, 1928).
6   Translator's note: This seems to be a paraphrase from Cassirer: "The whole man is contained in his hair, his nail-cuttings, his clothes, his footprints. Every trace a man leaves passes as a real part of him, which can react on him as a whole and endanger him as a whole. And the same mythical law of 'participation' which holds for empirical things prevails for purely ideal relations (in *our* sense)." Ernst Cassirer, *The Philosophy of Symbolic Forms: Volume Two: Mythical Thought*, trans. Ralph Manheim (New Haven: Yale University Press, 1955), 64.
7   Lévy-Bruhl, *Les fonctions mentales*, 430ff.
8   Alfred Rosenberg, *Der Mythus des 20. Jahrhunderts* (Munich: Hoheneinchen Verlag, 1930).
9   Paul Valéry, *Petite letter sur les mythes*, *Variété II* (Paris: Gallimard, 1930), 255.
10 Translator's note: Here Miki mentions two words for imagination, *sōzō* and *kōsōryoku*. *Sōzō* (想像) has the connotation of "fancy" or "phantasy," while *kōsōryoku* (構想力) includes within it the character for creation or construction and hence connotes creative or productive imagination. Miki settles on using the latter term for most of this work, but occasionally uses the former term. I will translate *sōzō* as "imagination" or "phantasy" depending on the author whom he is discussing and how it has been rendered in English (whether in the original or in translation) in the discussed author's work.
11 Théodule Ribot, *La logique des sentiments* (Paris: F. Alcan, 1920), Préface.
12 Lévy-Bruhl, *La mythologie primitive*, xxiv–xxvi. See also Lévy-Bruhl, *La mentalité primitive* (Paris: F. Alcan, 1925), ch. 3.
13 Wilhelm Dilthey, *Diltherische Einbildungskraft und Wahnsinn, Gesammelte Schriften Band VI.: Die geistige Welt: Einleitung in die Philosophie des Lebens* (Göttingen: Vandenhoeck & Ruprecht, 1994).
14 Translator's note: This translation is based on the quotation worded in Japanese by Miki Kiyoshi. Presumably he took the quotation from Dilthey's book that he cites above, where the German reads: "Ich hatte die Gabe, wenn ich die Augen schloß und mit niedergesenktem Haupt mir in die Mitte des Sehorgans eine Blume dachte, so verharrte sie nicht einen Augenblick in ihrer ersten Gestalt, sondern sie legte sich auseinander und aus ihrem Innern entfalteten sich wieder neue Blumen aus farbigen, wohl auch grünen Blättern. Es waren keine natürlichen Blumen, sondern phantastische, jedoch regelmäßig wie die Rosetten der Bildhauer. Es war unmöglich die hervorsprossende Schöpfung zu fixieren." Quoted by Wilhelm Dilthey in Dilthey, 100. The English translation here was made by comparing Miki's Japanese translation and the original German.
15 Translator's note: This translation is made by consulting both the Japanese worded by Miki and the German original. Miki's rendition of the German in Japanese is quite loose and he skipped parts without indication and combined portions of separate sentences. The German original reads as follows: "Mein Verfahren ist dies. Es geht eine Stimmung voraus, eine musikalische; die wird mir zur Farbe; dann she' ich Gestalten, eine oder mehrere in irgendeiner Stellung und Gebärdung für sich oder gegeneinander ... Wunderlicherweise ist jene Gruppe gewöhnlich nicht das Bild der Katastrophe, manchmal nur eine charakteristische Figur in irgendeiner pathetischen Stellung ... Sondern bald vorwärts, bald nach dem Ende zu; von der erst gesehenen Situation aus schießen immer neue plastisch-mimische Gestalten und Gruppen an, bis ich das ganze Stück ... habe. Dieses alles in großer Hast, wobei mein Bewußtsein ganze leidend sich verhält ... hat." Quoted by Wilhelm Dilthey in Dilthey, 95.

16 See Karl Bühler, *Die Krise der Psychologie*, Zweite Auflage (Jena: Verlag Gustav Fischer, 1929).
17 Translator's note: It is possible to translate *keizō* as simply "image," but as a reminder that the term has the double significance belonging to both the German *Bild* and the Greek *eidos* of "form" and "image," I opted to translate it, for the most part, as "form-image." Miki was aware of this double sense and accordingly neologized the word *keizō* by combining the character *kei* (形) for "form/shape" and the character *zō* (像) for "image/picture." *Keizō* refers to the imagination (especially in Kant) and is thus more technical than a similar term *keishō* (形象), translated as "figure."
18 Translator's note: The term *keishō* (形象), translated here as "figure," refers to figures or shapes in the broader sense than the more technical term, *keizō* (形像), but is often associated with human beings, such as 1) a person's appearance, especially the face; 2) rhetorical flourishes; 3) geometrical figures; or 4) concrete aesthetic expressions.
19 Ernst Cassirer, *Philosophie der symbolischen Formen*, 3 Bunde (Berlin: B. Cassirer, 1923–29).
20 Translator's note: Here Miki uses both of the terms, translatable as "object," *taishō* (対象) and *kyakkan* (客観).
21 Translator's note: *Kata* here could have the connotations of "model" as well as "style."
22 Translator's note: We will render 生の哲学 in the German instead of the English, since as a school of thought, it is better known by its German title, and to render it in English may lead to misunderstanding.
23 Léon Brunchvicg, *Les âges de l'intelligence* (Paris: F. Alcan, 1937), 25.
24 Translator's note: The reference is to Georg Friedrich Creuzer (1771–1858), a German philologist and archaeologist, who wrote *Symbolik und Mythologie der alten Völker, besonders der Griechen* (3rd ed., 1837). The translator would like to thank Fernando Wirtz for identifying this author.
25 Jules Toutain, *Études de mythologie et d'histoire des religions antiques* (Paris: Librairie Hachette, 1909), 36.
26 Ernest Renan, *Études d'histoire religieuse* (Paris: M. Lévy frères, 1864), 26, 27. [Translator's note: The quotation is really Toutain's paraphrasing of Renan cited in the previous note. The translation of the quotation was made on the basis of comparing Miki's Japanese translation and consulting the French in Toutain's book.]
27 See J.A. Stewart, *The Myths of Plato* (London: Macmillan, 1905).
28 Edmund Husserl, *Logische Untersuchungen*, Dritte Auflage (Tübingen: Max Niemeyer Verlag, 1922), II, 1., 61ff.
29 Benjamin Jowett, *The Dialogues of Plato, Introduction to the Republic* (London: Oxford University Press, 1892), clxiv. [Translator's note: The quotation given here is from the English original.]
30 See Armand Petitjean, *Imagination et realisation* (Paris: Denoël et Steele, 1936), 27.
31 Translator's note: The Japanese term *chōetsu* can have the senses of "transcendence" as opposed to "immanence," as well as of "going beyond," whether construed in the Greek and medieval scholastic senses or phenomenological sense (as in Heidegger). On the other hand the adjective, *chōetsuronteki* (an adjective of the noun for *chōetsuron* or "transcendentalism") is a Japanese Kantian term for "transcendental," having the significance of an a priori condition necessary for experience or cognition.
32 Translator's note: This is a tacit reference to Nishida Kitarō's concept of the "place of absolute nothingness" (*zettai mu no basho*, 絶対無の場所) as a self-forming formlessness that forms itself into forms.

33 Translator's note: The German reads, "Alles, was geschieht, ist Symbol, und indem es vollkommen sich selbst darstellt, deutet es auf das Übrige." It appears in a letter Goethe wrote to Karl Ernst Schubart from April 3, 1818. The translator would like to thank Professor Eric Klaus of German Area Studies, Hobart and Smith Colleges for helping to trace the source.
34 Hermann Usener, *Mythologie* in *Vorträge und Aufsätze*, Zweite Auflage (Leipzig: Druck und Verlag B.G. Teubner, 1914), 58ff.
35 Théodule Ribot, *Essai sur l'imagination créatirice* (Paris: F. Alcan, 1926).
36 Georges Sorel, *Réflexions sur la violence* (Paris: Rivière et Cie, 1908). See the present author's *Yuibutsu shikan to gendai no ishiki* (『唯物史観と現代の意識』; *The Materialist View of History and Contemporary Consciousness*) [Translator's note: In Miki, *Miki Kiyoshi zenshū* (*Collected Works of Miki Kiyoshi*) (Tokyo: Iwanami shoten, 1966–68), vol. 3, 105f].
37 Translator's note: This quotation is given in the Japanese original without bibliographical reference. The translator here presents the English quotation in full from John Henry Newman, *Grammaire de l'assentiment* (Paris: Bloud, 2907), 69, as it appears in the English translation of Georges Sorel's *Reflections on Violence*, ed. Jeremy Jennings (Cambridge, MA: Cambridge University Press, 1999), 28.n.37.
38 Translator's note: One might contrast Miki's view here with Paul Ricoeur's Kant-reading in his *Lectures on Ideology and Utopia*, where he associates utopia with the productive imagination as opposed to ideology which he associates with the reproductive imagination. See Ricoeur, *Lectures on Ideology and Utopia* (NYC: Columbia University Press, 1986), 3, 302, 310.
39 Georges Sorel, *Introduction à l'économie modern*, Deuxiène edition (Paris: Marcel Rivière, 1922), 383ff.
40 Translator's note: The original reads: "Si celle-ci [sociologie] est demeurée si souvent stérile, c'est qu'elle a été surtout cultivée par des gens dépourvus d'imagination créatrice" (Sorel 1922, 388).
41 Translator's note: The original reads: "Je me demande s'il est possible de fournir une exposition intelligible du passage des principes à l'action sans employer des mythes" (Sorel 1922, 394).
42 Leopold Ziegler, *Gestaltwandel der Götter*, Dritte Auflage (Darmstadt: Otto Reichl Verlag, 1922).
43 See Ernst Bertram, *Nietzsche, Versuch einer Mythologie* (Berlin: G. Bondi, 1922).
44 Translator's note: *Gleichnis* actually means allegory or simile but the Japanese Miki uses here for the German is *shōchō* 象徴, meaning "symbol."
45 Ribot 1920, 71–75.
46 Henri Delacroix, *La psychologie de Stendhal* (Paris: F. Alcan, 1918), 100.
47 Jean-Paul Sartre, *L'imagination* (Paris: Alcan, 1936), Introduction.
48 Translator's note: This word is ambiguous in Japanese as it has been used to translate both "transcendental" in the Kantian and epistemological sense as well as "transcendence" in the sense of the transcendence of God in medieval Christian thought or the transcendence of the other in contemporary Continental philosophy. Here, Miki seems to have both the senses in mind as creation transcends the world created in the ontological or metaphysical sense, and yet its logic also logically precedes the empirical (the created) even if it does not precede the process of creation itself.
49 Malinowski 1926, 18. [Translator's note: In the Japanese original Miki refers to page 21 but the passage appears in page 18.]

50 K. Th. Preuss, *Der religiöse Gehalt der Mythen* (Tübingen: J.C.B. Mohr, 1933), 12, 23.
51 Lévy-Bruhl 1935, 1–12.
52 Lévy-Bruhl 1935, 80, 81.
53 Lévy-Bruhl 1935, 223, 224.
54 Aristotle, *Metaphysica*, 982b. [Translator's note: This line appears in 982b18–19.]
55 F.W.J. Schelling, *Über die Gottheiten von Samothrake* vol. 8 in *Sämtliche* Werke I (Stuttgart: Cotta, 1856–61).
56 F.W.J. Schelling, *Philosophische Untersuchungen über das Wesen der menschlichen Freiheit und die damit zusammenhängenden Gegenstände* vol. 7 in *Sämmtliche Werke* I (Stuttgart: Cotta, 1856–61), 358, 359.
57 Translator's note: This quote appears in sec. 23 of *The Birth of Tragedy*.
58 Arthur Liebert, *Mythus und Kultur* (Berlin: R. Heise, 1925).
59 Karl Reinhardt, *Platons Mythen* (Bonn: Friedrich Cohen, 1927), 26.
60 *Timaios* [*Timaeus*], 29bc.
61 *Timaios* [*Timaeus*], 37d.
62 See Ernst Hoffman, "The Activity of the Good in Plato's Doctrine," cited in *Shisō*, 1923, December issue.
63 *Phaidros* [*Phaedrus*], 245c–246a; *Nomoi* [*Laws*], 891e–892a, ff.
64 Augustine, *Confessions*, X 8.
65 Augustine, *Confessions*, X 18.
66 Augustine, *Confessions*, X 15, 16.
67 H. Hubert and M. Mauss, *Étude sommaire de la representation du temps dans la religion et la magie* Mélanges d'histoire des religions, Deuxième edition (Paris: F. Alcan, 1929).
68 See Miki, 'Kiki ishiki no tetsugaku kaimei' [「危機意識の哲学的解明」; 'A Philosophical Elucidation of the Consciousness of Crisis'] (in *Kiki ni okeru ningen no tachiba* [『危機に於ける人間の立場』; *The Standpoint of Man Placed in Crisis*] in Miki 1966–1968, vol. 5.
69 Ribot 1926.
70 Henri Bergson, *L'énergie spirituelle* (Paris: F. Alcan, 1919), 91–116.
71 Johannes Volkelt, *Die Traum-Phantasie* (Stuttgart: Meyer und Zeller, 1875).
72 Ribot 1926, 114, 115.
73 Malinowski 1926, 24. [Translator's note: In the original Miki refers to p. 30 but the quoted passage appears on p. 24 in the 1926 edition.]

Chapter 2

1 Paul Valéry, *Regards sur le monde actuel* (Paris: Librairie Stock Delamain et Boutelleau, 1933), 89. [Translator's note: The reference is to Paul Valéry (1871–1945), French poet. Miki's Japanese translation of the original slightly alters what is in the French text, which runs as follows: "La société, les langages, les lois, les "moeurs", les arts, la politique, tout ce qui est fiduciaire dans le monde, tout effet inégal à sa cause exige des conventions, c'est-à-dire des relais—par le détour desquels une réalité seconde s'installe, se compose avec la réalité sensible et instantanée, la recouvre, la domine—se déchire parfois pour laisser apparaître l'effrayante simplicité de la vie élémentaire."]
2 See Paul Valéry, "Prèface aux Lettres Persanes" in *Variété II* (Paris: Gallimard, 1930), 53–73.

3. Translator's note: Miki does not give the precise source of this quotation but it is found in "Petite letter sur les mythes" in Valéry 1930, 243–58, 252.
4. "Petite letter sur les mythes" in Valéry 1930, 256.
5. As an example of a text that makes use of the concept of institution in this broad sense, see Charles Hubbard Judd, *The Psychology of Social Institutions* (NYC: MacMillan Co., 1927).
6. Rudolf von Jhering, *Der Zweck im Recht*, Zweiter Band (Leipzig: Breitkopf, 1923), 21. [Translator's note: Casper Rudolf von Jhering (1818–1892) was a German sociologist.]
7. Translator's note: An alternative translation to these words may be "mythical existence" and "institutional existence."
8. Fustel de Coulanges, *La cite antique* (Paris: Librairie Hachette, 1948), 226.
9. G. Tarde, *Les lois de l'imitation: étude sociologique* (Paris: Librairie Félix Alcan, 1921a), 381, 382.
10. Tarde 1921a, 375. [Translator's note: I am basing the translation mainly on Miki's Japanese, but the French reads as follows: "Les devoirs, si simples qu'ils paraissent à ceux qui les pratiquent depuis longtemps, ont tous été des inventions individuelles et originales à leur début; inventions successivement apparues comme les autres, et successivement réapndues."]
11. Henri Bergson, *L'evolution créatrice* (Paris: Félix Alcan, 1910), 178. [Translator's note: For the English, see Henri Bergson, *Creative Evolution*, trans. Arthur Mitchell (NYC: Barnes & Noble Books, 2005), 134–35. I modified the English translation of the original French to accord with Miki's Japanese translation.]
12. Henri Bergson, *Les deux sources de la morale et de la religion* (Paris: Presses Universitaires de France, 1962), 42.
13. Bergson 1910 179f [translator's note: Bergson 2005, 135f].
14. William James, *The Principles of Psychology*, vol. II (NYC: Henry Holt, 1890), 393.
15. Translator's note: This quotation from James (1890, 393), is set in Miki's original text without quotation marks. However, it is clearly a direct quotation and so I have taken the liberty to placing it in quotation marks and using James' original English within the quotation.
16. James 1890, 402.
17. Félix Ravaisson, *De l'habitude*, Nouvelle edition (Paris: Alcan, 1933). [Translator's note: A bilingual edition with English translation has been published as an Ebook: Félix Ravaisson, *Of Habit*, trans. Clare Carlisle and Mark Sinclair (NYC: Continuum, 2008) https://ebookcentral-proquest-com.ezproxy.hws.edu/lib/hws/detail.action?docID=601495. In rendering Miki's translation of Ravaisson into English, I have consulted this bilingual edition. The passage appears in Ravaisson 2008, 30–31.]
18. P. Guillaume, *La formation des habitudes* (Paris: Librairie Félix Alcan, 1936). [Translator's note: Miki does not provide pagination for this reference.]
19. Translator's note: Ravaisson 2008, 69–70, 72–73.
20. Translator's note: Ravaisson 2008, 58–59.
21. Translator's note: Ravaisson 2008, 74–75.
22. Translator's note: Ravaisson 2008, 74–75.
23. Translator's note: Ravaisson 2008, 70–71.
24. Blaise Pascal, *Pensées*. [Translator's note: Miki or Iwanami publisher here fails to provide proper bibliographical citation. For the English translation here I use Pascal, *Pensées*, trans. W.F. Trotter (Adelaide: University of Adelaide Library, 2014), §89, https://ebooks.adelaide.edu.au/p/pascal/blaise/p27pe/complete.html. I have, however, substituted "habit" for "custom" as Miki uses the Japanese term we have been translating as "habit."]

25 Pascal 2014, §93.
26 Pascal 2014, §91.
27 Pascal 2014, §92.
28 Pascal 2014, §97.
29 Translator's note: The reference is to Étienne Émile Boutroux (1845–1921), a French philosopher of science and religion.
30 Aristoteles, *De memoria*, 452a28 [Translator's note: The passage appears in Aristotle, *The Basic Works of Aristotle*, ed. Richard McKeon (NYC: Random House, 1941), 614. The English translation by J.I. Beare renders the passage as "Custom now assumes the role of Nature," but I am basing my translation on Miki's Japanese translation.]
31 These suggestive words were made into an epigraph by A. Cournot for his book, *De l'origine et les limites de la correspondence entre l'algèbre et la géométrie* (Paris: L. Hachette, 1847). [Translator's note: The reference is to Antoine Augustin Cournot (1801–77), a French philosopher and mathematician.]
32 Pascal 2014, §119. Brunschvicg relates this idea to Hegel's following formula, "a tree grows like a syllogism." We can probably say that this follows the logic of imagination. [Translator's note: Brunschvicg refers to Léon Brunschvicg (1869–1944), a French idealist philosopher.]
33 Pascal 2014, §120.
34 Tarde 1921a, 95.
35 See G. Tarde, *Les lois sociales: esquisse d'une sociologie* (Paris: Librairie Félix Alcan, 1921b).
36 Tarde 1921a, 85.
37 Th. Ribot, *La psychologie des sentiments* (Paris: Félix Alcan, 1986), 228. [Translator's note: The Japanese in the *Miki Kiyoshi zenshū* (*Miki Kiyoshi Collected Works*) has the pagination as p. 238 but this appears to be a typographical error, whether on Miki's own or the Japanese editor's part.]
38 Armand Petitjean, *Imagination et realization* (Paris: Les Éditions Denoël et Steele, 1936), 124ff.
39 Tarde 1921b, 81.
40 Translator's note: The reference is to Numa Denis Fustel de Coulanges (1830–89), a French historian.
41 Translator's note: Miki's text has "Manu" instead of "Numa," but Coulanges' original French text Miki quotes has "Numa", which probably refers to Numa Pompilius the legendary second king of Rome. This would make more sense than Manu since Manu refers to the Manuscmṛti, the ancient legal text of Hinduism. Rendering "Numa" (ヌマ) as "Manu" (マヌ) could simply be a typographical error on the part of Miki. Therefore I have taken the liberty of correcting the error.
42 Coulanges 1948, 220.
43 Pascal 2014, §116.
44 Jhering 1923, 17ff.
45 Translator's note: The reference is to Georg Friedrich Puchta (1798–1846), a German jurist.
46 Wilhelm Arnold, *Kultur und Rechtsleben* (Berlin: Ferd. Dümmlers Verlag, 1865), 359ff.
47 See Pierrs Guérin, *L'idée de justice dans la conception de l'universe chez les premiers philosophes grecs* (Paris: Librairie Félix Alcan, 1934). And in particular concerning law, see for example Maine, *Ancient law*, ch. 1. [Translator's note: Miki is referring to Henry Sumner Maine, *Ancient Law: Its Connection with the Early History of Society and its Relation to Modern Ideas* (London: John Murray, 1905). Chapter One is titled, "Ancient Codes."]

48 See Johann Sauter, *Die philosophischen Grundlagen des Naturrechts: Untersuchungen zur Geschichte der Rechts- und Staatslehre* (Wien: Julius Springer, 1932), 6.
49 See Hozumi Nobushige, *Kanshū to hōritsu* [*Convention and Law*] (Tokyo: Iwanami shoten, 1929), chapter 5.
50 See my *Koten ni okeru rekishi to hihyō* [「古典における歴史と批評」; "History and Criticism in the Classics"], *Bungaku*, April 1937 issue. [Translator's note: This is included in *Miki Kiyoshi zenshū* (*Miki Kiyoshi Collected Works*) vol. 11 (Tokyo: Iwanami shoten, 1967), 445–63.]
51 Robert E. Park and Ernest Watson Burgess, *Introduction to the Science of Sociology* (Chicago: University of Chicago Press, 1921), 796–97.
52 Charles Horton Cooley, *Social Organization: A Study of the Larger Mind* (NYC: Charles Scribner's Sons, 1909), 313–14.
53 Translator's note: The reference is to François Simiand (1873–1935), French sociologist and economist.
54 See C. Bouglé, *Leçons de sociologie sur l'évolution des valeurs* (Paris: Librairie Armand Colin, 1922).
55 Émile Durkheim, *Les forms élémentaires de la vie religieuss* (Paris: Bibliothèque nationale de France, 1912), 603. [Translator's note: The English can be found in Émile Durkheim, *The Elementary Forms of Religious Life*, trans. Carol Cosman (NYC: Oxford University Press, 2001), 317.]
56 Theodor Lipps, *Leitfaden der Psychologie*, Zweite Auflage (Leipzig: Verlag von Wilhelm Engelmann, 1906), 14ff.
57 Hans Freyer, *Theorie des objektiven Geistes* (Leipzig: Verlag und Druck von B.G. Teubner, 1923), 20.
58 Translator's note: Available in *Oeuvres de Maine de Biran* II (Paris: Libraire Félix Alcan, 1922). https://babel.hathitrust.org/cgi/pt?id=uiug.30112063375155&view=1up&seq=11. The English translation is available as: Maine de Biran, *The Influence of Habit on the Faculty of Thinking*, trans. Margaret Donaldson Boehm (Baltimore, MD: Williams & Wilkins Co., 1929).
59 Vilfredo Pareto, *Traité de sociologie Générale*, French translation by Pierre Boven, 2 vols. (Paris: Librairie Payot & C., 1917, 1919). [Translator's note: Miki does not provide pagination for these references to Pareto's book.]
60 "Selbsttäuschung," which Klages viewed as the fundamental theme in Nietzsche, resembles in many points Pareto's idea of *derivation*. See Ludwig Klages, *Die psychologischen Errungenschaften Nietzsches* (Leipzig: Johann Ambrosius Barth, 1926).
61 Pareto, Op. cit., I, p. 67. [Translator's note: The Japanese version in *Miki Kiyoshi zenshū* has the pagination here as p. 66, but the more precise page in which the passage to which this refers is page 67 so I have corrected this page reference.]
62 See Georg Simmel, *Lebensanschauung: Vier Metaphysische Kapitel* (Munich & Lepizig: Verlag von Duncker & Humblot, 1922, 1918). [Translator's note: His second chapter is title, "Wendung zur Idee."]
63 Tarde 1921a, 265ff.
64 Jhering 1923, 180ff.
65 H. Judd, *The Psychology of Social Institutions* (NYC: MacMillan Co., 1927), 59ff.
66 Translator's note: See Judd 1927, 64f.
67 T. S. Eliot, *The Sacred Wood: Essays on Poetry and Criticism* (NYC: Alfred A. Knopf, Inc., 1930), p. 49.

68 William Graham Sumner, *Folkways: A Study of the Sociological Importance of Usages, Manners, Customs, Mores, and Morals* (Boston: Ginn & Co., 1906), 56. http://www.gutenberg.org/files/24253/24253-h/24253-h.htm#Page_75
69 Sumner 1906, 33–34, 54.
70 John Dewey, *Human Nature and Conduct: An Introduction to Social Psychology*, 12th printing (NYC: Henry Holt & Co., 1935), p. 16. [Translator's note: The actual quotation is "They are working adaptations …" "They" refers to "honesty, chastity, malice, peevishness, courage, triviality, industry, irresponsibility …" in the previous sentence. And in the sentence following the quotation, Dewesy says "All virtues and vices are habits …"]
71 J. Segond, *Traité de psychologie* (Paris: Librairie Armand Colin, 1930), 27f.
72 Gustave Mercier, *Le transformisme et les lois de la biologie* (Paris: Librairie Félix Alcan, 1936).
73 Ravaisson 1933, 23 [Translator's note: Ravaisson 2008, 42–43].
74 Translator's note: Ravaisson 2008, 42–43. He actually says, "Effort is realized in the sense of touch" ("L'efforts' accomplit dans le tact.").
75 Translator's note: Ravaisson 2008, 42–43.
76 Rudolf Kassner, *Melancholia: Eine Trilogie des Geistes* (Leipzig: im Insel-Verlag, 1915), 147. [Translator's note: The German reads, "… die Einbildungskraft, durch welche des Menschen Körper und Seele ganz bestimmt irgendwie zusammenhängen …"]
77 Translator's note: See Judd 1927, 66.
78 Translator's note: Ravaisson 2008, 44–45.
79 Translator's note: Judd 1927, 5ff.
80 Translator's note: See Judd 1927, 275.
81 See Maine 1905. [Translator's note: Chapter two of the book is titled "Legal Fictions."]

Chapter 3

1 Translator's note: It is good to bear in mind that *gijutsu* has a very broad sense for Miki and hence in some cases could be translated as "technics." Heidegger, for example, noted in his "Question Concerning Technology," that *teckhnē* for the ancient Greeks meant both art and technology. On this see Martin Heidegger, *The Question Concerning Technology and Other Essays*, trans. William Lovitt (NYC: Harper & Row, 1977), 12–13. We will resort however to the more familiar "technology."
2 Translator's note: The reference is to Werner Sombart (1863–1941) who was a German economist and sociologist.
3 Werner Sombart, *Technik und Kultur, Verhandlungen des Ersten Deutschen Soziologentages* (Tübingen: Mohr, 1911).
4 Thorstein Veblen, *The Instinct of Workmanship and the State of the Industrial Arts*, 3rd reprint (NYC: Viking Press, 1937). [Translator's note: Veblen (1857–1929) was an American economist and sociologist.]
5 Bertrand Russell, *Religion and Science* (London: Thornton Butterworth, 1935).
6 Preuss in "Globus", LXXXVII, 419 cited in Sumner 1906, 5.
7 Veblen, Op. cit., 52–62. [Translator's note: But the more specific page in which this quote appears is 52. By 52–62, Miki seems to mean the page numbers in which this and the following quotations and paraphrase are taken from. Miki himself has not provided the exact pages for the following quotations but I was able to locate them.]

8   Ibid., 52.
9   Ibid., 54.
10 Léon Brunchvicg, *De la connaissance de soi* (Paris: Alcan, 1931), 60.
11 See H. Hubert and M. Mauss, "Esquisse d'une théorie Générale de la magie," *L'année sociologique* VII (1902–1903), 85.
12 Ibid., 143.
13 See ibid., 59.
14 Ibid., 145.
15 See ibid., 84.
16 Ibid., 128.
17 Ibid., 128.
18 Hubert and Mauss, *Mélanges d'histoire des religions*, Deuxième edition (Paris: Alcan, 1929), 134–35.
19 Hubert and Mauss 1902–03, 60–61.
20 See Daniel Essertier, *Les formes inférieures de l'explication* (Paris: Alcan/Université de Paris, 1927). [Translator's note: Essertier (1888–1931) was a French sociologist and psychologist. Miki does not provide a page reference here, but Essertier talks about "forms of explanation" in the first chapter.]
21 See ibid., 105.
22 See J.G. Frazer, *The Golden Bough* (NYC: MacMillan, New-one-volume edition, 1935). [Translator's note: James George Frazer (1854–1941) was a Scottish social anthropologist and folklorist who was influential in the study of mythology and comparative religion. In the 1956 printing of the abridged edition, the reference to sympathy appears on p. 43]
23 See Hubert and Mauss, 1902–03.
24 E.B. Tylor, *Anthropology*, vol. II (Thinker's Library) (London: Watts & Co., 1930), 84. [Translator's note: The reference is to Edward Burnett Tylor (1832–1917), an English anthropologist and founder of cultural anthropology.]
25 Henri Delacroix, *La religion et la foi* (Paris: Alcan, 1922), 30. [Translator's note: Delacroix (1873–1937) was a famous French psychologist.]
26 See E.R. Jaensch, *Die Völkerkunde und der eidetische Tatsachenkreis* in *Über den Aufbau der Wahrnehmungswelt und die Grundlagen der menschlichen Erkenntnis*, Zweite Auflage (Leipzig: Barth, 1927). [Translator's note: The reference is to Erich Rudolf Ferdinand Jaensch (1883–1940), a German psychologist.]
27 Essertier 1927, 84.
28 Translator's note: or "reflection" in more standard English.
29 Hubert and Mauss 1902–03, 73.
30 Ibid., 73.
31 "Un est le tout, et le tout est dans un." Ibid., 71.
32 Ibid., 71.
33 Ibid., 72. [Translator's note: The above was almost a direct quotation but without quotation marks.]
34 Ibid., 117.
35 See Egon Friedell, *Novalis als Philosoph* (Munich: F. Bruckmann, 1904), 53ff.
36 See Karl Joël, *Der Ursprung der Naturphilosophie aus dem Geiste der Mystik* (Jena: Dietrichs, 1926).
37 Essertier 1927, 167.
38 Translator's note: The verb here is 嫌う which literally means "dislike" or "hate," but it would seem to make more sense that Miki really means an inability to recognize

chance rather than disliking chance since for their psychology chance would be unthinkable and hence cannot be a matter of liking or disliking. Thus I am taking the liberty to alter the word in English slightly.

39 Essertier 1927, 49f.
40 H. Delacroix 1922, 37 [Translator's note: also for the following paraphrasing as well].
41 Lois Weber, *Le rythme du progress* (Paris: Alcan, 1913), 196.
42 Translator's note: I have been unable to locate this quotation. The original states "Ibid., 46," which would refer to Delacroix's text from the preceding endnote (as the Weber reference was an in-text reference). But the text says, "Essertier." I have been unable to locate the quotation in either text.
43 Alfred Espinas, *Les origins de la technologie* (Paris: Alcan, 1897), 45.
44 Essertier 1927, 144–45.
45 Louis Weber, *Le rythme du progress* (Paris: Alcan, 1913), 138–39.
46 Ludwig Noiré, *Das Werkzeug und seine Bedeutung für die Entwickelungsgeschichte der Menschheit* (Mainz: J. Diemer, 1880), 107.
47 See Viktor Engelhardt, *Weltanschauung und Technik* (Leipzig: F. Meiner, 1922).
48 Translator's note: Miki probably has in mind what is translated in English usually as "pure duration," but uses the Japanese word *ryūdō* (流動) which means "flux" or "flow."
49 Despite the fact that it is not considered so significant a work, Walter Pater, *Plato and Platonism* (London: MacMillan, 1902) is quite interesting when viewed from this perspective. Could Plato's philosophy—including its form of expression—ever have been built without an outstanding imagination?
50 See Nicolai Hartmann, *Die Philosophie des deutschen Idealismus*, II Teil (Hegel) (Berlin: De Gruyter, 1929).
51 Gabriel Séailles, *Essai sur le genie dans l'art* (Paris: Alcan, 1897), Introduction, viii–x. [Translator's note: Séailles (1852–1922) was a French philosopher, who wrote in a variety of subjects.]
52 Ibid., viii.
53 Ibid., x.
54 From out of Ribot's lectures on the creative imagination, this is according to Frederic Paulhan, *Psychologie de l'invention* (Paris: Alcan, 1901), 166.
55 Ibid., 166.
56 Julien Pacotte, *La pensée technique* (Paris: Alcan, 1931), 10.
57 Aristotle, *Physics* II, 8. [Translator's note: This appears in lines 199a15–17. I have based my translation on Miki's Japanese translation. But in the English translation by R.P. Hardie and R.K. Gaye, the line is as follows: ". . . generally art partly completes what nature cannot bring to a finish, and partly imitates her." Richard McKeon, ed., *The Basic Works of Aristotle* (NYC: Random House, 1941), 250.]
58 See Joseph-Marie Montmasson, *Le role de l'inconscient dans l'invention scientifique* (Paris: Alcan, 1928), xxxii–xxxviii [Translator's note, the pagination here is for the general paraphrase in the following. The pagination for the following quotation is the following endnote.].
59 Ibid., xxxiv.
60 Édouard le Roy, *La pensée intuitive* vol. II: *Invention et verification* (Paris: Boivin & Cie, 1930), 8. [Translator's note: Éouard Louis Emmanuel Julien Le Roy (1870–1954) was a French philosopher and mathematician. He was interested in the relations between science and morality, and was close to Bergson.
61 Ibid., 63.

62　Translator's note: Miki does not provide a reference for this quotation. Although it is most likely from Le Roy's text, I have not been able to locate the page number.
63　See Friedrich Dessauer, *Philosophie der Technik*, Dritte Auflage (Bonn: F. Cohen, 1933). [Translator's note: Dessauer (1881–1963) was a German physicist, philosopher, entrepreneur, and journalist. He is noted for working on the medical application of X-rays.]
64　J.S. Haldane, *The Philosophical Basis of Biology* (Garden City, NY: Doubleday, Doran & Co., 1931). [Translator's note: "The life of an organism is ultimately just as much bound up with its external as with its internal environment" (67). John Scott Haldane (1860–1936) was a Scottish physician and physiologist, famous for his discoveries about the human body and the nature of gasses.]
65　See Émile Durkheim, *Les règles de la méthode sociologique* (Paris: Alcan, 1904).
66　The reference is to Hermut Plessner (1892–1985), a German philosopher and sociologist and advocate of philosophical anthropology.
67　Tarde 1921b, 129.
68　Paulhan 1901, 167. [Translator's note: Frédéric Paulhan (1856–1931) was a French philosopher.]
69　Ibid.
70　Le Roy 1930 (vol. II), 13.
71　Le Roy 1930 (vol. II), 21–22.
72　Paulhan 1901, 172.
73　Ibid.
74　Ibid.

Chapter 4

1　Translator's note: In Japanese the human "subject" can be rendered as *shukan* or *shutai*. *Shukan* (主観) means specifically the subject of cognition or perception, and *shutai* (主体) means the subject of bodily activity. So I will translate *shukan* as "(epistemological) subject" and *shutai* as "(embodied) subject," and then drop the parenthetical additions when the meaning is obvious from the context of the discussion.
2　David Hume, *An Enquiry Concerning Human Understanding* (Indianapolis, IN: Hackett Pub., 1977), 105. [Translator's note: David Hume (1711–1776) was a Scottish Enlightenment philosopher, historian, economist, and essayist.]
3　David Hume, *A Treatise of Human Nature*, edit. Selby-Bigge (Oxford: Clarendon Press, 1978), 67–68. [Translator's note: Less than a quarter of the quotations in this text have proper citations. Moreover, there are numerous passages without quotation marks that paraphrase passages from other texts almost word for word. I have tried to locate and identify the textual sources for all quotations without proper citations as well as such paraphrases. However there were quite a few that I was unable to locate and identify.]
4　George Berkeley, *The Principles of Human Knowledge* (Cleveland, OH: Meridian Books, 1963), sections 4–5, 66–67. Take note that the last clause ("In truth the object and the sensation are the same thing") is withdrawn in the second edition. [Translator's note: George Berkeley (1685–1753) was an Irish philosopher who advanced the theory he called "immaterialism," also known as "subjective idealism." Hume and Berkeley, together with John Locke (1632–1704) are generally considered

representatives of British empiricism. That last sentence, which should be from section 5 while the rest of the quotation is from section 4, does not appear in this edition. Miki provides the original English sentence in the footnote of the Japanese edition.]

5   Buber (Martin Buber, *Ich und Du* (1922)), distinguishing between the world as experience (*die Welt als Erfahrung*) and the world of relation (*die Welt der Beziehung*), states that the former belongs to what he calls his basic words (*Grundwort*) of I-thing [it] (*Ich-Es*) and the latter is established through the basic contrasting words of I-you [thou] (*Ich-Du*). But experience is also already the relationship between independent things. Presumably we already see in what we call experience a trace of the fact that "every actual life is an encounter" (*Alles wirkliche Leben ist Begegnung*). Empirical science is also empirical by recognizing the independence of individual things. The world of real encounter, real relationships, furthermore, is realized from a moral or religious standpoint. [Translator's note: Martin Buber (1878–1965) was an Austrian Jewish and Israeli philosopher, scholar, literary translator, and political activist, known philosophically for his existentialism centered on the I-thou relationship distinguished from the I-it relationship.]

6   Translator's note: Miki here writes the words *experience* and *experiment* in English, followed by *experiri* in Latin.

7   Cf. John Dewey, "The Need for a Recovery of Philosophy" in Dewey et. al., *Creative Intelligence: Essays in the Pragmatic Attitude* (NYC: Henry Holt: 1917), 3–69, 7. In this essay Dewey summarizes his critical views on empiricism in five points, but we shall eventually touch upon the other three points. [Translator's note: The above is almost an exact word-for-word rendition of what Dewey says although Miki does not insert the passage in quotation marks. I therefore amended my original translation of Miki by following what Dewey says in the English. John Dewey (1859–1952) was an American philosopher, psychologist, and educational reformer. In philosophy he is known as one of the early founders of American pragmatism.]

8   Translator's note: Miki gives this phrase in English.

9   According to M.P. Follett, *Creative Experience* (NYC: Longman's Green & Co., 1924), 59 quoting S.T. Bok, *The Reflex-Circle* in *Psychiatrische en Neurologische Bladen*, Amsterdam, July-August, 1917. [Transalator's note: Both quotations, as well as the paraphrase in-between the two quotations, above are of Bok as given in Follet's book.]

10 Translator's note: Miki may be responding here to Watsuji's theory of the milieu or climate (*fūdo* 風土) in speaking of *fūdoshikan* (風土史観) ("climatological-historical view").

11 Translator's note: *Behavior pattern* is here given in English in the original.

12 Translator's note: *trial and error* is written in English in the original.

13 See the present author's *Tetsugaku nyūmon* [『哲学入門』 ; *Introduction to Philosophy*], 108ff [in *Miki Kiyoshi zenshū* (*Miki Kiyoshi Collected Works*) vol. 7 (Tokyo: Iwanami shoten, 1967), vol. 7, 109ff]. I regard the concept of form as the synthesis of the ancient concept of substance and the modern concept of relation (the concept of function).

14 Robert Bruce Raup, *Complacency* (NYC: Macmillan, 1925), 13, 16, 17. [Translator's note: Raup was a well-known philosopher of education in the 1930s, influenced by his mentor John Dewey.]

15 Dewey, "The Need for a Recovery of Philosophy," 7. [Translator's note: This passage is also almost an exact word-for-word rendition of what Dewey says in the English but without quotation marks and given without citation in the original.]

16 Paul Guillaume, *La formation des habitudes* (Paris: F. Alcan, 1936), ch.2. Guillaume raises adaptation by conditioning and reflex and trial and error as principle forms of

habit. Although the former [conditioning and reflex] can also be called experience in the broad sense, what can be called experience in the outstanding sense is the latter [trial and error].
17 Raup, *Complacency*, 113ff. [Translator's note: *Complacency* here is written in English.]
18 Guillaume, ch.3.
19 Dewey, "The Need for a Recovery of Philosophy," 13.
20 Dewey, "The Need for a Recovery of Philosophy," 13. [Translator's note: The italicized phrase is given in English.]
21 Dewey, "The Need for a Recovery of Philosophy," 14. [Translator's note: The italicized is given in English.]
22 Translator's note: The italicized words are given in English.
23 C.f. Samuel Taylor Coleridge, *Biographia literaria* (London: J.M. Dent & Sons, 1906), 140–46. Coleridge's distinction between *imagination* and *fancy* is famous. Without being affected by that terminology I defined *memory* and *fancy* as operations, in two directions, of the *imagination*. [Translator's note: Samuel Taylor Coleridge (1772–1834) was an English poet, literary critic, philosopher, and theologian. He co-founded the Romantic movement in England. All italicized words were given in English and the Greek words were given in Greek.]
24 Albert Spaier, *La pensée conrète* (Paris: Librairie Félix Alcan, 1927), 208. [Translator's note: The reference is to Albert Spaier (1883–1934), a Romanian French philosopher. The part in parentheses was added by Miki and is not a part of the original quotation.]
25 Translator's note: Miki translates *particularism* with the Japanese word meaning *exclusivism* or *exclusionism* (排他主義) and then provides the English in parenthesis after the Japanese. The rendition of *particularism* as *exclusivism* does not seem to make sense so I have opted to leave it out in place of the original English.
26 Dewey, "The Need for a Recovery of Philosophy," 7–8. [Translator's note: Here the paraphrase is not exactly word for word but closely follows what Dewey says and I have thus based my translation of Miki on Dewey's English.]
27 William James, *Essays in Radical Empiricism* (NYC: Longmans, Green, & Co., 1912), 42.
28 Dewey, "The Need for a Recovery of Philosophy," 8. [Translator's note: Here while closely following what Dewey says, the paraphrase is not quite word for word as it skips sentences or parts of sentences. But since it is nevertheless based on what Dewey says, I based my translation on Dewey's English.]
29 Even someone like Dilthey attempted what he called "analytic logic" (*analytische Logic*) from the standpoint that sees logic as contained within experience itself and not as something beyond experience. See Wilhelm Dilthey, *Erfahren und Denken* in *Gesammelte Schriften* V. Band (Stuttgart: B.G. Teubner, 1957), 74–89. [Translator's note: Wilhelm Dilthey (1833–1911) was a German hermeneutic philosopher, historian, psychologist, and sociologist.]
30 Hume, *Treatise*, 19.
31 Hume, *Treatise*, 22.
32 Hume, *Treatise*, 24.
33 Félix Ravaisson, *De l'habitude*, Nouvelle edition (Paris: Librairie Félix Alcan, 1933), 58. [Translator's note: This paraphrase is almost a direct quote although Miki does not provide quotation marks here.]
34 Aristotle, *De Anima*, 431a17. [Translator's note: See Aristotle, *The Basic Works of Aristotle*, ed. Richard McKeon (NYC: Random House, 1941), 594.]
35 Metz stresses that one feature running through Hume's thinking was the approach to life, the connection to life. See Rudolf Metz, *David Hume: Leben und Philosophie*

(Stuttgart: Fr. Frommanns, 1929), 95. [Translator's note: Metz (1891–?) was a philosopher who wrote in German and specialized in British philosophy.]
36 René Descartes, *The Principles of Philosophy* [*Principia philosophiae*] in Descartes, *The Philosophical Works of Descartes* vol. 1, trans. by Elizabeth S. Haldane & G.R.T. Rowe (Cambridge: Cambridge University Press, 1931), Second Part, Principle III, 255.
37 Cf. John Dewey, *Reconstruction in Philosophy* (NYC: Henry Holt & Co., 1920), 87.
38 Hume, *Treatise*, 14–15.
39 Hume, *Treatise*, 170.
40 Hume, *Treatise*, 13.
41 Hume, *Treatise*, 170.
42 Hume, *Treatise*, 13–14.
43 Malebranche, in his theory of the imagination, spoke on "natural connections" (*liaisons naturelles*) and states that "they are universally the same for all human beings. They are absolutely necessary for the preservation of life." Cf. N. Malebranche, *De la recherche de la vérité* (Paris: Garnier Frères, 1893) [Translator's note: Miki provides no pagination and I was unable to find what page the quotation is from. The reference is to French rationalist philosopher Nicolas Malebranche (1638–1715), known for synthesizing the thoughts of Augustine and Descartes.]
44 Hume, *Treatise*, 13. [Translator's note: What has been translated here from Miki as "principle of association" in Hume's English is "principles of union or cohesion."]
45 Hume, *Treatise*, 70. [Translator's note: In the Japanese text, Miki places the ending of the sentence, "... which we can compare with one another" as part of the quotation, but there is nothing like it in this particular passage of Hume. It appears that this was Miki's addition and hence I am placing it outside of the quote marks.]
46 Hume, *Treatise*, 73–74.
47 Hume, *Treatise*, 74.
48 Hume, *Enquiry*, 15.
49 See Alois Riehl, *Der philosophische Kritizismus* Erster Band, Zweite Auflage (Leipzig: W. Engelmann, 1908), 117.
50 Hume, *Enquiry*, 16.
51 Hume, *Enquiry*, 16.
52 Moreover the first issue was dealt with only in the *Treatise*. See Riehl, Op cit., 124.
53 Hume, *Treatise*, 79–80.
54 Hume, *Treatise*, 18.
55 Hume, *Treatise*, 10.
56 Hume, *Treatise*, 87.
57 Hume, *Treatise*, 88.
58 Hume, *Treatise*, 88.
59 Hume, *Treatise*, 93. [Translator's note: Miki wrote the italicized part in English.]
60 Hume, *Treatise*, 94.
61 Hume, *Treatise*, 156.
62 Hume, *Treatise*, 165.
63 Hume, *Treatise*, 164.
64 Hume, *Treatise*, 165.
65 Hume, *Enquiry*, 28–29.
66 Blaise Pascal, *Pensées*, §§93, 92. [Translator's note: I am basing my translation on the English translation in Pascal, *Pensées*, trans. W.F. Trotter (London: J.M. Dent & Sons., 1908).]
67 Hume, *Treatise*, 198.

68 Cf. Ralph W. Church, *Hume's Theory of the Understanding* (Ithaca: Cornell University Press, 1935), 136, 160.
69 In this connection Schopenhauer, *Über die vierfache Wurzel des Satzes vom zureichenden Grunde* is interesting. [Translator's note: Miki provides no bibliography but this text is currently available through a number of publishers as well as online.]
70 See my manuscript, *Benshōhō no sonzaironteki kaimei* (「弁証法の存在論的解明」; "The Ontological Elucidation of Dialectics") [Translator's note: in Miki, *Miki Kiyoshi zenshū* vol. 4.].
71 Hume, *Treatise*, 134.
72 Hume, *Treatise*, 136.
73 Hume, *Treatise*, 118.n.1. [Translator's note: The italics are mine and designate the portion of the quotation that Miki renders in the original English.]
74 Hume, *Treatise*, 225.
75 Hume, *Treatise*, 265. [Translator's note: The italics are mine and designate the portion of the quotation that Miki renders in the original English.]
76 Hume, *Treatise*, 225.
77 Hume, *Treatise*, 267. [Translator's note: The italics designate that the quotation was rendered in English by Miki.]
78 Hume, *Treatise*, 175.
79 Hume, *Treatise*, 175.
80 Hume, *Treatise*, 265.
81 Coleridge, 146. [Translator's note: This paraphrase is almost a direct quote but without quotation marks.]
82 Hume, *Treatise*, 109.
83 Hume, *Treatise*, 102.
84 Coleridge, 140.
85 Translator's note: Miki seems to be referring to Afrikan Aleksandrovich Spir (1837–90), a Russian Neo-Kantian philosopher.
86 Translator's note: Throughout this text, Miki does not place *Critique of Pure Reason* or Kant's other books such as the *Anthropology* or *Critique of Judgment* in Japanese square brackets 『』 that normally would indicate the title of a book. I have proceeded to place these titles nonetheless in italics and with capital letters when the context indicates that he is talking about the books.
87 Translator's note: The reference is to Johann Friedrich Herbart (1776–1841), a German philosopher and psychologist and founder of pedagogy as an academic discipline.
88 The phrase, "metaphysics of experience" (*Metaphysik der Erfahrung*) is also used by the author of *Kants Theorie der Erfahrung*, Cohen himself. See Hermann Cohen, *Kommentar zu Kants Kritik der reinen Vernunft* (Hildesheim: Georg Olms Verlag, 1978, 1925), 4. [Translator's note: Hermann Cohen (1842–1919) was a German Jewish philosopher and one of the founders of the Marburg school of Neo-Kantianism.]
89 That part on empirical psychology (*Psychologie empirica*) in Baumgarten's *Metaphysica* (4th edition) (Halae Magdeburgicae: Impensis Carol. Herman. Hemmerde, 1757) that Kant had used is reprinted along with Kant's commentary in the 15th volume of the Akademie edition of Kant's *Works*. [Translator's note: The reference here is to German philosopher Alexander Gottlieb Baumgarten (1714–62).]
90 See Raymund Schmidt, *Kants Lehre von der Einbildungskraft* (Leipzig: Verlag von Felix Meiner, 1924).

91 This formula was later taken up by Stout. Cf. G.F. Stout, *Analytic Psychology*, Fourth edition (London: George Allen & Unwin, 1918), vol. 1, 270. [Translator's note: George Frederick Stout (1860–1944) was an English philosopher and psychologist.]
92 Immanuel Kant, *Vorlesungen über die Metaphysik* (Erfurt: Keyserschen Buchhandlung: 1821). [Translator's note: Karl Heinrich Ludwig Pölitz (1772–1838) was a German historian of the modern age. Miki actually refers to the second edition. But I am here citing the pagination of the first edition, which was the edition available to me.]
93 Translator's note: Miki uses 先験的 (*sen'ken'teki*) to translate both "*transzendental*" and "*a priori*" in Kant. Depending on the context or the Kant passage Miki discusses, I thus translate this as either "transcendental" or "*a priori*."
94 Translator's note: The original has the German *Willkürlichkeit* placed after the Japanese *yūisei* (有意性), but *yūisei* means "meaningfulness," so this seems to be a typographical error and *Willkürlichkeit* should instead go after *muisei* (無意性), translated here as "arbitrariness."
95 Immanuel Kant, *Anthropologie in pragmatischer Hinsicht*, §28 in *Kants Werke: Akademie Textausgabe* (Berlin: de Gruyter, 1968), vol. 7, 167 [Translator's note: for the English rendering I also consulted Immanuel Kant, *Anthropology from a Pragmatic Point of View*, trans. Mary J. Gregor (The Hague: Martinus Nijhoff, 1974).]
96 Kant, *Anthropologie*, §28, 167.
97 Kant, *Anthropologie* §28, 168–69. [Translator's note: The above few lines follows what Kant writes almost word for word.]
98 Kant, *Anthropologie*, §28, 169. [Translator's note: These lines are also very close to the original.]
99 Kant, *Anthropologie,* §28, 169.
100 Kant, *Anthropologie*, §30, 172 and also see §57, 224.
101 Kant, *Anthropologie*, §31C, 177. This word affinity (*Verwandtschaft, affinitas*) is something he took from chemistry, but Kant says that this phenomenon exists in animate as well as in inanimate things, the mind as well as in material things (loc. cit., note). We can probably say that the logic of imagination is manifest everywhere in the world. The concept of affinity eventually came to possess a fundamental significance in the worldviews of those like Goethe.
102 Translator's note: Miki seems to be referring to Kant, *Anthropologie*, §34, 182, where Kant speaks of memory and foresight as "... based on our *associating* ideas of our past and future state with our present state; and ... they serve to connect our perceptions *in time*—to connect, in a coherent experience, *what no longer exists* with *what does not yet exist* through *what is present*. They are called the powers of *memory* and *divination*, of the retrospective and the prospective ..."
103 Translator's note: See *Miki Kiyoshi zenshū* vol. 8 (Tokyo: Iwanami shoten, 1967), 50; and in the present volume, it is in page 37 in the "Myth" chapter.
104 Kant, *Anthropologie*, §35, 185, and 186 on the following paraphrase.
105 The problem of emblems or signs (*signatio*) is an important issue omitted in modern epistemology and is a vast domain involving the imagination. It is interesting that recently Heidegger and Jaspers have taken up this problem, though from a standpoint different from ours.
106 Kant, *Kritik der reinen Vernunft*, B833 [Translator's note. For this text I consulted Immanuel Kant, *Kritik der reinen Vernunft* (Hamburg: Felix Meiner Verlag, 1993); English: *Critique of Pure Reason*, trans. Norman Kemp Smith (NYC: St. Martin's Press,

1929). The original pagination appears in the margins of these German and English editions.]
107 See Immanuel Kant, *Logik*, ed. Walter Kinkel (Leipzig: Dürr'schen Buchhandlung, 1904), 27.
108 Hume, *Treatise*, Introduction, xvi. [Translator's note: The italicized part designate that it was rendered in English by Miki.]
109 See A. Riehl, Op. cit., 503–504.
110 Kant, *Kritik der reinen Vernunft*, Axvi–xvii.
111 Kant, *Kritik der reinen Vernunft*, Axvii. [Translator's note: The pagination is wrongfully put in the Japanese *Zenshū* edition as Ax and xi.]
112 See Schmidt, Op.cit., 18.
113 Kant, *Kritik der reinen Vernunft*, A115, A94.
114 Kant, *Kritik der reinen vernunft*, B170.
115 Kant, *Kritik der reinen vernunft*, B87, 170.
116 Kant, *Kritik der reinen vernunft*, B185.
117 Kant, *Kritik der reinen Vernunft*, B104.
118 Kant, *Kritik der reinen Vernunft*, A94.
119 Kant, *Kritik der reinen Vernunft*, A115.
120 Kant, *Kritik der reinen Vernunft*, A99. [Translator's note: The paraphrase prior to the part inserted in quote marks is almost a direct quotation of the original, which begins in A98.]
121 Kant, *Vorlesungen über die Metaphysik*, a.a.O.s., 141. Also see Martin Heidegger, *Kant und das Problem der Metaphysik* (Frankfurt: Vittorio Klostermann, 1951, 1929), 165ff.
122 Kant, *Kritik der reinen Vernunft*, A99.
123 Translator's note: Miki generally uses 現象 to mean phenomenon/a but also uses it to translate *Erscheinung* in Kant. In English *Erscheinung* is usually translated as "appearance." Thus for the most part I have kept 現象 as "phenomenon/a," but depending on the context and especially in passages and quotations of Kant and discussions of Kant's thought, I render it as "appearance," to conform to standard English translations of Kant. I will also occasionally place the alternative translation in brackets after the other.
124 Translator's note: Although I have been generally translating Miki's term 形像 literally as "form-image," and although it certainly does have the meaning of *both* "form" and "image," when Miki uses the term to translate's Kant's *Bild*, I will nevertheless revert to the convention of Kantian English by translating it as "image." I will do this especially in quotations of, and discussions of, Kant. But occasionally, in Miki's discussions of Kant, I render it by placing "form" in parenthese, as in "(form-)image" to remind ourselves of the double meaning of *Bild* and *keizō* (形像).
125 Kant, *Kritik der reinen Vernunft*, A120.
126 Kant, *Kritik der reinen Vernunft*, A120.n.
127 See Kant, *Kritik der reinen Vernunft*, B204.
128 Kant, *Kritik der reinen Vernunft*, B151. [Translator's note: The *Zenshū* edition wrongfully has the page as B120.] This definition is in perfect agreement with the definition in the *Anthropology*.
129 Kant, *Kritik der reinen Vernunft*, A101.
130 Kant, *Kritik der reinen Vernunft*, A101.
131 Kant, *Kritik der reinen Vernunft*, A101.
132 Kant, *Kritik der reinen Vernunft*, A102.
133 Kant, *Kritik der reinen Vernunft*, A102.

134 Kant, *Kritik der reinen Vernunft*, A103. [Translator's note: The following is also a very close paraphrase of the following sentences in A103.]
135 Kant, *Kritik der reinen Vernunft*, A103.
136 Translator's note: The above few lines were a paraphrase of Kant, *Kritik der reinen Vernunft*, A104–105.
137 Kant, *Kritik der reinen Vernunft*, A105.
138 Translator's note: The above lines paraphrase, almost word for word, Kant, *Kritik der reinen Vernunft*, A105.
139 Translator's note: These lines as well, following the last paraphrase, are a paraphrase from Kant, *Kritik der reinen Vernunft*, A106.
140 Translator's note: The above lines paraphrase, almost word for word, *Kritik der reinen Vernunft*, A107.
141 See Heidegger, Op. cit., 175–77.
142 "[The understanding] is ... occupied in investigating phenomena, in order to detect some rules in them." Kant, *Kritik der reinen Vernunft*, A126.
143 "It must be possible for the 'I think' to accompany all [my] representations." Kant, *Kritik der reinen Vernunft*, B131.
144 Kant, *Kritik der reinen Vernunft*, A123. [Translator's note: {} indicates the original German but which Miki himself had inserted in his Japanese translations as part of the quotation. On the other hand square brackets [] will indicate my own insertions into the quotation, not in the Miki's text.]
145 Kant, *Kritik der reinen Vernunft*, A123.
146 Kant, *Kritik der reinen Vernunft*, A107.
147 Kant, *Kritik der reinen Vernunft*, A143, B183. [Translator's note: the *Zenshū* edition had the wrong pagination of A144 instead of 143.] This quality of time shapes its conceptuality and is significant in the schematism.
148 Hume, *Treatise*, 267.
149 Kant, *Kritik der reinen Vernunft*, A116.
150 Kant, *Kritik der reinen Vernunft*, A116–17.
151 Kant, *Kritik der reinen Vernunft*, A118.
152 Heidegger, *Kant und das Problem der Metaphysik*, 34.
153 Characterizing the above three modes of synthesis respectively as synopsis (*Synopsis*), synthesis (*Synthesis*), and unity (*Einheit*), Kant accordingly expresses the mode by means of the imagination in particular with the word *synthesis* and the mode by means of apperception in particular with the word *unity*. See A94.
154 Kant, *Kritik der reinen Vernunft*, B103.
155 Kant, *Kritik der reinen Vernunft*, A118. [Translator's note: Miki leaves out the part in square brackets.]
156 Kant, *Kritik der reinen Vernunft* A119. [Translator's note: The part in square brackets is what Miki had substituted for "this same unity".]
157 Kant, *Kritik der reinen Vernunft*, A122.
158 Kant, *Kritik der reinen Vernunft*, A123.
159 See Kant, *Kritik der reinen Vernunft*, A113–14 [Translator's note: This paraphrase is almost a direct quotation but the paraphrase alters and skips a few words.]. Incidentally, we ought to note that although in the *Anthropology* (174ff), the sensible fancy of productive imagination is differentiated into that of formation, association, and affinity, affinity (*Verwandtschaft, affinitas*) belongs to the imagination here as well. Furthermore it will become clear in the following discussion that the concept of affinity in the *Anthropology* and in the *Critique of Pure Reason* are not directly identical.

160 Kant, *Kritik der reinen Vernunft*, A123.
161 Kant, *Kritik der reinen Vernunft*, A124.
162 Kant, *Kritik der reinen Vernunft*, A124.
163 Kant, *Kritik der reinen Vernunft*, B151.
164 Kant, *Kritik der reinen Vernunft*, A124.
165 Kant, *Kritik der reinen Vernunft*, A119.
166 Kant, *Kritik der reinen Vernunft*, A124.
167 Heidegger, *Kant und das Problem der Metaphysik*, 148.
168 Kant, *Kritik der reinen Vernuft*, A15, B29.
169 Kant, *Kritik der reinen Vernuft*, A835, B863.
170 See this book (chapter 4), sec. 8, page 151 [Translator's note: MKZ 8: 131, 132 in the Japanese original].
171 Kant, *Anthropologie*, §31C, 176–77.
172 Kant, *Anthropologie*, §31C, 177.
173 Kant, *Anthropologie*, §31C, 177.
174 Kant, *Anthropologie*, §31C, 177.n.
175 Kant, *Kritik der reinen Vernunft*, B104.
176 Kant, *Kritik der reinen Vernuft*, A50, B74.
177 Kant, *Kritik der reinen Vernuft*, A294, B350. [Translator's note: The parenthetical clause is inserted into the quotation by Miki.]
178 Kant, *Kritik der reinen Vernunft*, B151–52.
179 Kant, *Kritik der reinen Vernunft*, B154.
180 Kant, *Anthropologie*, §30, 172 and also see §57, 224. See this book Chapter 4, section 8 above.
181 A noteworthy essay that conceives this sort of distinction by starting from Heidegger's Kant interpretation is Wakisaka Kōji's "On the Ontological Reading of the 'Critique of Pure Reason': One Preparatory Consideration in Regard to the Analysis of the Imagination" [*Junsui risei hihan no sonzaironteki kaishaku* 「『純粋理性批判」の存在論的解釈について：構想力の分析に関する一つの準備的考察」] (*Tetsugaku kenkyū* 1931 February). [Translator's note: I have added the subtitle here, which was not in the original Japanese. The paper is available here via Kyoto University: https://repository.kulib.kyoto-u.ac.jp/dspace/handle/2433/271644.]
182 Kant, *Kritik der reinen Vernunft*, A124.
183 Kant, *Kritik der reinen Vernunft*, A127.
184 Kant, *Kritik der reinen Vernunft*, B134.n.
185 Kant, *Kritik der reinen Vernunft*, B794.
186 Kant, *Kritik der reinen Vernunft*, A114.
187 Kant, *Kritik der reinen Vernunft*, A138, B177.
188 Kant, *Kritik der reinen Vernunft*, A140, B179.
189 Kant, *Kritik der reinen Vernunft*, A141, B180.
190 Kant, *Kritik der reinen Vernunft*, A141, B180.
191 See Christoph Sigwart, *Logik* vol. 1 (Tübingen: Verlag von J.C.B. Mohr (Paul Siebeck), 1911), 334–35. [Translator's note: Christoph von Sigwart (1830–1904) was a German philosopher and logician.]
192 Kant, *Kritik der reinen Vernunft*, A140, B179–80.
193 Kant, *Kritik der reinen Vernunft*, A140–41, B180.
194 Kant, *Kritik der reinen Vernunft*, A141, B180.
195 Kant, *Kritik der reinen Vernunft*, A141, B180–81.
196 Kant, *Kritik der reinen Vernunft*, A124.

197 Kant, *Kritik der reinen Vernunft*, B151–52.
198 Kant, *Kritik der reinen Vernunft*, B152.
199 Translator's note: Norman Kemp Smith, the English translator, has this as "reproductive imagination," but the original German (as well as Miki) has it as "productive imagination."
200 Kant, *Kritik der reinen Vernunft*, A141–42, B181.
201 Kant, *Kritik der reinen Vernunft*, A142, B181.
202 Kant, *Kritik der reinen Vernunft*, A140, B180.
203 Kant, *Kritik der reinen Vernunft*, A142, B182.
204 Kant, *Kritik der reinen Vernunft*, B377 [Translator's note: The original ends with "... is called *notio*" but Miki instead puts it as "... is called a concept of the understanding (*notio*)."
205 See Martin Heidegger, *Kant und das Problem der Metaphysik*, 103. [Translator's note: The Japanese *Zenshū* has the wrong pagination as 104 instead.]
206 Kant, *Kritik der reinen Vernunft*, A132, B171.
207 Kant, *Kritik der reinen Vernunft*, A137–38, B176–77. [Translator's note: Instead of "empirical ... intuitions" and "pure concepts of understanding," the German original has "latter" and "former," referring to those words that appeared in the previous sentence. Miki inserted those words into the quotation for obvious reasons.]
208 Kant, *Kritik der reinen Vernunft*, A132, B171.
209 Fritz Heinemann, *Der Aufbau von Kants Kritik der reinen Vernunft und das Problem der Zeit* in *Philosophische Arbeiten*, eds. Hermann Cohen & Paul Natorp (Gießen: Verlag von Alfred Töpelmann, 1913), 23 (85). [Translator's note: Fritz Heinemann (1889–1976) was a German philosopher..]
210 Kant, *Kritik der reinen Vernunft*, B134. [Translator's note: Miki inserts the portion in the parenthese.]
211 Kant, *Kritik der reinen Vernunft*, B137.n.
212 Kant, *Kritik der reinen Vernunft*, A123.
213 Kant, *Kritik der reinen Vernunft*, A113.
214 Translator's note: The reference is to Wilhelm von Humboldt (1767–1835), a Prussian philosopher and linguist.
215 Ernst Cassirer, *Die Begriffsform im mythischen Denken*, Studien der Bibliothek Warburg (Leipzig: B.G. Teubner, 1922), 6. [Translator's note: The former is "*Logik der Einbildungskraft*" and the latter is "*Logik der Phantasie*." Baumgarten's students, referred to here, are Georg Friedrich Meier (1718–77), a German philosopher and aesthetician, and Johann Nikolaus Tetens (1736–1807), a German–Danish philosopher and scientist.]
216 Kant, *Kritik der reinen Vernunft*, A132, B171.
217 Immanuel Kant, *Kritik der Urteilskraft* in *Kants gesammelte Schriften* (Berlin: Königlich Preußliche Akademie der Wissenschaften, 1902~), vol. 5 & vol. 20, vol. 5, Introduction, IV, 179; see also vol. 20, First Introduction, IV, 209–10. [Translator's note: To translate this text I also consulted the following English translations: Kant, *The Critique of Judgment*, trans. James Creed Meredith (Oxford: Clarendon Press, 1952); *Critique of Judgment*, trans. J.H. Bernard (Mineola, NY: Dover Pub., 2005); and *Critique of Judgment: Including the Introduction*, trans. Werner S. Pluhar (Indianapolis: Hackett Pub., 1987). The pagination refers to the original German pages in vol. 5 of the *gesammelte Schriften* for the main part of the *Kritik der Urteilskraft* and in vol. 20 for the First Introduction (*Erste Einleitung*) to the *Kritik der Urteilskraft*, and are placed in the margins of Meredith's and Pluhar's English translations.]

218 Kant, *Kritik der Urteilskraft*, §77, 407. [Translator's note: Also see §35, 287, where Kant speaks of the subjective power of judgment as containing a principle of subsumption which is the subsumption "of the faculty of intuitions or exhibitions ... under the faculty of concepts ..."]
219 Kant, *Kritik der Urteilskraft*, Introduction, VIII, 192.
220 Kant, *Anthropologie*, §28, 167.
221 Kant, *Kritik der Urteilskraft*, Introduction, VIII, 192–93.
222 Kant, *Kritik der Urteilskraft*, §50, 319.
223 Kant, *Kritik der Urteilskraft*, §61, but also Introduction, VIII, 192–93 cited above.
224 Translator's note: The reference is to Anthony Ashley Cooper, Third Earl of Shaftesbury (1671–1713), English politician, philosopher, and writer.
225 Kant, *Kritik der reinen Vernunft*, A141, B180–81.
226 See Kant, *Kritik der reinen Vernunft*, A832ff, B860ff.
227 Kant, *Kritik der reinen Vernunft*, A832, B860.
228 Kant, *Kritik der reinen Vernunft*, A833, B861.
229 Kant, *Kritik der reinen Vernunft*, A833, B861.
230 See Alfred Baeumler, *Kants Kritik der Urteilskraft, Ihre Geschichte und Systematik*, Erster Band (Halle-Saale: Max Niemeyer, 1923) that deals with the formation of Kant's *Critique of Judgment* in relation to eighteenth century intellectual history, particularly the history of aesthetics, shows the historical significance of this book in detail, and is a work of interest. [Translator's note: Alfred Baeumler (1887–1968) was a German philosopher.]
231 Kant, *Kritik der reinen Vernunft*, Axi.n.
232 The German word *Erkenntnis* includes the meaning of decision in a judicial court. (See Hermann Cohen, *Logik der reinen Erkenntnis* (Hildesheim: Georg Olms Verlag, 1977), 1.). It is said that in Kant, the word *erkennen* is always accompanied by such an alternative judicial meaning, i.e., *entscheiden, urteilen* (Baeumler, Op. cit., 7). [Translator's note: Miki borrows the idea of a new method of objectively cognizing from Baeumler here in the same page as well.]
233 A. Stadler, *Kants Teleologie und ihre erkenntnistheoretische Bedeutung* Neuausgabe (Berlin: Ferd. Duummlers Verlangsbuchhandlung, 1912).
234 John Dewey, *Art as Experience* (NYC: Minton, Balch & Co., 1934).
235 Baeumler, 12.
236 Kant, *Kritik der Urteilskraft*, Introduction, IV, 179.
237 Kant, *Kritik der Urteilskraft*, §77, 407.
238 Kant, *Kritik der Urteilskraft*, Introduction, IV, 179; First Introduction, II, 201.
239 Kant, *Kritik der Urteilskraft*, Introduction, IV, 179.
240 Kant, *Kritik der Urteilskraft*, §9, 217–18.
241 Kant, *Kritik der Urteilskraft*, §9, 217–18.
242 Kant, *Kritik der Urteilskraft*, Introduction, VIII, 192.
243 Kant, Erste Einleitung in *die Kritik der Urteilskraft*, VII, 220.
244 Translator's note: I have failed to locate the exact source of the quote but Kant says similar things throughout the book, for example, where he says on A141–42/B181 that "the image is a product of the empirical faculty of reproductive imagination," and follows this by saying, "the schema ... is a product ... of pure *a priori* imagination."
245 Kant, *Anthropologie*, §28, 167.
246 Kant, *Kritik der Urteilskraft*, §20, 238.
247 Kant, *Kritik der Urteilskraft*, §20, 238.

248 *"Also ist der Gemeinsinn, von dessen Urteil ich mein Geschmacksurteil hier als ein Beispiel angebe,...."* Kant, *Kritik der Urteilskraft*, §22, 239.
249 Kant, *Anthropologie in pragmatischer Hinsicht*, §28, 167.
250 Kant, *Kritik der Urteilskraft*, First Introduction, VII, 220–21.
251 Kant, *Kritik der Urteilskraft*, §17, Definition of the Beautiful, 236.
252 Kant, *Kritik der Urteilskraft*, §15, 226, 228; General Comment on the First Section of the Analytic, 241.
253 Kant, *Kritik der Urteilskraft*, §10, 220.
254 Kant, *Kritik der Urteilskraft*, §9, 217-18.
255 Kant, *Kritik der Urteilskraft*, §9, 218.
256 Kant, *Kritik der Urteilskraft*, First Introduction, VIII, 223.
257 Kant, *Kritik der Urteilskraft*, §48, 311.
258 See Otto Schlapp, *Kants Lehre vom Genie und die Entstehung der Kritik der Urteilskraft* (Göttingen: Vandenhoeck & Ruprecht, 1901). Also see my manuscript, "On Genius" [「天才論」] (included in *Philosophical Notes* [『哲学ノート』]) [Translator's note: included in Miki, *Miki Kiyoshi zenshū* (Collected Works of Miki Kiyoshi) (Tokyo: Iwanami shoten, 1966–68), vol. 12.].
259 Kant, *Kritik der Urteilskraft*, §46, 307.
260 Translator's note: The above was a very close (almost word for word) paraphrase from Kant, *Kritik der Urteilskraft*, §46 of the lines following the above cited quotation.
261 Kant, *Kritik der Urteilskraft*, §17, 233.
262 Kant, *Kritik der Urteilskraft*, §45, 306.
263 Kant, *Anthropologie*, §30, 172.
264 See Wilhelm Lange-Eichbaum, *The Problem of Genius*, trans. Eden and Cedar Paul (London: Kegan Paul, Trench, Trubner, 1931). Also see my "Myth" in this volume (chapter 1). [Translator's note: Wilhelm Lange-Eichbaum (1875–1949) was a German psychiatrist who devoted himself to the issue of genius, for which he attempted to give sociological and socio-psychological explanations.]
265 See Kant, *Kritik der Urteilskraft*, §46, 308.
266 See Kant, *Kritik der Urteilskraft*, §47, 308.
267 Translator's note: The above lines are a close paraphrasing of Kant, *Kritik der Urteilskraft*, §47, 308.
268 See my above mentioned manuscript, "On Genius."
269 Kant, *Kritik der Urteilskraft*, §18, 237.
270 Kant, *Kritik der Urteilskraft*, §47, 309. [Translator's note: Miki does not translate *Idee*, but rather leaves the word in its original German form.]
271 Kant, *Kritik der Urteilskraft*, §49, 318.
272 Kant, *Kritik der Urteilskraft*, §49, 317.
273 Kant, *Kritik der Urteilskraft*, §49, 319.
274 Kant, *Kritik der Urteilskraft*, §49, 313–14. [Translator's note: for both the above quotations and paraphrasing.]
275 Kant, *Kritik der Urteilskraft*, §49, 313.
276 Kant, *Kritik der Urteilskraft*, §49, 313.
277 Kant, *Kritik der Urteilskraft*, §49, 316–17.
278 Kant, *Kritik der Urteilskraft*, §49, 317–18.
279 Kant, *Anthropologie*, §30, 172.
280 Translator's note: The reference is to Wilhelm von Humbolt (1767–1835), Prussian philosopher, linguist, and diplomat.
281 Kant, *Kritik der Urteilskraft*, General Remark, 240.

282 Kant, *Kritik der Urteilskraft*, Introduction, VIII, 192.
283 Kant, *Kritik der reinen Vernunft* A120. See chapter 4, sec. 9 above.
284 Kant, *Kritik der Urteilskraft*, Introduction, VIII, 192.
285 Kant, *Kritik der Urteilskraft*, §45, 306.
286 Kant, *Kritik der Urteilskraft*, First Introduction, V, 214.
287 Kant, *Kritik der Urteilskraft*, First Introduction, II, 203.
288 See Kant, *Kritik der Urteilskraft*, First Introduction, II, 203.
289 Translator's note: Miki uses the term *muen* (無縁), which means "irrelevant" or "unrelated," to translate the German *fremd*, meaning "strange" or "foreign."
290 Kant, *Kritik der Urteilskraft*, Introduction, V, 186.
291 Translator's note: I have failed to find the exact source of this quotation but Kant says something close to this in *Kritik der Urteilskraft*, Introduction, V, 186.
292 Kant, *Kritik der Urteilskraft*, First Introduction, II, 201.
293 Kant, *Kritik der Urteilskraft*, Introduction, V, 186.
294 Kant, *Kritik der Urteilskraft*, Introduction, VI, 187.
295 Translator's note: I have added italics here to clarify Miki's point.
296 Translator's note: The reference is to Benedikt Stattler (1728–1797), a German Jesuit theologian and opponent of Kant.
297 Kant, *Kritik der reinen Vernunft*, A645, B673.
298 Kant, *Kritik der reinen Vernunft*, A654, B682.
299 Kant, *Kritik der reinen Vernunft*, A654–55, B682–83.
300 Kant, *Kritik der reinen Vernunft*, A656–58, B684–86.
301 Kant, *Kritik der reinen Vernunft*, A657–58, B685–86.
302 Kant, *Kritik der Urteilskraft*, First Introduction, V, 214.
303 Kant, *Kritik der reinen Vernunft*, A654, B682.
304 Kant, *Kritik der reinen Vernunft*, A656, B684.
305 Kant, *Kritik der Urteilskraft*, §77, 407.
306 Kant, *Kritik der reinen Vernunft*, A657–58, B685–86.
307 Translator's note: I cannot find the exact source of this quotation but the general idea of it is in Kant, *Kritik der Urteilskraft*, §77.
308 Kant, *Kritik der Urteilskraft*, First Introduction, II, 205.
309 Translator's note: I have been unable to locate the exact source of this quotation but Kant says something similar to it in *Kritik der Urteilskraft*, First Introduction, II, 202.
310 Kant, *Kritik der Urteilskraft*, First Introduction, V, 214.
311 Translator's note: The reference is to Otto Liebmann (1840–1912), a German Neo-Kantian philosopher.
312 Hermann von Helmholtz, *Wissenschaftliche abhandlungen* (Leipzig: Johann Ambrosius Barth, 1882), 13. [Translator's note: The reference is to German physician and physicist Hermann von Helmholtz (1821–94).]
313 Jules Lachelier, *Du fondement de l'induction suivi de psychologie et métaphysique* (Paris: Félix Alcan, 1896). [Translator's note: The reference is to Jules Lachelier (1832–1918), a French idealist philosopher.]
314 Kant, *Kritik der Urteilskraft*, First Introduction, V, 213.
315 Kant, *Kritik der Urteilskraft*, First Introduction, IV, 209.
316 Kant, *Kritik der reinen Vernunft*, A123. See present volume, chapter 4, sec. 10.
317 Kant, *Kritik der Urteilskraft*, First Introduction, V, 213–14.
318 Kant, *Kritik der Urteilskraft*, First VII, 220.
319 Kant, *Kritik der Urteilskraft*, First Introduction, V, 212.
320 Kant, *Kritik der reinen Vernunft*, B180–81.

321 See the chapter on technology (ch. 3 in this volume) and my *Philosophy of Technology* [『技術哲学』 *Gijutsu tetsugaku*] [in *Miki Kiyoshi zenshū* vol. 7, 197–299].
322 Kant, *Kritik der Urteilskraft*, First Introduction, I, Comment, 201. See also §23, 246.
323 Kant, *Kritik der Urteilskraft*, First Introduction. [Translator's note: Like most of these references, Miki fails to provide an exact citation here and I have been unable to locate its exact source. However Kant makes this general point in V, e.g., 214 and 216.]
324 Kant, *Kritik der Urteilskraft*, IX, 234.
325 See Dr. Yamauchi Tokuryū [山内得立], *Anarogia shisō no ichi* [「アナロギア思想の位置」; "The Position of the Idea of Analogy"] (in *Taikei to Tensō* [『体系と展相』] (Tokyo: Kōbundō, 1937)), also Erich Przywara, *Analogia entis* (Munich: Kösel & Pustet, 1932). [Translator's note: The English translation is published as Przywara, *Analogia Entis. Metaphysics: Original Structure and Universal Rhythm*, trans. John R. Betz, David Bentley Hart (Grand Rapids, MI: Wm. B. Eerdmans Pub., 2014).]
326 Immanuel Kant, *Logik: Ein Handbuch zu Vorlesugnen*, ed. Gottlob Benjamin Jäsche (Leipzig: Verlag der Dürr'schen Buchhandlung, 1904), §84. [Translator's note: For the English I also consulted Kant, *Logic*, trans. Robert S. Hartman and Wolfgang Schwarz (Indianapolis, IN: Bobbs-Merrill Co., 1974).]
327 For example, in Duns Scotus, the one God and the many creatures, while utterly distinct, simultaneously have something in common, but this relationship of one and many is grasped by analogy. What he calls the metaphysical species (*genus metaphysicum*) manifests the one in the many and the many in the one, and its foundation is the logic of analogy. See Martin Heidegger, *Die Kategorien-und-Bedeutungslehre des Duns Scotus* (1916) in *Martin Heidegger Gesamtausgabe* Band 1: *Frühe Schriften* (Frankfurt: Vittorio Klostermann, 1978), 258ff.
328 Translator's note: Miki is here borrowing and appropriating the concept (enactive intuition) of his mentor, Nishida Kitarō (西田幾多郎).
329 Richard Kroner, *Zweck und Gesetz in der Biologie: Eine logische Untersuchung* (Tübingen: Verlag von J.C.B. Mohr (Paul Siebeck), 1913), 100. [Translator's note: Richard Kroner (1884-1974) was a German neo-Hegelian philosopher.]
330 Kant, *Kritik der reinen Vernunft*, B696.
331 Kant, *Kritik der Urteilskraft*, First Introduction, V, 214.
332 Kant, *Kritik der Urteilskraft*, §79, 417.
333 Kant, *Kritik der Urteilskraft*, §80, 418–19.
334 Kant, *Kritik der Urteilskraft*, §80, 419.
335 Kant, *Kritik der Urteilskraft*, §65, 372.
336 Translator's note: The above lines is a paraphrase of a passage appearing in Kant, *Kritik der Urteilskraft*, §65, 372.
337 Kant, *Kritik der Urteilskraft*, §65, 373.
338 Kant, *Kritik der Urteilskraft*, §65, 373.
339 Kant, *Kritik der Urteilskraft*, §65, 373–74.
340 Translator's note: Kant says something close to this, though not exactly in these terms, in *Kritik der Urteilskraft*, §80, 418.
341 Kant, *Kritik der Urteilskraft*, §78, 410.
342 Kant, *Kritik der Urteilskraft*, §80, 418.
343 Kant, *Kritik der Urteilskraft*, §79, 417.
344 Kant, *Kritik der Urteilskraft*, §78, 412.
345 Kant, *Kritik der Urteilskraft*, §78, 412–13.
346 Kant, *Kritik der Urteilskraft*, §78, 413.

347 Kant, *Kritik der Urteilskraft*, §77, 410; §81, 422; §87, 448.n.
348 See my work, "Organicism and Dialectics" [*Yūkitaisetsu to benshōhō* 「有機体説と弁証法」] in *Preliminary Concepts for Social Science* [*Shakai kagaku no yobi gainen* 『社会科学の予備概念』] [in *Miki Kiyoshi zenshū* vol. 3].
349 See Kant, *Kritik der Urteilskraft*, §71, 388–89: ".... And for things as genuine natural ends [purposes] (as we must necessarily estimate them to be), founded upon a completely different kind of original causality {*eine ganz andere Art von ursprünglicher Kauslität*}, that is, an architectonic understanding {*ein architektonischer Verstand*} that cannot be included within material nature or its intelligible substrate—concerning these questions, our reason, exceedingly restricted in respect to the concept of causality, to the extent that it ought to be specified *a priori* {*a priori spezifiziert warden soll*}, can give absolutely no instruction."
350 Kant, *Kritik der Urteilskraft*, §75. [Translator's note: I have been unable to locate this exact quotation within this section. I suspect that Miki is loosely paraphrasing what Kant says here on page 398.]
351 Kant, *Kritik der Urteilskraft*, §80, 418.
352 See Kant, *Kritik der Urteilskraft*, §§ 68, 78, 80, 81.
353 Kant, *Kritik der Urteilskraft*, §78, 414.
354 Kant, *Kritik der Urteilskraft*, §78, 414–15.
355 Johann Gottlieb Fichte, *Grundlage der gesamten Wissenschaftslehre* in *Fichtes Werke* vol. 1, ed. Fritz Medicus (Leipzig: Felix Meiner, 1911), 402.
356 Translator's note: I add the italics here.
357 Fichte, *Grundlage*, 420.
358 Translator's note: Both titles were given in the Japanese original without the brackets 『 』 that would indicate they are book titles. But I am assuming that Miki is referring to Schelling's and Hegel's books, similar to how he treated the titles of Kant's books without putting them in brackets, which would be equivalent to italicizing them in English.
359 Translator's note: Miki fails to provide any bibliographical reference here but he seems to be referring to Ernst Kuno Fischer, *J.G. Fichte und seine Vorgänger* (Heidelberg: Carl Winter's Universitätsbuchhandlung, 1890). Ernst Kuno Berthold Fischer (1824–1907) was a German philosopher, historian of philosophy, and critic.
360 See the present volume, chapter 4, section 10.
361 Kant, *Kritik der reinen Vernuft*, A15, B29.
362 Translator's note: I have not been able to locate this exact quotation, but Kant says something similar in *Kritik der reinen Vernuft*, A50–51, B74–75.
363 See Kant, *Kritik der Urteilskraft*, §78, 412–13.
364 Kant, *Kritik der Urteilskraft*, §75, 387.
365 Kant, *Kritik der Urteilskraft*, §67, 380–81.
366 Translator's note: I have added the italics here and the previous sentence.
367 Kant, *Kritik der Urteilskraft*, §66, 376.
368 Kant, *Kritik der Urteilskraft*, §66, 377.
369 Kant, *Kritik der Urteilskraft*, §77, 407.
370 Kant, *Kritik der reinen Vernunft*, B386.
371 The following words are noteworthy: "This systematic unity of ends ... unites practical reason with speculative reason." See Kant, *Kritik der reinen Vernunft*, A815, B843.
372 Kant, *Kritik der Urteilskraft*, First Introduction, VI, 217.
373 Kant, *Kritik der Urteilskraft*, §76, 402.

374 Kant, *Kritik der Urteilskraft*, §82, 425.
375 Kant, *Kritik der Urteilskraft*, §67, 378.
376 Kant, *Kritik der Urteilskraft*, §67, 378.
377 Kant, *Kritik der Urteilskraft*, §84, 435.
378 See Kant, *Kritik der Urteilskraft*, §84, 435–36.
379 Translator's note: Kant says something close to this in *Kritik der Urteilskraft*, §83, 431.
380 Kant, *Kritik der Urteilskraft*, §83, 431.
381 Kant, *Kritik der Urteilskraft*, §83, 429.
382 Kant, *Kritik der Urteilskraft*, §83, 430.
383 Kant, *Kritik der Urteilskraft*, §83, 430.
384 Kant, *Kritik der Urteilskraft*, §83, 431. [Translator's note: It is possible that Miki here is mixing up or reversing the meanings of ultimate end (究極目的) and final end (最後の目的).]
385 Kant, *Kritik der Urteilskraft*, §83, 431.
386 Kant, *Kritik der Urteilskraft*, §83, 431.
387 Translator's note: Miki does not provide an exact citation for this but Kant says something close to this in *Kritik der Urteilskraft*, §66, 376.
388 Kant, *Kritik der Urteilskraft*, §83, 431.
389 Kant, *Kritik der Urteilskraft*, §83, 433.
390 Kant, *Kritik der Urteilskraft*, §83, 431–32.
391 Kant, *Kritik der Urteilskraft*, §83, 432 [Translator's note: For both this quotation and the lines paraphrased above it.]
392 Translator's note: The above sentences paraphrase Kant, *Kritik der Urteilskraft*, §83, 432–33.
393 Kant, *Kritik der Urteilskraft*, §83, 433.
394 See Kant, *Idee zu einer allgemeinen Geschichte in weltbürgerlicher Absicht* in *Kants Werke* (Akademie Ausgabe), vol. 8, 18. [Translator's note: For this text I also consulted the English translation: Kant, "Idea for a Universal History from a Cosmopolitan Point of View" in Kant, *On History*, trans. Lewis White Beck, Robert E. Anchor, and Emil L. Fackenheim (NYC: Macmillan Pub., 1985), 11–26. The German pagination appear in the margins of the English translation.]
395 Kant, *Idee zu einer allgemeinen Geschichte*, 20–21. [Translator's note: The German for "unsocial sociability" is *ungesellige Geselligkeit*.]
396 Kant, See *Zum ewigen Frieden* in *Kants Werke* (Akademie Ausgabe), vol. 8, 360. [Translator's note: For an English translation, see Kant, "Perpetual Peace" in Kant, *On History*, 85–135.]
397 See Emil Lask, *Fichtes Idealismus und die Geschichte* (Berlin: Druck von Imberg und Lefson, 1902).
398 Kant, *Kritik der Urteilskraft*, §75, 398.
399 Kant, *Kritik der Urteilskraft*, §65, 374.
400 Kant, *Kritik der Urteilskraft*, §76, 403–404.
401 Translator's note: Both *tendency* and *propensity* translate the Japanese *keikō* (傾向). While Hume spoke of "propensity," Ranke's English translations usually have him speaking of "tendency."
402 Kant, *Kritik der reinen Vernunft*, A644, B672, A647, B675.
403 Kant, *Kritik der praktischen Vernunft* in *Kants Werke* (Akademie-Ausgabe), vol. 5, 69. [Translator's note: The Japanese in the *Zenshū* edition wrongfully puts the pagination as 68. For the English, I also consulted the translation in Kant, *Critique of Practical Reason*, trans. Lewis White Beck (Chicago: University of Chicago Press, 1960).]

404 Translator's note: Miki seems to intentionally play on the ambiguity of the meaning of *chōetsuteki* (超越的), which can be translated as either "transcendental" or "transcendent." Here he seems to mean both, referring to both the supersensible and imagination in Kant.
405 Translator's note: Miki uses the Japanese word *sayō* (作用), meaning "act" or "operation" to translate the German *Wirksamkeit* meaning "efficacy" or "effectiveness."
406 Johann Gottlieb Fichte, *Grundriss des Eigentümlichen der Wissenschaftlehre in Rücksicht auf das theoretische Vernmögen* in *Fichtes Werke* vol. 1, ed. Friz Medicus (Medicus-Ausgabe) (Leipzig: Felix Meiner, 1911), 578.

Index

abstract ideas 131–3
accident 105
action 22, 23, 84 *see also* philosophy of action
   autonomy 127
   environment 80, 126
   experience 124–5, 127
   form 127–8
   instinct 86
   logical 75, 76–7
   memory 52
   non-logical 75–7
   thought 114–15
adaptation 65, 66, 83, 127–8
   instinct 86
   technology 85–6
aesthetics 22, 23, 179, 180, 184, 186, 190, 192–3, 194–5 *see also* taste
   idea 190
affinity 151, 165, 166–7, 199–200
affinity of appearances 164, 165
Akamatsu Tsunehiro 12
   cosmopolitan humanism 225 n. 5
alchemy 104
analogy 202–3, 204
ancestors 42–3
animals 106
animism 95–6
anthropology 152–3
Anthropology (Kant, Immanuel) 150, 152, 154, 155, 157, 166, 168, 173, 177, 183, 184, 187, 191, 212
anthropomorphism 95–6
anticipation of experience 106
apperception 160, 161, 162–3, 164, 165–6, 169–70, 176
apprehension 156–7, 159, 160, 192–3
architechtonic, the 178
Aristotle
   logic 17
   Metaphysics 2

Nichomachean Ethics 2
Arnold, Wilhelm 69
art 187, 188, 189, 221
   nature 201, 202
association 142, 143, 148, 151
atomism 130–1
Augustine, Saint 49–50
autonomous activity 84

Baumgarten, Alexander Gottlieb 22, 23, 148–50
beauty. *See* aesthetics
becoming 47, 48–9
behaviour 126–30
Bergson, Henri 52, 53
   creation 61
   instinct 61, 86
   intellect 61
   morality 189
   transcendence 86
Berkeley, George 124
Bertram, Ernst 39, 40, 41
Birth of Tragedy, The (Nietzsche, Friedrich) 46
blood relationships 59–60
body, the 108, 109
Bok, S.T. 126
Bololo people 25
Bouglé, C. 72–4
Brunchvicg, Léon 96
Buber, Martin 239 n. 5

Cassirer, Ernst 21, 30, 177
causality 110, 136, 137–42
   Hume, David 134–5, 136, 137–42, 143, 144–7
   inference 146
   Kant, Immanuel 206, 208–9, 212, 221
   organisms 205, 206
cause and effect 100, 134, 135, 136, 137–42, 143–4, 146–7, 205

ceremony 99, 100
change 144–5
classics 70–1
classification 203–4
cognition 153, 154, 155, 156, 159–60, 166, 167–8, 193
cognitive faculties 148–50
Coleridge, Samuel Taylor 130, 147
collective representation 24–5, 26–7, 31
common sense 94, 183–4
Communist Party 4
complacency 127, 128
concepts 171–2, 174–5, 182–4
Conjectural Beginning of Human History (Kant, Immanuel) 218
consciousness 124–5, 160, 211
constancy 144–5
constant conjunction 140–1, 142–3
constraint 73, 74, 75, 76
contiguity 137–8, 142
contingency 219–20
continuous being 144
contradiction 120, 145
convention 57–8, 64–5, 68–70, 81–2, 86–7
  see also habit
  Tarde, G. 65, 77
  technology 94
  Valéry, Paul 57–8
cosmopolitan humanism 225 n. 5
coutume (custom) 58, 64
craftsmen 95, 96, 107–8
creation 42, 43, 45, 46, 61, 103, 112–13
  technology 116, 120–1
creative societies 90–1
critique 179–80
Critique of Judgment (Kant, Immanuel) 8, 11, 112, 116, 151, 162, 177, 178–9, 180, 181, 183, 185–6, 187, 189, 191, 192, 193, 195, 196, 197, 198–9, 200, 201, 204, 212, 215, 218, 219, 220
Critique of Practical Reason (Kant, Immanuel) 116, 188, 189, 223
Critique of Pure Reason (Kant, Immanuel) 8, 11, 112, 116, 148, 149, 150, 152, 153, 154, 155, 157, 162–3, 164, 166, 167, 168, 169, 170, 172, 176, 177, 178, 179, 180–1, 182, 183, 185–6, 192, 193, 195, 197, 199–200, 204, 212, 219, 222

crystallization processes 40–1
culture 18, 46, 121, 217, 218
custom. *See* convention; habit

demonisch 117–18
demonstrative knowledge 145–6
derivation 76
descriptive science 118
Dessauer, Friedrich 115–16
determinant judgment 181–2, 200, 208
Dewey, John 125, 128, 129–30, 131
dialectics 102, 104, 111, 112, 115
dikē (convention; judgment) 69–70
Dilthey, William 2, 28, 29, 30, 102
discovery 114
distinguishable/separable 139, 140
dreams 28, 29, 52–4, 106–7
dualism 12
Durkheim, Émile 73

effort 84
ego, the 210–11
emanation 45
emotional, the 35, 36 *see also* emotions
emotions 41, 106–7
empirical laws 193–4
empiricism 123–5, 128, 129, 130–4, 137, 139, 146
enactive intuition 17, 18, 203, 223
Encyclopedia (Hegel, Georg Wilhelm Friedrich) 3
environment, the 80, 84, 87, 89, 113, 116
  action 80, 126
  adaptation 127–8
  behaviour 126
  habit 83, 84
  human beings 117
  life 113, 116
  power 98
  transcendence 117
equilibrium 83, 84, 127–8
Essertier, Daniel 100, 102, 106, 108
eternal truth 145
ethics. *See* morality
existence 41–2
expectations 79
experience 11, 123–224
  action 124–5, 127

cause and effect 134, 135, 136, 137–42, 143–4
consciousness 124–5
creative 128
empiricism 123–5, 128, 130–4, 137
experiments 222
form 127
future, the 128, 129–30
habit 129, 147–8
Hume, David 131, 137, 138, 140, 141–2, 143, 144, 146, 147–8
independent beings 125
Kant, Immanuel 154, 155, 158, 162, 169–70, 181, 193, 195
knowledge 124–5, 130, 137
meaning 123
past, the 128, 129
perception 123–4
reality 126, 130
stimulus/response 126, 128
temporality 223
trial and error 127, 129
experiments 222
external figures 30

facts 136–7
　knowledge of 145–6
faculties 148–50
fashion 77–8
Fichte, Johann Gottlieb 224
　Science of Knowledge 210–12
fiction 57–60, 71, 78, 89–90
folkways 81–2
foresight 152
form 8–9, 10, 77–8, 81, 110–13, 130, 224
　see also formal logic
　action 127–8
　analogy of 204–5
　equilibrium 84–5
　experience 127
　form-images 35, 41, 42, 171–2, 173–4
　formless 18, 33
　Greece 18
　philosophy of form 17
　system of 204
　technology 109–10, 115–16, 118–19
　transformation 10, 113, 118
form-images 35, 41, 42
　schematism 171–2, 173–4

formal logic 8, 16, 17, 18, 21–3, 110–11, 203
formation 151
"Foundation of Induction" (Lachelier, Jules) 198
Frazer, James George 100–2
freedom 110, 214, 215, 219
Freyer, Hans 74

genius 112, 169, 186–91
Gewohnheit (habit; social convention) 68–9
God 46
Goethe, Johann Wolfgang von 29
good, the 47–8
Greek mythology 44–5
Greek philosophy 111, 112
greetings 60
Guillaume, Paul 129

habit 62–5, 68–9, 79, 82–6, 87, 132, 143–4
　experience 129, 147–8
　Hume, David 147–8
　idea 133
　perception 129
　technology 83, 85, 86, 120
Haldane, J.S. 116
hallucination 52–3, 75, 102
happiness 217
harmony 183, 184, 185
Hatano Seiichi 1
Hegel, Georg Wilhelm Friedrich 198–9
　dialectics 23, 112
　Encyclopedia 3
　logic 17, 119
　Logic 8
　Phenomenology of Spirit 8, 211
Heidegger, Martin 2, 160, 161–2, 192
hermeneutic ontology 2–3
Historical Materialism and Contemporary Consciousness (Miki Kiyoshi) 3, 15
historical nature 219, 222
historical-social ontology 4–5
historical world 10
history 10, 17, 18, 22–3, 38, 218–20, 222
　fiction 89
　myth 39–40, 43, 56
　nature 105
　transformation 113

Holt, B.E. 126
Hubert, H. 51, 96, 97–8, 99–100, 101, 102–3, 104
human beings 80, 81, 91, 117, 179, 223
  see also individual, the
  animals, in relation to 106
  as *demonisch* 117–18
  end of nature 216–17
  environment, the 117
  happiness 217
  as moral beings 216, 217–18
  nature 119
  transcendence 117
human technology 18, 113, 117–18, 119
humanism 10–11
Humboldt, Wilhelm von 176–7
Hume, David 131–3, 134–7, 138–48
Husserl, Edmund 32, 42, 154
hyperadaptation 106

idea 41–2, 46–7
  abstract 131–3
  aesthetic 190
  association of 102
  becoming 47
  good, the 47–8
  habit 133
  Locke, John 124, 125
  Plato 47–9, 50
  relations of ideas 136
  representationism 123
  soul, the 48–9
Idea for a Universal History with a Cosmopolitan Purpose (Kant, Immanuel) 218
Ideal 72, 73
Idee 72, 77, 78, 111, 220
  art 221
  Kant, Immanuel 214, 221, 222
idée 41, 47, 111
  Ribot, Théodule 113
images 32–3, 41–3, 47, 100–2, 133
  anticipation of experience 106
  form-images 35, 41, 42, 171–2, 173–4
  mental images 28–30, 32, 33
imitation 65–8, 84, 90, 120, 121
immanentism 79, 220
impressions 133, 144

individual, the 65–6, 69, 84, 90–1 *see also* human beings
  independence of 105
  transcendence 117
induction 198, 203
inference 131, 135–6, 140, 141–2, 146
Inquiry into the Good (Nishida Kitarō) 1, 4
insects 86
instinct 61–2, 63, 86, 95, 112–13
institutional societies 90, 91
institutions 9, 58–91
  concept 71, 72, 74, 80
  convention 58, 63–5, 68–70, 86–7
  coutume (custom) 58, 64
  definitions 71–2
  enacted 82
  environment 80, 87, 89
  expectation 79
  expressive meaning 77
  fiction 59–60, 78, 88–90
  foundation 74–5
  greetings 60
  habit 62–5
  hallucination 75
  imitation 90
  immanent 79
  individual, the 90
  instinct 61–2, 63
  institutional being 59
  intellect 59–61, 63
  logical action 75
  materiality 80
  myths 59
  nomos (law) 58–9, 68, 69, 70, 71, 78
  norms 68–9, 71–2
  objective apprehension 74
  rationality 76–7, 80, 82
  repetition 81
  society 90
  spirit of 75
  structure 71–2, 74, 80–2
  technology 86–8, 94
  temporality 79
  transcendence 78–9
instrumental technology 93, 94
instruments 107–8, 109
  magic 99
integration 126
intellect 59–61, 63

intellectual, the 35, 36
internal states 30
Introduction to Philosophy (Miki Kiyoshi) 6
intuition 17, 111–12, 156–7, 224 *see also* synthesis
  apprehension 192–3
  enactive intuition 17, 18, 203, 223
  intuitive understanding 191–2, 199, 208, 210, 212, 214–15, 221
Intuition and Reflection in Self-Awareness (Nishida Kitarō) 1
intuitive understanding 191–2, 199, 208, 210, 212, 214–15, 221
invention 65, 85, 108, 114–15, 119–21
Investigation of Man in Pascal, The (Miki Kiyoshi) 15
irrationality 76–7

James, William 61, 62, 130–1
Judd, H. 79
judgment 175–86, 199–201, 203

Kabeiroi cult 44–5
Kant, Immanuel 8, 11, 37, 112, 148–210, 212–24
  aesthetics 179, 180, 184, 186, 190, 192–3, 194–5
  affinity 151, 165, 166–7, 199–200
  affinity of appearances 164, 165
  analogy 202, 204–5
  Anthropology 150, 152, 154, 155, 157, 166, 168, 173, 177, 183, 184, 187, 191, 212
  apprehension 192–3
  Baumgarten, Alexander Gottlieb 148–50
  causality 206, 208–9, 212, 221
  classification 204
  cognition 153, 154, 155, 156, 159–60, 166, 167–8
  common sense 183–4
  concepts 171–2, 174–5, 182–4
  Conjectural Beginning of Human History 218
  contingency 219–20
  Critique of Judgment 8, 11, 112, 116, 151, 162, 177, 178–9, 180, 181, 183, 185–6, 187, 189, 191, 192, 193, 195, 196, 197, 198–9, 200, 201, 204, 212, 215, 218, 219, 220
  Critique of Practical Reason 116, 188, 189, 223
  Critique of Pure Reason 8, 11, 112, 116, 148, 149, 150, 152, 153, 154, 155, 157, 162–3, 164, 166, 167, 168, 169, 170, 172, 176, 177, 178, 179, 180–1, 182, 183, 185–6, 192, 193, 195, 197, 199–200, 204, 212, 219, 222
  end of nature 216–18
  experience 154, 155, 158, 162, 169–70, 181, 193, 195
  foresight 152
  genius 169, 186–91
  harmony 183, 184, 185
  Idea for a Universal History with a Cosmopolitan Purpose 218
  Idee 214, 221, 222
  imagination classification 149–50
  intuitive understanding 191–2, 199, 208, 210, 214–15, 221
  judgment 175–86, 199–201, 203
  laws of nature 223
  Lectures on Metaphysics 150, 156, 159, 160
  Logic 152
  mechanism 206–8, 209, 212
  morality 223
  nation-states 218
  nature 193–4, 200–2, 203, 204–10, 213–14, 215–19
  object/objectivity 184, 185
  organisms 202, 205–7, 208–9, 213–14, 215, 220
  Perpetual Peace 219
  phenomena 164–5
  productive imagination 8, 11, 37, 150–1, 157, 183
  Prolegomena 219
  purposiveness 192–8, 199, 201, 205, 212–13, 215, 219–20, 221
  reason 166, 220–1
  reproductive imagination 151–2
  schematism 170–8, 185, 200–1, 223
  sensation 151
  sensibility 165, 166–9, 172–4, 212
  sensible imagination 151
  spirit 190, 191

subject/subjectivity 183–4, 185
subsumption 170, 175, 181–2
synthesis 155–63, 164–6, 168, 169, 172–4, 175, 176, 185
system of ends 213–14
taste 179, 180, 183–4, 185, 186
teleology 178, 207–9, 212, 214–15, 221
time 149, 156, 157, 161, 224
transcendence 220, 223–4, 223–4
transcendental anthropology 153
transcendental apperception 160, 161, 162–3, 164, 165–6, 169–70, 176
transcendental logic 153–5
transcendental philosophy 150, 152–5
understanding 153, 163, 165–70, 172–4, 176, 182, 183, 184–5, 190–1, 212
universal, the 181–3
war 218
Kassner, Rudolf 85
Kawakami Hajime 3
knowledge 124–5, 130, 136–7, 138
   demonstrative knowledge 145–6
   of facts 145–6
Kroner, Richard 204
Kyoto School of philosophy 1
"Kyoto University incident" 5

Lachelier, Jules
   "Foundation of Induction" 198
law 58–9, 69, 70
   legal fiction 89–90
   nomos 58–9, 68, 69, 70, 78
law of accumulation 40, 41
Le Roy, Édouard 114–15
Learning and Human Life (Miki Kiyoshi) 7
Lectures on Metaphysics (Kant, Immanuel) 150, 156, 159, 160
legal fiction 89–90
legends 39–40, 55
Leibniz, Gottfried Wilhelm 66–7, 145–6, 189
Lévy-Bruhl, Lucien 24, 27, 31
Liebert, Arthur 46–7
life 84, 112–13
   environment, the 113, 116
"Literature of Contemporary Class Struggle, The" (Miki Kiyoshi) 5
Locke, John 124, 125
logic 17–18
   laws of 30
   pre-logical, the 24, 26
   transcendental 153–5
Logic (Hegel, Georg Wilhelm Friedrich) 8
Logic (Kant, Immanuel) 152
logic of emotions. *See* emotions
logic of form. *See* form
logic of history. *See* history
Logic of Imagination (Miki Kiyoshi) 6, 7–12, 15–19 *see also* experience; institution; myth; technology
logic of symbols. *See* symbolism
logical action 75, 76–7
logos 3–4, 8, 9, 10, 15–16, 23, 46
   classics 71
   creation 45
   fiction 89
   form 115
   formal logic 21–2
   history 222
   institutions 77, 89
   myth 47
   propensity 222
   technology 115, 118
   transcendence 78, 117, 118
   value 74
longing 44, 45, 46
love, romantic 40–1
Löwith, Karl 2
Ludwig, Otto 29

magic 44, 45, 46, 94–100
   contagious 100, 101
   foundation of 104–5
   Hubert, H 101, 102–3
   hyperadaptation 106
   imagination 100–3
   imitative 100–1
   law of contiguity 101
   law of contrariety 101
   law of similarity 100–1
   laws of 100–1
   mana 99, 104
   Mauss, M. 101, 102–3
   pantheism 104–5
   power 97–9, 105
   science 105, 108
   sympathy 100–2
   tradition 103

Maine, Henry Sumner 89–90
Malinowski, Bronisław 55
mana 99, 104
Marx, Karl 3–5, 37–8
"Marxist Form of the Humanistic
  Sciences, The" (Miki Kiyoshi) 3
mathematical natural science 118, 119
matters of fact 136–7
Mauss, M. 51, 96, 97–8, 99–100, 101,
  102–3, 104
mechanism 206–8, 212
memory 49–51, 52–3, 63, 120–1, 129, 148
  Baumgarten, Alexander Gottlieb 149
mental images 28–30, 32, 33
Mercier, Gustave 84
Metaphysics (Aristotle) 2
Miki Kiyoshi 8–12, 16
  anthropology 4
  biography 1–7
  contribution and relevance of 11–12
  hermeneutic ontology 2–3
  *Historical Materialism and
    Contemporary Consciousness* 3, 15
  historical-social ontology 4–5
  ideology 4
  Introduction to Philosophy 6
  Investigation of Man in Pascal, The 15
  Learning and Human Life 7
  "Literature of Contemporary Class
    Struggle, The" 5
  Logic of Imagination. See *Logic of
    Imagination*
  Marx studies 3–5
  "Marxist Form of the Humanistic
    Sciences, The" 3
  Neo-Kantianism 2
  Notes on a Theory of Human Life 6–7
  Notes on Philosophy 7
  On Anthropological Literature 16
  Philosophical Anthropology 6
  philosophy of 10–11
  Philosophy of History 4, 15
  Philosophy of Knowledge 7
  philosophy of technological-
    productive action 5–6
  Philosophy of Technology 7, 9
  philosophy of the imagination and
    forms 5, 6, 8
  Reading and Human Life 7

Shinran 7
Socrates 6
Standpoint of Man in Crisis, The 15
Study of Man in Pascal, The 3
mimesis 77
morality 59, 60, 68–9, 71, 189, 216, 217–18,
  223
mores 68–70, 77, 81–2 *see also* convention
morphology 17
mystical, the 24–5, 26
myth 8–9, 23–56, 71 *see also* magic
  Bertram, Ernst 39, 40, 41
  common structure of 31
  context of 55–6
  crisis periods 51
  culture 46
  dreams 28, 29, 52–4
  ensouling 34–5
  figuration 34–5
  Greek mythology 44–5
  history 39–40, 43, 56
  idea 46–7
  imagination, relationship with 27–8,
    31, 32–4, 36–7, 38
  institutions 59
  intellectual, the 36
  legends 39–40, 55
  Liebert, Arthur 46–7
  Malinowski, Bronisław 55
  mythe 39
  mythical being 59
  mythologie 39
  Plato 47–51
  polytheism 33
  as primitive 23–4, 25–7
  primitive people 24–6, 31, 33, 42–3, 55
  Ribot, Théodule 54–5
  Schelling, F.W.J. 44–5
  Sorel, Georges 35–6, 37, 38, 39, 57
  supernatural, the 42–3
  symbolism 30, 31–2
  technology 94, 95
  time 42–3, 51
  transcendence 33, 42, 43–4
  Valéry, Paul 57
mythos 71

nation-states 218
natural relations 134–5

nature 9–10, 12, 18, 104–5
    art 201, 202
    causality 206
    classification 203–4
    custom 144
    end of 213–14, 215–18
    form 113
    genius 187
    habit 63–5
    hidden plan 219
    historical 219, 222
    human beings 119
    imitation 68
    instinct 86
    judgment 208
    laws of 223
    mechanism 206–8, 209
    organisms 202, 205–7, 208–9, 213–14, 215, 220
    purposiveness 193, 195–8, 199, 201, 205, 213, 215, 219
    Schelling, F.W.J. 44
    supernatural, the 42–3
    as a system 193–4
    technology 87, 109, 113, 177–8, 193, 200–2, 203
necessity 143
Neo-Kantianism 2
Nichomachean Ethics (Aristotle) 2
Nietzsche, Friedrich
    Birth of Tragedy, The 46
Nishida Kitarō 1, 2
    historical world 10
    historical-social ontology 5
    Inquiry into the Good 1, 4
    Intuition and Reflection in Self-Awareness 1
    Nishidian philosophy 16
non-logical action 75–7
nomos (law) 58–9, 68, 69, 70, 78
    classics 71
Notes on a Theory of Human Life (Miki Kiyoshi) 6–7
Notes on Philosophy (Miki Kiyoshi) 7
nothingness 6, 11

object/objectivity 16, 17, 33, 110
    cognition 159–60
    deduction 153, 154
    dreams 54
    ego, the 210–11
    experience 123–4
    Fichte, Johann Gottlieb 210
    form 18, 23
    good, the 47–8
    individual, the 90
    institutions 77
    instruments 109
    Kant, Immanuel 184, 185
    logical action 75
    objective apprehension 74
    objective spirit 74
    reality 126
    sensation 52
    taste 180
    technology 85, 88, 109, 110, 115
    transcendence 117
    understanding 153
    value 73–4
On Anthropological Literature (Miki Kiyoshi) 16
organisms 202, 205–7, 208–9, 213–14, 215, 220

pantheism 104–5
Pareto, Vilfredo 75–7
participation 33
Pascal, Blaise 3, 15, 64, 68
passion 84
pathos 8, 9, 10, 11, 15–16, 23
    creation 45
    culture 46
    of distance 118
    fiction 89
    form 115
    formal logic 21–2
    history 222
    human 118
    instinct 61
    institutions 77, 89
    magic 45
    myth 46, 47
    propensity 222
    sympathy 68
    technology 115, 118
    transcendence 78, 117, 118
Paulhan, Frédéric 120, 121
periods 51

perception 123–4, 129, 132, 145, 163–4
Perpetual Peace (Kant, Immanuel) 219
personality 121
petites perception 67
phantasy 21, 27, 52, 149, 151
    Baumgarten, Alexander Gottlieb 22, 23, 149
    dreams 53
    Husserl, Edmund 32
    memory 63
phenomena 164–5
Phenomenology of Spirit (Hegel, Georg Wilhelm Friedrich) 8, 211
Philebus (Plato) 49
Philosophical Anthropology (Miki Kiyoshi) 6
philosophical relations 134–6
philosophy of action 16–17
philosophy of form 17
Philosophy of History (Miki Kiyoshi) 4, 15
Philosophy of Knowledge (Miki Kiyoshi) 7
philosophy of technological-productive action 5–6
Philosophy of Technology (Miki Kiyoshi) 7, 9
philosophy of the imagination and forms 5, 6, 8
Plato/Platonism
    idea 49–50
    myth 31, 32, 47–51
    Philebus 49
    Timaios 49
    time 51
pleasure 194–5
poets 28
poiesis 8, 17, 22, 93
polytheism 33
power 97–9, 105
pre-logical, the 24, 26
primary imagination 147
primitive people 24–6
    accident 105
    ancestors 43
    blood relationships 59–60
    dreams 28
    images 102
    myth 24–6, 31, 33, 42–3, 55
    supernatural, the 42–3
    time, concept of 42–3

probability 141–2
production 9, 10, 17, 93
    ego, the 211
    magic 96
production technology 93, 94
productive imagination 8, 55, 102, 210–11
    Kant, Immanuel 8, 11, 37, 150–1, 157, 183
Prolegomena (Kant, Immanuel) 219
propensity 222
psychology 153, 155
Puchta, Georg Friedrich 69
purposiveness 192–8, 199, 201, 205, 212–13, 215, 219–20, 221

rationality 15, 27, 36, 60, 76–7, 80, 82
Ravaisson, Félix 62–4, 84
Reading and Human Life (Miki Kiyoshi) 7
reality 72, 73, 126, 130
reason 61–2, 145–6, 166, 178, 220–1
recognition 159, 160–2
recollection 49, 50
reflective judgment 181–2, 184, 185, 186, 194, 199, 200, 203
relation of association 134–5
relation of comparison 134
relations 134–6
relations of ideas 136
religion 35, 59, 97
    magic 96
    technology 109
Renaissance, the 179
Renan, Ernest 32
repetition 62, 65, 142–3
representation 24, 28, 30, 123, 157–8 *see also* collective representation; mental images
reproduction 157–9, 160
reproductive imagination 37, 151–2
resemblance 143
residue 76
response/stimulus 126, 128
Ribot, Théodule 27–8, 40, 41, 54–5, 112–13
Rickert, Heinrich 2

Samothrace 44–5
Sartre, Jean-Paul 41, 42
Scheler, Max 2
Schelling, F.W.J. 44–6

schematism 170–8, 185, 200–1, 223
science 17–18, 35, 94, 105–6, 119
    descriptive 118
    genius 188
    magic 105, 108
    mathematical natural science 118, 119
    technology 107–10, 118–19
Science of Knowledge (Fichte, Johann Gottlieb) 210–12
Séailles, Gabriel 112
secondary imagination 147
sensation 52–3, 106, 133–4, 148
    Kant, Immanuel 151
sensibility 165, 166–9, 165, 166–9, 172–4, 212
sensible imagination 151
separable/distinguishable 139, 140
Shinran (Miki Kiyoshi) 7
Sitte (mores) 68–9
sleep 53–4
social imperatives 77
social phenomena, research rules 37–8
society 5, 22, 38, 57, 60, 61–2, 90–1, 218 *see also* primitive people
    Durkheim, Émile 73
    expectations 79
    imitation 65, 67, 68
    institutions 87–9
    language 39
    technology 91
    themis 69
    transcendence 117
    Valéry, Paul 57–8, 78
Socrates (Miki Kiyoshi) 6
Sorel, Georges 35–6, 37–8, 39, 57
soul, the 47, 48–9
spatiality 150
species 196–7, 204
Spengler, Oswald 118
spirit 190, 191, 211
Standpoint of Man in Crisis, The (Miki Kiyoshi) 15
Stendhal (Henri Beyle) 40
stimulus/response 126, 128
Study of Man in Pascal, The (Miki Kiyoshi) 3
stylized projections 37
subject/subjectivity 16, 17
    action 127

deduction 153, 154
dreams 54
ego, the 210–11
experience 123–4
Fichte, Johann Gottlieb 210
form 18, 23
good, the 47–8
imagination 33
individual, the 90
institutions 77
instruments 109
Kant, Immanuel 183–4, 185
logical action 75
reality 126
sensation 52
society 90
technology 9, 85, 88, 109, 110, 115
transcendence 117
understanding 153
value 73–4
substance 144
subsumption 170, 175, 181–2
succession 138, 142
sufficient reason 145–6
Sumner, William Graham 71, 72, 78, 81, 82, 88
supernatural, the 42–3
symbolism 30, 31–2, 51, 103–4
sympathy 61, 67, 68
    Frazer, James George 100–2
synthesis 9, 16, 146
    integration 126
    Kant, Immanuel 155–63, 164–6, 168, 169, 172–4, 175, 176, 185
    magic 104
    technology 115
system of ends 213–14
systems 193–4, 195–7

tact 88
"Takigawa Incident" 5
Takigawa Yukitoki 5
Tanabe Hajime 1
Tarde, G. 65–8, 77, 84, 90, 120
    invention 65, 119
taste 179, 180, 183–4, 185, 186
technological philosophy 88
technology 5–6, 9–10, 12, 17–18, 93–121
    adaptation 85–6

changes 115
convention 94
dialectical 115
form 109–10, 115–16, 118–19
habit 83, 85, 86, 120
human 18, 113, 117–18, 119
imitation 120
institutions 86–8, 94
instruments 93, 94
invention 114–15, 120
Kant, Immanuel 178
life 112–13
magic 94–6, 97
myth 94, 95
natural laws 115
nature 87, 109, 113, 177–8, 193, 200–2, 203
production 9, 10, 93, 94
reconciliation 119
religion 109
science 107–10, 118–19
single best solutions 115–16
society 91
synthesis 115
transcendence 86, 115–16
teleology 110, 178, 207–9, 212, 214–15, 221
themis (judgment; law) 69–70
things 72–3, 74
thought 107, 111–12
action 114–15
Timaios (Plato) 49
time 42–3, 50–1
crisis periods 51
habit 64
Heidegger, Martin 161
institutions 79
Kant, Immanuel 149, 156, 157, 161, 224
myth 42–3, 51
periods 51
Plato 47
schematism 170–1
tradition 103

transcendence 3, 42, 43–4, 110, 118, 165
environment, the 117
human beings 117
institutions 78–9
Kant, Immanuel 220, 223–4, 223–4
technology 86, 115–16
transcendental anthropology 153
transcendental apperception 160, 161, 162–3, 164, 165–6, 169–70, 176
transcendental judgment. *See* judgment
transcendental logic 153–5
transcendental philosophy 150, 152–5
Transcendental Schematism. *See* schematism
transformation 10, 113, 118
transitive, the 147
transmission 46
truth 154–5
types 30–1

understanding 146–7, 153, 165–70
intuitive understanding 191–2, 199, 208, 210, 212, 214–15, 221
Kant, Immanuel 153, 163, 165–70, 172–4, 176, 182, 183, 184–5, 190–1, 212
unity 159–60
unity of apperception 160, 163, 164, 165–7, 169
universal, the 34, 181–3
universal principle of alchemy 104
utopia 35, 36, 37
Usener, Hermann 34–5

Valéry, Paul 57–8, 78
value 72–4
Veblen, Thorstein 94, 95, 98
Volkelt, Johannes 53–4

war 218
will 63
words 99
workmanship 95